Book for Everyone, Everywhere

Living Well: The Art of Simplicity and Success

Volume I: Foundations of a Simple, Happy and Healthy Life

A Practical Guide to Living with Clarity, Balance and Inner Peace

Sandeep Shah

Clever Fox® PUBLISHING

Chennai • Bangalore

Dedication

To my wife, **Jagruti Shah**—

Your steadfast support, love and belief in the power of simplicity have been my guiding light. Your approach to minimalism has been the wellspring of inspiration behind this book.

To my daughter, **Isha Shah** and my son, **Neev Shah**—

You see me as your role model and that fills my heart with purpose. I authored this book to pass on the lessons I have gathered in life, hoping they serve you as well as they have served me.

And to everyone searching for peace and purpose—
may you find the courage to live a life that is true to yourself.

Acknowledgments

I am deeply grateful to everyone who has supported me throughout the journey of writing *Living Well: The Art of Simplicity and Success*.

To my wife, **Jagruti Shah**, thank you for being my unwavering pillar of strength, my friend, philosopher and guide. Your wisdom, encouragement and belief in simplicity and minimalism gave me the confidence to bring this book to life. You have been my sounding board and my greatest inspiration throughout this journey.

To my children, **Isha Shah and Neev Shah**, you are my greatest motivation. Your curiosity and admiration remind me every day why living well matters.

A special note of gratitude to **Isha Shah**, whose patient and thoughtful support in proofreading strengthened this book in countless ways. Your keen eye, clarity of thought and genuine involvement added depth, refinement and grace to these pages.

I also extend my heartfelt thanks to my family, friends and mentors who offered guidance, feedback and encouragement at every stage.

Finally to my readers—thank you for choosing this book. Your trust and willingness to embrace simplicity and success make this effort meaningful.

Copyright © 2026 by Sandeep Shah

ISBN (Print Edition): [978-93-7500-277-2]

ASIN (Kindle Edition): [978-93-7500-862-0]

First Edition: 2026

Published by: CLEVER FOX PUBLISHING 2026

Disclaimer:
This book is intended solely for informational and motivational purposes. The author and publisher do not provide medical, legal, financial or professional advice. The contents should not be relied upon as a substitute for consultation with qualified professionals in these fields.

While every effort has been made to ensure accuracy, the author and publisher make no representations or warranties regarding the completeness, reliability or suitability of the information contained herein. Any actions taken based on this material are at the sole discretion and responsibility of the reader.

Neither the author nor the publisher shall be held liable for any loss, injury or damages arising directly or indirectly from the use of this book. Readers are encouraged to seek independent professional guidance before making decisions related to health, finances, legal matters or other areas requiring expert input.

Cover Design: Sandeep Shah

Printed in India

Preface

Living Well: The Art of Simplicity and Success
Volume I: Foundations of a Simple, Happy and Healthy Life

Life today feels heavier than it should. Many of us wake up already tired inside—carrying stress, noise and expectations that are nowhere visible but always felt. We rush through our days but somewhere in the speed, we lose the gentle art of simple living.

This book is a reminder

To pause.
To breathe.
To return to what truly matters.

Living Well: The Art of Simplicity and Success — Volume I is written for **every person** who wishes to live a **Happy, Healthy and Peaceful life**. Whoever you are, wherever you are, whatever your background—these pages are meant to sit beside you like a quiet source of strength and clarity.

- It is intentionally simple.
- It is easy to open at any moment—morning, night or whenever life feels overwhelming.
- It offers small practices, gentle truths and practical wisdom that help you feel lighter, calmer and more grounded.

This book is a life companion that walks with you quietly, guiding you toward a simpler way of living. Not by changing everything at once but by helping you shift just one thought, one habit or one small part of your day.

- You do not need to follow every idea.
- You do not need to transform your entire life.
- Allow just one insight to touch you—and let that be your beginning.
- Simplicity grows softly, one step at a time.

Each page of this book carries gentle guidance, simple practices and small truths that help you return to balance and peace.

This book is also a wonderful gift for your loved ones.

A gift of calm.
A gift of clarity.
A gift of a lighter, happier life.

As I continued writing and reflecting on these learnings, I realised that once we simplify the inside, the natural next step is to strengthen the outside—by aligning purpose, discipline, productivity and intentional action with daily life.

At its heart, ***Living Well: The Art of Simplicity and Success*** carry a simple promise: inner clarity should translate into wise, steady action. When the inside is light, the outside can move with focus and grace.

That understanding led to the continuation of this journey:

Living Well: The Art of Simplicity and Success
Volume II: Mastering Success, Productivity & Personal Discipline

a practical companion for focus, deep work and sustainable performance—built upon the inner foundation created in ***Living Well: The Art of Simplicity and Success — Volume I.***

Together, these two volumes offer a natural progression within the ***Living Well: The Art of Simplicity and Success*** journey:

Peace within. Progress outside.
Simplicity in living. Strength in doing.

My hope is that you feel supported, understood and gently encouraged as you read this **Volume I**. And when inner simplicity begins to take root, **Volume II** will walk with you naturally guiding you toward clarity in action, consistency in effort and strength in execution.

Important Essence of This Series

Living Well: The Art of Simplicity and Success are written for every person on this planet who wants to live a **Happy, Healthy and Prosperous life** regardless of age, background or life situation. Wherever you are in life, this series is designed to sit in your hands like a small source of strength, clarity and encouragement. These volumes are crafted as pocket companions—easy to open at any moment when life feels confusing, noisy or overwhelming.

Guided by the philosophy of ***Six Essential Dimensions of a Meaningful and Successful Life***, ***Living Well: The Art of Simplicity and Success*** begin with inner foundations **(this volume)** and then disciplined execution **(Volume II).** As your journey unfolds, *further dimensions* will gently deepen and broaden this framework—helping you integrate simplicity with strength across the whole arc of a well-lived life

— **Sandeep Shah**

Why I authored this book

This book was born from a simple but powerful desire: **to help people live lighter, calmer and more meaningful lives in a world that is becoming increasingly complex.**

For years, I watched how stress, speed and constant comparison were taking away people's peace. I saw how most of us chase success yet forget happiness, accumulate more yet feel emptier and move faster yet lose touch with ourselves. I felt these pressures in my own journey too—until I discovered the profound strength hidden in living simply.

As I began simplifying my thoughts, routines and lifestyle, life itself started opening beautifully.

- Clarity improved.
- Confidence grew.
- Peace returned.

And I realised that the answers people seek are often not in "more"—but in **less**.

Over the years, my habit of taking notes became a constant companion. I collected learnings from books I read, YouTube videos I watched, online content, professional experiences and everyday observations. These simple notes—recorded across journals, diaries and digital apps—slowly grew into a treasure of insights and clarity. They became the very roots from which this series "***Living Well: The Art of Simplicity and Success***" eventually blossomed.

I realised that millions of people silently long for simplicity—for a life that feels peaceful and purposeful again. This understanding led me to write **Volume I**, a gentle guide designed to bring clarity and calm to anyone who holds it. My intention is not to overwhelm you with information but to offer simple truths, timeless principles and practical habits that make life better—one small step at a time.

My intention behind writing these books is simple: to help you live a happy, healthy, balanced and successful life— a life built on clarity, simplicity and conscious choices.

If even one page of this book helps you feel lighter, breathe easier or see your life with new clarity, then it has fulfilled its purpose.

— **Sandeep Shah**

Contents

Introduction

Why This Book

Modern life has become faster, louder and more demanding than ever before. Almost everyone today feels overwhelmed caught between responsibilities, expectations, digital noise and the silent pressure to "keep up." I wrote this book to offer a gentle alternative. A simpler path. A path back to peace, clarity and balance. Through years of learning, observing and applying simplicity in my own life, I discovered a truth: **life becomes lighter not by adding more but by removing what weighs us down.** This book was born from that truth—first for my children, then for my family and now for every reader who seeks a calmer, happier and healthier life.

What Problem This Book Solves

Most people today live in a constant state of **mental overload**—too many choices too much information too much comparison and too little peace. We have convenience yet lack clarity. We have access yet lack presence. We have comfort yet lack calm. This book helps you understand **why modern life feels chaotic** and provides a practical roadmap to reclaim your time, your focus and your emotional well-being.

It solves problems such as:

- Stress and burnout
- Digital distraction
- Consumerism and clutter
- Emotional imbalance
- Lack of direction or purpose
- Relationship strain
- Health neglected in the rush of life
- Feeling overwhelmed despite "having everything"

Through simple principles and real-life examples, this book offers clarity in a world full of noise.

Who This Book Is For

This book is for **anyone who wants to live a Happier, Healthier and more Meaningful life**.

It is written for:

- Professionals feeling drained by constant pressure
- Homemakers carrying invisible emotional weight
- Students overwhelmed by expectations
- Parents seeking peace in family life
- Leaders looking for clarity and balance
- Young adults confused by comparison, choices and digital overload
- Anyone who wants to simplify their mind, home, habits or lifestyle

Whether you are at a crossroad, feeling stuck or simply wanting a life with more peace and purpose—this book is your companion.

How to Use This Book

This is not a book to rush through. It is not meant to be read once and kept aside. Think of it as a **life companion**—something you return to whenever life feels heavy or confusing.

Here is how you can use it:

- **Read one chapter at a time** and let the ideas sink in.
- **Pause** whenever you feel a connection—reflection is part of the journey.
- **Apply one small change** instead of trying to change everything.
- **Revisit chapters** whenever you face stress, burnout, clutter, emotional imbalance or decision fatigue.
- **Share insights** with family—simple living becomes easier when done together.

Every section is intentionally short, practical and designed for busy lives. Even one idea can create a powerful shift. Simplicity grows slowly—one gentle step at a time

Part I: Modern Life – Understanding the Chaos

Understand the pressures of today's fast-paced world and why modern living often feels overwhelming

Chapter 1: The Speed Trap — When Life Becomes a Race

Modern Life: More Convenience, Less Peace

"We simplified our tasks but complicated our minds."

Modern life has given us levels of convenience that past generations could never imagine. With a single tap, we can order food, book a ride, check global news, entertain ourselves, transfer money or communicate instantly. Tasks that once required planning, travel, waiting and effort are now completed in seconds. Yet despite this dramatic rise in comfort, peace has quietly declined. People today live with more anxiety, more distraction and more emotional exhaustion than ever before. Convenience has solved physical problems but created psychological ones. Our external life became easier but our inner life became heavier.

The modern mind now carries burdens the body never experiences — continuous notifications, constant comparison, endless decisions and a nonstop stream of information that demands attention. Instead of enjoying free time, people often feel guilty for not being productive. Instead of feeling satisfied with enough, they feel pressured by the endless options available. Instead of resting, they scroll. Instead of connecting deeply, they multitask. The physical world has become light; the mental world has become overloaded.

Consider the real-life example of **Neev**, a 34-year-old IT professional. His day begins not with calm but with chaos. Before he even gets out of bed, he checks emails, responds to overnight messages, scrolls through updates, glances at stock tickers and replies to group chats. His phone becomes the first conversation he has every morning. On the way to work, traffic navigation apps keep rerouting him, adding micro-stress to an already tense commute. At the office, he juggles multiple tools—Slack, Teams, WhatsApp, email, Jira—and has to switch between them hundreds of times. Each app simplifies one task while collectively overwhelming his mind. During lunch, instead of resting, he scrolls through social media, comparing his life with curated versions of others. At night, he streams shows to "relax," but stimulation keeps his mind active, delaying sleep. Although his life is overflowing with convenient tools, Neev feels more drained and disconnected than ever. His day is full of activity but empty of peace.

Stories like Neev's are now the norm. Many people live in a continuous state of mental "open tabs." Convenience has made everything faster but has also trained the mind to remain constantly alert. The human brain, designed for moments of stillness, now rarely gets a pause. Even leisure has become stressful — too many movies to choose from too many food options to decide among too many opinions and updates to consume. Simpler times offered fewer choices but more clarity. Today's world offers everything but makes it difficult to enjoy anything deeply.

Even relationships are affected. Convenience replaced slow, meaningful conversations with quick messages and emojis. Staying connected became easy but staying emotionally present became difficult. Families sit together physically but live separately through screens. Friends communicate more but bond less. Children grow up surrounded by devices that entertain them instantly but reduce patience, imagination and mental resilience.

Work life reflects the same paradox. Digital tools increase efficiency but also increase expectations. Because tasks can be completed faster, people are expected to handle more. Because communication is instant, response time is expected to be instant. Because information is always available, the pressure to stay updated never ends. Convenience doesn't give more time; it often steals time quietly. What was meant to simplify life ends up complicating our thoughts, schedules and emotions. Modern conveniences are beneficial but they come with hidden psychological costs. The convenience-driven world tends to push individuals into speed without direction, stimulation without rest, connection without presence and consumption without satisfaction. The result is a life where everything feels accessible but nothing feels enough. We live in an age where comfort is abundant but calm is rare. Convenience has given us unmatched freedom but often at the expense of the mental space we desperately need.

Modern life is filled with conveniences our grandparents could never have imagined. Tasks that once required effort, time or physical presence can now be done instantly—ordered with a tap, delivered with a click, accessed within seconds. We have smart devices, fast transportation, instant communication, on-demand entertainment, automated reminders, online shopping and AI tools ready to assist anytime.

On the surface, life has never been easier. But beneath this convenience lies a growing sense of restlessness. People today are overwhelmed, mentally exhausted and emotionally scattered. The world has become faster, louder and more demanding—even as it promises ease. Convenience was meant to free us. Yet in many ways, it has taken over our attention, our energy and our inner quiet.

Why This Happens in Modern Life

Technology and innovation have transformed our routines but they've also altered our rhythm. The pace of life no longer matches the pace of human emotion. Everything accelerates—even things that once grounded us. Tasks that took time now happen instantly; conversations that once unfolded slowly now happen at lightning speed. Expectations rise alongside convenience. If something is easy, people expect it *immediately*. If everything is available instantly, patience becomes rare. Convenience has reduced effort but increased **mental noise**. It has created a world where people have more options, more access, more stimulation—yet less calm, less rest and less presence. Modern living has become a strange paradox: The easier life becomes externally, the more difficult it feels internally.

The Reality of Today's Convenient Yet Chaotic Life

- **Instant Everything, Constant Stimulation -** Everything—messages, deliveries, information—arrives instantly. The brain barely rests, moving from one notification to the next.
- **Convenience Turning into Dependency -** Many people rely heavily on digital tools for memory, reminders, decisions and even emotions. Life feels difficult without them.
- **Faster Pace, Shorter Patience -** As services speed up, expectations follow. Waiting feels frustrating, even when the delay is small.
- **Noise Filling Every Moment -** People rarely experience silence. Music, videos, alerts and updates fill even the smallest gaps during the day.
- **Convenience Increasing Pressure -** When things are easy to do, people are expected to do more. More replies, more availability, more productivity—faster.

Real-Life Examples:

- **Ethan: The Manager Who Couldn't Disconnect -** Ethan appreciated the convenience of having work emails on his phone—it allowed him to respond quickly. But over time, he noticed he was never truly "off." Even during dinner or while watching a movie with his family, he checked messages out of habit. Convenience blurred the boundary between his work and life until both felt mixed together. **He felt accessible to everyone—except himself.**
- **Olivia: The Woman Overwhelmed by Endless Choices -** Olivia loved the convenience of online shopping. But with endless products, deals and recommendations, even simple decisions—like choosing a pair of shoes—felt mentally exhausting. What used to take 10 minutes now took an hour of comparisons. The convenience that promised ease ended up draining her energy. **She felt tired before she even made a choice.**
- **Daniel: The Man Who Became Dependent on Instant Deliveries -** Daniel enjoyed the comfort of getting anything delivered to his home—food within minutes, groceries within an hour and household items the same day. At first, it felt magical. But soon, he noticed something unsettling: even small delays made him impatient. If a delivery took 20 minutes instead of 10, he felt irritated. The speed that once amazed him slowly became an expectation. **Convenience reshaped his patience without him realizing it.**

Conclusion: The Cost of Convenience

Modern life has given us incredible comfort and efficiency. Tasks are faster, communication is easier and access is immediate. Yet peace—the one thing convenience was supposed to create—often feels farther away.

This chapter is not about rejecting convenience; it is about recognising how it shapes today's emotional landscape. A world full of easy options has quietly become a world full of inner tension.

And so the question arises:

If life keeps getting more convenient, why aren't we feeling more peaceful?

Life is a Race Without a Finish Line

"We live in an age where speed is celebrated and stillness feels like a luxury. The question is—are we moving forward or just moving faster?"

As I look at modern life, I often feel like I'm running a marathon with no finish line. I wake up to alarms, not sunrises. I measure my days in deadlines, not moments. Productivity is praised everywhere I turn but I rarely pause to ask myself: **At what cost?**

Technology promised me convenience but it tethered me to constant notifications. Global connectivity opened endless opportunities but it also erased the boundaries between my work and my home. The world runs 24/7—and some days, I feel like I do too mentally if not physically.

Modern life often feels like an endless race—one without a starting signal, without a clear direction and, most importantly, without a finish line. People run not because they know where they are going but because everyone else seems to be running. The pace keeps rising, the noise keeps growing and the pressure keeps intensifying.

There's a quiet expectation today that we must always be improving, achieving and outperforming—moving from one milestone to the next without pause. Somewhere along the way, life transformed from a journey into a competition. And in this competition, there is no "enough."
No moment to breathe. No space to simply exist.
Just a constant pull to keep going.

Why This Feeling Exists Today

Society glorifies speed—fast responses, fast results, fast progress. People celebrate busyness as if it were a badge of honour. Technology accelerates everything: work,

communication, expectations and comparisons. In this environment, slowing down feels risky and stillness feels almost rebellious.
Everywhere, people feel the pressure to achieve more—financially, professionally, socially. The world sends a constant message: **"Do more, earn more, become more."**

But as the pace increases, fulfillment does not. Achievements quickly lose meaning. Accomplishments fade faster than they used to. Life becomes a series of deadlines, targets and goals stacked so close together that people barely notice when one ends and the next begins. The result is a life lived in constant urgency—moving fast but rarely feeling present.

A Day in the Life

To help you understand this reality, let me walk you through a day I've seen many people live—and I've lived versions of this myself. Step with me into **Lucas's** shoes.
His alarm vibrates at 6 a.m. but he's already awake—his mind rehearsing the day's tasks. Before his feet touch the floor, he has checked overnight emails, a client's urgent message and a school update about his son.

In the kitchen, he scrolls while sipping tea, half listening to his daughter talks about her science project. During his commute, he jumps between Slack pings, WhatsApp groups and productivity articles he'll never read.
By 10 a.m., his calendar looks like a Tetris board—back-to-back meetings, a quick sync that runs long and "focus time" that evaporates under new requests. Lunch becomes an energy bar at his desk.

At 7 p.m., Lucas carries work home. His laptop opens on the dining table while his family eats. He promises himself he'll stop working by nine but a "five-minute fix" becomes forty. Later to relax, he scrolls reels—but his mind races even faster. In bed, he wonders why he feels both accomplished and empty.

When I look at Lucas's life, I see a reflection of what many of us experience. The world's pace keeps rising until life feels like running on a treadmill that never slows down.

The Illusion of "More Is Better"

I grew up in a culture that glorifies busyness. Maybe you did too.
I was taught to measure success by how packed my calendar is, how many emails I answer, how many tasks I juggle. *Do more. Earn more. Achieve more.*

But I've learned something the hard way:

Doing more rarely leads to being better. Instead, it traps me in a cycle of exhaustion where I confuse activity with progress and busyness with purpose.

The Pressure to Keep Up

Technology was supposed to liberate me but many days it feels like it has chained me to constant alerts. Social media magnifies comparison, making me feel like I'm falling behind if I'm not achieving at the pace I see online.

I've felt that pressure—to keep up professionally, socially, personally. Maybe you have too.

The Reality of Today's Endless Race

- **Always Preparing for the Next Step -** People finish one task and immediately think about the next. Even after reaching a milestone, the mind jumps ahead, never pausing to acknowledge the moment.
- **Constant Fear of Falling Behind -** With so many people showcasing success online, many individuals feel pressured to keep up—even when they don't want the same life.
- **The Disappearing Boundary Between Work and Life -** With phones, laptops and digital platforms, work follows people everywhere. The race continues long after office hours.
- **Life Becoming Measurable Instead of Meaningful -** Progress is tracked in numbers—income, promotions, likes, achievements—while emotional well-being, peace and joy get overshadowed.
- **The Illusion of Forward Movement -** People feel busy and productive yet many quietly sense they aren't moving any closer to what truly matters.

Real-Life Examples:

- **David: The Executive Who Kept Raising the Bar -** David worked hard for years, chasing promotions and recognition. Every time he reached a goal, he felt satisfied for a day or two—but soon, the excitement faded. He set new targets immediately, not because he wanted them but because slowing down felt unsafe. Eventually, he realised he had been running for so long that he forgot why he started. **He wasn't moving toward something—he was running from stillness.**
- **Elena: The Student Who Never Felt "Enough" -** Elena excelled academically yet she constantly felt behind. She compared her achievements with others online—better grades, better internships, better lives. Even after securing a great opportunity, she felt anxious about the next one. Her success never brought peace—only pressure. **The race she was running had no finish line, only more lanes to sprint through.**

Key Features of Today's Busy Life

Here are the forces I see shaping our daily fatigue.

- **Constant Connectivity -** I can be reached anytime, anywhere—through email, WhatsApp, calls, social media. This flexibility is useful but it blurs the boundary between my work life and personal life. Disconnecting feels almost impossible.
- **Overloaded Schedules -** Work, family, social commitments, personal goals—it often feels like everything demands my attention at the same time. Rest becomes a luxury instead of a necessity.
- **Pressure to Achieve -** The world rewards results. I've often felt the need to prove myself through productivity—career milestones, financial goals, academic success. But sometimes that pressure pushes me toward burnout more than fulfillment.
- **Information Overload -** Every day, I'm bombarded with news, trends and updates. Keeping up feels overwhelming. Even choosing what to pay attention to drains my energy.
- **Decline in Face-to-Face Interaction -** Even though I can message anyone instantly, I sometimes feel more disconnected than ever. Digital interaction has replaced real human interaction, weakening the emotional bond I crave.
- **Reduced Time for Self-Care -** In the rush to do everything, my sleep, hobbies, health and peace are often the first things I sacrifice. Over time, I pay the price—physically and mentally.
- **Desire for Instant Gratification -** Modern life conditions me to expect immediate results—fast delivery, fast responses, fast updates. This makes patience difficult and deep satisfaction rare.

The Impact of Today's Busy Life on Well-Being

- **Stress and Burnout -** When every day feels like a race, rest becomes guilt and burnout becomes inevitable. I've seen how chronic stress affects my mood, my focus, my relationships and even my physical health.
- **Loss of Personal Fulfilment -** I sometimes find myself achieving goals yet feeling empty. Without time for relationships, hobbies or reflection, life can feel mechanical.
- **Decreased Attention Span -** Multitasking and constant notifications have trained my mind to jump instead of focus. I struggle to be fully present.
- **Reduced Creativity and Innovation -** Creativity requires stillness and space. When my mind is overloaded, fresh ideas rarely appear.

- **Disconnection from Nature -** My modern routine often keeps me indoors, behind screens. But every time I reconnect with nature, I feel my stress melt and my clarity return.

Conclusion: A Look at Today's Pace

Many people today live in a mental and emotional sprint—always striving, never arriving. Life has become an endless race, where rest feels like weakness and speed is mistaken for progress. The finish line keeps moving, goals keep shifting and expectations keep expanding.
This chapter is not about slowing down or changing pace—that comes later. This is about understanding the reality we live in: A world where movement is constant, achievement is expected and peace is postponed endlessly.

And so the question quietly emerges:

If life is a race without a finish line… what exactly are we running toward?

Busyness has become a badge of honour. But I ask myself often—**at what cost?** The treadmill of modern life promises progress yet so often delivers stress, emptiness and disconnection. I've learned that awareness is the first step toward reclaiming balance.

And here's the truth I've come to see clearly: **this is not just my life—it's everyone's life today.** So, as you read this, I invite you to pause for a moment and ask yourself, just as I ask myself:

Is my life truly moving forward—or am I simply moving faster?

Chapter 2: Choice Overload — The Hidden Stress We Don't Notice

Identity in a Material World: Who Are We Really?

"When the world measures worth in possessions, it becomes harder to hear the quiet truth of who we actually are."

We live in a time where identity is increasingly shaped not from within but from the outside. The modern world constantly sends signals—through advertisements, social media, lifestyle trends and cultural expectations—telling us who we should be, how we should look and what we must own to "belong." In this environment, the line between **who we are** and **what we have** quietly blurs. Many people find themselves caught between their authentic self and the version of themselves they feel pressured to present.

Today, identity is often constructed like a display—curated, polished, filtered. The need to appear successful, stylish or "ahead" has become a silent competition. Possessions turn into status symbols, achievements into performances and online personas into masks. And beneath all of this, a simple question lingers: **Who am I when no one is watching?**

Why This Topic Matters Today

In the modern material-driven world, identity can be fragile. People increasingly define themselves through:

- their job titles
- their lifestyle choices
- their gadgets and clothes
- their social media image
- their achievements
- their financial status

Instead of asking, "What kind of person am I?" many are asking, "How do I look compared to others?" This shift creates an internal disconnect. People may appear confident but feel uncertain inside. They may appear successful yet feel hollow. The more identity becomes tied to external markers, the easier it is to lose sight of inner truth.

At the same time, constant exposure to others' highlight reels makes individuals question their own worth. Social comparison—once limited to small social circles—is now global and constant. Everyone seems better, richer, happier or more "put-together," creating pressure to upgrade not just possessions but identity itself.

In this environment, identity becomes something many people struggle to understand. It feels shaped by trends, influenced by algorithms and measured by reactions.
The question "Who am I?" becomes more complicated than ever before.

The Reality of Today's Identity Landscape

- **Possessions As Identity -** Many people unconsciously tie their identity to what they own. The phone they use, the clothes they wear, the car they drive or the locations they visit become symbols of who they believe they are—or who they want to be perceived as.
- **Social Media as a Mirror -** For many, online profiles have become a second identity—filtered, enhanced, edited. It reflects more of how they want to be seen than how they truly feel.
- **Comparison as a Daily Habit -** Scrolling through success stories, luxury lifestyles and curated perfection makes individuals question if their own life is enough. Identity becomes tangled in comparison.
- **Achievement as Self-Worth -** People often chase degrees, promotions, awards and recognition not for personal growth but to feel worthy in the eyes of others. Identity becomes conditional—"I am valuable only if I achieve."
- **External Validation as Fuel -** Likes, comments and praise become the new currency of self-esteem. Without external approval, many feel unseen and unsure of their identity.
- **Emotional Disconnect -** Even when someone owns everything that "should" make them feel confident, they may still feel insecure—because identity built externally lacks stability.

Real-Life Examples:

- **The Man Who Felt Successful but Empty -** Rohan worked hard to build a luxurious lifestyle. He owned the latest gadgets, wore premium brands and lived in a stylish apartment. Outwardly, people admired him. But privately, he often felt a strange emptiness—because the image he projected was not the person he felt himself to be. **He wondered why success on the outside didn't feel like confidence on the inside.**
- **The Student Who Lost Herself in Comparison -** Nisha followed influencers who displayed perfect lives—travel, fashion, celebrations. She started buying things she didn't need just to feel "included." Over time, she noticed that her self-worth was tied to likes and comments. She no

longer knew whether her preferences were truly hers or shaped by what she saw online. **She felt disconnected from her own identity.**

Conclusion: A Question We All Face Today

In a world that constantly tells us who we should be, it is easy to drift away from who we truly are. Identity today is shaped by noise—trends, expectations, comparisons, images and possessions. People are surrounded by influences that quietly mold their inner sense of self.

This chapter is not about solutions yet—it is about awareness. A mirror held up to modern life. A gentle reminder that many people today are living with an identity built more from the outside than the inside. And so, in this material-driven world, the real question becomes:

Are we living as ourselves—or as the version the world wants us to be?

The Happiness Trap: Searching in Material Things

"We buy things to feel happy, only to discover that happiness was never for sale."

We live in a world where happiness is often packaged, priced and promoted. Everywhere we look—on screens, in stores, on billboards—we are told that joy can be purchased. New gadgets promise excitement, fashionable clothes promise confidence and luxury purchases promise status. The message is subtle but constant: **"You will feel better once you buy this."** Over time, this belief becomes a quiet trap. Not because possessions are wrong but because we start associating happiness with things rather than experiences, meanings or feelings. Modern life conditions us to expect emotional fulfilment from material upgrades. But the more we chase it, the more fleeting happiness becomes.

Why This Trap Exists Today

In our hyper-consumer culture, desire is no longer natural—it is manufactured. Companies spend billions crafting images that connect buying with belonging, comfort, success and self-worth. Social media amplifies this further. We see curated lifestyles, luxury holidays, stylish homes and perfectly framed moments. Even when we don't consciously compare, a part of us whispers, **"I should have that too."**

This creates a cycle where happiness becomes dependent on the next purchase, the next upgrade, the next "high." But material joy is short-lived. The excitement fades quickly and what was once new becomes ordinary. Then the search begins again—another item, another distraction, another rush.

In this loop, happiness becomes something people **pursue**, not something they **experience**. And the pursuit keeps moving the finish line.

The Reality of Today's Material-Driven Happiness

- **The Thrill That Fades Quickly -** New things feel exciting at first—fresh, shiny, satisfying. But the feeling rarely lasts. Once the novelty wears off, the desire for the next new thing quietly returns.
- **Comparing What We Have to What Others Display -** Online, people showcase their best possessions, not their ordinary days. This creates an illusion that everyone else is living a richer, more exciting life.
- **Shopping as Emotional Comfort -** For many, buying becomes a way to escape stress, boredom or loneliness. It feels like relief—but only for a moment.
- **Possessions Becoming Identity Markers -** People often associate their worth with what they own. Cars, phones, clothes, homes—these become signals of "success," while the person behind them remains unseen.
- **Happiness Delayed Until the Next Purchase -** Instead of enjoying the present, many find themselves waiting for the next delivery, upgrade or celebration to feel joy.

Real-Life Examples:

- **The Man Who Mistook Luxury for Fulfilment -** Malik always believed that owning premium items would make him feel accomplished. He saved for months to buy the luxury car he had admired for years. And for a few weeks, it did feel magical—people noticed, admired and praised him. But slowly, the excitement faded. The loan remained. The pressure increased. Malik realised he didn't feel any happier than before—just more burdened. **He had chased excitement, not fulfilment.**
- **The Young Woman Who Confused Buying with Belonging -** Tara followed influencers who showcased beautiful clothes, travel and décor. She wanted her life to look just as perfect, so she bought things she didn't need—just to feel relevant. But her home filled up while her heart did not. She felt more anxious, not more confident and more disconnected from herself than ever. **She found that buying created moments—but not meaning.**

Conclusion: A Quiet Question Behind Every Purchase

In a world where material things are marketed as the gateway to happiness, it becomes easy to confuse desire with joy, excitement with fulfilment and possession with self-worth. The happiness derived from material things is often brief—pleasant but temporary. It fades as quickly as it arrives, leaving behind a lingering desire for more.

This chapter is not about finding solutions or changing habits yet—it is about recognising the pattern that so many people today live within. A pattern where happiness feels close but never quite enough.

And so the deeper question remains:

Are we truly seeking happiness—or simply collecting things that distract us from its absence?

The Paradox of Choice: Too Many Options too Little Peace

"Choice was meant to give us freedom. Instead, it often leaves us frozen, confused and overwhelmed."

We live in a world overflowing with options—endless brands, infinite entertainment, limitless decisions at every step. What to eat, what to watch, what to buy, where to live, which career path to follow, whom to trust, how to spend time... Almost everything now comes in dozens, sometimes hundreds, of variations. On the surface, this abundance looks like freedom. But for many people today, it quietly becomes a source of confusion, anxiety and emotional exhaustion.

Modern life has reached a point where choosing feels heavier than doing. Even simple decisions—like selecting a pair of shoes or picking a restaurant—can turn into long mental marathons. And behind every choice lies a subtle fear: **"What if I choose wrong?"**

Why This Paradox Exists Today

In earlier times, choices were limited and life felt simpler—not because everything was perfect but because decisions were fewer and clearer. Today, we are

surrounded by endless possibilities: hundreds of cereals on a shelf, thousands of movies to stream, countless products one click away. What used to require little thought now demands analysis, comparisons and reviews.
This constant decision-making overloads the brain. The pressure to make the "best" choice in everything—from careers to relationships to purchases—creates tension instead of satisfaction. Even after choosing, many people feel unsure, second-guessing themselves and wondering if a better option was missed.

Ironically, the more options people have, the less confident and peaceful they feel. Choice, once a gift, has become a mental burden.

The Reality of Today's Choice-Driven Lifestyle

- **Overthinking Every Decision -** Whether it's picking a phone, a streaming show or even a simple meal, people often feel overwhelmed by too much information. Decisions that should take seconds now take minutes—or hours.
- **Fear of Missing Out on a Better Option -** With so many choices available, people constantly worry that a better deal, better job, better partner or better experience exists somewhere else.
- **The Pressure to Choose "Perfectly" -** Reviews, ratings and public opinions create invisible pressure to make flawless decisions. Even small choices feel high-stakes.
- **Constant Switching of Plans -** Many people change their minds frequently—cancelling, shifting or rethinking plans—because every alternative seems tempting.
- **Dissatisfaction After Choosing -** Even when a choice is made, satisfaction is low. The mind still imagines the other possibilities that "might have" been better.

Real-Life Examples:

- **Michael: The Professional Paralyzed by Too Many Career Paths -** Michael, a talented marketing specialist, had multiple job offers from different companies. Each role came with its own advantages, perks and uncertainties. Instead of feeling excited, he felt stressed. He spent weeks comparing salaries, growth paths, work cultures, commute times and online reviews. The more he analysed, the more confused he became. Even after choosing a job, he felt anxious and wondered if he had made the right choice. **He realised the weight of choice had drained the joy from opportunity.**
- **Sofia: The Shopper Who Couldn't Decide -** Sofia entered a store to buy a simple jacket. But in front of her were racks of dozens of styles, colors

and fits. She tried one after another, checked prices, compared fabrics and scrolled through her phone to read brand reviews. What should have been a 10-minute purchase took over an hour, leaving her mentally exhausted. Even after buying the jacket, she wondered if she should have chosen a different one. **The abundance of options left her feeling unsure instead of satisfied.**

Conclusion: A Quiet Question Behind Every Choice

In a world overflowing with possibilities, choosing has become more stressful than freeing. People face decision fatigue daily—not because their lives are harder but because their minds are overloaded. The paradox of choice is a defining experience of modern life: the more options we gain, the less peace we feel.
This chapter is not about solutions—it is about understanding today's reality. A reality where freedom of choice often becomes a mental maze.

And so the deeper question emerges:

Are we making choices that serve us—or are choices consuming us?

Consumerism: Buying More Than We Require

"We don't just buy things—we buy stress, debt and distraction."

If the Paradox of Choice is about deciding, Consumerism is about acquiring—and what happens after. Modern life nudges us to buy beyond need, turning homes, calendars and minds into storage units.

Consumerism is a significant factor complicating the pursuit of a simpler life. While consumerism offers convenience, variety and constant innovation, it can also trap us in a cycle of buying, accumulating and desiring more, often at the cost of clarity, financial well-being and inner peace. Here's how consumerism contributes to complexity

Person works hard to get paycheck to buy things which he does not need in life.

The tendency to buy more than we need is a widespread phenomenon in modern society. Several psychological, social and economic factors contribute to this behaviour, leading people to purchase more items than necessary.

Why We Over-Buy (Drivers of Acquisition)

- **Advertising & scarcity cues -** Modern marketing is designed to trigger urgency—countdowns, "only 2 left," and curated imagery that promises a better life. These signals make us feel we're missing out unless we act immediately. Even when we don't need the product, the emotional pull can override rational thinking.

- **Emotional spending -** Shopping often becomes a quick escape from stress, boredom or loneliness. The excitement of buying something new provides a temporary mood boost, which the brain quickly starts craving again. This cycle leads to purchases driven by emotion, not genuine need.
- **Frictionless checkout -** One-click buying, saved cards and instant delivery erase the natural pauses that once made us reconsider a purchase. With no time to reflect, impulsive decisions feel effortless and harmless. The convenience makes buying easier than thinking.
- **Discount traps -** Sales and promotions create the illusion of saving money, even when the item adds clutter and future cost. "Buy one, get one" deals trick the mind into feeling smart and rewarded. In reality, we often end up owning more than we can use.
- **"Just in case" mindset -** People often buy things for hypothetical scenarios that rarely arrive. These items sit untouched, taking up space and creating guilt. What begins as preparedness turns into silent accumulation.

The Hidden After-Costs (After You Own It)

- **Money drain -** The financial weight doesn't end at the checkout—EMIs, insurance, maintenance and upgrades continue month after month. The initial thrill fades quickly but the payments stay. Small purchases accumulate into long-term pressure.
- **Time tax -** Every item you bring home demands time: research, setup, repairs, cleaning and organization. Weekends quietly disappear into managing possessions rather than enjoying life. Stuff doesn't just take space—it takes hours.
- **Attention clutter -** Each possession occupies a small corner of your mind—needing care, tracking, cleaning or remembering. This creates a continuous low-grade mental load. Over time, attention becomes scattered and peace becomes harder to access.
- **Space pressure -** Homes expand around belongings—drawers, shelves and cabinets fill faster than we imagine. Rooms feel tighter, movement becomes restricted and living spaces feel more like storage units. More things slowly reduce the space meant for living.
- **Value trade -** Money spent on unnecessary items is money not invested in experiences, skills, health or meaningful goals. Every purchase is a choice between short-term pleasure and long-term well-being. Over-buying quietly steals from what enriches life most.

"Buy now, pay later," same-day delivery and one-click checkouts make spending effortless while ownership remains heavy—EMIs, maintenance and mental clutter. The cart empties in seconds; the cost lingers for months, stealing space, bandwidth and the quiet you need to feel alive.

When Things Start Owning You: The Burden of Possessions

"We think we own things. But often, they own us."

At first, possessions feel like tools that make life easier. A new car promises freedom, a bigger house offers comfort and the latest gadget delivers convenience. But over time, these very possessions begin to demand our attention. They need maintenance, repairs, upgrades, insurance and storage. What once felt like liberation slowly becomes obligation.

The truth is that ownership often comes with invisible strings. The more we accumulate, the more our time, money and energy are tied up in caring for what we own. Instead of serving us, our possessions begin to dictate our choices. We work longer hours to pay for them, worry about protecting them and feel anxious about losing them. In this way, things start owning us.

Story: Arjun's Upgrade

Arjun is a 36-year-old manager at a manufacturing firm. He lives with his family in a comfortable apartment, earns well and prides himself on being "up to date." One Friday, after a long week, he decides he deserves a reward: the newest flagship smartphone.

The First Domino

At the store, the salesperson praises the phone's camera and speed. Arjun buys it, feeling a rush of satisfaction. On the way home he thinks, *"This will make my life easier."* But the **chain effect** begins within minutes:

- **Premium case** and **tempered glass**— "to protect the investment."
- **Wireless earbuds**—the old ones don't pair as seamlessly.
- **Fast charger** and **power bank**—because the new battery supports "super charging."
- **Cloud storage subscription**—those high-res photos eat space.
- **Streaming upgrade**—to enjoy the larger, brighter screen.

By Sunday evening, Arjun has spent far more than the phone's sticker price. He's also invested **time**: unboxing, updating, customizing, transferring data, setting passwords, syncing devices, reading how-to guides. The phone was supposed to save time but ironically, it has already consumed several hours.

Owning Begets More Owning

The beautiful new device changes other choices too.

- **Work bag**: The old messenger bag feels bulky; Arjun buys a sleek backpack with a padded laptop/phone sleeve.
- **Desk accessories**: A wireless charging pad, a multi-port hub and cable organizers—because a premium phone should sit on a tidy desk.
- **Home internet**: The video buffering seems more annoying now; he upgrades to a faster (and costlier) plan.
- **Smartwatch**: He wants to reply to messages hands-free during meetings.

Every item **demands attention**—firmware updates, battery charging cycles, warranty registrations, invoices stored "just in case." Notifications multiply. Arjun notices a subtle anxiety: *"What if I scratch the screen? Where did I put the earbuds case? Did I cancel the old subscription?"*

Lifestyle Echoes

On Monday, colleagues admire the phone. Someone mentions an upcoming **smart TV** sale: "The phone mirrors beautifully to certain models." Arjun files that away. Another colleague showcases a **home automation** app: "You can control lights and AC from your phone!" A third suggests a **digital camera**: "With your phone, you'll love tethered shooting."
Arjun doesn't purchase those immediately—but the **desire seeds are planted**. When payday arrives, he buys the smart TV. That leads to:

- A **soundbar** for better audio.
- **Wall mount and installation** service.

- A **streaming bundle** with add-ons he didn't want last month.

The living room looks modern yet there's a new weekend routine: app updates, device pairing, troubleshooting. When his child misplaces a remote, a movie night turns into a fifteen-minute hunt. **Peace gives way to micro-stresses.**

Maintenance Tax

Six months later, Arjun's earbuds battery degrades. The **replacement** costs surprisingly high. A cable frays. The cloud subscription auto-renews. The internet provider raises prices. The phone's OS update breaks a favourite app; he spends an evening on forums, installing patches.
Each item carries a **maintenance tax**:

- **Time**: updates, repairs, warranty claims, reading manuals.
- **Money**: accessories, service fees, replacements, extended warranties.
- **Attention**: remembering passwords, managing notifications, protecting fragile gear.

Arjun notices another change—**household clutter**. Tech boxes "kept for warranty" pile up. Old devices "kept as backup" squat in drawers. Chargers breed in a tangle. The home gradually shifts from a sanctuary to a **warehouse**.

The Car Cascade

When Arjun's office announces flexible hours, he rationalizes buying a **new car**: "Safer, more comfortable, better mileage." The chain effect escalates:

- **Loan** with EMIs and insurance premium upgrades.
- **Accessories**: seat covers, dash cam, phone mount, fast charger for the car, air purifier.
- **Services**: detailing, annual maintenance plans, alignment checks.
- **Parking**: a reserved spot fee at work; a storage solution at home for car cleaning supplies.

Commuting feels pleasant at first but soon traffic steals time. EMIs trim savings. Add-ons push monthly expenses up. The car "owns" weekends—service appointments, washing, polishing—while Arjun's **free time shrinks**.

Invisible Costs

Arjun's spreadsheet shows rising costs but the **invisible costs** sting more:

- **Peace** → notifications, upgrades, decisions, micro-repairs.
- **Time** → setup, maintenance, shopping, comparisons, returns.
- **Energy** → attention scattered across gadgets and services.
- **Space** → drawers and shelves turn into storage for "maybe useful" items.

One night, Arjun looks at his living room—beautiful yet **busy**—and recalls how calm life felt before the upgrade spiral. He realizes: ***"I don't own these things; these things own me."***

The Burden of Possessions

"*Why having more often gives us less.*"

I was taught—like most of us—that having more means living better: more things, more upgrades, more choice. But here's what I've learned: **the more I own, the more I carry**. Every possession quietly asks for my time, my energy, my money—and often, my peace of mind. As you read this, I invite you to reflect with me on how owning more than we need slowly becomes a burden.

1. **Mental Clutter and Stress** — Every item requires attention—space, care and decisions. Cluttered rooms create cluttered thoughts. It becomes harder to think clearly, relax or focus. Repeated decisions about what to store, fix, clean or organize create decision fatigue that drains energy from the work and relationships that matter most.
2. **Financial Pressure** — More stuff isn't just a one-time cost; it is a lifestyle cost: buying, maintaining, repairing, insuring and eventually replacing things. "Just one more" can compound into debt, reduced savings and long-term stress.
3. **Losing Focus on What Truly Matters** — Attention gets trapped by things—tracking, cleaning, comparing, upgrading. As this grows, it drifts attention away from what genuinely nourishes life: relationships, meaningful work, learning, health and simple joy. Many people feel strangely empty after getting "more."
4. **Increased Responsibility** — Each extra possession adds hidden tasks: cleaning, storing, fixing, arranging. These tasks quietly consume hours that could have supported rest, family or personal interests.
5. **Emotional Dependence on Things** — Identity can become attached to brands, gadgets and appearances, making confidence fragile. Scratches, losses or missed upgrades can translate into feeling "less," as worth begins to lean on what is owned rather than who one is.
6. **Environmental Impact** — Over-consumption strains resources and creates pollution and waste. Most purchased items eventually become trash, externalizing costs to the planet.
7. **Reduced Flexibility and Freedom** — Possessions can anchor people to one lifestyle. Stuff makes it harder to move, travel or say yes to new opportunities; mobility and adaptability shrink as ownership grows.

8. **Social Comparison and Pressure** — The comparison trap—scrolling, upgrading, chasing trends—keeps desires open-ended. Someone always has more, newer, better, turning "enough" into a moving target.
9. **Loss of Creativity and Gratitude** — When everything is available, appreciation dulls. Abundance without intention can make satisfaction harder and creativity can fade amid endless, low-friction options.
10. **The Psychological Weight of Ownership** — Letting go is hard. People overvalue what they own (the "endowment effect") and often keep unused items, feeling an outsized attachment despite lack of use.
11. **The Illusion of Security** — Things can project safety or success yet real security rests more in skills, resilience, health, relationships and purpose. When possessions are mistaken for security, the sense of safety becomes fragile.
12. **Impact on Health and Relationships** — Clutter affects sleep, mood and patience. It can also create friction at home—what to buy, where to keep it, what to discard—adding emotional strain to shared spaces.
13. **Reduced Capacity for New Experiences** — Money and time directed toward things reduce what's available for experiences—travel, learning, new skills and meaningful moments—narrowing life's richness.
14. **Disconnect from the Present** — Excess pulls attention into the past ("I might need this someday") or the future ("I'll use this later"), making it harder to inhabit the present moment.
15. **Cultural and Environmental Disconnect** — Overconsumption can hide real costs—labour conditions, ecosystem damage, waste streams—numbing awareness of broader impacts.

The Real Cost of "More"

I once believed possessions would serve me. Often, they enslaved me. Every item I own quietly asks for my time, money and mental space. The more I accumulate, the more I trade **freedom for responsibility**.

Conclusion: The Hidden Weight Behind What We Own

In an age of abundance, ownership often feels like progress—but quietly behaves like pressure. Each new possession adds small demands that accumulate into a mental load: more to manage, more to maintain, more to think about. What promises comfort can, over time, convert into cognitive strain, financial drag, relational friction and environmental cost. This is not a question of morality—it is a question of mental space.

This chapter is not about fixing anything. It is about **seeing** the true footprint of "more": how objects occupy mindshare, shape routines and narrow freedom, often without our noticing. The burden rarely arrives loudly; it gathers slowly—item by item, payment by payment, decision by decision—until life feels heavier than it should.

And so, a quieter question surfaces beneath every purchase and possession:

Are the things we own supporting our life—or quietly owning pieces of it?

Needs vs. Wants: Where We Lost Balance

"We learned how to satisfy our wants but forgot how to understand our needs."

The difference between **needs** and **wants** is fundamental in understanding personal priorities and making mindful decisions, especially when it comes to living a minimalist lifestyle. Here's a breakdown of both concepts:

Needs:

Needs are essential requirements for survival and well-being. These are the basic things that are necessary for a person to live, function and maintain a healthy life. Needs are not optional—they are things you must have to sustain your life or meet essential physical and emotional needs.

Examples of Needs: Food and water, Safe shelter, Basic clothing, Healthcare, Physical and emotional safety.

Wants:

Wants, on the other hand, are not necessary for survival but enhance the quality of life, provide comfort or are desired for pleasure. Wants are optional and although they can bring joy or satisfaction, they are not essential for basic survival.

Examples of Wants: Luxury items and gadgets, Entertainment subscriptions, Trendy fashion, Exotic travel, High-end home décor.

Key Differences:

1. Necessity vs Desire

Needs keep you alive and stable.
Wants enhance comfort but aren't essential.

2. Impact on Well-Being

Needs directly affect health, safety and functioning.
Wants to bring temporary happiness but do not sustain long-term well-being.

3. Duration of Importance

Needs remain constant throughout life.
Wants shift quickly with trends, mood and lifestyle.

4. Dependency

Needs are non-negotiable.

Wants are flexible and often influenced by culture and comparison.

Needs are essential to your survival and well-being, like food, shelter and healthcare. **Wants** are desires that enhance life but aren't necessary for survival, like luxury items or entertainment.

We Lost Balance

Modern life has blurred the line between what we truly need and what we think we need. The world around us constantly promotes comfort, luxury, upgrades and instant gratification. As a result, wants—once occasional desires—have quietly transformed into expectations. And needs—basic elements of well-being—often get overshadowed or neglected.

Today, people feel pressure to live a certain lifestyle, buy certain things and keep up with trends that promise happiness or status. In this environment, the difference between needs and wants becomes increasingly unclear. This confusion shapes how people spend their time, money and emotional energy—and influences how fulfilled or exhausted they feel.

Why This Imbalance Happens Today

Our surroundings encourage consumption. Advertisements, social media and online culture send a constant message: **"More is better."** A larger home, a newer car, the latest phone, the trendiest fashion—wants are presented as if they are essential for living a good life. Over time, this shapes expectations: what was once considered a luxury becomes a "necessity."

Meanwhile, real needs—rest, connection, purpose, simplicity, emotional health—receive less attention. People often overlook them because they are not marketed, sold or highlighted in the same dramatic way.

This imbalance creates a silent conflict: people chase wants believing they will bring satisfaction, while their deeper needs remain unfulfilled.

The Reality of Today's Needs vs. Wants Confusion

- **Wants Masquerading as Needs -** Modern marketing cleverly blurs the distinction. People begin to feel they "need" what they merely desire—upgrades, trends, comfort-driven purchases.
- **Constant Exposure to Better Options -** Seeing others live beautifully curated lifestyles makes ordinary life feel inadequate. Wants quickly turn into expectations.

- **Emotional Decisions Driving Consumption -** Stress, boredom, comparison and loneliness push people to buy things hoping for relief or validation.
- **Neglect of Real Needs -** Basic emotional, mental and relational needs—such as rest, attention, stability and connection—often remain unmet because the focus shifts to external markers of success.
- **Lifestyle Inflation Becoming Normal -** As incomes rise, wants rise even faster. What felt luxurious becomes "normal," and simplicity feels insufficient.

Real-Life Examples:

- **James: The Professional Trapped in Lifestyle Expansion -** James received a promotion and a significant salary increase. Instead of feeling secure, he immediately upgraded his apartment, bought a new car and started spending more on dining and travel. These wants felt like needs—the natural "next step." But over time, his expenses grew as fast as his income. Despite earning more dollars, he felt financially stressed. **His wants expanded so quickly that his needs remained unmet.**
- **Clara: The Woman Who Filled Emotional Gaps with Purchases -** Clara loved buying small luxuries—skincare, décor, trendy gadgets. Whenever she felt lonely or stressed, shopping gave her a momentary boost. But her home slowly filled with items she rarely used, while her deeper needs—companionship, rest and self-understanding—remained untouched. **She realised her purchases were wants but her emptiness came from unmet needs.**

Conclusion: A Mirror Reflecting Today's Reality

In a world driven by consumption and comparison, the boundary between needs and wants has quietly dissolved. People upgrade lifestyles faster than they upgrade inner well-being. Wants are louder, brighter and more tempting; needs are quieter, softer and easily ignored. This chapter isn't about choosing simplicity or analyzing habits—that comes later. It is about seeing clearly how modern life shapes our perception of what we "must have."
And ultimately, it invites a deeper reflection:

Are we chasing what we truly need—or what the world has taught us to want?

Chapter 3: Digital Drowning — Always Connected, Rarely Present

Digital Overload: Information Without Wisdom

"Technology promised freedom. Instead, it gave us chains we can't see."

Digital Overload is a modern challenge that has intensified as technology has become deeply integrated into every aspect of life. While digital tools and platforms offer immense convenience, the constant flow of information, notifications and entertainment can lead to mental fatigue, distraction and stress, making it harder to live a simple, balanced life.
We live in a time where information arrives faster than we can process it. News updates, social media posts, notifications, emails, reels, messages, articles, ads—content flows toward us every second, from every direction. What once required effort to access now demands effort to escape. The world has never been more connected yet our minds have never felt more crowded.

Digital convenience has turned into digital overload. People scroll endlessly, consume rapidly and react instantly. There is always something new to watch, something trending to follow, something urgent to check. The constant inflow keeps the mind alert but drained, stimulated but unfocused. We know more than ever yet understand less than before.

Why This Happens Today

Technology has made information abundant—far more abundant than the human brain is designed to handle. Every minute brings new updates, opinions and content demanding our attention. The internet offers unlimited knowledge but unlimited knowledge also creates a silent pressure: **to keep up to stay informed to stay relevant.**

This constant input interrupts our thoughts, shortens our attention span and reduces the space needed for reflection. Information arrives faster than wisdom can form. People switch between apps, tabs and notifications without noticing how fragmented their mind becomes. The mind remains active but rarely still. Busy but not necessarily better.

Digital overload shapes the emotional landscape of modern life—quietly, continuously and often unconsciously.

The Reality of Today's Information-Saturated World

1. **Information Overload -** In the digital age, information is available at our fingertips but this ease comes at a price. The sheer volume of information we encounter daily—from news feeds to social media to emails—can feel overwhelming. Our minds are constantly processing new data, which can lead to cognitive fatigue, reducing our ability to focus and make thoughtful decisions.
2. **Constant Connectivity and the "Always On" Culture -** Smartphones, emails and instant messaging apps have created a culture of constant connectivity, where people feel they need to always be available. This can lead to stress and anxiety, as individuals find it challenging to disconnect, even after work hours.
3. **The Erosion of Attention and Focus -** Digital platforms, particularly social media and news apps, are designed to capture and hold our attention as long as possible. This constant interruption of notifications, updates and messages trains the mind to seek short bursts of information, eroding our ability to focus deeply on a single task.
4. **The Pressure of Social Comparison -** social media amplifies the tendency to compare ourselves with others, as we are constantly exposed to curated images of others' lives, achievements and possessions. This pressure to "keep up" can lead to feelings of inadequacy, envy and anxiety.
5. **Decision Fatigue from Too Many Digital Choices -** With the rise of apps and platforms, we face endless decisions about which tools to use, what content to consume and how to manage our digital lives. This constant decision-making contributes to decision fatigue, a state where making even simple choices becomes mentally exhausting.
6. **Sleep Disruption and Poor Health -** Excessive screen time, particularly before bed, disrupts natural sleep patterns. Blue light from screens can interfere with melatonin production, making it harder to fall asleep. Over time, poor sleep can lead to decreased mental health, productivity and general well-being.

7. **Superficial Connections over Deep Relationships -** Digital communication has made it easier to stay connected with a larger network of people but these connections are often shallow. Constantly interacting through texts and social media can prevent people from forming meaningful, face-to-face relationships, which are essential for emotional well-being.
8. **Loss of Personal Privacy -** In the digital world, personal information is constantly being collected, analysed and shared by companies. This erosion of privacy can create unease and anxiety, as people worry about their data being exposed or misused.
9. **Digital Hoarding and Clutter -** Just as people accumulate physical clutter, digital hoarding—accumulating unnecessary files, emails, apps and media—can lead to a cluttered mind and reduced productivity. A cluttered digital space mirrors the clutter of the mind, creating a sense of chaos and distraction.
10. **The Dangers of Digital Multitasking -** With digital tools, multitasking has become easier but more distracting. Switching between apps, messages and tasks prevents deep focus, creating a fragmented and scattered mindset.

People are exposed to crises, debates, tragedies and controversies around the world—events they cannot control but still absorb emotionally.

Real-Life Examples:

- **Benjamin: The Analyst Lost in Endless Updates -** Benjamin worked in finance and felt compelled to stay updated constantly—market alerts, news, expert opinions. Throughout the day, he checked multiple sources, worried he might miss something important. But the flood of information left him anxious and mentally scattered. Even after work, he found himself scrolling through financial updates out of habit. **He knew more every day—but felt less clear.**
- **Sophia: The Student Overwhelmed by Online Learning -** Sophia loved learning but the internet offered too much. She saved articles, subscribed to channels, enrolled in online courses—never finishing most of them. The abundance made her feel behind, even when she was doing well. Her brain was full yet her understanding felt shallow. **She confused access to information with actual wisdom.**

Conclusion: Information Without Stillness

We live in an age where information comes easily and continuously. The world delivers data, opinions and updates faster than the mind can filter them. While this chapter does not explore solutions yet, it reflects a reality many people feel every day:

A life filled with information but low in insight.
A mind filled with noise but low in clarity.
A world filled with connection but low in peace.
And so the question emerges:
In the midst of so much information, what are we truly learning?

Living Like Robots: Automation of Human Life

"We have mastered efficiency—but forgotten how to live."

Modern life has reached a stage where almost everything can be automated—our schedules, our homes, our purchases, our entertainment and even our conversations. With smart devices, apps, reminders and AI-driven tools, daily life runs on pre-set routines and digital commands. On the surface, this seems like progress. Tasks are faster, decisions easier and actions efficient. But beneath this efficiency, something deeper is happening. People are beginning to live on autopilot—moving, reacting and functioning without fully engaging.

Many individuals today go through entire days without intentional thought: waking up to automated alarms, following pre-programmed routines, responding to algorithm-curated content and relying on devices to tell them what to do next. Life feels smooth but also strangely mechanical. The world has become more convenient than ever yet humans increasingly feel disconnected from themselves.

Why This Feels True in Today's World

Technology was designed to make life simpler but it also subtly influences how we think and behave. Automation removes friction—but it also removes awareness. Every automated process creates one less moment of choice, one less pause for reflection.

From calendar alerts telling us where to be to apps suggesting what to watch to platforms recommending what to buy, modern life often feels pre-scripted. The more systems we create to help ourselves, the more we adapt ourselves to those systems.

Human beings, without noticing, become predictable in their routines—checking the same apps, reacting to the same triggers, following the same patterns daily. Life becomes efficient but not always meaningful.

The Reality of Today's Automated Living

- **Daily Routines Becoming Pre-Programmed -** People wake, work, eat and sleep at the same times, following routines shaped more by notifications and tasks than by intention.
- **Decisions Outsourced to Algorithms -** What to watch, where to eat, what to buy, even whom to follow—many choices are driven by automated recommendations rather than personal thought.
- **Reduced Human Effort in Basic Tasks -** Lights switch on automatically, groceries reorder themselves, devices remind us to drink water or stand up.
- **Emotional Reactions Becoming Automated -** Many people react instantly to notifications, messages or triggers without conscious awareness—like reflexes.
- **Life Feeling Fast but Unfelt -** Days pass quickly, filled with activity yet people often struggle to recall what they actually experienced.

Real-Life Examples:

- **Lucas: The Man Whose Day Ran on Notifications -** Lucas didn't plan his day—his phone did. His alarms woke him, his calendar told him where to be, his apps told him what to buy and his reminders told him what to do next. Even his entertainment was decided by algorithmic suggestions. Everything worked smoothly yet Lucas sometimes felt like he was living someone else's script. **His life was efficient but not fully lived.**
- **Maria: The Homemaker Guided by Smart Devices -** Maria used smart assistants to manage her home—lights adjusted automatically, groceries arrived through subscription services and appliances operated on timers. While this saved her time, she noticed that her days felt repetitive. The more her home ran itself, the less connected she felt to the rhythm of her own life. **She moved through routines without noticing how little she was engaging.**
- **Aaron: The Professional on Autopilot -** Aaron lived by his productivity apps. His meals were delivered, his workouts tracked, his meetings scheduled and his finances automated. Over time, he realised he rarely

made spontaneous decisions. He wasn't choosing his life—he was executing it. **He functioned like a perfectly optimized machine yet felt strangely empty inside.**

Conclusion: The Human Cost of Automation

Automation simplifies life—but it also shapes it. As more tasks become automatic, people risk losing the awareness, presence and intentionality that make life genuinely human. Modern living often resembles a perfectly running system with humans as its operators.
This chapter is not about reducing automation—that comes later. It is about recognising a reality many experience silently: A world where life runs smoothly but feels strangely robotic.

And so the question arises:

Are we living with technology—or living according to it?

Seeking Social Media Approval: The New Addiction

We measure our worth in likes—but forget that real value can't be counted."

There was a time when people lived their moments quietly, without needing to prove anything to anyone. But today, much of life feels like a performance. Social media has turned ordinary experiences into public displays and personal achievements into content. Every photo, every thought, every celebration carries an unspoken question: **"How will others react?"**

Approval—once something we sought from the few people close to us—is now something we chase from hundreds or thousands of strangers. A like, a comment, a share has quietly become the new currency of emotional validation. The more connected the world becomes, the more individuals feel driven to seek recognition through screens.

Social media promised expression. Instead, it often fuels insecurity. It promised connection. Instead, it often amplifies comparison. It promised freedom. Instead, it creates dependence on approval.

Why This Happens in Today's Digital World

Human beings naturally want to feel seen, valued and appreciated. Social media magnifies this desire by offering instant feedback—hearts, likes, emojis, reactions—tiny signals that make people feel validated. But this feedback is unpredictable and addictive. It conditions people to measure their worth through numbers and algorithms.

Instead of asking, "Do I like this photo?" people ask, "Will others like it?" Instead of feeling joy for themselves, many feel joy only when others approve. The line between real self and online self becomes blurry.

Every post becomes a silent test: *Am I interesting enough? Attractive enough? Successful enough? Worthy enough?*

This pursuit of approval shapes behaviour, emotions and identity—often without people noticing.

The Reality of Today's Approval-Driven Social Culture

- **Posting for Validation Instead of Expression -** People share not because they want to but because they want reactions. The thrill of approval becomes the purpose.
- **Self-Worth Measured in Numbers -** Likes, followers and views become indicators of value. Low engagement feels like rejection.
- **Constant Comparison to Curated Lives -** People compare their real lives to others' filtered perfection—leading to insecurity, envy and dissatisfaction.
- **Anxiety Around How Posts Will Be Received -** Many hesitate, re-edit or delete posts based on anticipated judgment.
- **Emotional Dependence on External Feedback -** The absence of likes or comments creates feelings of emptiness or doubt.

Real-Life Examples:

- **Hannah: The Teenager Who Measured Happiness in Likes -** Hannah loved taking photos but over time, she noticed her mood depended on how many likes her posts received. If a picture performed well, she felt confident for a moment. If it didn't, she spent hours wondering what was wrong with her. Instead of enjoying her life, she started curating it for approval. **Her self-esteem rose and fell with numbers on a screen.**
- **Marcus: The Professional Obsessed With Online Image -** Marcus built a successful career but he craved the image of success even more. He posted photos of achievements, vacations, gifts and lifestyle upgrades—not to celebrate them but to maintain a digital identity. Every post brought a momentary high, followed by a deeper need for more approval. **He was admired online but felt invisible offline.**
- **Emily: The Content Creator Stuck in a Validation Loop -** Emily enjoyed sharing her creative work but gradually her focus shifted from passion to performance. She checked analytics obsessively—views, comments, watch time. When numbers dropped, she felt anxious.

Her joy slowly turned into pressure to stay relevant. **She wasn't creating anymore—she was competing.**

Conclusion: The Quiet Cost of Digital Validation

Social media has changed how people express themselves, how they view their lives and how they measure their worth. What began as a platform for connection has evolved into a source of emotional dependence. People seek approval not from within but from invisible audiences they may never meet.
This chapter does not offer solutions yet—it simply reflects a truth of our time: A world where validation is instant, addictive and often empty. A world where people feel pressured to perform instead of simply live.

And so the question remains:
Are we sharing our lives—or seeking permission to feel good about them?

Social Proof — When Other People Decide for Us

"We think we are choosing freely—until we realise how much we are copying."

Modern life increasingly shapes choices not through personal reflection but through observation of others. This behaviour, known as **social proof**, leads people to believe that if many individuals are choosing something, it must be right, valuable or necessary. What once helped communities learn and survive now operates on a much larger and more intense scale.

Social media, advertising, digital platforms and public metrics constantly display what others are buying, achieving and celebrating. Over time, these repeated images begin to influence decisions quietly. Preferences form externally. Goals feel urgent because others are pursuing them. Life choices start resembling imitation rather than intention.

Many people today do not consciously decide the direction of their life. They absorb it.

Why This Feels True in Today's World

Modern society has turned visibility into validation. Popularity is often mistaken for correctness. Repetition replaces reflection. When people are constantly exposed to how others live, the mind naturally adopts those patterns as reference points.
Instead of asking, *"Is this right for me?"* individuals begin asking, *"Why am I not there yet?"* Comparison becomes continuous. Satisfaction becomes fragile. Confidence slowly shifts from inner clarity to external approval.

In such an environment, even a peaceful or stable life can begin to feel insufficient— not because something is missing but because something else appears louder or faster.

The Reality of Today's Social-Proof-Driven Living

- **Comparison Becoming the Default Lens** – People evaluate their lives against visible achievements and lifestyles rather than personal values or circumstances.
- **Borrowed Desires Replacing Real Needs** – Wants and aspirations are shaped by exposure, not inner clarity.
- **Identity Shaped by Trends** – Career paths, spending habits and success timelines feel imposed rather than chosen.
- **Constant Fear of Falling Behind** – Progress feels mandatory, even when direction is unclear.
- **Short-Lived Satisfaction** – Achievements bring brief relief but not lasting fulfilment, as external reference points keep shifting.

Real-Life Examples:

- **Daniel: The Professional Who Expanded Without Intention** – Daniel was financially stable and reasonably content. But constant exposure to peers upgrading lifestyles and achievements made him feel behind. He began taking on bigger commitments and higher expenses without clearly knowing why. Over time, stress replaced stability. His life grew heavier— not because of necessity but because comparison quietly dictated his pace.
- **Claire: The Woman Who Questioned a Peaceful Life** – Claire enjoyed a simple, balanced routine. Yet repeated exposure to curated online lives made her question her choices. Gradually, contentment turned into self-doubt. Nothing was wrong with her life—but it started feeling inadequate simply because other lives looked more impressive.

Conclusion: The Quiet Cost of Social Proof

Social proof works silently. It rarely forces. It gently redirects. When choices are guided more by visibility than by clarity, people move quickly— often without direction. Life becomes crowded with borrowed goals and unexamined expectations.

This reflection does not explore how to break free from social proof—that comes later. It simply names a reality many live inside today: a world where individuality fades slowly under constant comparison.

And the question quietly remains:

Are we living our own lives—or repeating the lives we keep seeing around us?

Chapter 4: The Price of Success: What We Sacrifice for More

Burnout: The Silent Epidemic

"You can't pour from an empty cup—but modern life keeps asking you to."

Burnout is not a sudden collapse; it's a slow erosion. It creeps in quietly, disguised as dedication, ambition and hard work. At first, it feels like progress—late nights, early mornings and the thrill of achievement. But over time, the body whispers, the mind protests and the soul begin to fade.

What is Burnout?

Burnout is more than fatigue. It's a state of emotional, physical and mental exhaustion caused by prolonged stress and relentless demands. Unlike ordinary tiredness, burnout drains your motivation, dulls your creativity and leaves you feeling detached from work and life.

Why It's Silent—and Dangerous

Burnout rarely announces itself with a bang. It starts with small compromises: skipping lunch, ignoring sleep, saying "YES" when you should say "NO." You tell yourself it's temporary, that you'll rest after the next deadline. But deadlines multiply and rest becomes a distant dream.

The danger lies in its invisibility. Society glorifies hustle, so exhaustion feels like a badge of honour. People wear stress like a trophy, unaware that they're trading health for hollow victories.

Signs You're Burning Out

- **Constant Fatigue:** Even after sleep, you feel drained.
- **Loss of Joy:** Work feels meaningless; hobbies lose appeal.
- **Irritability and Anxiety:** Small issues trigger big reactions.
- **Declining Performance:** Despite longer hours, output suffers.
- **Detachment:** You feel disconnected from colleagues, family and even yourself.

The Cost of Burnout - Burnout doesn't just affect productivity—it impacts life itself. Chronic stress weakens immunity, raises blood pressure and increases the risk of depression. Relationships suffer as irritability replaces empathy. Creativity dies, leaving you stuck in survival mode.

Why Modern Success Fuels Burnout

- **Always-On Culture:** Technology keeps us tethered to work 24/7.
- **Comparison Trap:** Social media amplifies pressure to achieve more.
- **Unrealistic Expectations:** Organizations reward output, not well-being.
- **Loss of Boundaries:** Home becomes office; weekends become workdays.

Burnout is the tax we pay for ignoring balance. Success without sustainability is failure in disguise.

The question isn't ***"Can I keep going?"*** **It's** ***"Should I?"***

"Some people collapse from doing too much. Others collapse from trying too hard. Most collapse quietly."

In today's world, burnout has become a silent epidemic—an experience so common that many people mistake it for a normal part of modern life. Exhaustion, emotional numbness, irritability and a constant feeling of being "on edge" have become everyday realities. People push themselves endlessly while pretending everything is fine. Behind smiles, deadlines and routines, there is a quiet struggle—the struggle of a mind and body running far beyond their limits.

Burnout doesn't announce itself dramatically. It creeps in slowly: a tired morning, a restless night, a lost interest, a forgotten joy. Bit by bit, energy turns into fatigue, motivation into pressure and passion into survival. People are functioning but not truly living.

Why Burnout Feels Universal Today

Modern life demands more than humans are built to handle. Work expectations rise. Personal responsibilities expand. Digital connectivity erases any sense of "off time." The result is a constant state of mental load—thinking, worrying, planning, reacting. The world celebrates productivity, hustle and achievement, creating social pressure to always do more. People fear slowing down, afraid of falling behind professionally, financially or socially.

Rest feels guilty.
Pauses feel risky.
Stillness feels unearned.

Burnout thrives in this environment, where people ignore early signs because "everyone else is also struggling." Instead of recognizing burnout as a warning, many treat it as a lifestyle.

The Reality of Today's Burnout-Driven World

- **Exhaustion Becoming the New Normal -** People wake up tired and go to bed wired. Rest no longer restores them; it only maintains survival.
- **Emotional Numbness Replacing Enthusiasm -** Activities that once brought joy now feel like obligations. People stop feeling fully—they simply function.
- **Work Spilling into Personal Spaces -** Phones, messages and digital platforms keep the mind working long after office hours.
- **Constant Pressure to Perform -** Expectations rise, deadlines tighten and achievements quickly lose their meaning. There is always another target.
- **Losing Sense of Purpose -** Many keep moving out of habit, not intention. They don't know whether they are progressing or just exhausting themselves.

Real-Life Examples:

- **Alexander: The High-Performer Running on Empty -** Alexander loved his job but over time, the constant demands drained him. He worked late nights, skipped breaks and stayed reachable 24/7. His colleagues admired his dedication but privately he felt disconnected and emotionally flat. Even small tasks felt overwhelming. **His body moved but his mind felt exhausted long before the day began.**
- **Isabella: The Caregiver Who Forgot Herself -** Isabella balanced work, family and household responsibilities. She cared for everyone—except herself. Her days were packed from morning to night, leaving no room for rest or reflection. Over months, she noticed she was becoming irritable,

drained and detached. Yet she kept going, believing she "had no choice." **Her burnout grew silently behind her daily responsibilities.**

- **Noah: The Student Crushed by Expectations -** Noah pushed himself to excel academically. He juggled assignments, projects, extracurriculars and constant comparisons with peers. He stopped enjoying learning and started surviving it. Even when he achieved high grades, he felt nothing—just relief followed by new pressure. **He was burning out before his adult life had even begun.**

Conclusion: The Quiet Crisis of Our Time

Burnout is not loud.
It doesn't always look dramatic.
It doesn't always look broken.
Often, it looks like a person who is functioning well on the outside and falling apart on the inside.

This chapter does not explore solutions—that comes later. For now, it simply holds a mirror to modern life: A world where exhaustion is common, boundaries are blurred and emotional depletion is silently endured.

And it leaves us with an important question:
If burnout is everywhere, why are we still pretending it means we are strong?

Declining Health: Physical and Mental Toll

"We have more conveniences than ever—but less well-being than ever."

Modern life has slowly changed how people feel in their bodies and minds. Most sleep less, sit more, worry more and move less than they once did. Tired mornings, short patience, shallow focus and constant restlessness have become normal—dismissed as just part of a busy life.

Health rarely collapses overnight. It fades quietly. Days keep moving, work gets done, responsibilities are met—yet something inside feels thinner, slower, less restored.

Why This Decline Feels Normal Today

Life now moves faster than the human system can comfortably follow. Work stretches into evenings. Screens steal moments meant for rest. Expectations grow while pauses disappear. Worry, comparison, and uncertainty are carried silently. Because people continue to function, the strain often goes unnoticed. Everything looks fine from the outside, even as energy quietly drains within.

Everyday Health Patterns

Many days pass mostly seated—at desks, in traffic, indoors. Natural light is limited. Bodies stay tense without release. Screens keep the mind alert when it should soften. Notifications interrupt attention. Late nights shorten sleep. Over time, small changes appear. Memory feels less sharp. Patience runs thin. Motivation flickers. Small challenges feel heavier than they used to. Meaning feels distant, even when life looks full.

Eating in Modern Life

Eating has become flexible—but also distracted. Meals blur into snacks. Hunger mixes with boredom. Food is quick and available at any hour, yet satisfaction often feels missing. Traditional rhythms—unhurried meals, regular timing, simple balance—slowly fade. People eat more yet feel less nourished than before.

Stress and Emotional Well-Being

Work and life no longer feel separate. Rest carries guilt. Quiet moments feel unfamiliar. Connection happens often—but not always deeply. Many move through their days capable and responsible yet emotionally underfed. Present in roles but slightly absent within themselves.

Real-Life Examples:

- **Idris: The Quietly Tired Achiever** - Idris met deadlines and delivered results. Morning headaches and restless evenings felt normal to him. Over time, he noticed something subtle—the work continued, but the feeling of being rested never returned.
- **Yelena: Carrying Too Much, Too Quietly** - Yelena managed work, caregiving, and expectations without complaint. She answered every message and ignored her limits. Slowly, joy faded from daily moments. Nothing broke—but energy and patience slowly thinned.

Conclusion: A Mirror to Today's Health Crisis

This chapter is not a solution; it is a recognition. Physical and mental health are eroding not because people are weak but because life demands constancy without recovery. The decline is slow, steady and hidden by competence. A world where convenience rises while well-being falls creates a population that functions while fraying. And the question remains:

If health is the foundation of life, why does it feel so fragile in everyday living?

Quiet Collapse — Lifestyle Diseases and Obesity in a Fast-Living World

"When the body is forced to adjust endlessly, disease becomes its way of surviving."

Modern routines do not simply tire the body—they rewire it. Lifestyle diseases rarely arrive with alarms; they enter quietly and settle as part of daily life. Blood pressure inches up, blood sugar drifts, digestion grows erratic and weight creeps—life continues, adjusted and medicated. Illness doesn't interrupt living; it embeds within it.

Why This Feels True in Today's World

Days are designed for output, not rhythm. Meals are delayed or rushed; sleep is fragmented; movement is optional; stress hums in the background. The body, kept in a state of subtle alert, adapts by storing more and repairing less. What looks like "normal busyness" becomes the soil in which disease takes root—not as a single event but as a lifestyle condition.

Common Triggers That Push the Body Toward Disease

These forces often overlap and compound until compensation turns into illness:

- Continuous pressure with little recovery
- Long sitting hours and minimal muscle use
- Irregular eating and tense digestion
- Short, light or disrupted sleep

- Emotional numbing and comfort-driven eating
- Early warning signs dismissed as "age" or "seasonal"

The Reality of Bodies Living with Slow Disease

- **Diseases that accompany life** — Hypertension, type 2 diabetes, high LDL cholesterol, high triglycerides, elevated uric acid, thyroid imbalance, fatty liver, GERD/acidity, IBS and constipation, migraine, sleep apnea, osteoarthritis, PCOS and obesity are managed around meetings, family plans and travel.
- **Weight as an outcome** — Obesity reflects deeper hormonal and behavioural drift rather than mere excess.
- **Life organized by numbers** — Readings, refills and "safe foods" shape choices quietly.
- **Acceptance before urgency** — By the time concern rises, disease already feels like identity.

Real-Life Examples:

- **Luca: Living by Readings** — Promotions came; so did new numbers: cholesterol up, pressure medicated, sugar "borderline," reflux nightly. He packed antacids, avoided stairs and tracked levels before outings. Nothing looked catastrophic; everything felt narrower.
- **Farah: Digesting a Demanding Life** — Farah's days were relentless. Meals slid late; sleep came light; stress stayed. Over years, acidity became routine, weight settled stubbornly and fatigue lingered. Tests showed no emergency—only parameters inching upward, a quiet confirmation that her body had been absorbing the cost of pace.

Conclusion: When Illness Becomes a Lifestyle Artifact

This chapter does not define recovery; it names a reality. In a world that won't slow, the body copes by turning imbalance into chronic conditions. Blood pressure, sugar, cholesterol, triglycerides, uric acid, digestion issues, thyroid shifts, fatty liver, sleep apnea, osteoarthritis, PCOS, migraine and obesity begin to **walk with life** rather than stopping it. And so the question stands: **What happens when life keeps accelerating—and the body has nowhere left to adjust?**

Fear and Anxiety: Living in Constant Stress

"When the mind does not feel safe, even ordinary moments feel heavy."

Fear and anxiety have become regular companions in modern life. What used to be occasional emotions are now daily experiences for many people. The world moves fast, uncertainties rise, expectations grow and digital noise never stops. As a result, people live in a state of constant alertness—thinking, worrying, overanalyzing and anticipating problems that may never happen.

Fear today is not always about danger. Anxiety is not always about crises. They often arise from pressure, instability, comparison and emotional overload. They linger in the background—quiet but persistent—shaping how people think, act and feel.

Many individuals go through life carrying an invisible tension in their chest, a restlessness in their thoughts and a heaviness they cannot explain. The mind is racing even when the body is still.

Why This Constant Stress Exists Today

The modern world offers comfort but it also creates emotional instability. Information spreads rapidly, bad news travels instantly and people constantly compare their lives with others online. Workplaces demand speed. Society demands results. Families demand responsibility. Social circles demand relevance. With so many expectations pressing from every direction, the mind struggles to find a sense of safety. People fear falling behind, fear being judged, fear failing, fear losing control. Even small uncertainties feel magnified. Anxiety grows silently fed by overstimulation, overthinking and constant mental noise.

The world has become more advanced yet inner peace has become harder to find.

The Reality of Today's Fear-Driven and Anxiety-Filled Life

- **Overthinking Becoming a Daily Habit -** People analyze conversations, replay events and imagine negative outcomes long before anything happens.
- **Emotional Restlessness Without a Clear Reason -** A vague feeling of worry or tension remains throughout the day, even during calm moments.
- **Fear of Judgment, Rejection and Imperfection -** Every decision feels tied to how others might respond or what they might think.
- **Fear of Missing Out (FOMO) Creating Constant Pressure -** Seeing others' highlight moments—travel, achievements, celebrations—makes people feel inadequate or behind, even when their own life is perfectly fine.
- **Fear of Uncertainty Becoming a Daily Weight -** People struggle with not knowing what will happen next—financially, professionally, emotionally—leading to constant mental tension.
- **Future Worries Making the Present Uncomfortable -** Even during peaceful moments, the mind anticipates potential problems, making it difficult to relax or feel safe.

Real-Life Examples:

- **Matthew: The Professional Living in Constant Anticipation -** Matthew had a good job but he always feared something would go wrong. He checked his emails repeatedly, worried about small mistakes and replayed conversations in his head long after work. Even when nothing was wrong, his mind imagined problems. Nights felt long and restless; mornings felt heavy. **He wasn't stressed by events—he was stressed by anticipation.**
- **Grace: The Woman Overwhelmed by Invisible Pressure -** Grace appeared calm on the outside but her mind was constantly racing. She worried about disappointing others, missing expectations or not doing enough. Even quiet days felt tense because she was mentally preparing for things that might happen. Her anxiety didn't come from crises—it came from carrying emotional weight alone. **She lived in a storm that no one else could see.**

Conclusion: The Hidden Struggle of Modern Minds

Fear and anxiety have become part of the emotional landscape of modern life—not as rare moments but as daily companions. People are outwardly functioning but inwardly fighting battles no one else notices. The stress is constant, quiet and deeply exhausting. This chapter does not explore solutions—that comes later. For now, it simply describes a truth many live in silence:

A world where the mind rarely rests, where fear hides in ordinary days and where anxiety becomes a shadow that follows everywhere.

And it leads to a deeper reflection: **If the world has advanced so much, why does the mind still live in survival mode?**

Daily Disappointments: The Emotional Rollercoaster

"Life rarely unfolds as planned—each day brings its own sting"

We start each morning hoping the day will run smoothly. Instead, small snags—late trains, overlooked work, a plan derailed by one email—chip away at calm. Each moment seems minor yet together they create an emotional swing of irritation, deflation and self-doubt.

"Some days break us in big ways but most days bend us in small, quiet ways we never talk about."

Modern life is filled with small, constant disappointments—minor letdowns, unmet expectations and tiny emotional dips that accumulate without notice. While major setbacks are rare, it is the everyday frustrations that quietly shape how people feel. A delayed message, an ignored effort, a broken plan, an unexpected comment, a missed opportunity—these moments seem insignificant individually yet collectively create emotional turbulence.

People today experience more emotional fluctuations than ever before. The pace of life, social comparisons, high expectations and constant connectivity intensify the impact of even the smallest disappointments. Everyday life becomes an emotional rollercoaster—not because everything is terrible but because so much feels unpredictable, unstable and out of our control.

Why This Emotional Rollercoaster Exists Today

Modern life sets the stage for constant micro-disappointments. Social media shows perfect days, flawless achievements and curated happiness—making ordinary days feel lacking. Workplaces expect quick responses, personal lives demand balance and society celebrates constant progress. When reality doesn't match these expectations, disappointment follows. Daily stress, rushing, pressure and digital noise reduce emotional resilience. People feel less capable of handling small setbacks, so minor issues feel heavier.

A small inconvenience becomes irritation.
A small delay becomes frustration.
A small silence becomes doubt.
This cycle continues silently, making emotional ups and downs a part of everyday experience.

Real-Life Examples:

- **The delayed train:** You've planned your morning down to the minute but a signal failure throws the schedule off. You arrive flustered—already behind before the day begins.
- **Invisible effort:** You prepare a clear, data-backed proposal. In the meeting, attention pivots elsewhere and your work barely gets mentioned. The sting isn't just about the idea—it's about being unseen.
- **The dinner that didn't land:** You plan a special meal but your teenager arrives late and distracted. You feel the distance more than the delay.
- **The interrupted start:** You set out for a morning jog; rain arrives unannounced. The day feels off kilter, as if momentum was stolen at the first step.

- **Quiet comparisons:** You see a friend's promotion on LinkedIn or flawless vacation on Instagram. Your perfectly ordinary Tuesday suddenly feels inadequate.

The Reality of Today's Constant Emotional Swings

- **Small Setbacks Feeling Bigger Than They Are -** A plan changes, a message is delayed or something doesn't go as expected—yet it triggers deeper frustration than the situation deserves.
- **Mood Fluctuating Throughout the Day -** People shift between hope, stress, irritation and relief multiple times, often without understanding why.
- **Constant Expectation vs. Reality Gap -** What people imagine rarely matches what actually happens—and even small mismatches create emotional dips.
- **Sensitivity to Social Responses -** A short reply, lack of acknowledgment or change in tone can impact mood significantly.
- **Emotional Exhaustion from Repeated Micro-Letdowns -** Small disappointments accumulate, creating a quiet sense of heaviness by the end of the day.

Conclusion: The Weight of the Small Things

Daily disappointments rarely make headlines but they shape emotional well-being more than people realise. Modern life, with its speed and expectations, magnifies the impact of even the smallest letdowns. This chapter does not explore solutions—that comes later. It simply mirrors today's emotional reality: **a world where tiny cracks appear throughout the day, forming a quiet emotional fatigue.**
And it leaves us with a reflective question:

If small disappointments affect us so deeply, what does that say about the weight we silently carry every day?

Unbearable Life — Extreme Reactions in a Disconnected World

"When pain has no language and life feels cornered, people don't choose wisely—they choose desperately."

Modern life has created a silent emotional crisis. Beneath the surface of success, connectivity and opportunity, many individuals feel overwhelmed, trapped and disconnected from life itself. When internal pressure crosses a personal threshold, some people take **extreme steps**—not because they seek ruin but because they no longer see a livable way forward.

These extremes appear in multiple forms: addiction, repeated self-destructive behaviour, involvement with harmful people, moral compromise, withdrawal from life and, in tragic cases, the wish to escape life entirely. These are not sudden decisions. They are the end result of **accumulated stress, unresolved pain and prolonged frustration**.

People rarely fall apart overnight. They deteriorate quietly—under pressure that keeps building.

Why This Feels True in Today's World

Modern living exposes people to constant evaluation, uncertainty and emotional strain while simultaneously reducing support systems. Many individuals carry heavy responsibilities but lack emotional safety, understanding or relief.
Failures and losses that were once absorbed by family or community are now borne alone. Expressing vulnerability feels risky. Asking for help feels like weakness. As a result, pressure turns inward.

Life begins to feel like a narrow corridor with no exits—and desperation grows not from weakness but from **exhaustion**.

Common Triggers That Push People Toward Extremes

While each story is unique, certain experiences repeatedly appear behind extreme reactions:

- **Failure in Relationships** – Breakdowns in marriage, long-term partnerships or emotional bonds often leave people feeling rejected, guilty or worthless, especially when identity was deeply tied to the relationship.
- **Loss of Job or Career Collapse** – Employment is not only income; it is identity, structure and self-respect. Sudden job loss or prolonged unemployment can create shame, fear and a sense of falling behind irreversibly.
- **Harassment or Humiliation at the Workplace** – Continuous pressure toxic leadership or harassment from superiors erodes confidence slowly. Many endure silently until the emotional damage becomes unbearable.
- **Conflict With One's Own Children** – Disconnection, disrespect or rejection from children deeply affects parents, often breaking their sense of purpose and dignity.
- **Extreme Debt and Financial Pressure** – Mounting loans, failed businesses or constant financial stress create a feeling of entrapment. Debt doesn't only strain money—it compresses hope.

- **Involvement in a Wrong Act or Moral Failure** – Guilt, fear of exposure or regret from past actions can isolate individuals psychologically, making them feel undeserving of recovery or understanding.

These pressures rarely exist alone. They overlap, compound and intensify—until clarity collapses underweight.

The Reality of Lives Pushed to Extremes

- **Emotional Pain Without Expression** – Feelings of failure, shame and fear remain unspoken and unresolved.
- **Loss of Meaning and Direction** – Life continues mechanically but internally feels empty or pointless.
- **Tunnel Vision Under Stress** – The mind narrows; possibilities disappear; choices feel reduced to escape or endurance.
- **Gravitation Toward Harmful Escapes** – Substances, destructive habits or damaging associations provide brief relief from mental overload.
- **Disconnection From Life Itself** – Long before extreme acts occur, individuals withdraw emotionally, losing interest, hope and attachment.

Real-Life Examples:

- **David: Crushed by Work Pressure and Debt** – David lost his job unexpectedly while carrying heavy financial obligations. Continuous calls, mounting dues and rejection eroded his self-worth. What appeared externally as irresponsibility was internally a collapse under fear and shame he never spoke about.
- **Laura: Broken by Relationships and Family Conflict** – Laura faced repeated relationship failures and growing distance from her own children. Each conflict chipped away at her sense of belonging. Though surrounded by people, she felt invisible and deeply disconnected from life's meaning.

Conclusion: When Despair Goes Unrecognized

Extreme reactions are rarely a desire for harm. They are **responses to prolonged, unrelieved suffering**. When pain accumulates without understanding, people don't search for wisdom—they search for relief.
This reflection does not describe how recovery happens—that comes later in the journey. Here, it acknowledges a difficult truth of modern life:

Many people who take extreme paths are not weak, immoral or broken. They are **overloaded, isolated and emotionally cornered**.

And the quiet question remains:**What happens when life feels like a closed door—and a person no longer sees a way to breathe inside it?**

Lack of Emotional Intelligence: Why We Struggle to Connect

"In a world obsessed with IQ, we forgot the power of EQ."

What Is Emotional Quotient (EQ)?

Emotional Quotient, often called Emotional Intelligence, is the ability to recognize, understand and manage our own emotions while also perceiving and responding to the emotions of others. Unlike IQ, which measures cognitive ability, EQ reflects how well we navigate relationships, handle stress and make decisions with empathy and self-awareness. High EQ allows people to communicate effectively, resolve conflicts peacefully and build meaningful connections. In essence, EQ is the foundation of living well in both personal and professional life.

Human connection is one of the deepest needs of life—yet today, many people find themselves struggling to relate, understand or truly communicate. Even in a world full of messages, calls, chats and constant interaction, emotional distance is quietly growing.

People know how to talk but not always how to listen. They know how to react but not always how to understand. They know what to say but not how to feel.

Modern life rewards speed, efficiency and information—but emotional intelligence grows only in awareness, patience and presence. As a result, many individuals move through relationships not with understanding but with assumptions, defensiveness or emotional disconnect.

This gap makes relationships—professional, personal and social—fragile and easily strained.

Why Emotional Intelligence is Weakening Today

Life today is rushed. People move quickly through tasks, conversations and responsibilities. There is little time to slow down and reflect on feelings—either their own or others'. Digital communication shortcuts emotional cues; text messages replace tone, emojis replace expression and online reactions replace empathy.
Comparison, pressure and stress also make people more self-focused—leaving less emotional space for understanding others. Many individuals don't learn to express emotions clearly. Others don't know how to manage them. Most were never taught to recognise them in themselves, let alone in others.

In this environment, emotional intelligence—once a natural part of human interaction—becomes rare.

Real-Life Examples:

- **Workplace Example**: A manager notices declining performance but fails to ask about the employee's stress. Instead of support, criticism is given, causing resentment and turnover.
- **Family Example**: A parent, overwhelmed by work, snaps at their child without realizing the emotional damage. The child withdraws, feeling unheard.
- **Social Example**: A friend posts about their struggles online but others scroll past without offering empathy. Digital connection replaces genuine care.
- **Education Example**: A student receives poor grades and reacts with anger rather than reflection, missing the chance to learn resilience.
- **Health Example**: Someone ignores their stress signals, pushing through exhaustion until illness forces them to stop.

The Reality of Today's Emotionally Disconnected World

- **Difficulty Understanding Personal Emotions -** People feel overwhelmed, irritated or anxious but cannot explain why, creating confusion inside and distance outside.
- **Low Empathy in Daily Interactions -** With everyone coping with their own stress, understanding others' feelings becomes harder.
- **Communication Becoming Transactional -** Conversations often focus on tasks and outcomes, not emotions or meaning.
- **Emotional Reactions Instead of Emotional Awareness -** People react quickly—anger, defensiveness, withdrawal—without understanding what triggered them.
- **Misinterpretation Becoming Common -** Tone is missed, intentions are assumed and simple messages create unnecessary conflict.

Conclusion: The Quiet Disconnect of Our Time

People today communicate constantly yet understand each other less. The lack of emotional intelligence creates misunderstandings, weakens relationships and amplifies loneliness. This chapter does not offer solutions—that comes later. It simply describes the emotional reality of the modern world: **A time where people express more, react more and connect less. A world where emotions run high but emotional understanding runs low.**

And it leaves us with a quiet question: **If we are more connected than ever, why do we feel so emotionally far apart?**

Absence of Life Purpose: Drifting Without Direction

"A life without purpose isn't empty—it's heavy with confusion."

What Is Life Purpose?

Life purpose is the sense of meaning and direction that guides our choices, fuels our motivation and connects us to something larger than ourselves. It is not simply about career or achievement but about knowing *why* we live the way we do. A clear purpose gives resilience in hard times and joy in everyday living.

Absence of Life Purpose: Drifting Without Direction

Many people today live without a clear sense of purpose—not because they lack dreams but because modern life pulls them in countless directions. Days pass quickly, schedules stay busy, responsibilities pile up—yet a quiet emptiness lingers beneath it all.

People work, earn, achieve and survive but rarely feel deeply connected to *why* they are doing any of it. Life becomes a cycle of routines without meaning, productivity without fulfilment and movement without direction. In the noise of the modern world, the inner voice that once guided people grow faint. Without purpose, even success feels incomplete and even progress feels directionless. The result is a generation drifting—busy, active, overwhelmed yet unsure where they are truly heading.

"When life has no anchor, even calm seas feel unsettling."

Why Purpose Feels Absent Today

Life today is filled with distractions, expectations and pressures. People are conditioned to chase achievements—degrees, promotions, milestones, possessions—without pausing to ask what truly matters to them. The world pushes speed and results, not reflection and clarity. In this rush, individuals lose connection with their inner desires and long-term vision. Social comparison also blurs internal direction. People measure their worth not by their own values but by the visible success of others. When everyone seems to be achieving something extraordinary ordinary life feels insignificant. The mind constantly questions: *"Am I doing enough? Am I on the right path?"*
Without a sense of purpose anchoring their actions, people feel emotionally unsteady—floating from task to task, goal to goal, without a deeper meaning tying their life together.

The Reality of Living Without a Clear Purpose

- **Going Through Days on Autopilot -** People wake up, work, return home, repeat—without feeling connected to their actions.
- **Feeling Busy but Emotionally Empty -** Even with full schedules, many sense a quiet inner void that productivity cannot fill.
- **Constantly Switching Goals or Interests -** Without direction, individuals shift paths frequently, hoping the next change will spark meaning.
- **Difficulty Feeling Fulfilled or Satisfied -** Achievements bring temporary relief, not lasting contentment.
- **A Sense of Drifting Through Life -** Life feels like motion without destination—a journey without a map.

Real-Life Examples:

- **Caleb: The High Achiever Who Felt Lost Inside -** Caleb had a successful career, a stable income and the respect of his peers. But despite these achievements, he felt emotionally disconnected from his daily life. He couldn't understand why his accomplishments didn't bring fulfilment. Every morning felt routine, every evening felt empty. **He wasn't struggling with goals—he was struggling with the absence of direction.**

- **Lily: The Young Woman Unsure of Her Path -** Lily tried different jobs, hobbies and interests, hoping something would spark meaning. But nothing felt right for long. She admired others who seemed confident about their future, while she felt stuck in uncertainty. Her days were filled with activity yet she felt she wasn't moving anywhere. **She wasn't lacking potential—she was lacking purpose.**

Conclusion: The Quiet Drift of Modern Life

The absence of purpose is one of the most silent emotional struggles of our time. People appear functional on the outside but feel directionless within. Days blur together, decisions lose meaning and progress feels hollow. This chapter does not offer solutions—that comes later. For now, it simply reflects the reality many live with quietly: **a life full of motion but missing a sense of meaning, a journey without a compass.**

And it leaves us with a deeper question:
If life keeps moving forward, why do so many hearts feel stuck in place?

Modern Mindsets: How Our Thinking Shapes Our Reality

"We don't just live in a fast world—we think fast, compare fast and burn out fast."

The way we think today is shaped by a culture that values speed, visibility and constant achievement. Modern life pushes people to chase more, do more and become more—often without pausing to ask whether these pursuits align with their values or well-being. This mindset is not accidental; it is the product of societal pressure, competitive environments and the belief that worth must always be proven.

Below are the defining patterns of the modern mindset—and how they quietly shape our reality.

- **Achievement-Oriented Thinking -** Success is increasingly measured by external milestones: promotions, income, awards or public recognition. People feel they must constantly "level up" to stay relevant. This mindset often leads individuals to sacrifice rest, relationships and health in pursuit of bigger goals—yet the finish line keeps shifting. When achievement becomes identity, slowing down feels like failure.

- **Comparison as a Default Lens -** Instead of celebrating their own journey, many people evaluate their progress through comparisons—who is ahead, who achieved more, who looks more successful. This constant measurement creates pressure and dissatisfaction, making personal accomplishments feel small or "not enough," even when they are meaningful.
- **Scarcity & FOMO Mindset -** Many operate with a subtle belief that opportunities are limited and life is a race. This scarcity thinking leads to fear-based choices: saying yes to everything, taking on more than necessary or

chasing trends just to avoid feeling left behind. Even when choices don't align with personal values, people feel compelled to participate.

- **Short-Term Gratification Over Long-Term Growth -** In a world trained for instant results, patience has become rare. Quick wins often seem more appealing than slow, steady progress. This mindset pushes people toward shortcuts—fast outcomes, quick learning hacks, immediate returns—while long-term habits like consistency, discipline and mastery feel "too slow."
- **Low Inner Awareness -** Modern minds are busy but not always reflective. Many people struggle to notice their emotional state, understand their triggers or recognize when they need rest. Without inner awareness, reactions replace responses, leading to stress, misunderstandings and burnout—especially when life becomes demanding.
- **Material Success as Identity -** For many, self-worth is tied to career titles, lifestyle upgrades or financial standing. People worry more about how they are perceived than how they truly feel. This mindset pushes individuals to pursue status symbols rather than inner alignment—a cycle that looks successful on the outside but feels empty within.

Consequences of the Modern Mindset

- **Stress & mental strain** from constant comparison and competition
- **Shallow or fragile relationships** built more on image than authenticity
- **Burnout** from chasing goals misaligned with personal values
- **Emptiness despite abundance** because achievements alone cannot fulfil
- **Loss of purpose** as life becomes performance rather than meaning

Today's world pushes us to think fast, move fast and prove ourselves constantly—but in the rush, we drift away from what matters. Pause and ask yourself: Is my thinking guided by my values or by the noise around me? When the mind slows, clarity returns—and life begins to feel like your own again.

Modern mindsets promise happiness through speed and status—but deliver stress and emptiness. The question isn't *"How much can I achieve?"* It's *"Can I achieve without losing myself?"* True success begins when we slow down and choose authenticity over applause.

Big Dreams Without Action: The Illusion of Success

"Dreams feel like progress—until we realise they moved only in our minds."

In today's world, big dreams are celebrated everywhere. People talk about goals, ambitions, visions and future achievements with pride. Social media is filled with inspirational quotes and success stories that make dreaming feel like the first step toward greatness. And for a moment, dreams do feel powerful. They bring hope, excitement and a sense of possibility. But without action, they remain imagination—beautiful but empty.

Many people today confuse dreaming with doing. They spend hours envisioning the life they want but little time building it. They enjoy the feeling of possibility but avoid the discomfort of effort. This creates an emotional illusion: the *sense* of progress without real progress. The imagination moves forward but life stays still.

Why This Illusion Exists Today

Modern culture glorifies aspiration. The idea of success is everywhere shared in videos, books, podcasts and stories of overnight breakthroughs. This constant exposure makes dreaming feel familiar and accessible. But real success requires consistency, discipline and long-term effort—qualities that develop slowly, not instantly.

People also feel pressured to appear ambitious. Talking about big goals creates admiration from others and boosts self-esteem temporarily. It's easier to dream than to act. Easier to plan than to start. Easier to imagine than to struggle.

In a world filled with motivation content, action feels like the slowest part of the process. Many individuals stay stuck in the comfort of big ideas while avoiding the discomfort of execution.

The Reality of Today's Dream-Heavy, Action-Light Lifestyle

- **Dreams Repeated but Never Started -** People talk passionately about their goals for months—or years—without taking the first step.

- **Planning Replacing Progress -** Endless research, discussions and "preparation" create the illusion of moving forward while standing still.
- **Excitement Without Commitment -** The initial rush of dreaming fades quickly when it's time to work consistently.
- **Comparing Dreams Instead of Building Them -** People measure their ambitions against others, feeling inspired but rarely acting.
- **Vision Without Effort Creating Emotional Friction -** The gap between imagined life and reality grows, leading to frustration, self-doubt and disappointment.

Real-Life Examples:

- **Oliver: The Man Who Dreamed More Than He Did -** Oliver often talked about starting his own design studio. He had ideas, plans and even a name for the business. But every time he considered beginning, he felt intimidated by the effort required. Months turned into years and the dream stayed exactly where it began—in his imagination. **He wasn't lacking ambition—he was lacking action.**
- **Ava: The Young Woman Caught in the Planning Loop -** Ava wanted to write a book. She bought journals, created outlines and watched countless writing tutorials. Her notebooks were full of ideas, quotes and chapter summaries. But she never wrote the actual chapters. She felt productive thinking about the book but the pages remained blank. **Her dream grew louder, while her actions remained silent.**

Conclusion: The Comfort and Cost of Dreaming

Big dreams are beautiful—they inspire, uplift and fuel imagination. But without action, they can become emotional traps, giving the illusion of progress while life stays unchanged. This chapter does not explore solutions—that comes later. For now, it simply highlights the truth of our time: **A world full of dreams but short on action. A world where hope feels like movement—but only movement creates change.**

And it raises an important reflection:

If we dream so big, why do our lives remain the same?

The Hidden Cost of Modern Success

"Success reveals what we gain but hides what we silently lose."

Success in the modern world appears glamorous—high salaries, recognition, promotions, achievements, respected titles and impressive milestones. From the outside, successful lives look polished and enviable. But behind these bright outcomes lies a quieter, heavier truth: modern success often comes with costs that are rarely acknowledged and almost never discussed openly.

People push themselves harder than their minds and bodies were designed to handle. They sacrifice sleep, time, health, relationships and emotional balance in the pursuit of progress. They meet expectations, exceed targets and maintain packed schedules, all while quietly carrying stress, guilt, exhaustion or loneliness. Success has become less about fulfilment and more about keeping up, staying ahead or proving oneself. While the world claps for achievements, it rarely sees the internal toll they take.

Why These Costs Exist in Today's World

Modern society rewards visibility, speed and output. People are encouraged—sometimes pressured—to reach milestones quickly, stay productive constantly and appear strong publicly. Expectations grow with every achievement; each success becomes a new standard to maintain. The pursuit never ends. Workplaces demand efficiency. Social environments demand relevance. Families expect responsibility. And digital culture amplifies it all—showing highlight reels that make others' success appear effortless. This creates a silent competition, pushing individuals to stretch themselves further, even when they feel emotionally or physically drained. In this environment, the true cost of success isn't failure—it's self-neglect.

The Reality of Today's Success-Driven Pressure

- **Success Increasing Expectations Instead of Peace -** Every achievement raises the bar, making people feel they must constantly perform at their highest level.

- **Emotional and Physical Exhaustion Hidden Behind Productivity -** People appear strong but carry silent stress, fatigue and burnout.
- **Loss of Personal Time and Relationships -** Long hours, constant responsibilities and continuous pressure leave little room for connection.
- **Identity Becoming Tied to Accomplishments -** People feel valuable only when they achieve, not when they simply exist.
- **Success Feeling Public but Struggle Remaining Private -** The world sees the outcome, never the internal cost.

Real-Life Examples:

- **Ethan: The High Performer Living Under Pressure -** Ethan climbed the corporate ladder quickly. He earned a great salary, received praises from leadership and became a role model for his peers. But the reality behind his success was different. He worked late nights, skipped family events and lived with a constant fear of falling behind. The more he achieved, the heavier the pressure became. **His success looked impressive—but it carried a quiet emotional price.**
- **Sophia: The Creative Who Lost Herself in the Pursuit of Excellence -** Sophia loved her work as a designer. As her fame grew, so did expectations from clients, audiences and even herself. She spent long hours perfecting every detail, rarely slept enough and felt anxious whenever she wasn't working. People admired her talent but she felt lonely and mentally exhausted. **The world saw her brilliance—not the burnout behind it.**

Conclusion: The Quiet Trade-Off of Achievement

Modern success demands more than it reveals. It offers recognition but hides exhaustion. It promises fulfilment but often brings pressure. It looks bright on the outside but can feel heavy within. This chapter does not explore solutions—that comes later. For now, it simply reflects today's reality: **Success is celebrated loudly but its cost is paid quietly.**

And a single question lingers beneath it all:
If success requires giving up parts of ourselves, is the victory truly ours?

Part II: The Power of Simplicity – A New Way of Living

Discover how simplicity restores balance, peace and happiness in everyday life.

Chapter 5: Simplicity Begins with Clarity

The Essence of Simple Living

"A simple life begins when we stop adding and start asking: does this truly serve me?"

Simple Life – What It Really Means - A simple life means creating arrangements that support you, not entangle you. Everything we do—studying, buying a house, building relationships, having children, doing business—should enhance life, not complicate it.

Why We Get Entangled - Many people feel weighed down today because they commit to things without pausing to ask, *"Do I truly need this?"* We buy because others buy. We collect items we never use. Slowly, our homes fill with clutter and our days fill with obligations that don't serve us. These choices don't enhance life—they complicate it.

The Essence of Simplicity - Simplicity is about living enhanced, not restricted. When you keep only what's essential—possessions, commitments, routines—you free time, energy and mental space for what genuinely matters. A simpler life strengthens health, peace, joy and financial freedom.

Why Simplicity Matters Today

In a world overflowing with noise, speed and endless options, simplicity becomes a source of clarity and calm. It isn't about owning less for the sake of it—it's about removing what dulls your mind and drains your energy. Earlier generations lived with fewer distractions and found deeper joy in everyday moments. We can do the same by embracing mindful routines, intentional choices and living in alignment with our values. Simplicity touches every part of life—health, relationships, spirituality and happiness—reminding us that fulfilment is often found not in *more* but in **less that truly matters**.

The Law of Simplicity: Less Is More

"The ability to simplify means eliminating the unnecessary so the necessary may speak." – Hans Hofmann

This entire book is about "The Law of Simplicity". This law teaches that clarity, peace and fulfilment arise when we strip away unnecessary complexity from our lives. At its heart, this law reminds us that life is not meant to be cluttered with endless distractions, possessions or obligations. Instead, true joy is found in focusing on what matters most—love, purpose and meaningful experiences.

Simplicity is not about deprivation; it is about alignment. When we simplify, we create space for clarity of thought, emotional balance and spiritual growth. Just as a sculptor removes excess stone to reveal the masterpiece within, the Law of Simplicity encourages us to let go of what does not serve us so that our true essence can shine.

"The ability to simplify means to eliminate the unnecessary so that the necessary may speak."

This law also emphasizes that simplicity is a choice. In a world overflowing with information, consumerism and noise, choosing simplicity means consciously prioritizing quality over quantity, depth over superficiality and presence over distraction. By doing so, we reduce stress, conserve energy and live with greater intention.

Real-Life Examples of the Law of Simplicity

- **Minimalist Living** - A family decides to declutter their home, keeping only items that bring joy or serve a purpose. With fewer possessions, they feel lighter, more organized and more focused on spending time together rather than managing things.
- **Relationships** - Instead of chasing superficial connections, a person invests in a few deep, meaningful relationships. By simplifying their social circle, they experience greater trust, intimacy and joy.

The Law of Simplicity reminds us that **life becomes richer when it becomes simpler.** By removing clutter—whether physical, mental or emotional—we create space for clarity, peace and authentic joy. Simplicity is not about having less; it is about living more fully, with focus and intention.

The Law of Clarity: Clear Vision Creates Powerful Results

"Clarity is the starting point of success."

The Law of Clarity teaches that success, fulfilment and manifestation begin with a clear vision. When your goals, values and intentions are vague, your actions scatter in many directions, producing little progress. But when you cultivate clarity—knowing exactly what you want, why you want it and how it aligns with your deeper purpose—you create a powerful focus that guides your energy and attracts the right opportunities.

Clarity is like turning on a light in a dark room. Suddenly, obstacles become visible, paths reveal themselves and decisions feel easier. Without clarity, confusion and indecision dominate, draining energy and creating frustration. With clarity, your mind, emotions and actions align, allowing you to move forward with confidence and precision.

This law also emphasizes that clarity is not a one-time achievement but a continuous practice. Life circumstances change, priorities evolve and new opportunities emerge. By regularly reflecting on your goals and refining your vision, you maintain alignment with your true self.

Real-Life Examples of the Law of Clarity

- **Career Direction** - A young professional feels stuck in their job until they take time to clarify their long-term vision. By defining that they want to move into leadership within five years, they begin seeking mentorship, training and projects that align with that path. Clarity transforms stagnation into momentum.
- **Health and Wellness** - A person wanting to "get healthier" finds little progress until they clarify what that means—losing 10 pounds, eating whole foods and exercising three times a week. With specific clarity, they create a plan and achieve results.

The Law of Clarity reminds us that **clarity precedes achievement.** When you know what you want and why you want it, your energy becomes focused, your actions purposeful and your results inevitable. By practicing clarity in every area of life—career, relationships, health and spirituality—you unlock the power to move forward with confidence and create the future you desire.

Why Life Was Happier in the Past

"We gained speed but lost stillness. We gained abundance but lost balance."

Looking back a few decades, life often felt simpler and more grounded. People lived with clearer boundaries, slower rhythms and deeper human connections. While life wasn't perfect, the structure of society supported contentment. Today, we can still learn from the values that created that natural sense of balance.

1. Stronger Community Ties & Social Support - People lived close to family and neighbours, creating a built-in support system. Community wasn't an effort — it was a lifestyle where people helped without being asked. People shared time tools, meals and conversations, creating trust and belonging that protected mental well-being. Daily life felt less isolating because human presence was a constant part of it.

2. A Slower Pace of Life - Without phones buzzing every minute, days unfolded more gently. People focused on one thing at a time and didn't feel pressured to multitask constantly. Slowness gave the mind space to breathe, notice details and enjoy simple moments without rushing. Life felt fuller because attention was whole, not divided.

3. Greater Work–Life Balance - Work stayed at work. Once people left the office or factory, the day truly shifted to home life. Evenings were for rest, family or personal interests, not unfinished tasks or pending messages. With stable jobs and clear schedules, life felt more predictable and peaceful.

4. Fewer Materialistic Pressures - People weren't driven by constant upgrades or trends. Things were repaired, reused and valued for longevity. Contentment came from utility and quality, not from comparison with others. Without social media, there was less pressure to look successful — being content mattered more.

5. Closer Connection to Nature - Daily routines included natural movement — walking to the market, gardening, time outdoors. Nature acted as a natural stress-reliever long before mental health became a topic. People slept better, felt calmer and lived more in tune with seasons and daylight.

6. Simpler Technology & Shared Entertainment - Entertainment was limited but meaningful — reading together, listening to radio, shared meals and activities. Leisure was communal instead of isolated, strengthening bonds and emotional closeness. People felt included because entertainment brought families together, not apart.

7. A Stronger Sense of Purpose - People found meaning through contribution — to family, work and community. Roles were clearer, responsibilities respected and daily routines felt valuable. Purpose wasn't something to search for; it naturally grew from living.

8. Healthier Work Environments - Jobs were demanding but the emotional pressure was lower. Expectations were realistic and human. People felt valued for loyalty and consistency, not speed or numbers on a screen. This reduced anxiety and encouraged steady, healthier effort.

9. Less Information Overload - Limited news and fewer opinion sources meant less emotional turbulence. People had time to think, form opinions and live without constant mental noise. Focus came easier when distractions were few.

10. Greater Self-Reliance - People knew how to fix, cook, mend and make. These skills-built independence and quiet confidence. Everyday tasks felt empowering rather than burdensome. Solving small problems yourself created dignity and capability.

11. Clear Boundaries Between Work & Home - There was no expectation to be reachable 24/7. When people got home, they were truly at home. This separation protected emotional energy and strengthened relationships. Life felt more balanced because roles didn't blur.

12. Financial Simplicity - Living costs were lower, spending was thoughtful and debt was rare. People lived within their means and valued savings, creating financial stability. Money supported life, not stress.

13. Healthier Social Expectations - Success wasn't about appearance but contribution and character. People felt free to live authentically without the pressure of curated perfection. Life felt simpler because validation came from real connections, not online approval.

14. Mindful Use of Resources - Reuse, repair and "make do" were natural habits. This created gratitude and respect for possessions, reducing waste and unnecessary consumption. Simplicity wasn't a trend — it was a lived philosophy.

15. Purpose in Daily Roles - Taking care of family or contributing to community brought pride and identity. Ordinary responsibilities felt meaningful, creating fulfilment in everyday routines. Purpose was found in doing, not showcasing.

16. Higher Resilience & Mental Strength - People faced difficulty with patience instead of seeking instant solutions. This built emotional toughness and practical wisdom. With fewer distractions, people learned to sit with discomfort and overcome it.

17. Life Rooted in Rituals & Traditions -Rituals — family meals, festivals, weekly gatherings — gave life rhythm and belonging. These traditions created continuity across generations and strengthened identity. Moments were shared, not streamed.

Conclusion: A Balanced Approach to Modern Living

When I look at how people lived 50 years ago, I see a life rooted in community, simplicity and purpose. Their days were shaped by personal connections, resilience and a mindful use of resources. I admire how they found satisfaction in simple pleasures and meaningful activities—not because life was easier but because it was more present.

Today, even though technology and the fast pace of modern life give me convenience, I still feel the value of reclaiming certain elements from the past. I find myself longing for stronger community ties, a healthier work–life balance and a deeper focus on gratitude.

It's no surprise that many people including myself are now seeking a more balanced way of living. I notice how practices like minimalism, mindfulness and intentional living are becoming more popular, as we collectively try to reconnect with what truly matters: happiness, contentment and inner peace.

Life may have seemed happier in the past not because it was perfect—but because people were more present. I may not be able to go back in time but I can bring forward the values that mattered most. Simplicity isn't nostalgia for me—it's timeless wisdom for the future.

Lessons from Monk Life: The Power of Needing Less

"Happiness doesn't come from adding more—it comes from removing what doesn't matter."

It was a quiet afternoon in the monastery when I sat down with one of the monks under a Bodhi tree. The air felt still, almost sacred. I had come seeking clarity about life, success and happiness. The monk smiled gently, as if he already knew what I was struggling with.

"**Master, why do people say monks are happier even though they have so little?**" I asked.

He paused for a moment, then said softly:

"Happiness doesn't come from adding more. It comes from removing what doesn't matter."

His words hit me immediately.

1. The Blue Box Lesson

The monk told me, "When a new monk joins, we give him one simple empty blue box. Everything he owns must fit inside that box."
I was surprised. "Only one box? How do you live like that?"

He smiled.

"Because needing less frees us. When we reduce the things that occupy our space, we also reduce the things that occupy our mind."

He explained how monks live in small tents with almost no space to accumulate belongings. It wasn't poverty—it was intentional simplicity.

2. Fewer Things, Fewer Distractions

The monk continued, "Most people think freedom comes from having more choices, more ownership, more luxury. But freedom truly comes from having fewer distractions."
He pointed to a group of monks meditating nearby. "With fewer things to manage, we spend our time on what matters—meditation, discipline, wisdom and purifying the mind. The world keeps people busy; simplicity keeps us grounded."

3. Hair, Clothes and the Burden of Too Much

I pointed to his shaved head and asked, "Why do monks remove their hair and even eyebrows?"
He laughed softly. "Hair brings maintenance—shampoo, conditioners, haircuts, decisions. When we shave it off, all those problems disappear. One choice removes 100 future choices."

Then he lifted his simple robe.

"We only have two sets of clothes. One for wearing, one for washing. Same robe for meals, ceremonies, meditation—even sleeping."

He looked at me kindly.

"You have wardrobes of clothes but how many do you truly need?"

4. The Burden of Ownership

The monk leaned forward and said, "People say they want time—for rest, for growth, for themselves. But they fill their lives with so much that their possessions start owning them."

He continued:

- "You buy a car and then you buy insurance, fuel, servicing, parking.
- You buy a house and then you spend a lifetime maintaining it.
- You buy gadgets and then you must update, charge, upgrade and repair them."

He paused.

"Monks don't have those burdens—so we have more time to live."

5. Minimalism Isn't About Giving Up—It's About Choosing Wisely

"Master," I asked, "Does practicing minimalism mean I must give up everything?"

He shook his head.

"No. You don't need to shave your head or live in a tent. The goal isn't deprivation—it's liberation."

He looked into the distance and said:

"Ask yourself: Do you own your things or do your things own you?"

6. A Practical Wisdom for Daily Life

He gave simple advice:

- "If you have four cars, do you need four?"
- "If you have ten pairs of shoes, could three be enough?"
- "If your home is full, how much of it do you really use?"

"Reducing clutter reduces expenses, stress and decisions. And that creates time—time for family, time for friendships, time for yourself."

7. The Hidden Truth

Before I left, I asked him one final question:
"Why does the modern world feel so exhausting?"

He answered gently:

"Because people chase more without realizing that more brings more problems.
Simple living isn't about less—it's about *enough*.
Minimalism isn't about taking away—it's about making space."

He concluded with a final lesson I will never forget:

"Don't ask 'What else can I add to my life?'
Ask 'What can I remove - so I can truly live?'"

Simple Living: Freedom, Not Restriction

"Simple Living: Embrace Freedom Through Clarity"

A simple life doesn't mean owning nothing or rejecting progress. It means choosing arrangements that support you rather than trap you. Every choice—career, relationships, home, possessions—should enhance life, not complicate it. When these decisions are made unconsciously, they turn into burdens instead of blessings.

True simplicity is clarity: asking yourself, *"Do I need this? Will it serve me—or entangle me?"* When the answer is honest, life becomes lighter, freer and more joyful.

"Simplicity is the ultimate sophistication." — Leonardo da Vinci

The Trap of Modern Arrangements

People often appear vibrant before responsibilities pile up. Later, stress lines deepen not because marriage, children or careers are wrong but because choices were made without awareness.

- **Shopping Without Need:** Buying because others buy fills homes with unused items and clutter.
- **Relationships Without Clarity:** Entering commitments without purpose leads to friction instead of fulfilment.
- **Possessions Without Use:** Keeping things "just in case" drains energy and mental space.

When choices are driven by comparison or trends, life becomes heavy instead of meaningful.

What Simple Living Truly Means

Simple living is not denial—it is intentional choice:

- **Enhancement, Not Entanglement:** Let every arrangement uplift your life.
- **Need Over Comparison:** Choose what serves *you*, not what others are doing.
- **Space Over Clutter:** Keep what adds value and release what doesn't.
- **Freedom Over Obligation:** Routines, possessions and relationships should feel supportive, not suffocating.

When life is simple, your choices support you instead of trapping you.

Real-Life Examples:

- Meera once filled her home with clothes, gadgets and décor she rarely used. Every corner felt crowded and so did her mind. One day, she kept only what she truly needed. She donated excess items, simplified her routines and focused on relationships. Within months, her home felt lighter, her mind calmer and her joy deeper. Her life didn't shrink—it expanded. Removing entanglements created space for peace and purpose.

Conclusion: The True Meaning of Simplicity

Simple living is not a limitation—it is an invitation. An invitation to create space to breathe freely and to experience life without the constant weight of excess. It is a shift from carrying too much to carrying only what supports peace and clarity.

You have seen how modern life becomes crowded, noisy and overwhelming and how simplicity can feel like a quiet doorway back to yourself. This chapter does not dive into the "how"—that comes steadily in the next chapters—but it marks the beginning of a deeper understanding:

Simplicity is not about reducing your life. It is about reclaiming it.

As you continue reading, the path ahead will unfold—showing how simple living can evolve from a longing into a practical, joyful reality.

Chapter 6: Daily Simplicity — Habits That Bring Peace

Building Simple and Sustainable Routines

"Clarity today creates success tomorrow."

Routines shape our days and gently guide our long-term success. When simplified, they reduce stress, save time and create space for what truly matters. A simple routine isn't rigid—it's intentional, balanced and easy to follow.
"Your day is your life in miniature. Master the day and you master your life."

Building a Simple Daily Routine

A good routine helps you:

- Lower stress and decision fatigue
- Balance health, work and relationships
- Build consistency for long-term growth

Core Principles

1. **Simplicity:** Keep routines practical and easy to repeat.
2. **Consistency:** Small daily habits create lasting change.
3. **Balance:** Include movement, mindfulness and meaningful work.
4. **Flexibility:** Adjust without guilt when life shifts.

Morning Routine (Start Strong)

- **Wake Early:** Begin calmly, not rushed.
- **Hydrate:** Drink water first thing.
- **Move Your Body:** 10–20 minutes of walking, stretching or yoga.
- **Mindfulness:** A few minutes of meditation or breathing.
- **Gratitude:** Note three things you appreciate.
- **Healthy Breakfast:** Fuel your body well.
- **Set 3 MITs:** Choose your Most Important Tasks.

Daytime Routine (Stay Focused & Energized)

- **Time-Block Work:** Use focused work intervals with short breaks.
- **Tackle MITs First:** Start with the most important tasks.
- **Active Breaks:** Move or stretch every hour.
- **Mindful Lunch:** Eat slowly without screens.
- **Connection:** A quick call or chat with someone you care about.
- **Creative Pause:** A short hobby or brainstorming moment.

Evening Routine (Recharge & Reflect)

- **Wind Down:** Transition away from work.
- **Balanced Dinner:** Light, nourishing food.
- **Reflect & Plan:** Review your day and set tomorrow's MITs.
- **Digital Detox:** Avoid screens before bed.
- **Relaxation:** Read, journal or do gentle movement.
- **Sleep Hygiene:** Aim for 7–8 hours.

Sample Daily Flow

- **6:00 AM:** Wake, hydrate, meditate
- **6:30 AM:** Exercise
- **7:00 AM:** Breakfast
- **8:00–11:00 AM:** Deep work on MITs
- **12:00 PM:** Mindful lunch
- **1:00–3:00 PM:** Meetings or lighter tasks
- **7:30 PM:** Dinner + family time
- **9:00 PM:** Reading or journaling
- **10:30 PM:** Sleep

Design your own routine based on your lifestyle, work rhythm and personal goals. What matters is intention, not perfection.

Conclusion: The Gentle Power of Daily Rhythm

Routines are not about doing more—they are about doing what matters most with ease. A simple, sustainable routine clears mental space, protects emotional energy and anchors the day in calmness. When your days flow smoothly, your life follows.

Time Management with Purpose

"Time is life's most precious currency. Spend it wisely."

When I think about what truly matters, I always return to this truth: **time is one of the most valuable resources you and I have**. Yet I've noticed how easily it slips away lost in distractions, unnecessary tasks or commitments that don't genuinely serve our goals or our peace.

For me, intentional time management means making conscious choices. It means **I decide how I spend my time**, instead of letting the world decide for me. And I want to help **you** do the same using your time deliberately so you can focus on what genuinely enriches your life, not just what fills your day. Purposeful time management turns days from chaotic to meaningful. It reduces mental fatigue, protects focus and ensures your energy is spent on what truly matters—not on what simply appears urgent.

Time becomes powerful when it is used intentionally, not accidentally.

"Time is not just minutes and hours. It is life in motion."

In this chapter, **I'll share with you** practical ways I've learned to prioritize, manage and enjoy my time with purpose—so **you and I** can both create days that feel meaningful, balanced and deeply fulfilling.

Prioritizing Your Time

- **Identify What Truly Matters** - Start by clarifying your core priorities. Understand the difference between what's urgent and what's important. When you know what matters most, you can align your actions with your values instead of reacting to constant demands.
- **The Art of Saying "No"** - Every "**Yes**" you give takes time away from something else. Learn to say "**No**" gracefully—without guilt—so you can protect your energy and avoid burnout. Setting boundaries is an act of self-respect.
- **Time-Blocking for Productivity** - Structure your day around your priorities. Time-blocking helps you allocate specific hours for focused work, rest and personal pursuits. Create a schedule that balances productivity with renewal.
- **Balancing Work and Life** - A healthy balance doesn't happen by accident—it's intentional. Define work hours, set physical boundaries and establish end-of-day rituals to protect personal time and prevent work from spilling into every corner of life.

Doing Less, Living More

- **Simplify Your Commitments** - Less can truly be more. Reduce obligations that don't align with your values. Regularly review your commitments and let go of activities that drain your energy without adding joy or meaning.
- **Eliminate Time-Wasters** - Identify common culprits—excessive screen time, unproductive meetings, procrastination—and take steps to minimize them. Reclaim those hours for things that matter.
- **Embrace Downtime** - Rest isn't a luxury; it's essential. Downtime fuels creativity, mental clarity and well-being. Explore restorative activities like reading, journaling or spending time in nature.
- **Overcome FOMO (Fear of Missing Out)** - FOMO often leads to overcommitment and stress. Combat it by focusing on your personal goals and finding contentment in intentional choices. Remember: saying "no" to one thing means saying "yes" to what matters most.

Cultivating Focus and Efficiency

- **Develop Deep Focus** - In a world full of distractions, focus is a superpower. Practice single-tasking, work in distraction-free environments and use tools that support productivity.
- **Set Achievable Goals** - Goals give direction. Use frameworks like SMART (Specific, Measurable, Achievable, Relevant, Time-bound) to create clear, realistic objectives that support long-term growth.
- **Break Down Big Tasks** - Large projects can feel overwhelming. Break them into smaller, manageable steps with time estimates. Progress becomes easier—and more motivating—when you tackle one piece at a time.
- **Review and Adjust Regularly** - Time management isn't static. Schedule weekly or monthly check-ins to assess what's working and what needs adjustment. Staying aligned with your priorities ensures lasting success.

Time is life's most precious resource.

The real question isn't: ***"How much can I do today?"***
It's: ***"Am I spending time on what truly matters?"***

Time is not something to manage—it is something to honour. When you use your hours with intention, life becomes simpler, calmer and more meaningful. Purposeful time management is not about discipline—it is about direction. Not about doing more—but about doing what matters. Not about filling time—but about living fully.

Aligning Life with Core Values

"When your life aligns with your values, decisions become clear and peace becomes natural."

Living meaningfully begins with knowing what you truly value. Without clear values, you may stay busy yet feel directionless moving but not moving with purpose. Values act as a compass: they guide choices, shape goals and create inner clarity. When your actions match your values, life feels lighter, more authentic and far more peaceful.

Why Values Matter

Values quietly influence how you spend time, respond to challenges and define success. When you live in alignment, you feel grounded. When you don't, stress and restlessness appear—even when life looks successful.

Real-Life Examples:

- Rohan had a great salary, status and comfort yet felt empty. His real values were family and well-being but his schedule ignored both. When he adjusted his lifestyle—setting work boundaries and putting health first—fulfilment returned.

Success without alignment is achievement without meaning.

Discovering Your Core Values

You can identify your values by recalling moments when you felt proud, alive or deeply connected. These experiences reveal what matters most.

Real-Life Examples:

- Sara realised her happiest memories were simple ones—family meals, helping others and meaningful conversations. Her true values were connection and kindness. Recognising this helped her stop chasing trends and start nurturing what gave her joy.

Common values include honesty, compassion, growth, simplicity, creativity and freedom.

Living by Your Values

Knowing your values is the first step; living by them is the shift. Before making decisions, ask yourself:

- *Does this choice match my values?*
- *Will this move me closer to the life I want?*

Real-Life Examples:

- Miguel valued health and learning but spent evenings lost in social media. When he noticed the misalignment, he replaced scrolling with short walks and online courses. His days felt calmer and more purposeful.

Values simplify decisions and remove unnecessary noise.

Designing a Values-Driven Life

Let your values appear in every area of life:

- If **simplicity** matters: declutter your home and schedule.
- If **growth** matters: set aside time to learn.
- If **family** matters: protect evenings and weekends.
- If **peace** matters: create quiet spaces in your day.

Create a simple mission statement to guide you: **"I live with honesty, nurture my well-being and choose actions that reflect my purpose."**

Letting Go of Misaligned Commitments

Living by your values means releasing what doesn't fit. Say no to obligations made out of guilt or pressure. Every "No" to misalignment becomes a "Yes" to authenticity, clarity and peace.

Building a Supportive Environment

Your environment should reinforce your values. Surround yourself with people who uplift you and respect your choices. If needed, set boundaries like: "I don't take work calls after 7 PM—I protect that time for my family."
Alignment isn't restriction—it's self-respect.

When Values Conflict

Sometimes values collide work vs rest, ambition vs presence. In those moments, pause, reflect and choose consciously. Values are a compass, not a cage.

Real-Life Examples:

- **Noah: The Professional Who Redefined Success Through Values -** Noah earned well but always felt restless. His real values were freedom, health and meaningful impact—but his schedule revolved around pressure and endless tasks. When he began aligning his days with these values—fewer late nights, more health routines and meaningful work—his stress fell and satisfaction grew. **He realised that success feels empty when it doesn't honour your values.**

- **Sofia: The Woman Who Reclaimed Her Life Through Alignment -** Sofia valued creativity, peace and connection. But her life was filled with noise—constant work deadlines, social obligations and online comparison. When she filtered her choices through her values, her life became calmer and more authentic. **She discovered that values are not goals—they are the foundation of a life that feels true.**

Values Make Life Simple. When your life aligns with your values, clarity replaces confusion, peace replaces stress and joy replaces emptiness.

The question isn't ***"Am I successful?"*** It's ***"Am I living true to what matters most?"*** Because real success is not about having more—it's about living with meaning.

The Law of Self-Awareness: Know Yourself to Grow Yourself

"The first step toward change is awareness."

The Law of Self-Awareness teaches that true growth, fulfilment and transformation begin with knowing yourself. It is the recognition that your thoughts, emotions, beliefs and behaviours shape your reality and that by becoming conscious of them, you gain the power to change and direct your life. Without self-awareness, you move through life unconsciously, reacting to circumstances rather than creating them. With self-awareness, you step into the role of an active participant in your destiny.

At its core, this law reminds us that **you cannot change what you do not acknowledge.** Self-awareness is the mirror that reflects your strengths, weaknesses, desires and fears. It allows you to see patterns in your life—both empowering and limiting—and gives you the clarity to choose differently. By observing yourself without judgment, you cultivate wisdom and authenticity.

"Self-awareness is the light that reveals who you are, who you're becoming and who you can be."

Self-awareness also deepens connection. When you understand yourself, you communicate more clearly, empathize more deeply and build healthier relationships. It is the foundation of emotional intelligence and the key to aligning your inner world with your outer actions.

Real-Life Examples of the Law of Self-Awareness

- **Career Growth** - A professional notices they often procrastinate on tasks requiring detail. Through self-awareness, they recognize that perfectionism is the root cause. By acknowledging this, they shift their mindset, set realistic standards and improve productivity.
- **Relationships** - A person realizes they become defensive during arguments. Instead of blaming others, they reflect on their fear of rejection. This awareness helps them respond calmly, strengthening their relationships.
- **The Leader Who Transformed His Communication Style** – Raj always felt his team didn't understand him. After reflecting on his tone and listening habits, he realised he spoke more than he listened. By practicing mindful pauses and asking questions, his relationships at work improved and conflicts reduced. **Lesson:** Awareness of behaviour creates meaningful change.

- **The Young Professional Who Discovered Her Stress Triggers** – Aakriti often felt overwhelmed but didn't know why. Through journaling, she identified that multitasking and lack of breaks increased her stress. She redesigned her routine with focused work blocks and short pauses. Her productivity increased and her anxiety decreased. **Lesson:** When you understand your triggers, you gain control over your emotions.

The Law of Self-Awareness reminds us that **the journey inward is the most powerful journey of all.** By observing your thoughts, emotions and behaviours with honesty and compassion, you unlock the ability to grow, transform and live authentically. Self-awareness is the foundation of wisdom, the key to emotional mastery and the doorway to creating a life aligned with your highest self.

Mindful and Intentional Living: The Power of the Present Moment

"Peace begins when you stop rushing through life and start living it."

Mindful and intentional living means engaging with life consciously instead of moving through it on autopilot. It is the practice of slowing down, paying attention and being fully present in whatever you're doing. In a world filled with speed, multitasking and constant stimulation, mindfulness brings you back to the richness of the present moment.

Mindful living is not about doing less—it's about **living more fully**. It transforms everyday routines into meaningful experiences and brings calm, clarity and emotional balance into your life.

What Mindful Living Really Means

Mindfulness is the ability to notice your thoughts, emotions, surroundings and responses—without judgment. It teaches you to respond thoughtfully instead of reacting impulsively. When you live mindfully:

- Stress reduces
- Clarity increases
- Focus improves
- Emotional balance strengthens
- Relationships become deeper and more empathetic

Mindfulness helps you experience life with awareness instead of allowing external noise, habits and triggers to control your reactions.

Simple Mindfulness Practices

1. Deep Breathing

A few slow breaths can calm your mind immediately. **Example:** Before replying to a tense message, pause and breathe deeply.

2. Body Awareness

Notice where you carry tension—shoulders, forehead or jaw—and release it. **Example:** Relax your posture each time you sit down.

3. Mindful Observation

Be fully attentive while walking, eating, listening or talking. **Example:** Enjoy a meal without a screen; savor every bite.

Starting a Meditation Habit

Meditation is the foundation of mindful living.

- Begin with **5 minutes a day**
- Focus on your breath
- Use guided sessions if helpful
- Gently bring your attention back when it wanders

Even a few minutes daily can rewire your mind for calmness and clarity.

Gratitude: The Heart of Mindful Living

Gratitude shifts your attention from worry to abundance. Write three things you're grateful for every morning or night. This small practice builds positivity, appreciation and emotional strength.

Clearing Your Mental Space

Mental clutter—overthinking, negativity, self-doubt—drains energy and blocks peace.
To declutter your mind:

- Identify limiting thoughts
- Replace them with empowering ones
- Journal to organize emotions and gain clarity
- Reduce unnecessary mental noise

A clearer mind makes better decisions.

Cultivate Positivity & Resilience

Positivity is not a personality trait—it is a practice.

- Use simple affirmations: **"I choose calm."**
- Stay close to uplifting people

- Focus on solutions, not problems
- Be gentle with yourself during tough moments

A positive mind sees possibilities even in challenges.

Mindful Relationships & Boundaries

Mindfulness also means being intentional with people.

- Prioritize meaningful connections
- Set healthy boundaries
- Protect your time and emotional energy
- Give with love but also receive with openness

Example: "Let's meet once a week instead of daily—I need time to recharge."

The One-Minute Pause: A Moment That Protects Peace

"A single minute of stillness can save you from hours of regret."

The one-minute pause is a micro-practice of mindfulness. It is the simplest way to bring awareness into daily life. When you pause for 60 seconds during stress, anger, confusion or excitement:

- Your breathing slows
- Emotions soften
- Perspective clears
- Reactions become thoughtful
- Decisions become wiser

It shifts you from impulse to awareness.

Why the One-Minute Pause Matters

Most people act first and think later. They react emotionally, speak quickly and regret later. Research shows that even a brief pause helps the mind shift from the **emotional brain** to the **rational brain**, improving judgment and emotional balance. A pause doesn't delay life—it **upgrades** it.

Key Benefits of the One-Minute Pause

- Prevents emotional reactions
- Improves decision quality
- Protects relationships
- Reduces stress instantly
- Builds self-control and awareness

This small habit has massive power.

Real-Life Examples:

- **Mira: A Life Rebalanced -** Mira felt overwhelmed by notifications and work pressure. She added three habits: 5-minute morning meditation, Gratitude journaling at night, No phone during meals.Within a month, her sleep improved, her focus increased and her family interactions became calmer.
- **Raghav: Avoiding Conflict with a Pause -** When a team member made a mistake, Raghav felt anger rising. Instead of reacting, he paused for one minute, breathed deeply and responded with clarity and respect. This strengthened trust and prevented conflict.
- **Priya: Creating a Peaceful Home -** Priya used to react quickly when overwhelmed. By practicing the one-minute pause, she communicated more patiently and reduced arguments. Her home atmosphere transformed.

Living Fully, Living Mindfully

Mindful and intentional living is not about escaping life—it's about experiencing it deeply. The real question is not: **"How much can I finish today?"** but **"How fully can I live today?"** And often, the difference between chaos and peace… Between reaction and wisdom… Between regret and clarity… is just **one mindful minute**.

Make a System - Build a Life That Runs Smoothly and Successfully

"Success doesn't come from willpower—it comes from systems that make good choices automatic."

A system is simply a set of small habits, routines and structures that help your life run without stress or confusion. When you rely only on motivation, your results vary. But when you rely on systems, your results become consistent. Systems remove daily decision fatigue, reduce emotional friction and create smooth pathways for progress. Making a system means designing your life intentionally—so that the right behaviours happen naturally and the wrong ones become difficult. A good system turns discipline into ease and progress into a habit.

Why Making a System Matters

Most people live reactively—waking up without a plan, doing things when they "feel like it," and relying on mood instead of method. This leads to inconsistency, stress, delays and emotional ups and downs. A system changes everything. It brings order, predictability and peace. It allows you to grow steadily, without burning out.

Research in behavioural science shows that systems create more long-term success than raw motivation. Routines reduce mental overload, conserve energy and make improvement sustainable.Life becomes calmer when your systems carry the weight. A system is not control—it is freedom from chaos.

How to Make a System (The Life-Friendly Way)

Begin by identifying one area of your life that feels messy or stressful—health, finances, work, routines, emotional habits or home management. Ask yourself: "What simple structure will make this easier?" Design a small routine around it. Fix a specific time. Fix a specific method. Reduce decisions. Automate what you can. Use checklists if needed. Make the system so simple you can follow it even on low-energy days. Systems grow slowly—start with one, refine it, then add another. Eventually, your life becomes a series of small, reliable routines that bring clarity and control. A good system removes thought from what should be automatic.

Real-Life Examples:

- **The Working Professional Who Turned Chaos Into Control -** Ramesh felt overwhelmed—emails, meetings, deadlines. He created a simple system: Morning = planning; afternoon = deep work; evening = follow-up. He fixed his tools, fixed his timings and fixed his rituals. Within weeks, stress reduced, productivity doubled and he ended each day with clarity instead of exhaustion. **Lesson:** Systems succeed where motivation fails.
- **The Homemaker Who Simplified Her Entire Day Through Small Systems -** Megha struggled with cooking, cleaning, children's routines and her own peace. She created micro-systems: pre-cut vegetables at night, fixed laundry days, a weekly planner and a Sunday reset routine. Her home became smoother, her mind became clearer and her energy returned. **Lesson:** Systems bring peace, not pressure.

When you create systems, life stops feeling heavy. You stop firefighting and start flowing. Systems don't make you rigid—they make you free. They reduce stress, increase consistency and turn good intentions into daily actions. Build one system at a time. Refine it. Trust it. Because when your systems grow stronger, **you** grow stronger.

Avoid the Strain of Perfection and Idealism

"A perfect life is an exhausting illusion; a real life is where peace lives."

Perfection and idealism often appear noble, disciplined and admirable on the surface. Many people believe that high standards will lead to success, happiness and respect. But beneath this pursuit lies a quiet strain. **The constant pressure to be flawless, right or ideal slowly drains joy, energy and inner calm**.

Perfectionism is not the desire to do well—it is the fear of doing wrong. Idealism is not vision—it is the refusal to accept reality as it is. Together, they create tension, self-criticism and chronic dissatisfaction. Letting go of this strain does not mean lowering values; it means living **humanly, realistically and peacefully**.

Why Perfection and Idealism Create Strain

Perfectionism keeps the mind in a state of "not enough." No matter how much is achieved, something always feels incomplete. Idealism adds another layer—expecting people, situations and even oneself to behave in ideal ways. When reality fails to match these expectations, frustration, disappointment and self-blame appear.

Psychological studies show that excessive perfectionism is linked to anxiety, burnout, emotional fatigue and reduced satisfaction. People who chase perfection rarely enjoy their progress. They live under internal pressure, postponing happiness until everything feels "right"—a moment that almost never arrives.
The mind becomes tired not from effort but from **unrealistic expectations**.

Key Principles to Release the Strain

- **Choose Progress Over Perfection:** Growth matters more than flawlessness.
- **Accept Human Limits:** Everyone learns through mistakes, not ideals.
- **Replace "Should Be" with "What Is":** Reality is the starting point of peace.
- **Allow Imperfection:** Imperfection is not failure—it is life.
- **Practice Self-Compassion:** Harsh self-judgment creates inner exhaustion.

Real-Life Examples:

- **The Professional Who Could Never Feel Satisfied** – Stefan set extremely high standards for himself and others. Even strong achievements felt inadequate. Compliments made him uncomfortable because he focused only on what could have been better. When he learned to appreciate progress instead of perfection, his stress reduced and work became more enjoyable. **Lesson:** Satisfaction begins when effort is valued, not just flawless results.

- **The Parent Trapped by Ideal Expectations** –Rina believed she had to be a perfect parent—always patient, always right. Small mistakes filled her with guilt. Over time, exhaustion replaced joy. When she accepted that being present mattered more than being perfect, her relationship with her children softened and her emotional health improved. **Lesson:** Idealism creates pressure; acceptance creates connection.

Perfection and idealism promise excellence but often deliver strain. Life becomes lighter when you allow space for mistakes, learning and adjustment. When standards soften, clarity strengthens. When expectations relax, peace enters.

Do your best—but do not demand impossible perfection.
Dream wisely—but stay grounded in reality.
Accept yourself—unfinished, learning and growing.

Because a peaceful life is not built on ideal versions of yourself or others—it is built on **acceptance, understanding and gentle effort**.

You Become What You Think About – The Silent Power of Thought

"Your thoughts are not harmless visitors—they are quiet architects of your life."

Every life is shaped first in the mind. Long before actions are taken or results appear, **thoughts set the direction**. What you think repeatedly becomes what you believe, how you behave and eventually who you become. This happens subtly, quietly and continuously—often without awareness.

Positive or negative, confident or fearful, calm or anxious—thoughts slowly condition the mind, body and outcomes. You may not control every external situation but you always influence your inner dialogue. And that inner dialogue shapes your reality more than circumstances ever will. You do not become what you wish for. You become what you consistently think about.

Why Your Thoughts Matter So Deeply

Thoughts are not just mental activity—they trigger emotional and physical responses. Repeated negative thinking keeps the body in stress mode and the mind in survival mode. Repeated positive and constructive thinking creates clarity, confidence and emotional balance.

Psychology and lived experience both show that when people constantly focus on fear, lack or failure, they unknowingly move toward those experiences. When they focus on growth, solutions and gratitude, their decisions, energy and behaviour begin to support better outcomes. Your mind believes what you tell it repeatedly. And your life follows that belief.

Key Principles of Thought Awareness

- **Thoughts Become Beliefs:** What you repeat internally becomes accepted as truth.
- **Beliefs Shape Actions:** You act according to what you believe about yourself and life.
- **Actions Create Results:** Daily behaviour builds long-term outcomes.
- **Unseen Thoughts Have Seen Consequences:** Even silent thinking leaves visible impact.
- **Awareness is the First Power:** You can change only what you notice.

Real-Life Examples:

- **The Man Who Thought He Was "Not Capable"** – Victor constantly told himself he was average and unlikely to succeed. He avoided challenges and opportunities without realizing why. When he became aware of this inner narrative and slowly replaced it with constructive thinking—"I can learn," "I can improve"—his confidence and performance changed. **Lesson:** When inner talk changes, outer results follow.

- **The Woman Who Learned to Redirect Her Mind** – Noura lived with constant worry, imagining future problems before they existed. This mental pattern kept her anxious and exhausted. When she consciously practiced shifting her thoughts toward what she could control in the present, her stress reduced and emotional clarity improved. **Lesson:** You gain peace not by changing life but by changing how you think about life.

Your thoughts shape how you speak, how you react, how you decide and how you treat yourself. A mind filled with fear builds a guarded life. A mind filled with growth builds possibility. A mind filled with gratitude builds peace.

You may not notice your thoughts shaping your life day by day—but over time, **they define the direction of your journey**.

Watch your thoughts gently.
Choose them wisely.
Feed the ones that strengthen you.

Because in the end, your life does not move in the direction of luck or chance—it moves in the direction of **your most repeated thoughts**.

Mental Mastery: Train, Protect & Reprogram Your Mind

"Master your mind and your life will follow"

Your Inner Engine: The Subconscious Mind

The subconscious mind is the silent powerhouse within you. It stores habits, beliefs, memories and emotional patterns. It operates without pause—day and night—shaping how you think, feel, respond and behave. While your conscious mind makes decisions, it is the subconscious mind that turns those decisions into actions. It influences confidence, fears, desires, creativity, intuition—and almost every result you create in life. When you learn to direct your subconscious mind with clarity and intention, your life begins to shift from the inside out. You don't live your life based on what you *want*—you live it based on what your **subconscious believes**.

Change doesn't happen only in the conscious mind; it happens in the deeper layer beneath it. The subconscious runs your automatic patterns—how you react to stress, how you speak to yourself, how you interpret situations and how quickly you bounce back. It absorbs repeated thoughts and experiences and then turns them into your reality. To change your life, you must change the programming that runs it. **You become what your subconscious repeatedly accepts as true.**

How the Subconscious Shapes Your Life

The subconscious mind does not argue. It simply obeys. Whatever you repeatedly tell it, imagine, fear or believe—slowly becomes your internal truth.

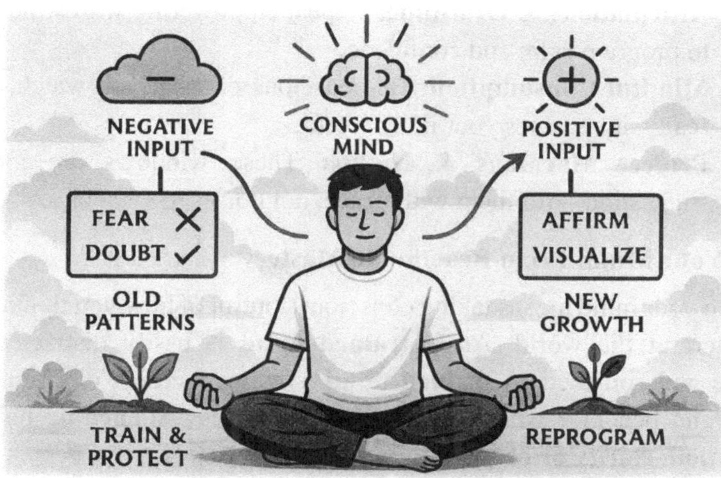

- If you repeat **"I can't,"** your subconscious blocks opportunities.

- If you declare **"I will learn,"** it begins creating pathways for growth.
- If you visualize **success**, your mind starts directing your behaviour toward it.
- If you dwell on **fear**, your life begins to shrink.

This mind responds to **emotion, repetition and belief**. When you consciously feed it empowering thoughts, better images and healthier stories, it begins to rewrite your life script. **The subconscious mind is the soil; your thoughts are the seeds.**

Guarding the Mind: Protect Your Inner World

The subconscious records everything you see, hear, repeat and believe—even when you are not paying attention. When you fill it with negativity, noise, fear, complaints, gossip or unhealthy content, your inner world becomes heavy, restless and confused. **Protecting your subconscious is an act of self-respect.** When you choose what enters your mind, you choose the quality of your future.

Why this matters: In the modern world, we consume massive amounts of information—social media, news, arguments, entertainment, comparison—without realizing how deeply it affects the inner world. Repeated exposure to negative input elevates stress and emotional instability, while meaningful, positive input strengthens confidence, motivation and peace.

Your subconscious becomes whatever you repeatedly allow into your mind.

Key principles to keep your subconscious clean:

- **Choose Positive Inputs:** Uplifting books, inspiring content, meaningful conversations.
- **Limit Negative Content:** Reduce gossip, violent media toxic news and draining people.
- **Affirmations & Gratitude:** Repeat empowering words; notice blessings to program calm and confidence.
- **Mindful Consumption:** Be conscious of what you watch, listen to and read—it becomes your inner world.
- **Protect Mornings & Nights:** These windows are most open to suggestion—fill them with peace, not noise.

Train Your Mind: From Reaction to Mastery

Training your mind means taking conscious control of how you think, react, decide and interpret the world. An **untrained mind** is easily distracted, emotional, reactive and confused. A **trained mind** is calm, focused, disciplined and wise. Your mind becomes what you repeatedly practice—**silence or noise, focus or distraction, clarity or chaos**.

Most problems in life do not come from situations—they come from the **mind's reaction** to those situations. Fear, overthinking, assumptions, anger, comparison and doubt are symptoms of an untrained mind. When you train your mind, you gain emotional freedom. You stop reacting to every trigger, reduce unnecessary stress and start thinking with clarity.

Your mind is the driver. Your life is the vehicle. Train the driver.

Foundational training practices:

- **Single-Task Focus:** Give your mind one task at a time and complete it fully.
- **Daily Silence:** Sit in quiet; observe thoughts without acting on them.
- **Self-Talk Upgrade:** Replace harsh inner talk with empowering dialogue.
- **The Emotional Pause:** Build a 10-second gap before responding.
- **Learn Something New:** Stretch mental flexibility regularly.
- **Digital Boundaries:** Limit unnecessary stimulation; your mind grows stronger in quiet.
- **Regular Reflection:** Review your patterns weekly and adjust with intention.

Reprogramming: Plant New Seeds, Harvest New Results

Reprogramming is simple: repeat the **right** stories with **feeling** until your subconscious adopts them.

Core tools:

- **Affirmations with Identity:** "I lead with clarity and courage." "I am worthy and capable."
- **Mental Rehearsal/Visualization:** See yourself acting as your best self; feel it as real.
- **Gratitude Imaging:** Picture the days you desire—and give thanks as if they already exist.
- **Environment Design:** Remove inputs that feed fear; add inputs that feed strength.
- **Morning & Night Scripting:** Speak your chosen identity and outcomes when your mind is most open.

Real-Life Examples:

- **Arvind — From Self-Doubt to Leadership:** - His inner loop said, "I am not leadership material." Through daily affirmations and mental rehearsal—"I lead with clarity and confidence"—he began speaking up, taking ownership and presenting ideas. His subconscious accepted the new identity; his results followed. **Lesson:** Change your inner story; your outer life follows.

- **Meera — Healing Through Rewriting the Script:** - Years of negative self-talk kept her stuck. She replaced the loop with, "I am worthy. I am capable. I am important," practiced gratitude and visualized calm mornings. Confidence rose; the family felt the shift in her presence. **Lesson:** Stop feeding pain; start feeding possibility.
- **Rohan — A Cleaner Mind, Sharper Decisions:** - Morning doom-scrolling made his mind heavy all day. He swapped it for positive reading and silence. Stress dropped; decisions became calm and clear. **Lesson:** What enters your mornings shapes your day.
- **Pooja — Peace by Ending Toxic Inputs:** - Gossip and arguments drained her. She reduced such interactions and chose uplifting activities. Emotional balance improved; the home grew happier. **Lesson:** Protecting your mind protects your peace.
- **Rajesh — Mastering the Reactive Moment:** - Anger and impatience hurt his work. He adopted a single rule: **Pause 10 seconds before responding.** Arguments declined; respect grew. **Lesson:** A trained reaction becomes a trained life.
- **Anita — Choosing Peace, Daily:** - Overwhelm and comparison faded as she gave herself 10 quiet minutes each morning, repeating, "I choose peace today." **Lesson:** The mind becomes what you feed it—choose nourishment.

The subconscious mind is the **engine** of your life. Train it, guide it, nourish it—and it will lift you higher than you imagined. Neglect it and it will run old programs on repeat. Speak to yourself with intention. Visualize the life you desire. Replace fear with purpose and doubt with belief. Because true change doesn't begin merely in action—it begins in the quiet space of the **subconscious mind**, where your future is silently being written.

The Law of Cause and Effect: Your Actions Shape Your Destiny

"Every action has consequences—choose wisely and you choose your future."

This law reminds us that success isn't luck—it is built through consistent actions, disciplined habits and conscious decisions. Change the cause and the effect must change. This law asserts that every action has an equal and opposite reaction. The more we simplify our actions and focus on good intentions, the more positive outcomes we will receive in return. If we live simply, focusing on meaningful relationships, work and experiences, we attract simplicity and clarity in return. By acting mindfully and intentionally, we create simplicity in our lives.

The universal law of cause-and-effect states that for every effect there is a definite cause, likewise for every cause, there is a definite effect. This means that everything we currently have in our lives is an effect that results from a specific cause.

Your thoughts, behaviours and actions create specific effects that manifest and shape your life as you know it. If you are not happy with the effects you have created, then you must change the causes that created them in the first place.

Change your actions and you change your life. Transform your thoughts and you will create a brand-new destiny. These causes are the decisions we make and the actions we take daily. Whether our decisions seem small and insignificant or whether they are significant and transformational in nature, it does not matter. Each decision we have made and action we have taken has set events into motion, creating predictable and specific effects that we are now experiencing in our lives.

The law of cause and effect stipulates that:

- Success is not built upon chance or luck.
- Success is not determined outside of you.
- Success is created within you.

In short, the law states that there are no accidents in this world and that the effects we create in our lives are a direct result of causes that come from within ourselves.

Real-Life Examples of the Law of Cause and Effect

- **Health** - A person who eats nutritious food and exercises regularly will enjoy better health and energy. On the other hand, neglecting these habits often leads to illness and fatigue.

- **Education** - A student who studies consistently, asks questions and practices daily will perform well in exams. The cause—dedication and effort—creates the effect of academic success.
- **Relationships** - When you show kindness, respect and honesty to your friends and family, those bonds grow stronger. If you ignore or mistreat them, the effect will be distance and conflict

The Law of Cause and Effect remind us that life is shaped from the inside out. When your choices are intentional and aligned with who you want to become, the results follow naturally. Every small action plant a seed—some grow quickly, others take time but none return empty.

Choose your causes wisely and your life will reflect the future you desire.

The Power of Honest Self-Reflection

"Accepting your limits creates wisdom; using your strengths creates success."

Honest self-reflection is the *practice* that turns awareness into wise action. Recognizing and accepting your weaknesses builds self-awareness; leveraging your strengths builds self-development. When you understand what limits you and what empowers you, you create a life rooted in clarity, balance and authenticity. Accepting weaknesses does not make you smaller—it makes you wiser. Building strengths does not make you arrogant—it makes you effective.

Why This Practice Matters

Most people ignore weaknesses out of fear or hide strengths out of doubt. This inner conflict breeds confusion, low confidence and emotional imbalance. Research in human performance consistently shows that people who accept their limits and cultivate their gifts are more resilient, successful and emotionally grounded. True growth happens when you know your limits without shame and your gifts without hesitation.

Key Principles to Recognize Weakness & Build Strength

- **Accept Without Judgment:** Weaknesses are not failures; they are areas for learning.
- **Identify Your Strengths:** Notice what energizes you and comes naturally—your power zones.
- **Work on Weakness Step by Step:** Small, steady improvements accumulate into real change.
- **Leverage Your Strengths Daily:** Using strengths consistently builds confidence and impact.

- **Let Go of Comparison:** Growth is personal; your path is unique.

Real-Life Examples:

- **The Leader Who Turned Self-Doubt into Emotional Strength** — Ramesh struggled to speak up in meetings. Acknowledging this weakness and practicing articulation—while leaning on his analytical strength—improved his communication and leadership.
- **The Homemaker Who Flourished by Using Her Natural Talents** — Kavita loved organizing but dismissed it as "simple." Naming it as a strength, she created systems at home, grew in confidence and began helping others.

Recognizing your weaknesses brings honesty. Accepting them brings peace. Working on your strengths brings power. When you stop pretending to be perfect and start embracing who you truly are, you open the door to genuine growth. In self-acceptance you find clarity and in your strengths you find the path forward. Grow not by denying your truth but by building upon it.

Mastering Your Emotions

"You cannot control the wind but you can adjust your sails."

Emotional Quotient (EQ), also called Emotional Intelligence, is the ability to recognize, understand and manage your own emotions — and to perceive and respond effectively to the emotions of others. Mastering your emotions means using this skill to stay calm under pressure, build stronger relationships and make better decisions.

What is Emotional Quotient (EQ)?

EQ is different from IQ. While IQ measures cognitive ability, **EQ measures emotional awareness and control.** High EQ means you can:

- Recognize your own feelings.
- Understand how emotions influence behaviour.
- Manage emotional reactions constructively.
- Empathize with others and respond appropriately.

Why Mastering Emotions Matters

- **Better Relationships:** People with high EQ communicate clearly and resolve conflicts peacefully.
- **Career Success:** Leaders with strong EQ inspire teams, handle stress and make balanced decisions.

- **Mental Fitness:** Managing emotions reduces anxiety, burnout and impulsive behaviour.

Real-Life Examples of EQs

1. **Workplace Stress -** Imagine your boss criticizes your work.
    - Low EQ reaction: Anger, defensiveness, damaged relationship.
    - High EQ reaction: Pause, listen calmly, ask clarifying questions and use feedback to improve.
2. **Parenting -** A child throws a tantrum.
    - Low EQ reaction: Shouting back, escalating conflict.
    - High EQ reaction: Recognizing the child's frustration, staying calm and guiding them to express feelings safely.
3. **Negotiation -** During a business deal, emotions run high.
    - Low EQ reaction: Impulsive decisions, loss of trust.
    - High EQ reaction: Reading the other person's emotions, staying composed and finding win-win solutions.

How to Master Your Emotions

- **Self-Awareness:** Notice your emotional triggers. Journaling or mindfulness helps.
- **Self-Regulation:** Pause before reacting. Practice deep breathing or short breaks.
- **Empathy:** Try to see situations from others' perspectives.
- **Social Skills:** Communicate clearly, listen actively and resolve conflicts constructively.

- **Continuous Learning:** Read, reflect and practice emotional intelligence daily.

The 90/10 Principle

The **90/10 Principle**, popularized by Stephen Covey, says that *10% of life is what happens to you and 90% is how you react to it.* You can't control events but you can control your response — and that determines your happiness, success and relationships.

Explanation

- **10% of life:** Events beyond your control — traffic jams, sudden delays, other people's actions, illness or accidents.
- **90% of life:** Your reaction to those events — whether you stay calm, adapt and move forward or let anger and stress take over.

This principle emphasizes **personal responsibility**. While circumstances are unpredictable, your response shapes the outcome.

Real-Life Examples:

- **Morning Mishap:** Spill coffee on your shirt. React with anger and ruin your day —or laugh it off, you change shirt and move on.
- **Traffic Jam:** Stress and honk—or use the time to listen to an audiobook.
- **Workplace Conflict:** Retaliate and create tension—or listen calmly and improve.

Mastering emotions doesn't mean suppressing them — it means **channelling them wisely.** By strengthening EQ, you gain resilience, build trust and create a balanced life where emotions serve you instead of controlling you. The **90/10 Principle** teaches that *life is less about what happens and more about how you respond.* By choosing calm, constructive reactions, you transform challenges into opportunities and live with greater peace and success.

The Law of Least Effort: Flow, Don't Force

"Nature achieves everything with ease—so can you."

The **Law of Least Effort** is a universal principle that teaches us that nature always follows the path of least resistance. Rivers flow around rocks, plants grow toward sunlight and energy moves in the simplest, most efficient way possible. In human life, this law reminds us that when we stop struggling against reality and instead align with it, things begin to flow more smoothly.

At its core, the Law of Least Effort is about **acceptance, responsibility and defencelessness**:

- **Acceptance** – Acknowledge situations as they are, without resisting or wishing they were different. Resistance drains energy, while acceptance allows clarity and creativity.
- **Responsibility** – Take ownership of your choices and actions without blaming others. This empowers you to respond constructively rather than react negatively.
- **Defencelessness** – Release the need to constantly prove yourself right or argue. By letting go of defensiveness, you conserve energy and open space for cooperation and solutions.

Real-Life Examples of the Law of Least Effort

- **Workplace Conflict** - Instead of arguing endlessly with a colleague, a manager accepts the situation, takes responsibility for their role and calmly seeks a solution. This approach resolves the issue faster than defensiveness or blame.
- **Parenting** - A parent trying to force a child to study may face resistance. But when they accept the child's perspective, take responsibility for creating a supportive environment and drop defensiveness, they find creative ways—like games or rewards—that make studying enjoyable.

In short: The Law of Least Effort teaches us that **ease, acceptance and flow are more powerful than struggle and resistance.** By conserving energy and aligning with reality, we create space for growth, creativity and success.

The Secret of Becoming Mentally Strong - Master Your Inner World

"Mental strength is not about avoiding storms—it is about learning to walk through them with steady steps."

Mental strength is the inner ability to stay calm, clear and grounded even when life becomes unpredictable. It is not about being emotionless or rigid. It is about being emotionally balanced, mentally disciplined and spiritually steady. People who are mentally strong are not born that way—they train themselves daily. They choose discipline over impulse, reflection over reaction and clarity over confusion. They protect their mind, manage their emotions and rise every time life knocks them down. A mentally strong person is not someone who never falls—but someone who always rises.

Why Mental Strength Matters

Life will always test you—through pressure, expectations, failures, losses and unexpected events. Without mental strength, even small challenges feel heavy. With mental strength, even big challenges become manageable. Research shows that mentally strong individuals make better decisions, recover faster from setbacks, maintain emotional balance and create healthier relationships. Mental strength gives you the power to pause, think and choose your response instead of letting situations control you. True strength begins where emotional control begins.

How to Become Mentally Strong (The Real Secret)

Mental strength is built slowly, like a muscle. When you practice small disciplines every day—pausing before reacting, choosing positive thoughts, staying consistent with habits, protecting your focus and setting boundaries—your mental resilience grows.Train your mind to observe, not absorb. To respond, not react. To endure discomfort, not escape it. Let go of what you cannot control. Focus on what you can. Read, reflect, journal, walk, breathe, pray and give your mind the silence it needs. Strength grows in stillness and shows in storms. Mental strength is not about harshness—it is about inner harmony.

Real-Life Examples:

- **The Athlete Who Turned Pressure Into Power -** A marathon runner always broke down halfway during races. Instead of blaming circumstances, she began mental conditioning—visualizing the run, practicing calm breathing, repeating affirmations and embracing discomfort. She didn't become stronger physically—she became stronger mentally. Her next race was her personal best. **Lesson:** The mind reaches the finish line before the body does.
- **The Soldier Who Mastered Emotional Control Under Fire -** A young soldier struggled with fear during training. His instructor taught him one principle: "Slow your breath. Slow your thoughts." Through repetition, he learned to stay calm under pressure. In real combat, that training saved not only his life but also the lives of his team. **Lesson:** Mental strength is built long before the moment that demands it.
- **The Nurse Who Stayed Steady During Medical Emergencies -** Working in the emergency ward, she faced chaos daily. Instead of panicking, she trained her mind to focus only on the next immediate step.

She became known for her calm presence and clear thinking, especially in critical moments. **Lesson:** Mental strength is the ability to stay composed when everyone else is overwhelmed.

Mental strength is built through small daily disciplines—choosing calmness over chaos, courage over fear, action over avoidance and clarity over confusion. When your inner world becomes strong, the outer world loses its power to disturb you.Strengthen your thoughts. Strengthen your responses. Strengthen your habits. Because the secret of becoming mentally strong is simple: **Train your mind until it becomes your strongest protector, not your greatest problem.**

Break Free from Unhealthy Habits - Protect Your Energy and Clarity

"The habits you avoid are as important as the habits you build."

Modern life brings stress, pressure, loneliness and the rush of daily responsibilities. In moments of overwhelm, people reach for quick relief—smoking to calm the nerves, drinking to soften the day, late-night eating for comfort, sugary drinks for a boost, mobile games and endless social scrolling to escape and "just tonight" sleep cuts to keep up. These feel soothing for a moment but they quietly erode clarity, weaken the body, disturb emotional balance and make life heavy. *Most people don't choose these habits to harm themselves; they choose them because they are exhausted and want relief.* **The relief is temporary. The cost is long-term**.

Why Unhealthy Habits Rise in Modern Life

Life moves faster than emotions can process. Expectations are heavy. Loneliness exists even in crowds. In that environment, **alcohol** becomes a social escape, **sugary drinks** a quick fuel, **late-night eating** an emotional filler, **smoking** a stress signal, **chronic sleep deprivation** a new normal, **no strength training** an accepted inertia, **mobile games** an easy distraction and **excessive social media scrolling** a digital refuge that quietly steals hours. These habits numb discomfort but create deeper inner chaos. They fog the mind, disturb digestion, weaken immunity, elevate anxiety and reduce motivation. A powerful, simple life needs a clear mind, strong body and steady emotions—unhealthy habits quietly break all three.

The Reality of Unhealthy Escapes

Unhealthy habits mute emotions instead of healing them, so dependency grows while problems remain. Clarity fades and decisions become reactive. Physical energy declines because the body spends more time recovering than growing. Gradually, the gap widens between who you are and who you want to be. "I need a break" turns into "I can't function without this," and the day starts revolving around the next hit of relief—another cigarette, another soda, another level in a mobile game, another scroll that turns minutes into hours.

Understanding the Red Flags

They arrive quietly as private justifications: *"It's only tonight." "Everyone does it." "I deserve a break." "I can stop anytime."* Slowly, "once in a while" becomes routine. Sleep quality drops, morning energy shrinks, confidence slides and relationships feel strained. The mind grows noisy, the body feels heavy and life becomes complicated instead of simple. You'll notice the signs: late dinners that steal rest, sweet drinks that spike and crash, screens that keep you awake, games that eat focus, cigarettes that become crutches, days without movement that make even stairs feel harder.

Real-Life Examples:

- **Roland — Reclaiming Energy from Late Nights and Quick Fixes** -= Roland had slipped into late dinners, sugary drinks to power through and chronic sleep cuts. A cigarette "only when stressed" became more frequent and mobile games filled the time he said he didn't have for exercise. His mornings felt dull, his mind foggy. He chose small changes—lighter earlier dinners, water instead of sweet drinks, a fixed bedtime and five minutes of body-weight moves before bed. The cigarette breaks shrank as his stress did. Within weeks, energy returned and clarity sharpened. **He discovered that life improves the moment your habits start respecting your body.**
- **Leona — Ending the Scroll-and-Snack Spiral** - Leona felt anxious and unfocused. Nights disappeared into "just a few minutes" on social media and mobile games, paired with mindless snacks. She introduced gentle shifts: a 20-minute evening walk, three short strength sessions a week, device-free wind-down with calming music and mindful meals. Her sleep deepened, cravings reduced and her mood steadied. **She realised that removing unhealthy inputs restores inner peace faster than chasing external fixes.**

How to Break Free Without Pressure

You don't need a perfect overhaul—just honest awareness and tiny upgrades. Move dinner earlier and lighter; swap one sugary drink for water; bring bedtime forward by 15 minutes; add a few minutes of strength moves most days; set a screen curfew and park the phone outside the bedroom; replace one cigarette break with deep, slow breaths; choose content that calms rather than agitates. Small steps, repeated gently, create big change without drama.

Unhealthy habits—smoking, late-night eating, excess sugar, chronic sleep loss, no strength training, mobile games that absorb hours and endless social scrolling—quietly drain your energy and blur your clarity. Choose awareness over autopilot and swap quick relief for small, steady upgrades. The moment your habits begin to honour your body and mind, life becomes lighter, calmer and unmistakably yours.

Part III: Spiritual Simplicity: Calm Mind, Clear Heart

Explore inner stillness, presence and spiritual clarity beyond religion

Chapter 7: Pathways to Inner Calm

The Essence of Spirituality - Beyond Religion toward Inner Truth

"Spirituality is not about believing in something outside you—it is about awakening to what already lives within you."

Spirituality, beyond religion, is the personal journey of understanding yourself, your purpose and your connection with life. It is not tied to rituals, symbols or doctrines—it is the experience of inner clarity, peace and awareness. True spirituality is the art of living consciously. It teaches you to observe your thoughts, listen to your inner voice, honour your values and live with compassion. It helps you rise above ego, fear and confusion, guiding you toward a life of meaning and inner balance.

Why Spirituality Matters

In a world filled with noise, speed and constant comparison, people often lose touch with their inner self. Spirituality brings you back to your center. It helps you understand your emotions, find purpose in challenges and stay grounded in chaos. Research in psychology shows that spiritual practices—like mindfulness, reflection, gratitude and compassion—reduce stress, improve emotional resilience and create a deeper sense of fulfilment. Spirituality is not about escaping life—it is about engaging with life more deeply, with clarity and awareness.

Key Elements of True Spirituality

- **Self-Awareness:** Understanding your thoughts, feelings and patterns without judgment.
- **Inner Peace:** Finding calm within yourself rather than depending on external situations.
- **Connection:** Feeling linked to nature, people, purpose and the universe.
- **Compassion:** Acting with kindness and seeing others with empathy.
- **Authenticity:** Living in alignment with your values, truth and inner wisdom.

Real-Life Examples:

- **The Professional Who Found Balance Through Mindfulness** – Rohan lived under pressure, juggling deadlines and responsibilities. He began practicing 10 minutes of silent awareness daily—simply observing his breath. Within weeks, he felt calmer, reacted less and made decisions with greater clarity. **Lesson:** Spirituality begins when you learn to pause and listen.

- **The Homemaker Who Reconnected with Herself Through Gratitude** – Sunita often felt overwhelmed by routine and expectations. She started ending each day by writing three things she was grateful for. Slowly, her attitude shifted—she felt lighter, more appreciative and more connected with herself. **Lesson:** Spirituality grows through simple acts of awareness and appreciation.

Spirituality is not about following a path—it is about discovering your own. It invites you to slow down, reflect and return to your inner truth. When you live spiritually, you live with depth. Every moment becomes meaningful, every experience becomes a lesson and every breath becomes a reminder of your connection with life. Spirituality doesn't take you away from the world—it helps you live in it with greater clarity, purpose and peace.

Meditation: The Gateway to Mindfulness

"In stillness, we find clarity."

In today's world, life moves at a frantic pace. Competition, deadlines and constant information overload keep our bodies and minds in a state of tension. Stress becomes the natural response, whether the threats we perceive are real or imagined. This stress is not only emotional; it is psychosomatic, affecting digestion, sleep, skin and even our ability to think clearly.

Meditation is one of the simplest yet most profound ways to filter the noise of the outside world. By training the mind to focus, we gradually achieve mindfulness — a state of calm awareness that reduces stress and extends the quality of life.

What Happens When You Start Meditating?

- **Less Reactionary** - Meditation teaches detachment. Instead of reacting impulsively, you observe situations with clarity. This temperament is essential for leadership and prevents rash words or actions you might later regret.
- **More Resilient** - Research shows that regular meditators bounce back faster from setbacks. They are more likely to quit harmful habits, stick to healthy routines and maintain discipline.
- **Less Fearful** - Meditation reduces anxiety and fear by calming the nervous system. It helps you face challenges with courage and composure.
- **More Present** - Meditation anchors you in the present moment. Instead of dwelling on the past or worrying about the future, you experience life as it unfolds.

3 Simple Ways to Begin Meditating

- **Guided Meditation** - Use YouTube or mobile apps to follow step-by-step sessions. A voice guides your breathing and focus, making it easy for beginners.
- **Breath Awareness** - Sit quietly, close your eyes and pay attention to your breath. Notice the inhale and exhale without trying to control it.
- **Body Scan** - Lie down and mentally scan your body from head to toe, releasing tension in each part.

Guided Meditation

Guided meditation is perfect for beginners and even more powerful for busy people. Someone's voice leads you step-by-step—helping you breathe, relax, visualize and focus. It removes confusion and makes meditation effortless.

A guided meditation can include:

1. Positive Affirmations

Repetitions like:
"I am calm."
"I am safe."
"I can handle today."
These rewire your mind with strength, confidence and peace.

2. Visualization

You may be guided to imagine:

- a peaceful beach
- a quiet forest
- a glowing light entering your body
- your future self-smiling with ease

Visualization activates the brain's natural ability to heal, relax and renew.

3. Gratitude Awareness

A guiding voice may remind you to appreciate: your breath, family, body, home, nature, opportunities. Gratitude softens the heart and shifts your energy into abundance.

4. Positive Energy Flow

Some guided journeys include imagining warm, healing light traveling: from head → to heart → to stomach → to legs → to the entire body. This creates a feeling of harmony and balance.

5. Story-Based Relaxation

A gentle story helps the mind let go—like walking through a garden, sitting by a river or watching stars. These soothing images calm the mind deeply.
Meditation is not about stopping life—it's about meeting life with clarity and strength.

In stillness, you reconnect with yourself. In silence, you rediscover your balance.

And through consistent practice, you begin to carry peace within you, wherever you go. A few minutes each day can change the way you think, feel and live. Meditation opens the door—mindfulness is what waits inside.

The Law of Presence: Live in the Now

"The present moment is all you ever truly have."

The Law of Presence teaches that true power and fulfilment are found in the present moment. Too often, our minds drift into the past, replaying regrets or into the future, worrying about what has yet to come. Presence is the practice of anchoring ourselves in the "now," where life unfolds. When we are fully present, we experience clarity, peace and connection. We stop scattering our energy across time and instead channel it into the only moment we can truly influence—the present.

At its core, this law reminds us that **the present moment is the gateway to transformation.** The past cannot be changed and the future is shaped by what we do today. By cultivating presence, we align our thoughts, emotions and actions with reality as it is, rather than as we fear or imagine it to be. Presence allows us to listen more deeply, act more intentionally and appreciate life more fully.

The Law of Presence also emphasizes awareness. When we are present, we notice the subtleties of life—the warmth of sunlight, the tone of a friend's voice, the rhythm of our breath. These small details enrich our experience and remind us of the beauty that is always available when we slow down and pay attention.

Why is the present so powerful?

- **Past Is History:** You can't change it, only learn from it.
- **Future Is Uncertain:** Planning is good but worrying steals energy.
- **Now Is Action:** Every achievement starts with what you do today.
- **Mind Clarity:** Living in the present reduces stress and increases focus.

Practicing the Power of Now means:

- Stop overthinking and start acting.
- Use mindfulness to stay grounded.
- Focus on today's priorities instead of tomorrow's fears.

Real-Life Examples of the Law of Presence

- **Relationships** - A parent playing with their child chooses to put away their phone and focus entirely on the moment. This presence strengthens the bond and creates memories that last far longer than distractions.
- **Work and Creativity** - An artist painting in full presence loses track of time, immersed in the colours and strokes. This state of flow produces work that feels authentic and inspired.
- **Sports Performance** - Athletes often speak of being "in the zone." This is presence—complete focus on the game, free from past mistakes or future worries. It allows them to perform at their highest level.

The Law of Presence reminds us that **life is happening now.** By grounding ourselves in the present, we release the weight of the past and the anxiety of the future. Presence is not just mindfulness—it is the foundation of joy, clarity and authentic living. When we live in the present, we discover that peace and fulfilment were never far away; they were always here, waiting for us to notice.

A Prayer for Peaceful Living

"A peaceful mind begins with a moment of stillness each day."

Daily prayer is more than a ritual; It is a moment of pause—a gentle space where the mind rests, the heart softens and the soul reconnects with its source. In a world filled with noise, pressure and constant motion, prayer becomes a quiet doorway to inner peace. It reminds you that life is bigger than your thoughts, kinder than your fears and stronger than your worries.

A prayer is not about religion—it is about returning to yourself. It is a breath, a whisper, a moment of stillness that resets the entire day.
When you pray, you anchor your mind.
When you pray, you release what you cannot control.
When you pray, you create emotional space for clarity and calm.

Why Prayer Brings Peace

Life today moves too fast. Minds stay crowded with responsibilities, doubts and expectations. Most people begin their mornings in a rush and end their nights with restless thoughts. Prayer slows the inner speed. Prayer quiets the noise of the world and reveals the truth of the moment. It shifts attention from chaos to clarity… from fear to trust… from pressure to presence. Even a small prayer—one minute, one line, one breath—can change the emotional temperature of your day.

Prayer gives you: a calm mind, a grounded heart, a sense of protection, a feeling of guidance, emotional renewal.

Prayer offers three powerful gifts:

- **Presence** — it anchors the mind in the current moment.
- **Clarity** — it creates space for reflection rather than reaction.
- **Positivity** — it sets the tone for peace, gratitude and purpose.

Here is a gentle daily prayer that supports mindfulness and a happier life.

How Daily Prayer Supports a Mindful Life

- **Creates a morning anchor** that sets a peaceful tone for the entire day.
- **Reduces stress** by shifting attention from chaos to clarity.
- **Improves emotional balance** through intentional reflection.
- **Strengthens gratitude** which directly increases happiness.
- **Enhances focus** by bringing awareness to thoughts and actions.

A short, sincere daily prayer has the power to transform how the day feels, unfolds and ends.

Practical Ways to Include Prayer in Daily Life

- Begin or end the day with a one-minute prayer.
- Pair prayer with breathing—slow, mindful inhales and exhales.
- Keep a "prayer corner" or quiet space for stillness.
- Combine prayer with gratitude journaling.
- Repeat a single line throughout the day, such as *"Let peace guide this moment."*

Real-Life Examples:

- **David: The Professional Who Found Strength in Silence -** David struggled with stress and constant deadlines. His mornings felt rushed and his nights restless. When he began starting his day with a one-minute prayer, his emotional state changed. He felt calmer, made clearer decisions and handled challenges with more patience. **Prayer didn't change his workload—it changed his inner world.**

- **Emma: The Homemaker Who Regained Emotional Balance -** Emma often felt overwhelmed with daily responsibilities. She began ending each day with a simple prayer of gratitude. Over time, her mindset softened. Her home felt lighter, her reactions gentler and her sleep deeper. **She realised that prayer is a soft place the heart can return to.**

A peaceful life is not built in grand moments—it is built in small pauses of awareness. Prayer is one of the simplest and most powerful pauses you can offer yourself. It grounds your thoughts, strengthens your heart and aligns your mind with clarity.

The Power of Music - Your Companion Through Every Season

"Music heals, connects, energizes and transforms the human spirit."

Music is more than sound. It is emotion in motion. A universal language that speaks to the heart without needing a single word. It can lift your mood, calm your mind, fuel your drive, deepen your relationships and heal your inner world. Whether you listen, sing, play or hum, music influences your brain, body and soul in ways few other things can.

From ancient chants to modern melodies, music has always been a companion of the human journey—guiding us through joy, grief, celebration, loneliness and hope.

Why Music Is So Powerful

- **Emotional Healing:** Music reduces stress, eases anxiety and helps release emotional pressure.
- **Boosts Mood & Energy:** Upbeat rhythms instantly raise energy levels and improve motivation.
- **Deepens Connection:** Shared music strengthens bonds, creating unity in families, groups and cultures.
- **Enhances Memory & Focus:** Certain sounds improve concentration, learning and recall.
- **Heals the Mind:** Music therapy is used worldwide for mental wellness and recovery.

How to Use Music in Everyday Life

1. **Start Your Day with the Right Vibe:** Calming or uplifting tracks set your emotional tone for the day.
2. **Use Music for Focus:** Instrumental or ambient music helps reduce distraction and improves productivity.
3. **Relax With Healing Sounds:** Soft melodies, nature sounds or slow rhythms soothe the mind and promote peace.
4. **Move Your Body:** Dance, walk or work out to music that energizes you—it improves stamina and mood.
5. **Express Emotions Safely:** When words fail, music becomes an outlet for feelings that need release.

Real-Life Examples:

- **Healing Grief:** People often use soft music during difficult times to reduce emotional pain and feel supported without words.
- **Better Study Habits:** Students who select calm background music often focus longer and recall more.
- **Stronger Workouts:** Athletes choose high-tempo tracks to push harder and maintain rhythm.
- **Family Bonding:** Singing or listening together creates harmony, laughter and a shared emotional experience.
- **Spiritual Growth:** Mantras, bhajans or devotional songs deepen meditation and inner connection.

Music is a companion, a healer and a silent teacher. It strengthens the mind, softens the heart and fuels the spirit. Whether you are happy, stressed, lonely or inspired music meets you exactly where you are.

Let music be your energy when you feel low, Your calm when you feel overwhelmed, your expression when you cannot speak and your joy when life feels heavy.

Listen deeply. Feel fully. The power of music can transform your life.

The Power of Solitude

"Solitude isn't loneliness—it's clarity. Time alone helps you reconnect with yourself."

The Power of Solitude lies in its ability to recharge your mind, deepen self-awareness and unlock creativity. Far from being isolation, solitude is a conscious choice to spend time with yourself, leading to clarity, resilience and emotional balance.

Why Solitude Matters

In today's world of constant notifications, crowded schedules and endless noise, solitude has become rare. Yet research shows that **spending intentional time alone improves mental well-being, fosters creativity and strengthens emotional resilience**.

Key Benefits of Solitude

- **Mental Well-Being:** Solitude reduces stress and allows your mind to reset.
- **Self-Discovery:** Alone time helps you reflect on values, goals and identity.
- **Creativity & Productivity:** Many breakthroughs happen in quiet moments without distraction.
- **Emotional Balance:** Solitude provides space to process emotions and regain perspective.
- **Resilience & Independence:** It builds self-reliance and confidence in your own decisions.

Real-Life Examples:

- **The Product Manager Who Found Clarity in Evening Walks -** After back-to-back meetings, Aisha felt mentally cluttered and reactive. She started a **20-minute phone-free walk** every evening—no podcasts, no calls—just breathing and noticing. Within a week, she slept better, distilled her top priorities and returned to work with calmer decisions and sharper ideas. **Lesson:** A small daily pocket of solitude resets the mind and upgrades choices.
- **The Student Who Used Quiet Mornings to Boost Creativity -** Rohan struggled to outline essays amid constant notifications. He began waking **30 minutes earlier** for silent journaling and mind-mapping before touching his phone. The quiet produced clearer arguments, stronger structure and less last-minute stress—grades rose as anxiety fell. **Lesson:** Solitude first, screens later—creativity grows where noise ends.

Solitude is not about escaping the world—it's about returning to yourself. By embracing quiet moments, you gain clarity, creativity and strength. In solitude, you don't lose connection—you deepen it, first with yourself and then with others.

Think Like a Monk - Master Your Inner World

"Peace is not found in the world—it is created in the mind."

To *think like a monk* means to live with clarity, calmness and inner strength—no matter what is happening around you. Monks are trained to quiet their mind, reduce ego, detach from noise and focus on what truly matters. You don't need to live in a monastery to think like a monk. You only need to adopt the mindset of simplicity, purpose and inner peace in daily life.

When you think like a monk, you stop reacting blindly, stop comparing constantly and start living intentionally.

Why Think Like a Monk

- **Reduces Stress:** A calm mind handles challenges without panic.
- **Improves Focus:** You learn to give full attention to one task at a time.
- **Strengthens Emotional Control:** Instead of reacting, you respond wisely.
- **Builds Inner Peace:** You stop letting outside noise disturb your inner world.
- **Creates Purpose:** You align your decisions with your inner values—not public pressure.

How to Think Like a Monk

- **Silence the Noise -** Spend a few minutes daily in quiet—no phone, no talking, no tasks. Silence sharpens self-awareness and resets your mind.
- **Observe Your Thoughts -** Do not fight your thoughts—watch them. The moment you observe them, they lose power over you. Awareness creates control.
- **Let Go of Ego -** Release the need to be right, admired or superior. Ego creates suffering; humility creates freedom.
- **Practice Detachment -** Detach from outcomes but stay committed to effort. Do your best but don't cling to results—you can control work, not destiny.
- **Serve Others -** Service removes selfishness and expands compassion. Helping others teaches gratitude and brings inner joy.

- **Live With Purpose -** Clarify your values, priorities and long-term direction. A monk mindset focuses on meaning, not distraction.
- **Choose Simplicity -**Reduce clutter, excess and chaos. A simple environment supports a simple mind and a simple mind supports deep peace.

Real-Life Examples:

- **In Work:** People who think like monks remain calm in high pressure, focus deeply and make balanced decisions without emotional noise.
- **In Relationships:** They listen more, react less, forgive quickly and communicate peacefully.
- **In Daily Life:** They avoid comparison, manage distractions and stay centered even when surrounded by chaos.
- **In Personal Growth:** Consistent meditation, journaling and reflection make them emotionally stable and self-aware.

You don't need a robe, a monastery or a spiritual title to think like a monk. You need **awareness**, **simplicity**, **purpose** and **inner silence**.

When you calm your mind, you rise above drama.
When you detach, you gain freedom.
When you simplify, you gain clarity.
When you think like a monk, you live like your highest self.
Peace is not given—it is trained. Master your mind and you master your life.

Unplug to Recharge: One Day of Silence Every Month

"Silence isn't empty—it's full of answers."

We live in a world of constant noise—notifications, calls, social media, endless chatter. This mental clutter drains focus, creativity and peace. Disconnecting for just **one day a month** is like pressing the reset button for your mind. It's not about isolation; it's about **reconnection**—with yourself, your thoughts and the present moment.

Why It Matters

- **Reduces stress**: Silence lowers cortisol and calms the nervous system.
- **Boosts clarity**: Without distractions, ideas flow freely.
- **Improves relationships**: You return more present and attentive.
- **Enhances productivity**: A clear mind works faster and better.

Real-Life Examples:

- **Elisa**, a marketing professional, felt overwhelmed by constant pings and deadlines. She started a monthly ritual: one Saturday offline—no phone, no TV, no social media. She spent the day reading, journaling and walking in a park. After three months:

- Her anxiety reduced.
- She felt more creative at work.
- Friends noticed she was calmer and more focused.

How to Practice

- Pick **one day a month**—mark it on your calendar.
- Inform family and colleagues in advance.
- Switch off devices or use airplane mode.
- Spend time on **mindful activities**: reading, gardening, journaling, nature walks.
- Reflect on your goals and gratitude.

Noise steals your peace; silence restores it. One day of disconnection each month is a small habit with a big impact.

Unplug from the world to plug into yourself.

Healing Inner Conflict - Finding Peace Within Yourself

"Healing begins the moment you stop fighting yourself and start listening to yourself."

Inner conflict is the silent battle between what you feel and what you show, what you want and what you choose, who you are and who you think you should be. It drains energy, creates emotional tension and keeps you stuck in patterns you don't fully understand. Healing inner conflict is not about ignoring the struggle—it is about acknowledging it with compassion. When you learn to listen to your inner voice instead of suppressing it, you gain clarity, peace and a renewed sense of direction.

Why Healing Inner Conflict Matters

In a world full of expectations, comparison and pressure to appear "perfect," many people carry hidden conflicts—unresolved emotions, unspoken desires, fears, regrets and unhealed memories. These inner tensions create stress, anxiety, self-doubt and confusion. Research in emotional psychology shows that unresolved inner conflicts reduce self-esteem, weaken decision-making and increase emotional fatigue. Healing brings alignment, strength and emotional freedom. When your inner world becomes peaceful, your outer world naturally improves.

Key Benefits of Healing Inner Conflict

- **Emotional Clarity:** You understand your feelings instead of fighting them.
- **Reduced Stress & Anxiety:** The mind relaxes when inner contradictions dissolve.
- **Better Decisions:** You choose based on truth, not confusion or fear.
- **Stronger Self-Confidence:** Healing builds self-trust and inner stability.
- **Healthier Relationships:** When you stop battling yourself, you connect more deeply with others.

Real-Life Examples:

- **The Executive Caught Between Ambition and Exhaustion** – For years, Vikram pushed himself to meet expectations at work, ignoring his need for rest. His conflict grew between wanting success and wanting peace. Through honest reflection and setting boundaries, he redesigned his schedule. His health improved, his work quality increased and the constant guilt faded. **Lesson:** When you acknowledge your limits, balance replaces burnout.
- **The Young Woman Torn Between Pleasing Others and Honouring Herself** – Shruti always said "yes" to avoid disappointing others, even when it meant suppressing her own needs. This created stress and hidden resentment. By practicing self-awareness and communicating gently, she began to honour her boundaries. She felt lighter, calmer and more authentic. **Lesson:** Inner peace grows when your actions match your truth.

Healing inner conflict is not about becoming perfect—it is about becoming honest. When you make peace with your thoughts, feelings and fears, you create space for growth, clarity and emotional strength. In healing yourself, you reclaim your power. And in that power, you find the freedom to live with authenticity, intention and deep inner peace.

The Art of Letting Go - The Inner Path to Peace

"When you release what weighs you down, you rise into who you truly are."

Letting go is not forgetting, suppressing or pretending. It is the gentle act of **releasing emotional weight**—the replayed hurts, the tight expectations, the old stories that keep pain alive. It is not weakness; it is **liberation**. Letting go is choosing peace over resistance and clarity over confusion.

We often believe that holding on gives us control but it is the opposite. Holding on keeps us stuck in yesterday's tension and tomorrow's fear. The mind becomes a storeroom of disappointments, what-ifs and "should have been" dialogues. Letting go begins the moment you decide: *I will not relive what is over; I will not fear what is unknown; I will rest in what is true now.*

It starts with **forgiveness within**. Forgiveness is not agreement; it is release. It does not force reconciliation or erase memory; it simply frees the heart to breathe again. You cannot edit the past but you can end its control over your present. Forgiveness says, *"My peace matters more than my pain."*

From forgiveness flows **acceptance**—the quiet strength of seeing reality as it is, not as the mind insists it must be. Most suffering emerges not from events but from **resisting** them. Acceptance is not settling; it is clarity. It stops the inner fight, calms the nervous system and reveals the next wise step. Acceptance whispers, *"What is, is. I will move with grace."*

With acceptance, **detachment** becomes possible. Detachment is not coldness; it is **healthy emotional freedom**. You care without clinging, love without losing yourself, give without demanding and show up without gripping outcomes. Attachment breeds fear; detachment restores balance and breath. In detachment, you stop forcing life and start flowing with it.

At depth, you meet **the Law of Detachment**: life works better when you release control. Do your best, set a sincere intention and then **allow**. Trust does what tension cannot. Certainty is not required for peace—**trust is**. When you let go of rigid outcomes, space opens for better possibilities to enter.

Letting go is not a single event; it is a gentle unfolding:

- you forgive the pain,
- you accept what is,

- you detach from outcomes,
- and peace returns—quietly, steadily.

Those who practice letting go walk differently: lighter, kinder, steadier. They look less to control and more to contribute. They do not rush what's meant to ripen. They don't chase what is not aligned. Their strength is quiet, their joy is calm and their confidence comes from trust, not from force.

Letting go does not end your story—It begins the chapter of lightness, clarity and inner freedom. It turns storms into soft skies and restless nights into restful breaths. Letting go is not losing; it is **returning**—to your calmness to your center to your true self.

When you let go, you don't fall. **You rise.**

Real-Life Examples:

- **Ansel — Closing the Loop With Grace** - After a painful fallout with a business partner, Ansel carried silent anger for months. He replayed every meeting, every sentence, every "what if." Sleep suffered, work dulled and joy disappeared. One evening, he wrote a single line in his journal: *"I release what I cannot rewrite."* He chose to forgive—not to excuse but to end the hold. He accepted the loss, stopped chasing a perfect closure and detached from the need to be understood. Within weeks, his mind quieted. He re-focused on craft, rebuilt slowly and felt lighter than he had in years. **Forgiveness released his energy; acceptance restored his clarity; detachment returned his peace.**
- **Nell — Trusting the Process After Rejection** - Nell was turned down for a role she'd dreamed about. For days, she refreshed email, analyzed every answer she gave and questioned her worth. Then she tried a different path: three breaths, a hand on the heart and the inner reminder, *"Do your best, then allow."* She forgave herself for not being perfect, accepted the outcome and detached from the story that "it must be this job now." She used the feedback, refined her portfolio and applied again elsewhere. Months later, she received a role that fit better than the first option—team, timing, growth. **When she stopped forcing life, the right door opened on its own.**

Letting go is the medicine for a heavy heart. **Forgiveness** heals the past; **acceptance** calms the present; **detachment** frees the future; and the **Law of Detachment** teaches you to trust the process after doing your best. Choose release over replay, trust over control and presence over pressure. When you let go, you don't lose—you make space for what truly belongs to you: **peace, clarity and a quietly joyful life.**

The Other is Not "Other" - He is My Divine Brother

"We are not separate souls—we are children of the same God, walking different paths to the same home."

The idea that "the other is not other" transforms the way we see people. Every person you meet—family, colleague, stranger, helper, neighbour—is not an outsider. He is a fellow soul, a fellow traveler, a fellow child of the same Supreme Power. When you see him as a divine brother, your heart softens, your reactions slow down and your relationships deepen. This understanding dissolves judgement, reduces conflict and awakens compassion. You stop seeing differences of status, wealth, role, caste, belief or behaviour. Underneath it all, the same divine spark lives in each of us. When you see God in others, you begin to live from a higher consciousness.

Why This Realisation Matters

Most of our conflicts, ego battles and misunderstandings arise from forgetting our shared spiritual origin. We divide people into "us" and "them," into categories and labels. This creates emotional distance and unnecessary suffering. But when you remember that every person comes from the same Divine Source, your interactions become gentler, your speech becomes kinder and your heart becomes broader. Spiritual traditions across the world teach the same truth: **We are one. We belong to the same Creator.** Seeing others as divine brothers elevates your consciousness and strengthens your inner peace.

Divinity becomes real when you see it in others—not only in temples, mosques, churches or any sacred place.

How to Practise This Divine Perspective

Begin by pausing before reacting. When someone speaks harshly, disappoints you or behaves differently, remind yourself: ***"He is not other; he is my divine brother on his own journey."*** This thought instantly reduces ego and increases empathy. Look at people beyond their roles—boss, employee, driver, customer, neighbour. Look at the soul behind the behaviour. Appreciate small acts of goodness. Forgive small mistakes. Treat everyone with dignity. Recognise that every person carries invisible struggles, dreams and fears just like you. When you shift from judgement to understanding, you rise above smallness and connect with higher truth.
Seeing divinity in others is the highest form of spiritual maturity.

Real-Life Examples:

- **The Leader Who Created Harmony by Changing His Lens -** A manager always felt irritated with his team's mistakes. One day, while reflecting spiritually, he realised he was seeing people only through their roles—not their humanity. He shifted his mindset: *"They are my divine brothers."* This softened his tone, improved his patience and strengthened trust. The team became more cooperative and committed. **Lesson:** When you see others as family, leadership becomes natural.
- **The Homemaker Who Healed Family Conflicts Through Spiritual Vision -** Meena struggled with tension in her extended family. But instead of reacting, she adopted one thought every morning: *"We are all children of the same God."* Her responses became calmer, arguments reduced and relationships softened. Her inner peace returned and her home atmosphere changed beautifully. **Lesson:** Spiritual perspective heals what logic cannot.

No one is separate from you. We all come from the same Divine Source and return to the same Divine Home. When you see every human as your divine brother, compassion becomes effortless, forgiveness becomes natural and love becomes your default state. Walk gently. Speak kindly. Treat everyone as a part of the same divine family.Because when you recognise the God in others, **you awaken the God within yourself.**

Believe in God - Trust the Supreme Power That Guides Your Life

"Faith does not change the situation—it changes the one facing the situation."

Believing in God or a Supreme Power gives your life an inner anchor. It reminds you that you are not alone, that there is meaning behind your journey and that a higher intelligence is guiding your steps even when the path feels unclear. Faith softens fear, steadies the heart and brings strength in moments when logic is not enough. It is the quiet inner knowing that someone bigger, wiser and kinder is watching over you. When you trust the Supreme Power, you walk with courage, calmness and hope.

"Faith does not remove challenges—it gives you the strength to rise above them."

Why Belief in a Higher Power Matters

Life is unpredictable. No amount of planning can prevent unexpected challenges. But faith creates emotional resilience. It gives you a sense of protection, purpose and peace. People who believe in a higher power do not break easily under pressure; they bend, adjust and rise again. Research in emotional well-being shows that faith reduces stress, increases optimism and supports mental balance. When you trust that there is a divine order behind your experiences, fear decreases, patience increases and decisions improve. Faith becomes the bridge between uncertainty and courage. Belief creates inner stability that no external situation can shake.

How to Strengthen Your Faith in the Supreme Power

Faith grows through awareness, gratitude and surrender. Begin your day with a moment of connection—silence, prayer, gratitude or simply acknowledging the presence of something greater. Speak to God in your own words. Share your worries, hopes and doubts. Trust life's timing. Trust delays. Trust redirections. Trust that every experience—good or difficult—is shaping you into the person you are meant to become. Whenever fear appears, remind yourself: "I am protected. I am guided. I am not alone." Let your faith lead your thoughts and your thoughts lead your actions. Faith is not asking God to do everything—faith is trusting God while you do your part.

Real-Life Examples:

- **The Professional Who Found Calm Through Faith -** After months of stress and uncertainty at work, Mehul felt exhausted. Instead of drowning in fear, he decided to surrender his worries to God. Every morning, he spent two minutes in silence, repeating, *"Whatever comes will be for my good."* With this inner shift, his anxiety reduced, his confidence returned and he handled challenges with surprising clarity. Soon, opportunities emerged where he once saw obstacles. **Lesson:** When you trust the Supreme Power, your mind becomes lighter and life becomes smoother.

- **The Homemaker Who Rebuilt Her Strength Through Devotion -** Neeta faced difficult times—family problems, financial pressure, emotional burden. She turned to prayer not as a ritual but as a conversation with the Divine. Her faith became her strength. She found patience where there was anger, clarity where there was confusion and hope where there was despair. Her inner transformation slowly transformed her outer world as well. **Lesson:** Faith creates strength even when circumstances have not yet changed.

Believing in God or the Supreme Power is believing that life has meaning, that you are guided and that you are supported. It gives you courage when you are afraid, direction when you feel lost and peace when your mind feels noisy. Trust the divine plan. Trust your path. Trust that you are exactly where you need to be. Walk with faith, act with sincerity and allow the Supreme Power to unfold the journey meant for you.

Because when your heart believes, your life begins to bloom.

Belief gives courage in uncertainty. But courage grows stronger when it is **nourished daily**. Faith is not a moment; it is a relationship. In the next chapter, we move from **trusting the Divine** to **staying connected** through silence, prayer, gratitude, surrender and right action—so your peace is sustained, not occasional.

Staying Connected to the Divine - Your Source of Strength

"Staying connected with God is not about rituals—it is about remembering the Source that guides, protects and strengthens you."

Remaining connected with Godor the central source of all poweris a way of living with awareness, humility and inner strength. It means aligning your thoughts, actions and emotions with something higher than your worries and larger than your limitations. When you stay connected to this divine power, you feel supported, grounded and guided especially during moments of uncertainty, confusion or fear. This connection becomes a silent anchor, reminding you that you are never alone.

Why Staying Connected With God Matters

In the rush of daily life, people often drift into stress, overthinking and emotional imbalance. Disconnect happens when the mind becomes louder than the soul. Spiritual research and ancient wisdom across cultures show that connection with the divine—through prayer, meditation, gratitude or silence—reduces anxiety, strengthens resilience and provides deep emotional comfort. When you tune into the Source, you access inner calm, clarity and courage that no external situation can take away.

Key Ways to Stay Connected With the Divine Power

- **Daily Moments of Prayer or Gratitude:** Expressing thanks aligns your heart with higher guidance.
- **Silence & Meditation:** Quiet moments help you hear the whisper of intuition—the voice of God within.
- **Faith During Challenges:** Trusting that life is unfolding with purpose gives strength during difficult times.
- **Right Actions & Compassion:** Living with kindness keeps your heart in alignment with divine energy.
- **Letting Go of Worry:** Surrendering what you cannot control strengthens your connection to the Source.

Real-Life Examples:

- **The Businessman Who Found Strength Through Daily Prayer** – Ketan experienced overwhelming stress during a challenging phase at work. He began spending five minutes every morning in silent prayer. This simple practice brought him clarity, steadiness and unexpected solutions. **Lesson:** When your mind is calm, you can hear divine guidance.
- **The Young Woman Who Regained Peace Through Surrender** – Ria struggled with constant anxiety. When she learned to surrender her fears to the higher power and trust the process, her mind relaxed. She became emotionally stronger and handled challenges with grace. **Lesson:** Surrender is not giving up—it is giving over to something wiser.

Staying connected with God means staying connected with your inner truth. It fills your heart with peace, your mind with clarity and your life with courage. When you remember your divine connection, you walk through life feeling supported and guided. The closer you stay to the Source, the more balanced, purposeful and peaceful your life becomes.

Chapter 8: Rituals, Faith & Inner Confidence

Ancient Rituals for a Happy and Healthy Life

"Rituals are the wisdom of our ancestors—simple practices that kept life balanced, minds calm and hearts connected."

Ancient rituals were created long before modern science yet they supported exactly what today's world struggles with: mental peace, emotional grounding, family bonding, community connection, discipline, gratitude and harmony with nature. These rituals were never meant to be followed blindly—they were designed as practical systems for living well.

A small lamp lit at dusk, a prayer before meals, receiving morning sunlight, taking evening walks, seasonal fasting, daily cleansing, eating together, offering gratitude, expressing respect to elders through meaningful gestures (in some traditions touching elders' feet), practicing silence, chanting, meditation or sharing food with others—these weren't just customs. They were intentional habits that shaped mindset, energy and inner stability. When we understand the meaning behind rituals—not just perform them mechanically—we discover that they exist to simplify life, protect values and create emotional strength. In a world filled with speed and noise, these rituals act like anchors that gently guide us back to ourselves.

Across cultures—Indian, Japanese, Middle Eastern, African, Western and beyond—rituals emerged as everyday wisdom: lighting a candle at dinner, sharing mindful tea, walking at sunrise or pausing in silence before a task. The forms differ; the purpose—presence, gratitude and connection—remains the same.

Why Ancient Rituals Still Matter Today

Modern life gives comfort but often removes grounding. Ancient rituals bring back what technology cannot—rhythm, meaning and emotional connection. Rituals slow the mind: a diya lit in silence, a mantra hummed softly, watering a plant or sitting with folded hands—all invite presence and quiet strength. They create bonding through shared meals, prayers, celebrations and simple traditions that connect generations.

Rituals also simplify decisions because healthy habits become automatic, reducing daily mental load. They align us with nature through sunrise practices, seasonal foods, fasting, herbal cleansing and mindful eating. And above all, rituals keep values alive—gratitude, respect, humility, service and discipline. They bring structure to moments, meaning to routines and soul to the ordinary.

Rituals That Build Happiness and Health

Rituals don't need to be grand—they need to be sincere. Morning rituals like sunlight exposure, simple cleansing or gratitude set the tone for clarity and energy. Meal rituals like mindful eating, a short prayer or eating together strengthen relationships and improve digestion. Evening rituals with soft lights, silence or reflection prepare the mind for rest. Community rituals such as festivals, gatherings or acts of service create belonging and emotional nourishment. Personal rituals—journaling, chanting, breathing practices—build consistency and inner stability. These small rituals weave peace into daily life.

Real-Life Examples:

- **Elias — Finding Calm Through Simple Rituals** - Elias lived a fast-paced urban life filled with deadlines and travel. Stress became his constant companion. During a visit to his childhood home, he noticed the quiet power of his grandparents' rituals—a small lamp at dusk, two minutes of silence, device-free meals. When he adopted these practices at home—a morning prayer, mindful eating and a brief gratitude pause—his stress softened, sleep improved and clarity returned. He realised ancient rituals were never old—they were **timeless tools for modern peace**.
- **Rania — Reconnecting Family Through Weekly Traditions** - Rania's family lived under one roof but rarely shared time together. Everyone had different routines. She revived a simple ritual from her childhood—a Sunday meal with one candle and each person sharing a highlight of their week. Slowly, conversations deepened, conflicts softened and laughter returned to the home. She understood that **rituals create connection in ways technology never can**.
- **Sam — A One-Minute Candle Pause** - Before dinner, Sam lights a small candle and invites a one-minute silence for gratitude. This tiny pause changes the tone of the evening—calmer conversations, slower eating, better sleep. A **simple signal** becomes a daily sanctuary.

How to Bring Ancient Rituals Into Modern Life

Choose simple rituals that resonate with you. Understand the meaning behind them rather than following blindly. Keep them short, sincere and consistent. Practice without pressure or perfection. Involve family gently—rituals work best when they come from love, not force. Their power comes from repetition, not complexity.

Ancient rituals hold the wisdom our modern lives have forgotten. They restore balance, strengthen bonds and bring calm to our days. When you honor rituals with awareness—not habit—you fill your life with gratitude, discipline, connection and inner peace. When ancient practices meet modern consciousness, life becomes simpler, healthier and far more joyful.

Living Your Religion - A Path to Inner Stability and Joy

"Religion is not about rules; it is about remembering who you are."

In a world filled with noise, speed and constant distraction, religion offers something rare—a place to return to. A quiet space where the heart feels anchored, the mind feels guided and life feels meaningful. Every religion, across cultures and continents, teaches the same universal foundations: kindness, gratitude, humility, discipline, service and living with purpose.

Following your religion does not mean rigid rituals or blind obedience. It means understanding its wisdom, embracing its values and allowing its teachings to shape your character gently. At its core, religion simplifies life. It offers clarity in confusion, steadiness during struggle and perspective during pressure. It reminds you to stay humble when ego rises, patient when anger grows, courageous when fear appears and grateful when life feels scarce.

Why Following Your Religion Brings Peace

Religion provides a rhythm in a chaotic world. Simple daily or weekly practices—prayers, readings, moments of silence or gathering with others—create emotional stability. It connects you to something larger than yourself, reducing anxiety and reminding you that you are supported and not alone. Religion protects your values, encouraging honesty, self-control, forgiveness and compassion—qualities that make life simpler, relationships warmer and decisions clearer. Faith also builds community: celebrations, festivals and acts of service bring people together in shared purpose. Most importantly, religion gives direction; its teachings answer deep questions about life, growth and responsibility, dissolving inner confusion and strengthening emotional resilience.

Religion and Simplicity — How They Connect

Every major religion teaches simplicity. Less greed and more gratitude. Less noise and more reflection. Less ego and more kindness. Less comparison and more compassion. Less desire and more contentment. Simplicity is not about owning fewer things—it is about carrying fewer inner conflicts. Religion reduces those conflicts by offering a framework for living meaningfully. It guides the mind away from chaos and towards clarity.

How to Follow Your Religion With Understanding

Begin with sincerity instead of pressure. Choose small, consistent practices that uplift your mind—morning prayers, mindful rituals, gratitude moments or silence. Focus on values rather than labels. Love, truth, compassion, presence and service are universal across all paths. Avoid rigidity or superiority; your religion is a personal journey, not a measure of others. Let your faith guide your decisions gently—shaping your character, not your ego. The goal is not to perform religion—it is to live it.

Real-Life Examples:

- **Imran — Finding Stability Through His Faith** - Imran lived a demanding corporate life. Deadlines, meetings and constant pressure left him restless. One day, he returned to the simple practices he grew up with: a short morning prayer, reading a verse and attending a weekly spiritual gathering. These small rituals steadied his mind. His reactions softened. His anxiety reduced. Days felt more grounded. He discovered that faith simplifies life by simplifying the heart.
- **Selina — Rediscovering Meaning Through Rituals** - When Selina moved abroad, she felt emotionally disconnected. Nothing felt familiar. She returned to her childhood traditions—lighting a small candle in the evening, offering gratitude before meals and spending a few minutes in silent reflection. These practices gave her comfort, identity and inner strength. She realised her religion wasn't a place—it was a feeling she carried within.

Religion is a path that aligns your inner and outer worlds. It brings clarity, steadiness and meaning to life's most confusing moments. You don't need grand ceremonies or perfect devotion—just sincerity, understanding and a quiet return to the values your faith teaches. When you follow your religion with an open heart, you gain peace, purpose and emotional balance. Follow your faith not out of duty—but out of the joy and stability it brings to your life.

God Is Within You - Live with Inner Confidence

"When you remember the divine within you, fear loses its power."

Most people go through life searching for confidence outside themselves. They look for motivation from others, approval from society, praise from family or inspiration from external sources. But the deepest strength you will ever find does not come from outside — it comes from within. The belief that **God lives inside you** gives you a steady inner foundation, reminding you that you are guided, supported and never truly alone.

When you recognize this inner divinity, your decisions become calmer, your actions become bolder and your mind becomes more peaceful. This awareness is not about religion or ritual — it is about remembering your own inner light.

Not fear but trust.
Not dependence but inner strength.
Not doubt but inner guidance.

When you realise the divine is within you, confidence becomes natural.

What It Really Means When We Say "God Is Within You"

It means you carry inner guidance that whispers the right direction.
It means peace lives inside you, waiting for your attention.
It means strength is within your reach, even when the world feels heavy.
It means intuition is your quiet compass, gently guiding you toward what is right.
It means courage is already in you — you only need to unlock it.
It means goodness, compassion and clarity are part of your true nature.
Everything you search for outside is already seeded inside you.

When you trust this inner presence, external problems lose their power to shake you.

How This Awareness Builds Confidence

The moment you believe something greater lives within you, your entire attitude shifts.
You speak with more calmness because fear shrinks.
You make decisions with clarity because doubt reduces.
You trust your instincts instead of drowning in overthinking.
You handle challenges with courage instead of panic.
You stop questioning your worth because you understand your inner strength.
You walk with dignity, humility and quiet power.
The divine within you becomes your emotional anchor — steady, silent and strong.

Why People Forget This Inner Divinity

Modern life forces the mind outward — toward screens, noise, expectations, comparisons and endless to-do lists. People become so busy reacting to life that they forget the strength resting in their own heart. Connection with oneself weakens. Silence disappears. Fear grows. Doubt rises. Insecurity increases. Not because people are weak but because they stop listening inward.

The truth is simple:

You were born with inner strength — you just learned to ignore it.

How to Reconnect With the God Within

You don't need complicated rituals or long hours of practice.
Small daily moments are enough:

- Sit silently for a minute and breathe slowly.
- Place your hand on your heart and remind yourself: *"I am guided."*
- Trust your instincts — they are messages from within.
- Speak kindly and act gently — that is how divinity expresses itself.
- Spend time in nature to reconnect with stillness.
- Do the right thing even when no one sees you.
- Listen to your inner voice before listening to the world.

When the inside becomes clear, the outside becomes easier.

Real-Life Examples:

- **Arvid — Discovering Courage Through Inner Faith** - Arvid often doubted himself during big decisions. An elder once told him, "Stop searching outside for strength — look within, the divine lives there." He began spending a minute each morning in silent breathing. Soon, his choices became clearer and fear reduced. He realised he had been looking everywhere for confidence except in the one place it always existed — inside him.
- **Soraya — Overcoming Anxiety by Trusting Her Inner Light** - Soraya felt overwhelmed by expectations from family and work. One evening, she whispered to herself, "There is divine strength in me." She repeated it daily. Slowly, anxiety softened, decisions felt lighter and clarity returned. She discovered that confidence grows not from approval but from trusting the divine energy already inside her.

You are never without strength and you are never truly alone. When you remember that God lives within you, fear loses its voice and doubt loses its force. Your inner world becomes calm, your actions guided and your confidence steady. Look inward when life feels uncertain — the guidance you seek is already there.

Trust the divine within you and walk through life with grace, courage and unshakeable peace.

Gratitude Today: The Dreams You Once Prayed For

"What you wished for yesterday is yours today—thank God for it."

Life moves fast and in the chase for more, we often forget what we already have. Pause for a moment and think many of the things you enjoy today—your home, your job, your family, your health—were once dreams you prayed for years ago. Gratitude is the bridge between past desires and present blessings. When you appreciate what you have, you invite peace, joy and even more abundance into your life.

Ten years ago, you might have wished for stability, a good career or a loving family. Today, you may have all or most of those things yet the mind keeps chasing the next milestone. This endless pursuit creates stress and dissatisfaction. Gratitude shifts the focus from what's missing to what's present. It reminds you that your current reality is the answer to your past prayers.

Appreciating God—or the higher power you believe in—doesn't mean you stop striving. It means you acknowledge the blessings along the way. Gratitude is not passive; it's active recognition that life has given you gifts worth cherishing. When you practice gratitude daily, you reduce anxiety, strengthen relationships and find happiness in simplicity.

Real-Life Examples:

- **The Home You Once Imagined -** Years ago, Neha prayed for a place of her own—somewhere peaceful, safe and warm. Today she cooks breakfast in her kitchen, waters her balcony plants and laughs with her family at the dinner table. It's easy to miss but this daily routine is the exact life she once asked for. Gratitude cue: Whisper *"Thank you"* when you turn the key at your door.

- **The Health You Hoped to Regain -** After a difficult period of illness, Arjun prayed simply to wake up pain-free and take long walks again. Now he jogs three times a week and plays in the park with his child. The ordinary feels extraordinary when you remember what it replaced. Gratitude cue: Say *"Thank you"* after every walk, workout or deep breath that feels easy.
- **Stable Job -** Think about the time you prayed for a stable job. Today, you have one. Or the time you wished for a home of your own—now you live in it. Maybe you longed for good health and today you wake up strong. These are not coincidences; they are answered prayers. Recognizing this truth fills your heart with peace and humility.

Stop for a moment and say, *"Thank you."* Gratitude is the secret to happiness—it turns ordinary days into blessings and dreams into reality

Chapter 9: Universal Laws: Living in Harmony

The Law of Harmony: Align with the Flow of Life

"Peace is not found in control but in alignment."

The Law of Harmony teaches that the universe is designed to operate in balance and when we align ourselves with this natural order, we experience peace, flow and fulfilment. Harmony is the state in which all parts of life—mind, body, spirit, relationships and environment—work together seamlessly. Just as an orchestra creates beautiful music when each instrument plays in tune, our lives become harmonious when our thoughts, emotions and actions are aligned with truth and purpose.

At its core, this law reminds us that **conflict and imbalance arise when we resist the natural rhythm of life.** When we fight against circumstances, cling to negativity or act out of ego, we create disharmony that manifests as stress, confusion or chaos. But when we cultivate harmony—through acceptance, compassion and alignment—we restore balance and invite greater joy. Harmony is not about perfection; it is about integration. It is the recognition that every part of life has its place and that peace comes from honouring the interconnectedness of all things.

Real-Life Examples of the Law of Harmony

- **Relationships** - In a marriage, harmony is achieved when both partners listen, compromise and respect each other's needs. Even disagreements can be resolved peacefully when approached with empathy and a desire for balance.

- **Nature** - Ecosystems thrive when plants, animals and resources coexist in balance. When humans disrupt this harmony through pollution or overconsumption, the environment suffers. Restoring harmony through sustainable practices heals the planet.

The Law of Harmony reminds us that **life is meant to be lived in balance.** When we align with the natural order of the universe, we experience peace within ourselves and connection with others. Harmony is not the absence of challenges—it is the ability to move through them with grace, knowing that balance can always be restored.

The Law of Rhythm: Flow with Life's Natural Cycles

"Life moves in waves—learn to ride them, not resist them."

The Law of Rhythm teaches that everything in the universe moves in cycles. Just as the tides rise and fall, the seasons change and the moon waxes and wanes, so too does human life follow patterns of highs and lows, growth and rest, beginnings and endings. This law reminds us that nothing stays the same forever—life is in constant motion and rhythm governs that motion.

At its core, the Law of Rhythm is about **balance and flow**. It tells us that every peak is followed by a valley and every valley eventually leads back to a peak. When we understand this, we stop resisting the natural ebb and flow of life. Instead of fearing downturns, we learn to accept them as temporary phases that prepare us for renewal and growth. Rhythm is not punishment—it is the universe's way of maintaining harmony.

This law also teaches patience. Just as farmers must wait for the right season to harvest, we too must trust the timing of our lives. By aligning ourselves with rhythm, we conserve energy during low cycles and maximize opportunities during high cycles.

Real-Life Examples of the Law of Rhythm

- **Personal Growth** - A student preparing for exams may experience periods of intense focus followed by fatigue. By respecting the rhythm—studying hard during peak energy and resting during low energy—they achieve better results than if they forced themselves constantly.
- **Business Cycles** -Economies naturally expand and contract. A business owner who understands rhythm doesn't panic during downturns but uses the time to innovate and prepare. When the cycle shifts upward, they are ready to seize opportunities.

The Law of Rhythm reminds us that **life is a dance of cycles.** By embracing the ebb and flow rather than resisting it, we find peace, patience and resilience. Rhythm teaches us that every setback is temporary, every winter gives way to spring and every low point is simply preparing us for the next rise.

The Law of Vibration: Align Your Energy, Shape Your Reality

"Your *vibration is your invitation—what you send out is what returns"*

The Law of Vibration states that everything in the universe—whether visible or invisible—is in constant motion, vibrating at its own unique frequency. By understanding and aligning with these vibrations, we can influence our reality and attract experiences that match our energy.

Understanding the Law of Vibration

The Law of Vibration is considered one of the foundational universal laws. It explains that **nothing rests; everything moves and vibrates**. From the smallest subatomic particles to vast galaxies, all matter is energy vibrating at different frequencies. What we perceive as solid matter is energy in motion.
Thoughts and emotions also carry vibrations. Positive emotions like love, gratitude and joy vibrate at higher frequencies, while fear, anger and resentment vibrate at lower ones.

These vibrations interact with the world around us, influencing what we attract into our lives. This is why the Law of Vibration is often seen as the foundation for the Law of Attraction.

How It Works in Daily Life

When you raise your vibrational frequency—through positive thoughts, gratitude, kindness or purposeful action—you align yourself with higher-frequency experiences. Conversely, dwelling in negativity lowers your vibration, attracting similar outcomes.
Key principle: *Your inner vibration sets the tone for your outer reality.*

Real-Life Examples of the Law of Vibration

- **Health and Wellness** - A person who constantly worries and lives in stress often experiences fatigue, illness or burnout. Their low vibration affects their body. On the other hand, someone who practices gratitude, meditation and positive thinking tends to feel more energetic and resilient. Their higher vibration supports better health.

- **Relationships** -Imagine two friends: one radiates positivity, kindness and encouragement, while the other constantly complains and criticizes. The positive friend naturally attracts more people and opportunities, while the negative one often finds themselves isolated. Their vibrations determine the quality of their relationships.

The Law of Vibration reminds us that **we are energetic beings in a universe of constant motion**. By consciously choosing higher vibrations—through our thoughts, emotions and actions—we can shape our reality and attract experiences that resonate with our true desires.

The Law of Inspired Action: Move with Purpose

"Dreams become reality when intention meets action."

The Law of Inspired Action teaches that manifestation requires more than thought and intention—it requires movement. While the Law of Attraction draws opportunities to us through energy and focus, the Law of Inspired Action reminds us that we must take steps toward those opportunities. Dreams remain dreams until they are paired with action.

At its core, this law emphasizes that **aligned action bridges the gap between desire and reality.** Inspired action is not about forcing or struggling; it is about listening to intuition and taking steps that feel natural, purposeful and energizing. These actions often arise from inner guidance, synchronicities or sudden bursts of clarity. When we follow them, we align ourselves with the flow of the universe and accelerate the manifestation of our goals.

Inspired action differs from ordinary action. Ordinary action is driven by obligation, fear or pressure, while inspired action feels exciting, effortless and aligned with our deeper purpose. It is the universe nudging us forward, showing us the path to our desires.

Real-Life Examples of the Law of Inspired Action

- **Career Opportunities** - A person visualizes a new career but feels uncertain about how to begin. One day, they feel a strong urge to attend a networking event. That single inspired action leads to meeting someone who connects them to their dream job.
- **Relationships** - Someone desiring love feels guided to join a community group or take a class. By following this inner nudge, they meet a partner who shares their values.

The Law of Inspired Action reminds us that **the universe responds to movement.**

When we act on intuitive nudges and align our steps with our desires, we open the door for manifestation. Inspired action is the bridge between thought and reality, the spark that transforms vision into experience.

The Law of Paradoxical Intent: Let Go to Receive

"The more you chase something, the faster it runs away."

The Law of Paradoxical Intent teaches that the harder you try to force something to happen, the more you push it away. True manifestation comes from relaxed confidence, not desperate effort.

What Is the Law of Paradoxical Intent?

This universal law explains that when we desperately chase or cling to an outcome, we create resistance. Our intense need signals fear, doubt and lack—low vibrations that repel the very thing we want. On the other hand, when we release attachment and trust the process, we align with higher vibrations that naturally attract our desires.
In simple terms: **wanting something too much can block it from happening.**

Why It Happens

- **Desperation lowers vibration:** When you're anxious or fearful, your energy communicates lack rather than abundance.
- **Pressure creates resistance:** Forcing outcomes often leads to stress and mistakes.
- **Relaxation opens flow:** When you trust, detach and act calmly, opportunities appear more naturally.

This paradox is why people often say, *"Things happen when you stop trying so hard."*

Real-Life Examples of the Law of Paradoxical Intent

- **Relationships** - Someone desperate to find love may come across as needy or insecure, unintentionally pushing potential partners away. When they shift focus to self-love and enjoying life, they naturally attract healthier relationships.
- **Job Search** - A candidate who anxiously over-prepares and pressures themselves during interviews may appear tense and inauthentic. Another candidate who prepares well but stays relaxed and confident often makes a better impression and lands the job.

- **Sports Performance** -An athlete who obsesses over winning may choke under pressure. But when they trust their training and play with ease, they perform at their best and often achieve victory.

The Law of Paradoxical Intent shows that life responds best to calm intention, not force. When you act sincerely and then release the pressure for results, opportunities flow more naturally.

Let go gently, trust deeply and allow what's meant for you to arrive in its own perfect time.

The Law of compensation: Rewards Reflect Effort and Value

"Life pays you back in proportion to the service you render"

The law of compensation re-establishes the concept of ***"you get as good as you give."*** The universe always compensates you for all your deeds, efforts and contributions—whether great or small.

Essentially, **you reap what you sow**. This law reminds you to be mindful of how you treat others and indeed the planet.

The law of compensation has a very simple motive: to balance the universe. Thus, when you spread love, you receive love; and if you spread hate, more hate will be returned to you.

Real-Life Examples of the Law of Compensation

- **Workplace Effort** - An employee who consistently goes beyond their basic duties—helping colleagues, showing initiative and delivering quality work—often receives promotions, recognition or unexpected opportunities. Their extra effort is compensated with career growth.
- **Community Service** - A person who volunteers time to teach underprivileged children not only helps others but also gains respect, gratitude and sometimes even new skills or networks that benefit their own life. The universe compensates their giving with fulfilment and opportunities.

By understanding and applying these universal laws, you can simplify your life, achieve greater peace and align with your true self, fostering a life of simplicity, purpose and fulfilment

The Law of Perpetual Transmutation of Energy: Change is Constant

"Energy cannot be destroyed—it only changes form."

The Law of Perpetual Transmutation of Energy teaches that energy is always moving, shifting and transforming. Nothing in the universe is static—every thought, emotion and action carries energy that can be elevated or diminished. This law reminds us that higher vibrations naturally transform lower ones and that we have the power to raise our own energy and influence the energy around us.

At its core, this law emphasizes that **we are not victims of stagnant circumstances.** Even when situations feel heavy or limiting, energy is constantly in motion, waiting to be redirected. By choosing uplifting thoughts, practicing gratitude or engaging in creative action, we transmute lower vibrations into higher ones. This process not only changes our inner state but also reshapes the external reality we experience.

The Law of Perpetual Transmutation of Energy empowers us to take responsibility for our vibration. It shows us that transformation is always possible and that even small shifts in energy can ripple outward to create profound change.

Real-Life Examples of the Law of Perpetual Transmutation of Energy

- **Personal Growth** - A person feeling stuck in negativity begins a daily gratitude practice. Over time, their energy shifts upward, attracting more positive experiences and opportunities.
- **Creativity** - An artist channels feelings of sadness into painting. The act of creation transmutes heavy emotions into beauty, uplifting both the artist and those who experience the artwork.

The Law of Perpetual Transmutation of Energy reminds us that **change is always possible because energy is always in motion.** By consciously raising our vibration, we transform not only ourselves but also the world around us. This law is a powerful reminder that we hold the ability to turn darkness into light, struggle into strength and limitation into possibility.

The Law of Relativity: Perspective Creates Meaning

"Nothing has meaning until you compare it."

The Law of Relativity teaches that nothing in life has meaning until we compare it to something else. Every situation, challenge or success is relative—it only appears "big" or "small," "good" or "bad" when measured against another experience or perspective. This law reminds us that perspective shapes reality and that by shifting how we view circumstances, we can transform our experience of them.

At its core, the Law of Relativity emphasizes that **life is neutral until we assign meaning.** A problem may feel overwhelming until we realise others face even greater challenges or until we see the hidden lesson within it. Likewise, achievements may feel small until we compare them to where we started. This law encourages humility, gratitude and resilience by teaching us to see our experiences in context rather than in isolation.

Real-Life Examples of the Law of Relativity

- **Challenges** - A student struggling with exams feels discouraged until they realise that their difficulties are part of growth and compared to past struggles, they are already stronger and more capable.
- **Daily Life** - Someone stuck in traffic feels annoyed until they reflect on the fact that they have a car, freedom of movement and safety—things others may lack.

The Law of Relativity reminds us that **perspective is power.** By seeing our experiences in context, we shift from frustration to gratitude, from despair to resilience. This law teaches us that meaning is not fixed—it is created by comparison and we have the ability to choose perspectives that empower us.

The Law of Polarity: Opposites Define Each Other

"Without darkness, we cannot know light; without contrast, life loses meaning."

The Law of Polarity teaches that everything in the universe has an opposite and these opposites are necessary for balance, growth and understanding. Light cannot exist without darkness; joy cannot be appreciated without sorrow and success cannot be measured without failure. This law reminds us that contrast is not a curse—it is a teacher. Opposites help us recognize value, develop resilience and expand our perspective.

At its core, the Law of Polarity emphasizes that **every challenge carries the seed of its opposite.** Within difficulty lies opportunity, within endings lie beginnings and within pain lies the potential for healing. By embracing polarity, we learn to see beyond extremes and discover the hidden gifts in every situation.

This law also teaches us that opposites are not enemies but partners. They work together to create wholeness, just as the yin and yang symbolize balance. When we accept polarity, we stop resisting life's contrasts and begin to use them as stepping stones toward growth.

Real-Life Examples of the Law of Polarity

- **Personal Growth** - A person facing failure in business learns valuable lessons that eventually lead to success. Without failure, the depth of success would not be fully appreciated.
- **Relationships** - Disagreements in a relationship highlight differences but they also create opportunities for deeper understanding and compromise.

The Law of Polarity reminds us that **life's contrasts are essential for growth and balance.** By recognizing that every negative carries the seed of a positive, we transform challenges into opportunities and pain into wisdom. Polarity is not opposition—it is the harmony of opposites working together to create wholeness.

The Law of Gender: Balance Creates Harmony

"Creation is born from the dance of opposites."

The Law of Gender teaches that everything in the universe contains both masculine and feminine energies and creation requires the balance of these two forces. Masculine energy is associated with action, logic and strength, while feminine energy is linked to intuition, nurturing and receptivity. Neither is superior; both are essential and together they create harmony and wholeness.

At its core, the Law of Gender emphasizes that **balance is the key to creation.** Just as seeds require time to gestate before becoming plants, ideas require both the masculine drive to act and the feminine patience to allow growth. When these energies are balanced within us, we live in alignment, creativity flows naturally and our relationships thrive.

This law also reminds us that imbalance leads to struggle. Overemphasis on masculine energy can result in burnout, aggression or rigidity, while overemphasis

on feminine energy can lead to passivity, indecision or stagnation. True fulfilment comes from honouring both energies and allowing them to work together.

Real-Life Examples of the Law of Gender

- **Relationships** - Healthy partnerships thrive when both partners honour masculine and feminine energies—balancing action with listening, strength with compassion.
- **Daily Life** - A leader balances masculine energy by making decisive choices and feminine energy by empathizing with their team's needs.

The Law of Gender reminds us that **creation is born from balance.** By honouring both masculine and feminine energies within us, we unlock harmony, creativity and fulfilment. This law teaches us that wholeness is not found in extremes but in the integration of opposites working together.

The Law of Reciprocating: What You Give Comes Back

"Life is like a mirror—what you send out reflects to you."

The Law of Reciprocating is a timeless principle that governs human relationships and success. At its core, it states that what you give to others—whether in kindness, respect, effort or value—will eventually return to you, often multiplied. Life operates like a mirror: the energy you project outward reflects back into your own experience.

This law is not about immediate rewards or transactional exchanges; it's about creating a cycle of goodwill and abundance. When you help others succeed, you plant seeds of trust and collaboration. When you show appreciation, you invite more reasons to be grateful. Conversely, negativity and selfishness tend to attract similar responses.

Why does this matter for living well?

Because simplicity and success thrive in environments of mutual benefit. By practicing reciprocity, you build stronger relationships, reduce friction and create opportunities that would never exist in isolation. It transforms competition into cooperation and scarcity into shared prosperity.

Real-Life Examples of the Law of Reciprocating

- **Relationships** - When a partner makes a conscious effort to appreciate small gestures—like thanking the other for cooking, listening or supporting their goals—the relationship naturally deepens. The appreciated partner begins returning the same warmth, creating a loop of respect, kindness and emotional safety. *What you give emotionally eventually comes back to you.*

- **Workplace** - An employee who consistently shares knowledge, helps colleagues solve problems and supports team members during difficult deadlines unknowingly builds a reservoir of goodwill. Later, when they need help—whether with a project, a tight timeline or career support—the same colleagues step forward enthusiastically. *Consistent contribution creates a network that reciprocates when you need it most.*

When you live by this law, success becomes a natural byproduct of your actions. The world responds to generosity with generosity and simplicity emerges when relationships are built on trust and mutual respect.

The Law of Gratitude: The Key to Abundance

"Gratitude turns what we have into enough."

The Law of Gratitude teaches that appreciation is the key to unlocking abundance, joy and fulfilment in life. Gratitude is more than a polite "thank you"; it is a powerful vibrational force that shifts our perspective from scarcity to abundance. When we focus on what we already have and express genuine appreciation, we raise our energy, attract more positive experiences and strengthen our connection to the universe.

At its core, this law reminds us that **what we appreciate, appreciates.** By acknowledging the blessings in our lives—big or small—we amplify them. Gratitude transforms ordinary moments into extraordinary ones, turning challenges into lessons and setbacks into opportunities for growth. It is the bridge between desire and manifestation, because when we are grateful, we signal to the universe that we are ready to receive more.

Gratitude also nurtures humility and compassion. It shifts our focus outward, helping us recognize the contributions of others and the interconnectedness of all things. In this way, the Law of Gratitude not only enriches our personal lives but also strengthens relationships and communities.

Real-Life Examples of the Law of Gratitude

- **Relationships** - A couple makes it a habit to express gratitude for each other's small acts—like cooking dinner or offering support. This practice deepens their bond, reduces conflict and creates a stronger foundation of love.
- **Career Success** - An employee who appreciates their team's efforts and acknowledges contributions fosters a positive work environment.

Gratitude motivates colleagues, builds trust and often leads to greater opportunities for leadership.

The Law of Gratitude reminds us that **gratitude is not just a reaction to receiving—it is a proactive choice to see the good in every moment.** By living with gratitude, we align ourselves with abundance, strengthen our relationships and cultivate inner peace. Gratitude is the seed from which joy, prosperity and fulfilment grow.

The Law of Difference – Understanding Why Everyone Is Unique

"Difference is not a flaw in life's design—it is life's greatest intelligence."

The **Law of Difference** reminds us of a simple but powerful truth: **no two people are meant to be the same**. Each individual is born with unique abilities, perspectives, rhythms and paths. Yet much of human suffering arises from forgetting this law—by comparing, judging or expecting sameness from ourselves and others.

Life functions beautifully because of difference. Just as nature needs different seasons, flowers and ecosystems, human society thrives on diversity of thought, talent and temperament. When we resist difference, frustration grows. When we accept it, understanding and peace follow.

Why Ignoring the Law of Difference Creates Conflict

Many people struggle because they unconsciously expect uniformity—expecting others to think like them, act like them or value what they value. When reality doesn't match expectation, judgment, disappointment and conflict arise.

Psychologically, comparison and forced conformity damage self-esteem and relationships. People begin to feel inadequate for being different or impatient with others for not matching their ideals. Stress increases, communication weakens and empathy fades. Inner peace begins the moment we realise: **Difference is natural. Resistance to difference is optional.**

Key Principles of the Law of Difference

- **Every Mind Is Wired Differently:** Thinking styles, emotional responses and priorities vary naturally.
- **Different Does Not Mean Wrong:** Other perspectives expand understanding; they don't threaten it.

- **Comparison Violates This Law:** Measuring yourself against others ignores unique design.
- **Acceptance Builds Harmony:** Peace comes from allowing people to be who they are.
- **Alignment Beats Imitation:** Growth happens when you honour your own path.

Real-Life Examples:

- **The Team Leader Who Expected Everyone to Work Like Him** – Arjun valued speed and efficiency and assumed his team should operate the same way. When some members worked more methodically, he grew frustrated. Once he recognised different working styles and aligned tasks accordingly, productivity and trust improved. **Lesson:** Results improve when difference is respected, not resisted.
- **The Woman Who Compared Her Life Constantly** – Sofia spent years comparing her journey with others—careers, lifestyles and timelines. This made her anxious and dissatisfied. When she understood that each life unfolds differently, she stopped racing others and started living more calmly and confidently. **Lesson:** Peace begins when you stop measuring your life by someone else's design.

The Law of Difference teaches maturity, patience and emotional intelligence. When you accept difference, you stop wasting energy on comparison and control. Relationships become lighter. Decisions become clearer. Self-respect grows.
You are not here to copy anyone.
Others are not here to match you.
Life flows best when uniqueness is allowed to breathe.

Accept difference in people.
Respect difference in paths.
Honour difference within yourself.

Because when you live in harmony with the **Law of Difference**, life stops feeling like a struggle—and starts feeling **balanced, respectful and deeply human**.

The Law of Mind – Where Life Is First Created

"Your life does not begin in the world outside—it begins in the mind within."

The **Law of Mind** states a simple yet powerful truth: **your mind is the primary creator of your life experience**. Long before actions take shape or results appear, the mind prepares the ground. Thoughts, beliefs, expectations and inner dialogue quietly shape how you see the world, respond to situations and move through life.

You may believe that circumstances control your happiness, stress or success—but the Law of Mind reminds us that **the same situation affects different people differently**, depending on how the mind perceives it. The outer world may present events but the inner world decides their meaning and impact.

Why the Law of Mind Governs Life

The mind is not a passive observer—it is an active interpreter. It filters every experience through belief systems built over time. When the mind is restless, even comfort feels heavy. When the mind is peaceful, even difficulty feels manageable. Psychology and lived experience consistently show that people suffer more from their **interpretation of events** than from the events themselves. A worried mind creates stress even in safety. A calm mind creates stability even in uncertainty. This is why mastering the mind is not self-improvement—it is **life mastery**.
You don't experience life directly. You experience life through your mind.

Key Principles of the Law of Mind

- **The Mind Interprets Reality:** Events are neutral; meaning is created mentally.
- **Thoughts Shape Emotional States:** Repeated thoughts create moods and patterns.
- **Belief Directs Behaviour:** You act according to what the mind accepts as true.
- **An Untrained Mind Creates Chaos:** Reaction replaces response when awareness is missing.
- **A Calm Mind Creates Clarity:** Peaceful thinking leads to balanced living.

Real-Life Examples:

- **The Man Whose Stress Came from His Thoughts** – Adrian believed pressure came from his job. Even on calm days, his mind anticipated problems. When he learned to observe his thinking—rather than automatically believe it—stress reduced without any external change. **Lesson:** Life becomes lighter when the mind stops creating unnecessary tension.
- **The Woman Who Changed Her Life by Changing Her Inner Dialogue** – Pema carried self-critical thoughts for years, believing she was never doing enough. This kept her emotionally exhausted. By consciously replacing harsh inner talk with supportive thinking, confidence and emotional balance returned. **Lesson:** When the mind becomes kind, life becomes manageable.

The Law of Mind teaches that **peace is not found by rearranging life—but by refining perception**. When the mind is clear, problems feel smaller. When the mind is cluttered, even simple tasks feel overwhelming.

Train the mind gently.
Observe thoughts without obeying them blindly.
Choose clarity over chaos.

Because when the mind is mastered,
life naturally begins to flow with balance, resilience and quiet confidence.

Part IV: Health & Well-Being: Your Real Wealth

Learn how true wealth begins with physical, mental and emotional health.

Chapter 10: Essentials of Strength & Calm

The Wellness Blueprint: Build a Life of Strength and Calm

"Take care of your body. It's the only place you have to live."

Good health is the foundation of a meaningful and successful life. It is the quiet force behind happiness, energy, clarity and resilience. When health is strong, everything else becomes easier — work flows, relationships flourish and daily life feel lighter. But health isn't achieved in a day; it is built through **simple, consistent habits** that support the body and calm the mind.

This chapter blends timeless wisdom with practical daily routines, creating a wellness blueprint that anyone can follow — regardless of age, income or background.

1. Understanding True Health

Health is far more than the absence of illness. It is a harmony of four essential pillars:

- **Physical Health** - Strength, stamina and freedom from disease.
- **Mental Health -** Clarity of thought, focus and emotional stability.
- **Emotional Health** - Balanced feelings, self-awareness and healthy relationships.
- **Social Health** - Connection with family, friends and community.

When these four work together, life feels abundant. When even one cracks, happiness quickly fades.

2. Why Health Is the Real Wealth

A wealthy person without health cannot enjoy anything. But a healthy person, even with modest means, can enjoy walks, friendships, hobbies, work, rest — everything life offers.

Health gives you:

- Energy to live your day fully
- Strength to pursue your goals
- Clarity to make wise decisions
- Peace to enjoy the present
- Resilience to face challenges

To care for your health is to safeguard your future.

3. Daily Habits for a Strong Body

You don't need complicated routines or expensive programs. Small habits done consistently create lifelong vitality.

- **Walk or Run Daily -** 15-minute run or 30-minute walk boosts heart health, burns calories and lifts mood.
- **Practice Yoga -** Yoga builds flexibility, improves posture and releases tension while calming the mind.
- **Breathing Exercises (Pranayama) -** Techniques like Anulom-Vilom or Kapalabhati improve lung capacity, reduce stress and balance emotions.
- **Strength Training -** Simple exercises — squats, push-ups, planks — maintain muscle and prevent age-related weakness.
- **Sleep 7–8 Hours -** Sleep restores the body and resets the brain. No habit can replace a good night's rest.

4. Daily Habits for a Healthy Mind

A calm mind is as important as a strong body. Emotional well-being shapes your reactions, decisions and relationships.

- **Meditation & Mindfulness -** Even 10 minutes reduces anxiety, improves concentration and builds emotional stability.
- **Journaling & Self-Reflection -** Write your thoughts, ideas or gratitude. It declutters the mind and strengthens self-awareness.
- **Digital Detox** - Limit screen time, especially before bed. Silence the noise so you can hear yourself again.
- **Learning & Reading** - Feed your mind with positive, growth-focused content for at least 15 minutes daily.
- **Social Connection** - Spend time with people who uplift you. Strong relationships are the backbone of mental health.

5. Daily Habits for Emotional & Social Health

Healthy emotions and meaningful relationships shape our happiness more than achievements, possessions or comfort. Emotional and social well-being are built through small intentional habits:

- **Express Gratitude Daily** – Appreciating people strengthens relationships and reduces negative emotions.
- **Share One Meaningful Conversation** – Talk to a friend, family member or colleague with full presence.
- **Practice Emotional Check-ins** – Pause for a minute and ask yourself: *"How am I feeling right now?"*

- **Offer Kindness** – A smile, a compliment or a small act of help lifts both you and others.
- **Set Healthy Boundaries** – Protect your peace by saying no to unnecessary stress and negativity.
- **Spend Time with Uplifting People** – Social connections are vitamins for emotional resilience.
- **Limit Emotional Overload** – Avoid unnecessary arguments, drama and overthinking; protect your inner balance.

Strong emotional habits make relationships richer, increase resilience and reduce the silent stress that drains health. Social and emotional wellness are not outcomes — they are daily practices.

6. Nutrition & Hydration

Your body becomes what you feed it.

- Eat more fruits, vegetables, whole grains and proteins
- Drink 7–8 glasses of water daily
- Reduce sugar and processed foods

Your diet fuels your energy, clarity and long-term health.

7. Rules for a Long and Healthy Life

These timeless principles, practiced across the world, form the backbone of longevity:

1. **Stay Active — Never Retire from Life -** Keep moving, learning and staying engaged. A busy mind and active body slow ageing.
2. **Take Life Slow** - Avoid rushing. Do one thing at a time. Enjoy the moment you are in.
3. **Eat Until 80%** Full - Practice moderation — it supports digestion, lightness and long-term health.
4. **Keep Close Friends** - Friendship reduces stress, boosts happiness and protects mental well-being.
5. **Exercise Daily** - Movement keeps the body young and the mind sharp.
6. **Smile and Laugh Often -** Joy heals. A cheerful attitude strengthens both immunity and relationships.
7. **Reconnect With Nature** - Fresh air, sunlight and greenery restore your inner balance.
8. **Practice Gratitude** - Gratitude multiplies joy and reduces stress.
9. **Live in the Present** - Let go of past regrets and future fears. Today is your life.
10. **Pursue What You Love** - Passion keeps you alive inside.

8. **Bonus Wisdom for a Healthier Life**
    - Avoid worrying — protect your peace
    - Build healthy routines — walk, stretch, rest
    - Stay optimistic — thoughts shape biology
    - Help others — service strengthens purpose
    - Celebrate life — dance, music, laughter
    - Stay meaningfully busy — purpose keeps you young
    - Try occasional fasting — rests the digestive system and builds discipline

A long and healthy life is not created by sudden changes — it is built through simple habits repeated with love and consistency. Sleep early, wake early, move daily, breathe deeply, eat mindfully, laugh freely and cherish the people who matter.

Health is not a part of life — it is the foundation of life. Protect it, nurture it and the rest of your life becomes naturally richer, calmer and more fulfilling.

Understanding Circadian Rhythm

"Your body has a natural clock—life becomes healthier and happier when you live in rhythm with it."

Understanding Circadian Rhythm means understanding the timing system that runs your entire body. This internal 24-hour clock controls your sleep, energy, digestion, hormones, mood and even your immunity. When your rhythm is aligned, life feels smooth, clear and balanced. When it is disturbed, everything from sleep to emotions to productivity becomes chaotic. Circadian Rhythm is not just biology—it is nature's blueprint for a healthy, focused and joyful life.

Why Circadian Rhythm Matters

In a world of late-night screens, irregular meals, odd sleep schedules and constant artificial light, our natural rhythm is more disrupted than ever. Yet research shows that aligning your lifestyle with your circadian clock dramatically improves physical health, emotional stability and long-term well-being. Your body functions best when it behaves in sync with day and night—just as nature designed.

Key Benefits of a Healthy Circadian Rhythm

- **Better Sleep Quality:** A consistent rhythm helps you fall asleep faster and wake up refreshed.
- **Higher Energy & Productivity:** Energy peaks align naturally with the day, improving focus and stamina.

- **Stronger Digestion & Metabolism:** Eating at proper times supports digestion, weight control and gut health.
- **Hormonal Balance:** Cortisol, melatonin, insulin and growth hormones flow in balance when your clock is steady.
- **Emotional Stability:** Aligned rhythms reduce stress, mood swings and irritability, fostering inner calm.

Real-Life Examples:

- **The Engineer Who Fixed His Sleep by Following Sunlight** – Aarav struggled with late-night work and constant fatigue. He began stepping into morning sunlight for 10 minutes daily and fixed his bedtime to 10:30 PM. Within a week, he woke up with more energy, felt focused at work and stopped needing mid-day caffeine. **Lesson:** Sunlight resets your biological clock more powerfully than any supplement.
- **The Homemaker Who Used Meal Timings to Improve Digestion** – Meera often felt bloated and tired. She aligned her meals with daylight—breakfast by 8, lunch by 1 and dinner before 7. Digestion improved, acidity reduced and her energy became steady throughout the day. **Lesson:** Your gut works best when it follows the body's natural rhythm.

Circadian Rhythm is not a rule—it is a reminder from nature. When you live in alignment with light, food, rest and movement, your body responds with clarity, vitality and peace. By honouring your inner clock, you do not restrict your life—you restore it. In rhythm, you find balance. In balance, you find health. And in health, you rediscover a happier, calmer, more vibrant version of yourself.

Japanese Technique for a Slim Body

"Small habits, practiced daily, create a naturally healthier life."

Japanese culture is known for its long-life expectancy, balanced lifestyle and naturally slim bodies—not through extreme dieting but through simple, mindful habits. These techniques focus on awareness, balance and sustainability rather than restriction. Here are the core principles behind Japan's natural approach to maintaining a healthy body.

1. **Train Your Taste Buds**
   Japanese eating habits are built on subtle flavours, mild sweetness and natural ingredients. Over time, the taste buds adjust to prefer fresh, lightly seasoned foods rather than processed or overly salty meals. Training the palate helps reduce cravings, overeating and dependency on sugar-heavy or oily foods.

2. **Healthy Convenience**
   Japanese households and stores offer easy access to healthy options—cut fruits, steamed vegetables, miso soup, rice balls and fresh bento boxes. This "healthy convenience" culture makes nutritious eating the default choice, not a difficult one. Having simple, ready-to-eat healthy foods at home encourages better habits.

3. **Walking as a Lifestyle**
   Walking is deeply embedded in daily life—commuting, shopping, school and neighbourhood routines. This consistent, low-intensity movement boosts metabolism, improves posture and keeps the body naturally toned without heavy workouts. Walking is seen as lifestyle medicine, not exercise.

4. **Hara Hachi Bu (Eat Until 80% Full)**
   This Okinawan concept encourages stopping before the stomach is completely full. Eating to 80% reduces overeating, improves digestion and supports long-term weight control. It trains the mind to listen to hunger cues instead of emotional impulses.

5. **Four Varieties of Food in Separate Bowls**
   A traditional Japanese meal uses multiple small bowls—each with a different item. This encourages:
   - Slow eating
   - Better portion control
   - Balanced nutrition
   - Visual satisfaction

   Instead of piling everything on one plate, separating food encourages moderation and mindful eating.

6. **Fermented Foods**
   Japanese cuisine includes miso, natto, pickles, kombucha and fermented vegetables. These foods support gut health, digestion, immunity and weight management. A healthy gut promotes better metabolism and reduces inflammation—key factors in staying slim.

7. **Sugar Awareness**
   Japanese diets are low in refined sugar. Desserts are smaller, less sweet and often fruit based. Sugar is consumed mindfully, not unconsciously. This awareness prevents energy crashes, mood swings and weight gain.

8. **Slow and Mindful Eating**
   Meals are eaten calmly, with full attention to taste, texture and satisfaction. This approach prevents overeating by giving the brain enough time to

register fullness. Mindful eating reduces stress-induced snacking and improves digestion.

9. **Do Not Mix Stress with Food**
   Emotional eating is strongly discouraged in Japanese culture. Meals are taken in peaceful environments—no arguments, no rushing, no phone scrolling. Eating under stress affects digestion, increases cravings and leads to overeating. By separating emotions from meals, the eating experience remains healthy and controlled.

The Japanese way to a slim body is built on balance, awareness and small daily habits—not restrictions or extreme diets. By training taste buds, choosing healthy convenience, walking regularly, eating mindfully and respecting the body's natural signals, a person can maintain health effortlessly.

These timeless principles prove one truth: **consistent, gentle habits create long-lasting results.**

Gentle Movement — The Discipline of Daily Motion

"The body does not ask for extremes; it asks to be moved, daily and with respect."

Gentle Movement is the quiet discipline of keeping the body in motion without turning health into pressure. It is the understanding that movement is not about fitness goals or competition but about **maintaining life flow**. Walking, light running, warm-ups, stretching, simple cardio or playful activity—all serve the same purpose: to keep the body awake, capable and responsive throughout life.

This chapter is not about how much you should do, how fast you should move or how hard you must push. It is about **choosing movement that suits your age, your body, your energy and your season of life** and then doing it consistently.

Why Gentle Movement Matters

The human body is designed to move regularly. When movement disappears, stiffness replaces ease, fatigue replaces vitality and imbalance slowly settles in. Most physical discomfort does not come from lack of intense exercise; it comes from **lack of regular motion**.

Gentle daily movement keeps joints lubricated, circulation active, digestion responsive and mood balanced. It preserves freedom—the freedom to walk without pain, climb without fear and live without constant physical limitation. Movement done with awareness becomes maintenance, not strain.

Understanding Movement by Life Stage and Body Type

There is no single "best" exercise for everyone. The right movement is the one that **your body accepts without resistance**.

- **Younger bodies** often respond well to brisk walking, light running, cycling, swimming, sports and general cardio.
- **Middle-aged bodies** often do best with walking, warm-up routines, stretching, moderate cardio, yoga and strength through body weight.
- **Older bodies** benefit most from walking, mobility work, balance exercises, chair movements, slow stretches and gentle breathing.
- **Sensitive or recovering bodies** need warm-ups, slow pace, low impact movement and consistency over intensity.

Listening matters more than copying.

Types of Gentle Movement (Choose What Fits You)

- **Walking** – The most underrated exercise. It nourishes the heart, clears the mind and suits all ages.
- **Warm-Up Movement** – Rotating joints, loosening shoulders, spine mobility and light stretches prepare the body for the day.
- **Light Running or Jogging** – Suitable for bodies that tolerate impact. It should feel energizing, not punishing.
- **Cardio at Comfort Pace** – Cycling, swimming, brisk walking or dancing where breathing increases but remains controllable.
- **Stretching and Mobility** – Keeps the body flexible and prevents stiffness from long sitting hours.
- **Playful Movement** – Sports, games, dancing, gardening—movement that does not feel like exercise at all.

The goal is not to do everything but to **do something regularly**.

Real-Life Examples:

- **The Mid-Career Professional Who Walked Back to Balance** Amit spent years sitting, working late and postponing exercise for "someday." Instead of joining a gym, he began a habit of 30 minutes of walking each morning. No gear, no targets. Over months, energy improved, stiffness eased and concentration returned. **Lesson:** Consistency restores what intensity often cannot.
- **The Retired Teacher Who Chose Chair Movement and Stretching** Meena felt exercise was no longer "for her." She started slow—joint rotations, seated stretches and gentle balance work near a wall. Her confidence in movement returned, along with better sleep and stability. **Lesson:** Movement adapts; dignity does not disappear with age.

Movement as Discipline, Not Force

Discipline here does not mean rigidity. It means **showing up gently, daily**.

- Some days your body will want to walk longer.
- Some days it will want only stretching.
- Some days rest itself is movement inward.

The mistake is not doing too little. The mistake is doing nothing for too long.

Gentle movement is a promise to your body: *I will not abandon you to inactivity, nor punish you with excess.* It is the discipline of honouring what the body can do today, not what it did yesterday or what others expect tomorrow.

Walking, warming up, running lightly, stretching or moving playfully—each keeps life circulating where stillness would allow decline.
Move with kindness.Move with respect.
And let daily motion quietly protect the health that makes everything else possible.

Sleep Like a Pro: Rest for Renewal

"Sleep is the golden chain that ties health and our bodies together."

Sleep is not a luxury — it is the foundation of health, clarity and emotional balance. Yet many people sacrifice it for work, entertainment or late-night distractions. High performers—from athletes to leaders—treat sleep as a non-negotiable tool for energy, focus and long-term success.

Why Sleep Matters

- **Repairs the Body:** Rest restores muscles, strengthens immunity and balances hormones.
- **Sharpens the Mind:** Deep sleep improves memory, creativity and focus.
- **Regulates Emotions:** Quality sleep reduces stress and emotional reactivity.
- **Boosts Performance:** Better sleep leads to better decisions and productivity.
- **Supports Longevity:** Consistent rest reduces chronic disease risk.

How to Sleep Like a Pro

1. **Keep a Consistent Schedule:** Sleep and wake at the same time daily.
2. **Create a Sleep-Friendly Space:** Cool, dark and quiet rooms promote deeper rest.
3. **Limit Stimulants:** Avoid caffeine, alcohol and heavy meals before bed.
4. **Reduce Screen Time:** Switch off devices at least an hour before sleep.

5. **Have a Wind-Down Ritual:** Read, stretch or meditate to signal your body to relax.
6. **Move Daily:** Regular exercise improves sleep quality (avoid intense workouts late).
7. **Calm the Mind:** Journal or practice deep breathing to manage racing thoughts.
8. **Respect Natural Cycles:** Aim for 7–9 hours so your body completes full sleep phases.

Real-Life Examples:

- Professional athletes don't only train their bodies—they train their sleep. By following consistent bedtimes, limiting late-night screens and practicing relaxation, they ensure their mind and body recover fully. Applying similar discipline in daily life can dramatically improve your focus, energy and mood.

To "sleep like a pro" is to honour rest as a priority, not an afterthought. When you protect your sleep, you unlock sharper focus, stronger resilience and deeper joy.

Healing Through Water - The Power of Hydration & Renewal

"Water heals in ways words cannot—cleansing the body, calming the mind and refreshing the spirit."

Water Therapy is the practice of using water consciously to restore balance, improve health and renew energy. From drinking warm water in the morning to taking relaxing baths, from staying hydrated to spending time near natural water bodies—water plays a powerful role in supporting both physical and emotional well-being. Just as water flows and adapts, it teaches you to soften, release and move through life with ease.

Why Water Therapy Matters

Modern lifestyles often lead to dehydration, sluggish digestion, dull skin, fatigue and toxin buildup—issues that silently affect energy and mood. Water is one of the simplest yet most powerful tools for healing. Research shows that adequate hydration improves brain function, boosts metabolism, regulates body temperature and enhances mood. Warm water stimulates digestion, while cool water reduces inflammation. Even listening to flowing water reduces stress and quiets the mind. Water is nature's most accessible and effective detoxifier.

Key Benefits of Water Therapy

- **Improved Digestion:** Warm water in the morning activates metabolism and clears toxins.
- **Better Skin & Hydration:** Proper water intake keeps skin glowing, soft and youthful.
- **Enhanced Energy Levels:** Hydrated cells produce energy more efficiently.
- **Detoxification:** Water flushes waste, supports kidneys and reduces inflammation.
- **Stress Relief:** Baths, showers and natural water sounds calm the nervous system.

Real-Life Examples:

- **The Professional Who Regained Energy with Warm Water Rituals** – Anand felt bloated, tired and mentally heavy. He began drinking a glass of warm water every morning and sipped regularly through the day. Within a week, his digestion improved, his energy became steady and his afternoon fatigue disappeared. **Lesson:** Small hydration habits can reawaken the body's natural vitality.
- **The Homemaker Who Found Calm Through Evening Foot-Soaks** – Reema often felt anxious at night. She introduced a 10-minute warm water foot-soak with a pinch of salt. It relaxed her muscles, slowed her thoughts and improved her sleep quality. **Lesson:** Water can heal both the mind and body through simple daily rituals.

Water Therapy reminds you that healing does not always require complexity. Sometimes, the most powerful solutions flow from the simplest sources. When you drink mindfully, bathe consciously and honour water as a source of life, you create space for clarity, energy and renewal. In every sip and every drop lies the possibility of healing—gentle, natural and transformative.

Why You Don't Feel at Your Best Today — The Discipline of the Mouth

"When taste leads the mind, the body pays the price."

Every day, your body quietly reflects how you treat it—especially through what enters it. Most people assume feeling tired, foggy, irritated, bloated or dull is "normal life." In reality, these states are often responses to **unchecked eating choices**, not medical conditions.

The stomach does not decide what enters the body. The **mouth does.**
And the mouth is guided not by need—but by **taste**.

The Mouth: The Main Gateway to Excess and Unnecessary Food

Most additional, unhealthy or unnecessary food does not enter the body because of hunger. It enters because the mouth enjoys taste—sweet, spicy, salty, crunchy, cold, indulgent. When taste takes charge, quantity increases, timing shifts and food quality drops.

This is how imbalance begins:

- Not with illness
- Not with disease
- But with **small, repeated loss of control at the mouth**

What you allow your mouth to demand, your body must process.

1. When Taste Overrules Hunger, Balance Is Lost

True hunger is simple. Taste cravings are demanding.
When eating is driven by taste:

- Meals become heavier than required
- Snacks appear between meals without need
- Late-night eating feels deserved
- Portion sizes silently expand

The digestive system is then forced to work beyond rhythm. Energy that could support clarity, patience and focus is redirected toward digestion. Over time, the

body expresses protest—through acidity, heaviness, bloating, thirst, cravings and discomfort.
The body always speaks first. We often listen last.

2. Overeating Begins at the Mouth, Not the Stomach

The stomach has limits. The mouth does not.
Overeating happens when taste refuses to stop even after the body has enough. The result is not strength—but **energy theft**.

Overeating often produces:

- mental dullness
- slow reaction and poor focus
- lack of motivation
- heaviness in both body and mind

Extra food does not become extra energy. It consumes the energy already available.

3. Taste Choices Affect the Stomach, Throat and Mind Together

Certain tastes excite the tongue but disturb the system.
Spicy excess, oily foods, excessive sugar, cold drinks, ultra-processed snacks and stale foods may feel satisfying for moments but irritate digestion over hours.

When food does not suit the system:

- The **stomach** feels heavy or acidic
- The **throat** becomes sensitive, dry or irritated
- The **mind** turns foggy and restless
- The **body** slows down

This is why food choices immediately affect mood, clarity and performance. The stomach and mind are not separate departments—they report to the same system.

4. Taste-Control Shapes Mood, Patience and Productivity

The emotional impact of food is underestimated.
When the stomach is disturbed, patience shortens.
When sugar spikes, emotions swing.
When meals are too heavy, sleep and alertness suffer.

This explains why:

- Some days feel calm, productive and light
- Other days feel sluggish, irritated or unfocused

Often, nothing changed except **what the mouth was allowed to choose**.

Real-Life Examples:

- **Karan** noticed that indulgent lunches made his afternoons meaningless. By stopping when taste said "more" and the body said "enough," his focus returned without effort.
- **Neha** struggled with throat irritation and morning heaviness. She observed that cold drinks at night pleased her mouth but punished her mornings. Warm choices restored comfort.
- **Arif** believed he lacked discipline. In truth, processed snacks controlled his taste and crashed his energy. Simpler food steadied both mood and motivation.
- **Simran** felt anxious without reason. Reducing sugar—without changing anything else—calmed her mind. Her body had been reacting faster than her thoughts.

None of these improvements began with medication or motivation. They began with **mouth awareness**.

Health often improves not by adding supplements, routines or remedies—but by **removing unnecessary intake**. Control of taste is not deprivation; it is respect.

When the mouth eats consciously:

- The stomach stays calm
- The mind stays clear
- Energy stays available
- Life feels lighter

Take care of what the mouth chooses and the body will take care of the rest. Control the entry—and you restore balance naturally.

The Gut–Mind Connection - Where Your Health and Emotions Begin

"The gut is not just where digestion happens—it's where emotions begin. A healthy mind starts with a healthy gut."

The connection between Gut Health and Mental Health is deeper than most people realise. Often called the **second brain**, the gut hosts millions of neurons and trillions of microbes that directly influence your mood, focus, stress levels and emotional balance. When your gut is healthy, you feel lighter, calmer and mentally clearer. When it is disturbed, you may experience anxiety, irritability, brain fog and fatigue. Understanding this gut–mind connection empowers you to build better emotional health through the food you eat and the habits you follow.

Why This Connection Matters

In today's lifestyle of fast food, stress, irregular meals and low-fiber diets, gut imbalances have become extremely common. Research shows that **over 90% of serotonin**, the "feel-good" hormone, is produced in the gut. This means your digestion affects your emotions far more than you think. A stable gut leads to stable emotions, better focus and greater mental resilience. Taking care of your gut is one of the simplest ways to improve both your physical and emotional well-being.

Key Benefits of a Healthy Gut

- **Better Mood & Emotional Stability:** A balanced gut microbiome supports the production of serotonin and reduces anxiety.
- **Sharper Mental Clarity:** Healthy digestion improves focus, memory and cognitive performance.
- **Lower Stress & Inflammation:** A strong gut lining reduces stress-induced inflammation in the body and mind.
- **More Energy & Motivation:** Efficient nutrient absorption enhances daily energy and reduces fatigue.
- **Stronger Immunity:** A healthy gut boosts immune strength, reducing sickness and improving overall vitality.

Real-Life Examples:

- **The Teacher Whose Anxiety Reduced by Fixing Her Diet** – For years, Priya struggled with irritability, stress and digestive discomfort. By increasing fibre, adding probiotics and reducing spicy late-night meals, her digestion improved, anxiety reduced and her mood felt more stable. **Lesson:** A calm gut supports a calm mind.

- **The College Student Who Overcame Brain Fog** – Aditya felt mentally dull, tired and unfocused during classes. When he cut down on sugary snacks, increased hydration and added fermented foods to his diet, his concentration improved and his energy became stable. **Lesson:** Clear thinking often begins with clean eating.

Your gut and mind are in constant conversation. When your gut is nourished, your mind becomes stronger, clearer and more peaceful. Taking care of your digestive health is not just a physical practice—it is an emotional investment. A healthy gut is the foundation of a stable, focused and joyful life.

Nourish to Flourish: Eating with Awareness and Joy

"Eat to nourish, not to numb."

In a world rushing from meal to meal, many people eat out of habit, emotion or convenience rather than care. Food is more than fuel—it affects mood, energy, clarity and overall, well-being. When you slow down, choose with intention and listen to your body, eating becomes a source of nourishment, gratitude and peace.

This chapter brings together three simple truths: **Eat consciously. Eat mindfully. Eat in a way that leaves you happier after the meal, not during it.**

1. What Is Intentional Eating?

Intentional eating means choosing food with awareness—what you eat, why you eat and how you eat. It moves you away from emotional or distracted eating and toward food that supports health and inner balance. Modern life promotes rushed meals, processed snacks and eating while scrolling. Over time, this disconnects leads to overeating, poor digestion and low energy. Intentional eating brings back clarity: food becomes nourishment, not escape.

2. The Power of Presence at the Table

Meals are ordinary moments with extraordinary potential. When you slow down, notice flavours and eat without screens or haste, food becomes a ritual of care. A simple meal eaten with presence offers more joy than a lavish one eaten mindlessly.

Mindful eating improves:

- Digestion
- Satisfaction
- Emotional calm
- Connection to food and nature

3. Choosing Foods with Purpose

Simplicity in food is not restriction—it is clarity. Whole ingredients, seasonal produce and minimally processed meals align with the body's natural needs.
A modest plate of rice and lentils, eaten consciously, nourishes more deeply than overeating rich, heavy foods. The goal is not calories—it's harmony.

4. Listening to Your Body

Your body is a guide. It signals hunger, fullness and imbalance. Intentional eating means honouring these signals instead of eating from habit, emotion or routine. *Eat when hungry, stop when satisfied*. Respecting your body's rhythm brings balance and freedom from guilt or overindulgence.

6. Principles of Intentional & Mindful Eating

- **Be Present While Eating** - Taste, chew and notice flavours. Avoid screens.
- **Honour Hunger & Fullness** - Eat according to your body's needs—not the clock.
- **Choose Quality Over Quantity** - Whole foods nourish more than processed ones.
- **Eat with Gratitude** - Pause to appreciate the people, effort and nature behind each meal.
- **Align with Your Value** - Choose foods that support health and sustainability.

7. A Real-Life Shift

Rajat, a busy manager, lived on fast food between meetings. He felt tired, unfocused and heavy after meals. He began packing simple homemade lunches, eating without screens and pausing after each meal to notice how he felt. Within weeks, he had better digestion, steadier energy and a calmer mind. Eating turned from stress to self-care.

8. Happiness After Eating: The Real Test

A powerful question to transform eating habits:

"How do I feel after eating?"

If you feel light, energized and satisfied—your food is serving you. If you feel heavy, sleepy or regretful—your choices need adjustment.

How to Use This Insight

- Pause after meals to notice your mood and energy
- Identify foods that make you feel good
- Build habits around meals that leave you happier afterward

The body always tells the truth. Listen.

Intentional eating is not about rules—it is about awareness. When you slow down, choose consciously and honour your body, food becomes a source of joy, energy and gratitude. **A simple meal, eaten with presence, can nourish the body and uplift the soul.**

The Cleanse Within - The Power of Fasting & Natural Detox

"Detoxification is not just about cleansing the body—it is about clearing space for energy, clarity and renewal."

Fasting & Detox are ancient practices designed to give your body the rest it needs to repair, heal and rejuvenate. When you stop overloading your system with constant food and stress, your body activates its natural cleansing mechanisms. Fasting calms digestion, balances hormones, reduces inflammation and boosts mental clarity. Detox removes accumulated toxins from poor diet, pollution, stress and irregular routines. Together, they help you return to lightness, balance and vibrant health.

Why Fasting & Detox Matter

In modern life, the body is constantly overstimulated—too much food too much sugar too many chemicals too little rest. The digestive system rarely gets a break. Over time, this leads to fatigue, weight gain, inflammation, dull skin, low immunity and reduced mental sharpness. Research shows that periodic fasting and natural detox practices improve cellular repair, balance blood sugar, enhance metabolism and support emotional well-being. Fasting is not starvation—it is conscious nourishment through rest.

Key Benefits of Fasting & Detox

- **Improved Digestion:** Fasting gives your digestive system time to recover, reducing bloating and discomfort.
- **Natural Cellular Repair:** The body activates autophagy—its internal cleaning process—during fasting.
- **More Energy & Mental Clarity:** Detox reduces inflammation, creating sharper thinking and stable energy.
- **Balanced Hormones:** Fasting helps regulate insulin, cortisol and hunger hormones.
- **Stronger Immunity:** A cleaner internal environment supports healthier immune function.

Real-Life Examples:

- **The Professional Who Regained Focus with Intermittent Fasting** – Rahul struggled with low energy and afternoon fatigue. He adopted a simple 14:10 fasting routine—eating between 9 AM and 7 PM. Within a week, his energy steadied, his cravings reduced and his concentration increased. **Lesson:** Even gentle fasting creates powerful changes.

- **The Homemaker Who Used Detox to Improve Skin & Digestion** – For months, Pooja experienced acidity and dull skin. She added warm water, lemon, herbal teas and early dinners to her routine. Her digestion improved, her skin brightened and she felt lighter throughout the day. **Lesson:** Detox is built through small, daily habits—not extreme diets.

Fasting & Detox teach you to pause, let go and trust your body's wisdom. When you give your system the rest it deserves, it rewards you with clarity, energy and healing. By embracing these gentle practices, you create space for renewal—physically, mentally and emotionally. In this space, you rediscover your natural vitality and a deeper sense of well-being.

The Expanded Practice of Fasting

"Fasting isn't just for the body—it's for the mind. Discipline creates clarity and strength."

The Essence of Fasting
At its core, fasting is about **voluntary restraint**. It is the conscious act of stepping back from consumption—whether physical, mental or emotional—to regain clarity, discipline and balance. When applied broadly, fasting becomes a lifestyle habit that strengthens self-control and nurtures inner freedom.

Dimensions of Non-Food Fasting

1. **Digital Fasting**

- **What it means:** Taking breaks from phones, social media and constant notifications.
- **Why it matters:** Reduces distraction, anxiety and comparison.

- **Practice:** Set aside hours or days where you disconnect from screens and reconnect with real life.

2. **Material Fasting**
   - **What it means:** Avoiding unnecessary purchases or consumption of goods.
   - **Why it matters:** Builds gratitude, reduces clutter and curbs consumerism.
   - **Practice:** Commit to "no shopping" days or weeks, using only what you already own.
3. **Emotional Fasting**
   - **What it means:** Choosing silence over reaction—stepping back from anger, gossip or negativity.
   - **Why it matters:** Preserves peace, strengthens emotional intelligence and prevents energy drain.
   - **Practice:** Pause before responding, avoid toxic conversations and cultivate calm reflection.
4. **Verbal Fasting**
   - **What it means:** Practicing restraint in speech—speaking less, listening more.
   - **Why it matters:** Encourages mindfulness, deepens relationships and reduces unnecessary conflict.
   - **Practice:** Dedicate time to silence, journaling or active listening instead of constant talking.
5. **Information Fasting**
   - **What it means:** Taking breaks from news, updates and endless input.
   - **Why it matters:** Prevents overload, reduces stress and allows deeper thinking.
   - **Practice:** Limit news checks to once a day or dedicate "no-information weekends."
6. **Sensory Fasting**
   - **What it means:** Reducing overstimulation—noise, entertainment or indulgence.
   - **Why it matters:** Restores balance, sharpens awareness and reconnects you with simplicity.
   - **Practice:** Spend time in quiet spaces, nature or meditation without external stimulation.

Benefits of All-Item Fasting

- **Clarity:** Creates mental and emotional space.

- **Discipline:** Strengthens willpower across different areas of life.
- **Balance:** Reduces dependence on external stimuli.
- **Renewal:** Restores energy and focus for meaningful pursuits.
- **Freedom:** Teaches that happiness is not tied to constant consumption.

Fasting is not deprivation—it is liberation. By extending fasting beyond food to digital, material, emotional, verbal, informational and sensory areas, you create a life of balance, clarity and discipline. The habit of fasting teaches that true strength lies not in constant consumption but in conscious restraint.

Strengthening Your Inner Shield - Daily Habits for Powerful Immunity

"Strong immunity is not built in a day—it is built every day, through conscious choices that protect your health and energize your life."

Immunity Boosting Habits are simple daily practices that strengthen your body's natural defence system. A strong immune system doesn't just prevent illness—it improves energy, sharpens thinking, reduces inflammation and supports emotional stability. In a world filled with stress, pollution, irregular routines and processed foods, strengthening immunity has become essential for long-term health and vitality. With the right habits, your body can heal faster, resist infections better and stay youthful for years.

Why Immunity Matters

Your immune system works silently to protect you from bacteria, viruses toxins and stress-related damage. Yet lifestyle choices—poor sleep, unhealthy food, dehydration, lack of movement and chronic stress—can weaken this shield. Research consistently shows that simple, consistent habits like good sleep, hydration, sunlight, movement and nutrition greatly enhance immunity and overall well-being. A strong immune system is the foundation of a healthy, active and resilient life.

Key Immunity-Boosting Habits

- **Prioritize Quality Sleep:** 7–8 hours of deep sleep supports healing, hormone balance and immune function.
- **Stay Hydrated:** Water helps flush toxins, support cells and maintain energy levels.
- **Eat Natural, Colourful Foods:** Fruits, vegetables, nuts and seeds provide antioxidants and essential nutrients.

- **Move Daily:** Regular walking or exercise increases circulation and strengthens immune cells.
- **Manage Stress:** Meditation, breathing exercises and breaks reduce stress-related inflammation.
- **Get Morning Sunlight:** Sun exposure boosts Vitamin D, a vital component of immune strength.
- **Limit Sugar & Junk Food:** These weaken immunity and increase inflammation.
- **Maintain a Healthy Gut:** Yogurt, fiber-rich foods and probiotics support digestion and immune health.

Real-Life Examples:

- **The Office Worker Who Recovered from Frequent Colds** – Kunal fell sick every month due to long hours and late nights. He began sleeping earlier, added fruits and nuts to his morning routine and started a daily 20-minute walk. Within a month, his sinus issues reduced and his energy levels improved. **Lesson:** Small, consistent changes create big immunity gains.
- **The Homemaker Who Reduced Stress-Related Fatigue** – Neeta struggled with fatigue and headaches. She introduced deep breathing twice a day, drank more water and added sunlight exposure every morning. Her mood stabilized, headaches reduced and she felt less tired during the day. **Lesson:** Immunity grows when stress falls and routines align with nature.

Immunity is not merely the absence of illness—it is the presence of strength, balance and vitality. By adopting simple, meaningful habits, you empower your body to protect you naturally. Strengthen your immunity and you strengthen your life. In these habits lie your health, energy and long-lasting well-being.

Sun Salutation: A Ritual of Strength and Serenity

"When you greet the sun with movement and breath, you awaken the light within."

The Sun Salutation (Surya Namaskar) is one of the most iconic sequences in Hatha Yoga. It is more than an exercise—it's a moving meditation that harmonizes body, breath and mind. This twelve-step flow energizes the body, improves flexibility and cultivates mindfulness.

Sun Salutation (Surya Namaskar) – 12 Steps

Note: After each step, pause for **1–2 seconds** to stay mindful and maintain balance.

1. **Pranamasana (Prayer Pose)**
   Stand straight, join palms at chest. **Exhale gently.**
2. **Hasta Uttanasana (Raised Arms Pose)**
   Raise arms overhead, arch back slightly. **Inhale deeply.**
3. **Padahastasana (Hand-to-Foot Pose)**
   Bend forward, hands toward feet. **Exhale fully.**
4. **Ashwa Sanchalanasana (Equestrian Pose)**
   Stretch right leg back, left knee bent, look forward. **Inhale deeply.**
5. **Dandasana (Plank Pose)**
   Take left leg back, body straight like a plank. **Exhale slowly.**

6. **Ashtanga Namaskara (Eight-Limbed Pose)**
   Lower knees, chest, chin to floor, hips raised. **Hold breath briefly.**
7. **Bhujangasana (Cobra Pose)**

Slide forward, lift chest, gentle backbend. **Inhale deeply.**

8. **Adho Mukha Svanasana (Downward Dog Pose)**
   Lift hips, form inverted "V". **Exhale fully.**
9. **Ashwa Sanchalanasana (Equestrian Pose)**
   Bring right foot forward, left leg back, look ahead. **Inhale deeply.**
10. **Padahastasana (Hand-to-Foot Pose)**
    Bring left foot forward, bend down. **Exhale slowly.**
11. **Hasta Uttanasana (Raised Arms Pose)**
    Raise arms overhead, arch back slightly. **Inhale deeply.**
12. **Pranamasana (Prayer Pose)**
    Return to standing, palms at chest. **Exhale gently.**

Benefits of Sun Salutation

- Improves flexibility and posture
- Boosts circulation and energy
- Enhances mental clarity and focus
- Promotes mindfulness through breath coordination

The Sun Salutation is not just a physical routine—it's a ritual of gratitude to the life-giving sun. Practiced daily, it awakens vitality, calms the mind and sets the tone for a balanced, harmonious day.

Stretch Your Limits - The Healing Power of Yoga

"Flexibility is not about touching your toes—it's about learning how to let go, breathe and create space within yourself."

Yoga & Flexibility go far beyond stretching the body. They help you release stiffness, ease tension, calm your mind and reconnect with your inner rhythm. When the body becomes flexible, the mind follows. Flexibility is a gentle reminder that life becomes lighter when we stop resisting and start flowing. Through yoga, you strengthen your muscles, open your joints and create harmony between breath, body and awareness. It becomes a moving meditation—bringing balance, energy and inner peace.

Why Yoga & Flexibility Matter

In today's lifestyle of prolonged sitting, constant screens and high stress, the body becomes tight and the mind becomes restless. Research shows that gentle stretching and mindful movement improve blood flow, reduce anxiety and enhance overall well-being. Flexibility is not about forcing the body—it is about listening to it. It teaches patience, presence and acceptance. A flexible body brings ease. A flexible mind brings freedom.

Key Benefits of Yoga & Flexibility

- **Reduced Stress & Muscle Tension:** Gentle stretches calm the nervous system and relax tight muscles.
- **Improved Mobility & Posture:** Flexible joints and stronger core create better alignment and pain-free movement.
- **Enhanced Breathing & Energy Flow:** Yoga opens the chest and lungs, improving oxygen flow and vitality.
- **Better Balance & Body Awareness:** Mindful movement strengthens coordination and stability.
- **Emotional Release:** Flexibility practices help release stored emotions and create inner lightness.

Real-Life Examples:

- **The Software Engineer Who Healed His Back Pain** – Arvind spent long hours sitting, which led to stiffness and recurring back pain. He started practicing 15 minutes of morning yoga—cat-cow, child's pose and gentle twists. Within weeks, his pain reduced, his posture improved and he felt more energetic throughout the day. **Lesson:** Small daily stretches can undo years of tension.
- **The Homemaker Who Regained Calm Through Evening Yoga** – Kavita often felt mentally overwhelmed and physically tired. She began a slow, calming flexibility routine in the evening—forward bends, hip openers and deep breathing. It helped her unwind, sleep better and feel emotionally balanced. **Lesson:** Flexibility is as healing for the mind as it is for the body.

Yoga & Flexibility invite you to slow down, breathe and reconnect with your body. They teach you to honour your limits, expand your comfort zone and move with grace. When your body becomes flexible, life becomes flexible. In that gentle flow, you find strength, balance and a deeper sense of well-being.

Breath of Life - The Power of Pranayama & Inner Balance

"Your breath is the bridge between the body and the mind. When you control your breath, you control your inner world."

Pranayama & Breathwork are ancient yet timeless practices that use the power of breathing to calm the mind, energize the body and balance the emotions. Your breath reflects your state—fast when stressed, shallow when anxious, steady when peaceful.

Through mindful breathing, you create space within yourself, reduce tension and bring clarity. It transforms stress into calm, restlessness into focus and confusion into balance. Breath becomes an anchor that stabilizes you, no matter what life brings.

Why Pranayama Matters

In today's fast-paced world, people breathe quickly, shallowly and unconsciously leading to stress, fatigue and emotional imbalance. Research shows that deep, controlled breathing activates the parasympathetic system, slows the heart rate, reduces anxiety and improves emotional regulation. Pranayama reconnects you to your most fundamental life force—your prana. It reminds you that peace is not found outside; it is created inside with every conscious breath.

Key Benefits of Pranayama & Breathwork

- **Stress Relief:** Slow breathing calms the nervous system and reduces cortisol.
- **Improved Focus:** Better oxygen flow sharpens memory, attention and mental clarity.
- **Emotional Balance:** Deep breaths help regulate emotions and reduce anxiety.
- **Increased Energy:** Breathwork enhances vitality and combats fatigue naturally.
- **Better Health:** Stronger lungs, improved circulation and enhanced immunity.

Real-Life Examples:

- **The Entrepreneur Who Used Breathwork to Reduce Anxiety** – Mehul often felt overwhelmed by deadlines and decisions. He started practicing 5 minutes of deep diaphragmatic breathing—inhale for 4 seconds, exhale for 6. Over days, his anxiety decreased, decision-making improved and he felt more grounded. **Lesson:** A few mindful breaths can shift your entire emotional state.
- **The Teacher Who Improved Sleep with Pranayama** – Lata struggled with late-night restlessness. By practicing Anulom-Vilom before bed, her mind felt calm and her sleep became deeper and more refreshing. **Lesson:** Balanced breathing creates balanced rest.

Pranayama is a reminder that peace is only one breath away. When you breathe with awareness, you slow down the noise of the mind, soften the tension in the body and awaken a deep sense of inner harmony. Through breath, you come home to yourself—calmer, clearer and more alive. In every inhale lies energy. In every exhale lies release. And in this rhythm, you rediscover your balance.

Reconnecting with Nature

"Return to your roots—nature is the ultimate healer."

In the rush of modern life, it is easy to forget that nature is our original home. Spending time outdoors—whether in a park, forest, beach or even a small garden—restores balance to the mind, body and spirit.

Why It Matters

- **Calm & Clarity:** Nature quiets the noise of daily life and helps you reconnect with yourself.
- **Health Benefits:** Fresh air, sunlight and movement in natural spaces boost physical and mental well-being.
- **Perspective:** Watching the cycles of seasons, rivers or trees reminds us of patience and resilience.
- **Creativity:** Time in nature sparks imagination and problem-solving by giving the mind space to wander.
- **Connection:** It deepens gratitude for the world around us and strengthens our sense of belonging.

How to Practice

- Take daily walks in green spaces.
- Spend weekends hiking, gardening or exploring new landscapes.

- Pause to notice small details—birds singing, leaves moving or the feel of wind.
- Use nature as a place for reflection, meditation or journaling.

Real-Life Examples:

- **The Corporate Professional Who Found Peace in Morning Park Walks -** Arvind worked long hours in a fast-paced corporate job and often felt mentally drained. At a friend's suggestion, he began taking a quiet 20-minute walk in a nearby park every morning—no phone, no music, just nature. Within a week, he noticed reduced stress, clearer thoughts and a renewed sense of calm. Those simple moments with trees, birds and fresh air became his daily reset button, bringing balance back into his life. **Lesson:** Even small doses of nature can restore clarity, energy and emotional well-being.
- Imagine sitting under a tree at sunset. The air is cool, the sky painted with colours and the world feels still. In that moment, stress fades, clarity returns and you feel recharged. That is the quiet power of nature.

Spending time with nature is not a luxury—it is a necessity. It reminds us of simplicity, restores our energy and keeps us aligned with the rhythm of life. In nature, we find peace, perspective and the strength to live fully.

Healing With Nature - Forest Walks, Sunlight & Pure Energy

"Nature heals quietly. A walk among trees or a moment in sunlight can restore what stress has taken away."

Nature Therapy is the practice of reconnecting with the natural world to renew your mind, body and emotions. Whether it is walking through a forest, sitting under a tree, watching the sky or soaking in gentle sunlight — nature brings a calm that modern life cannot offer. Trees, fresh air, sunlight and natural surroundings reset the nervous system, clear the mind and uplift your mood. Nature reminds you to slow down, breathe deeply and return to a simpler, more peaceful rhythm of life.

Why Nature Therapy Matters

In today's digital world, people spend more time indoors than ever before. Constant screens, artificial light and indoor environments slowly drain your energy and disturb your mental balance. Research shows that time spent in green spaces reduces stress hormones, boosts immunity, improves sleep and enhances emotional well-being. Sunlight, fresh air and natural surroundings act like a natural medicine

— improving mood, increasing Vitamin D levels and restoring your inner harmony.

Key Benefits of Forest Walks, Sunlight & Vitamin D

- **Stress Reduction:** Forest air lowers cortisol and relaxes the nervous system.
- **Improved Mood:** Sunlight increases serotonin — the "feel-good" hormone.
- **Stronger Immunity:** Trees release phytoncides, which enhance immune cell activity.
- **Better Sleep:** Sunlight exposure regulates your circadian rhythm for deeper sleep.
- **Healthy Vitamin D Levels:** Sunlight naturally boosts Vitamin D, supporting bones, immunity and overall vitality.
- **Mental Clarity:** Nature improves focus, creativity and problem-solving ability.

Real-Life Examples:

- **The Executive Who Found Calm Through Morning Sunlight** – Aman struggled with mental fatigue and irritability. He began spending 10 minutes in early morning sunlight before starting work. Within days, his mood felt lighter, his sleep improved and he felt more centered during stressful meetings. **Lesson:** A few minutes of sunlight can reset your emotional balance.
- **The Homemaker Who Healed Anxiety with Forest Walks** – After months of feeling overwhelmed, Sarita started taking slow evening walks in a nearby park filled with trees. The fresh air, greenery and silence reduced her anxiety, improved her breathing and restored her sense of peace. **Lesson:** Nature's presence heals gently but powerfully.

Nature is not a luxury — it is a necessity. Forest walks, fresh air and sunlight reconnect you with your natural rhythm. They calm your mind, strengthen your body and brighten your spirit. When you return to nature, you return to yourself. In the quiet of trees and the warmth of sunlight, you rediscover balance, clarity and a deeper sense of well-being.

Living in Balance - The Wisdom of an Ayurvedic Lifestyle

"Balance is not something you find—it is something you create daily through mindful living."

An Ayurvedic Lifestyle is the art of living in harmony with your body's natural rhythm. Rooted in ancient wisdom, Ayurveda teaches that health is not just the absence of illness—it is a state of balance between body, mind and spirit. By understanding your unique constitution (dosha) and choosing foods, habits and routines that support your inner nature, you create energy, clarity and long-lasting vitality. Ayurveda reminds you that well-being is built through small, consistent actions woven into everyday life.

Why an Ayurvedic Lifestyle Matters

In today's fast-paced world, people often ignore the signals of their body—leading to stress, digestive issues, poor sleep and emotional imbalance. Ayurveda offers a simple and timeless approach: live in alignment with nature, eat mindfully, rest adequately and follow routines that support your unique system. Research-backed habits like warm foods, proper hydration, timely meals and daily movement have shown positive effects on immunity, metabolism and emotional stability. Ayurveda brings you back to balance—gently, naturally and sustainably.

Key Principles of an Ayurvedic Lifestyle

- **Daily Rhythm (Dinacharya):** Waking early, oil pulling tongue cleaning and mindful morning rituals support physical and mental clarity.
- **Eating According to Your Constitution:** Choosing foods that balance your dosha helps digestion, energy and overall well-being.
- **Mindful Eating:** Warm, fresh meals consumed at regular times nourish deeply and prevent energy crashes.
- **Digestive Fire (Agni):** Maintaining strong digestion is central to Ayurveda—healthy agni means healthy body and mind.
- **Rest & Restoration:** Proper sleep and relaxation practices help rejuvenate and heal the body.
- **Herbal Support:** Turmeric, ginger, ashwagandha and other herbs strengthen immunity, calm the mind and improve vitality.

Real-Life Examples:

- **The Corporate Professional Who Regained Energy Through Routine** – For years, Neeraj lived with irregular meals and late nights. After adopting simple Ayurvedic practices—early dinners, warm water and a fixed sleep schedule—his digestion improved, his mood stabilized and his energy increased. **Lesson:** Consistency creates balance, even in a busy life.
- **The Homemaker Who Found Inner Calm Through Ayurvedic Rituals** – Meena started her days with oil pulling, light stretching and herbal tea. These gentle rituals reduced her stress, improved her digestion and gave

her a sense of inner stability. **Lesson:** Small daily rituals transform the mind as much as the body.

An Ayurvedic Lifestyle is not a strict discipline—it is a compassionate way of living in sync with your body's needs. It teaches you to listen deeply, choose mindfully and honour the natural rhythms of life. When you live with awareness and balance, your days flow with ease, your energy becomes steady and your inner world feels peaceful. In Ayurveda lies the wisdom to build a life that is simple, healthy and deeply fulfilling.

Healing Through Balance: Kapha, Vata and Pitta

"Health is harmony; imbalance is the root of disease."

Ayurveda, the ancient science of life, teaches that health is the result of balance—between body, mind and environment. When this balance is disturbed, illness arises. Cough, for example, is not just a standalone symptom but a signal that one or more of the body's three fundamental energies (doshas)—Vata, Pitta and Kapha—are out of balance. Understanding these doshas and their role in respiratory health helps us move beyond quick fixes and embrace holistic healing.

The Ayurvedic View of Cough

Cough in Ayurveda is often linked to disturbances in the doshas:

- **Vata Imbalance** – Causes dry, irritating cough, restlessness and fatigue.
- **Pitta Imbalance** – Leads to burning sensations in the throat, yellowish phlegm and inflammation.
- **Kapha Imbalance** – Associated with heavy mucus, congestion and sluggishness.

While **Kapha** is commonly involved in mucus-related coughs, **Vata** and **Pitta** imbalances often underlie chronic or seasonal respiratory issues.

Why Balance Matters

Ayurveda emphasizes that symptoms are surface indicators of deeper disharmony. Treating only the cough without addressing the root imbalance is like trimming weeds without removing their roots—they will return. True healing comes from restoring equilibrium through diet, lifestyle and natural remedies.

Practical Ways to Relieve Cough by Balancing Vata, Pitta and Kapha

For Cough Relief

- Drink warm herbal teas (ginger, tulsi, licorice).
- Use steam inhalation with eucalyptus or mint.

- Avoid cold, heavy or oily foods that aggravate mucus.

Balancing Vata

- Favour warm, moist and grounding foods like soups, stews, ghee and cooked grains.
- Maintain a regular routine with adequate rest.
- Practice calming activities like yoga, meditation and gentle breathing exercises.

Balancing Pitta

- Choose cooling foods such as cucumbers, melons, leafy greens and coconut water.
- Avoid excessive spicy, oily or fried foods.
- Engage in cooling practices—walks in nature, pranayama and staying hydrated.

Balancing Kapha

- Prefer **warm, light and dry foods**—vegetable soups, steamed greens, lentils; cook with minimal oil.
- Reduce **cold, heavy, sweet and dairy-rich foods**, especially at night, to limit mucus formation.
- Use **warming, stimulating spices**—ginger, black pepper, turmeric, cinnamon—to kindle digestion and clear heaviness.
- Stay **physically active** (brisk walks, yoga, light cardio) to counter Kapha sluggishness.
- Keep the body **warm and dry**; avoid prolonged exposure to cold and damp environments.

The Philosophy Behind Healing

Ayurveda teaches that health is not just about eliminating symptoms—it's about nurturing harmony. When **Vata** is calmed with warmth, **Pitta** cooled with moderation and **Kapha-related** respiratory heaviness is supported with natural remedies, the body regains its natural rhythm. This approach transforms healing into a holistic journey—one that strengthens immunity, restores energy and cultivates peace of mind.

Lifestyle Integration

- **Morning Rituals** – Begin the day with warm water and gentle breathing exercises.
- **Mindful Eating** – Choose seasonal, fresh foods that balance your dominant dosha.

- **Stress Management** – Meditation and yoga help stabilize Vata and cool Pitta.
- **Sleep Hygiene** – Adequate rest restores balance and supports immunity.

Herbal Allies

- **For Vata** – Ashwagandha, ginger and licorice soothe dryness and calm nerves.
- **For Pitta** – Aloe vera, coriander and fennel cool inflammation and reduce heat.
- **For Kapha** – Trikatu (dry ginger, black pepper, long pepper), tulsi, cinnamon and turmeric support digestion, reduce heaviness and help clear excess mucus.

Real-Life Examples:

- **Ethan**, a corporate executive, struggled with recurring dry cough and acidity. His irregular lifestyle—late nights, spicy meals and constant stress—kept worsening his symptoms. An Ayurvedic practitioner identified a **Vata-Pitta** imbalance. Ethan shifted to warm, grounding meals, cooling drinks and a simple daily meditation practice. Within weeks, his cough eased, digestion improved and his energy returned.

Healing begins with restoring balance, not suppressing symptoms. When we listen to the body, honour its needs and align with nature's rhythm, well-being becomes a natural state—not a battle.

The Power of Lighting for a Happy Life

"Lighting is a silent force that shapes your mood, energy and overall wellbeing."

Lighting is one of the most influential yet overlooked elements of daily living. Just as nutrition affects the body and habits shape behaviour, lighting plays a direct role in emotional stability, mental clarity, energy levels and overall wellbeing. The quality, temperature and timing of light significantly impact how we think, feel and function throughout the day.

In modern life, where people spend long hours indoors and constantly interact with digital screens, understanding how lighting influences mood and productivity has become essential. By using lighting intentionally, we can create environments that support happiness, calmness and effectiveness.

Why Lighting Matters

1. Lighting Influences Mood and Emotional Balance

Bright, natural light tends to increase alertness and uplift mood. Warm, soft lighting creates comfort and relaxation. On the other hand, harsh or dim lighting can contribute to irritability, stress or fatigue. The emotional tone of a space is often shaped by its lighting more than its design or furniture.

2. Lighting Regulates the Body's Internal Clock

Light exposure controls circadian rhythm—the body's natural sleep–wake cycle. Morning light signals the brain to become alert, while low, warm evening light prepares it for rest. Excessive exposure to strong artificial or blue light at night can disrupt sleep patterns and reduce overall wellbeing.

3. Lighting Shapes the Quality of Your Environment

Properly planned lighting supports the intended purpose of each area. A workspace requires bright, focused light for concentration, while living spaces benefit from softer tones to promote comfort. Lighting does not only illuminate your surroundings—it influences how you experience them.

4. Lighting Enhances Productivity and Mental Focus

Well-lit environments reduce eye strain, improve focus and support higher levels of cognitive performance. Natural daylight or daylight-simulated bulbs can significantly boost alertness and mental clarity, especially during demanding work hours.

5. Lighting Affects Interpersonal Atmosphere

Warm and balanced lighting fosters a sense of openness and ease, improving communication and connection. Overly bright or cold lighting can create tension or discomfort. Homes and workplaces that use lighting thoughtfully often report better interactions and stronger relationships.

Real-Life Examples:

- **Maria – Improving Sleep Through Evening Lighting -** Maria often struggled with restlessness and poor sleep quality. Her home remained brightly lit with white LED lights until late at night. After switching to warm, low-intensity lamps during the evening, she noticed improved relaxation and better sleep within a week. She understood that her lighting pattern was sending the wrong signals to her internal clock. **Lesson:** Proper evening lighting helped restore healthy sleep routines.

- **David – Increasing Morning Energy with Sunlight Exposure -** David experienced low motivation and sluggish mornings. He rarely saw natural light early in the day. By opening curtains immediately upon waking and spending 10 minutes in natural sunlight, he felt a noticeable improvement in his energy levels and mental alertness. **Lesson:** Morning light exposure became a simple and effective habit for increasing daily productivity.

How to Use Lighting Intentionally

1. **Prioritize Morning Sunlight**
   Expose yourself to natural light within the first hour of waking to support energy and circadian rhythm.
2. **Use Bright Light for Work and Focus**
   Daylight or cool-white bulbs are ideal for concentration and task-oriented activities.
3. **Reserve Warm Lighting for Evenings**
   Soft, warm lighting helps prepare the mind and body for rest.
4. **Minimize Screen Lighting at Night**
   Reduce exposure to blue light by lowering screen brightness or using night-mode settings.
5. **Create Purpose-Specific Lighting Zones**
   Assign lighting based on function: bright light for productivity areas, soft light for relaxation areas and dim light for sleep zones.

Evidence-Based Benefits of Appropriate Lighting

- Improved sleep quality
- Better mood stability
- Higher levels of focus and performance
- Reduced eye strain and mental fatigue
- Greater sense of comfort and emotional ease
- More intentional and pleasant living spaces

Lighting is a practical, controllable factor that significantly shapes daily wellbeing. By understanding how different types of light affect mood, focus and rest, individuals can design environments that support a happier and healthier lifestyle. Simple adjustments—exposure to morning light, using warm lighting in the evening and choosing the right brightness for work—can create meaningful improvements in both mental and emotional health.

The right lighting does not just brighten a room; it enhances the quality of life.

Green Living: How Plants Transform Health and Happiness

"Surround yourself with life—and watch your own life bloom."

Modern living often distances us from nature. Surrounded by screens, walls and artificial lighting, we forget how powerful greenery can be. Plants don't just beautify a space—they support mental clarity, emotional balance and physical well-being. Even a small garden on a balcony or a few pots indoors can reconnect you with calmness, patience and joy.

Benefits of Living Among Plants

- **Cleaner Air:** Indoor plants like snake plant and peace lily naturally filter toxins.
- **Lower Stress:** Greenery reduces cortisol levels and relaxes the mind.
- **Improved Focus:** Studies show plants boost concentration and creativity.
- **Gentle Exercise:** Gardening improves flexibility and encourages movement.
- **Mental Wellness:** Caring for plants builds mindfulness and a sense of accomplishment.

Real-Life Examples:

- **Isha**, an overworked professional, felt drained in her plain apartment. She started with one small plant on her desk. Over time, she added herbs in the kitchen and a flowering pot by the window. Weeks later, she noticed she was calmer during work, her home felt fresher and her weekend gardening became a peaceful ritual. Her mood lifted—simply because she brought a bit of nature indoors.

Simple Ways to Start Green Living

- Begin with easy plants like aloe vera, money plant or peace lily.
- Grow simple herbs—mint, basil, coriander—on a balcony or windowsill.
- Add air-purifying plants near workspaces.
- Use vertical planters if space is limited.
- Join a local gardening group for shared learning and community.

Plants don't just decorate a space—they heal it. Greenery brings freshness, reduces stress and reminds you to slow down. In a fast world, gardening teaches patience, presence and appreciation.

Move With Joy - Sports for Energy, Health & Happiness

"Sports don't just strengthen the body—they energize the mind, lift the spirit and reconnect you with joy."

Playing indoor and outdoor sports is one of the simplest and most powerful ways to improve overall well-being. Sports bring movement, enthusiasm, discipline and a sense of playfulness into life—qualities that adults often lose in the rush of responsibilities. Whether you're playing badminton at home, walking in a garden, joining a local cricket match or simply tossing a ball with children, sports refresh your energy, sharpen your focus and bring back the childlike excitement within you.

Why Sports Matter for a Happy & Healthy Life

Modern lifestyles involve long hours of sitting, screen time and mental overload, which slowly drain physical and emotional vitality. Sports counter this by activating the body, uplifting mood and clearing mental fog. Research shows that regular play—indoor or outdoor—reduces stress, improves cardiovascular health, enhances brain function and boosts emotional resilience. Sports become your natural medicine—keeping you active, alert and emotionally balanced.

Key Benefits of Indoor & Outdoor Sports

- **Better Physical Health:** Sports improve stamina, flexibility, coordination and overall fitness.
- **Stress Relief:** Physical activity releases endorphins—your natural feel-good hormones.

- **Stronger Mind:** Games requiring strategy boost focus, memory and mental clarity.
- **Social Connection:** Outdoor sports help you bond with family, friends and community.
- **Emotional Balance:** Playing regularly reduces anxiety and brings joy, confidence and lightness to life.

Real-Life Examples:

- **The Professional Who Found Daily Joy Through Table Tennis** – Vivek worked long hours and felt mentally tired. He began playing table tennis for 15 minutes during his break. The quick movement and fun competition refreshed his mind and improved his productivity. **Lesson:** Even short bursts of indoor sports can recharge your energy.
- **The Homemaker Who Reconnected with Life Through Evening Walks** – Meera felt stuck in routine. She began joining her neighbour's for evening walks and occasional badminton games in the park. Her mood lifted, her sleep improved and she felt more alive. **Lesson:** Outdoor sports reconnect you with fresh air, movement and community.

Sports remind you to move, play and breathe. They strengthen your body, clear your mind and nourish your emotional well-being. When you make time to play—indoors or outdoors—you bring balance, joy and vitality back into your life. Play not because you have to but because it brings you happiness, health and the freedom of feeling alive.

Joy in Motion — The Everyday Power of Dance

"Dance is not performance; it is permission—permission to feel to breathe and to be joyfully alive."

The power of dance lies in how simply it turns ordinary time into living energy. It brightens mood, softens tension and reconnects you to your body and to people around you. Beyond stages and steps, dance is the most human act of rhythm—available to every age, every ability, in any room with even a little music—or none at all. It supports both a **happy** and **healthy** life because it blends movement, emotion and belonging in a way that feels natural, playful and repeatable.

Why Dance Matters

Modern days are organized around tasks and talk. Dance brings us back to **felt experience**—timing, breath touch and flow. A single song can change the tone of an evening; two minutes of movement can reset an afternoon. Alone, dance reconnects you with yourself; together, it turns strangers into a circle. It is not another item on a wellness checklist; it is a small celebration that keeps returning you to the joy of being alive.

Key Benefits of Dance

- **Happier Mood, Lighter Mind** - Rhythm invites playfulness. As you move, the mind stops bracing and starts releasing and the emotional climate of the day shifts from effort to ease.
- **Everyday Health—Without the Pressure** - Dance builds stamina, balance and coordination yet never demands perfection. It is flexible by design: seated, standing, gentle or vigorous—choose what feels kind to your body today.
- **Embodied Presence** - Steps, sways and turns anchor attention in the present. You feel posture, breath and timing come back into alignment—the body's quiet way of saying "I'm here."
- **Confidence & Expression** - Small, repeatable wins—a rhythm learned, a pattern remembered—build self-belief. When words feel heavy, movement becomes your language.
- **Belonging & Culture** - From folk circles to family gatherings, shared movement creates trust. Traditions live through feet and drums; communities remember themselves in rhythm.
- **Accessible for Life** - No special gear, no perfect space. A hallway, a kitchen, a courtyard, a chair—dance meets you where you are.

Real-Life Examples:

- **The Three-Minute Reset** - After long shifts, **Nadia** reached home flat—present but not really *there*. She tried a simple rule: before anything else, play one song in the kitchen and move however the day allowed—sometimes just shoulders and hands, sometimes a full-room sway with her son. The house brightened in those three minutes; conversations softened; dinner felt less like duty, more like a small celebration. **Lesson:** A tiny ritual of dance can turn a tired evening into a warm one.
- **The Circle That Held Everyone** - At a community hall, **Ravi** helped start a monthly "open rhythm" evening. No choreography—just a loop of familiar songs where elders clapped seated, teenagers tried steps and little ones ran circles between them. Over months, neighbours who barely nodded in the lift began sharing snacks, stories and steps. - **Lesson:** Dance creates belonging first, polish later; people return for the feeling, not the form.

Simple Ways to Let Dance Support a Happy, Healthy Life

- **One-Song Rituals** - Pick one track for morning lightness or evening wind-down. Let the song be the timer—no negotiation, no guilt.
- **Kitchen Two-Step -** While waiting for the kettle or the pan, sway, step or shimmy. Small moments add up without stealing time.

- **Chair Dance for All Ages** - Hands, shoulders, head and torso—gentle movements to a favourite melody keep rhythm alive even on low-energy days.
- **Circle Moments** - Weekly family or friends' "song time." One person chooses, all join—standing, seated or clapping. Make it playful, not perfect.
- **Soundless Dance** - When music isn't possible, dance to your own breath. Count four steps in, four steps out—movement as quiet presence.

Dance asks for very little and gives back a great deal. It brightens mood without analysis, moves the body without pressure and gathers people without speeches. In a world of schedules and screens, dance is a small, stubborn act of humanity—joy made visible.

You do not need a studio or an audience; you only need a rhythm. Begin with one song. Let your body remember what your mind forgot: **you were made to move to feel and to belong.**

Family, Friends & Community: The True Pillars of a Good Life

"The best gift you can give your family is your time."

"A strong life is built not on possessions but on the people who stand beside us."

In the pursuit of achievement, many forget the relationships that make life meaningful. Family, friends and community form the foundation of emotional strength, belonging and happiness. When these bonds are strong, life feels balanced. When they weaken, even success feels empty.

1. Family: Your First Circle of Strength

Family offers identity, emotional safety and unconditional support. Quality time is less about hours and more about presence and attention.

Why Family Time Matters

- Builds emotional security
- Strengthens trust and communication
- Reinforces values and belonging
- Reminds us what true success means

How to Make It Meaningful

- Eat meals together
- Have real conversations
- Create small rituals — walks, weekend routines, game nights etc.

Even a few minutes of undistracted time can build lifelong connection. Family doesn't slow success — it strengthens you to achieve it.

2. Friends: The Family You Choose

Friends add joy, perspective and emotional balance. They celebrate your wins, support you through losses and help you grow.

Why Friendships Matter

- Reduce loneliness and stress
- Provide honest feedback and understanding
- Add laughter, learning and shared experiences
- Offer a safe space for emotional expression

A strong friendship often heals what work stress cannot.

3. Community: Belonging Beyond Home

Community widens your support network beyond family and friends — neighbours, colleagues, groups, shared spaces.

Why Community Matters

- Offers shared experiences and collective wisdom
- Creates purpose through contribution and involvement
- Expands your sense of belonging
- Provides support during difficult times

People thrive when they feel connected to something larger than themselves.

4. How These Bonds Improve Life

- **Emotional Stability -** Supportive relationships reduce anxiety and strengthen resilience.
- **Better Health -** Social connection improves longevity, mental well-being and recovery from illness.
- **Purpose & Fulfilment -** Caring for others — and being cared for — brings meaning beyond material success.
- **Resilience in Hard Times -** During crises, relationships act as emotional and practical support.
- **Shared Joy -** Every celebration, moment and achievement becomes richer when shared.

5. Strengthening Your Relationships

- **Be Present:** Show up emotionally, not just physically.
- **Give Time:** Consistent, intentional time deepens bonds.
- **Practice Gratitude:** Appreciate the people who support you.
- **Stay Connected:** Regular messages, calls or visits keep relationships alive.
- **Join Community:** Participate, contribute and take part in shared activities.
- **Offer Help:** Support others without expectation — kindness always returns.

Family roots you. Friends uplift you. Community surrounds you.

Together, they create emotional strength, mental peace and a fulfilling life. Material success adds comfort — but relationships add meaning. A good life is not built by standing alone but by standing together.

Chapter 11: Health Mindset & Protection

Your Greatest Wealth: Your Health

"A healthy body and a peaceful mind are life's greatest assets."

In a world where people chase careers, money, recognition and success, it becomes easy to forget the foundation that holds everything together: **your health**. Without health, even the simplest tasks feel overwhelming. With health, even the biggest challenges feel manageable. Health is not just the absence of illness—it is the presence of energy, clarity, balance and emotional stability. It is waking up refreshed, moving without pain, thinking without fog and living without constant exhaustion.

Health shapes your decisions, your confidence, your relationships and your overall happiness. You can always earn money again, rebuild your career or restart your life—but you cannot borrow health from anyone. You cannot replace your body. That is why health isn't just important—**it is your real wealth.**

Why Health Is the Real Wealth

Health makes every part of life easier. When your body is strong and your mind is clear, your productivity rises, your decisions improve and your mood stabilizes. Healthy living reduces irritability, protects emotional well-being and strengthens the bonds you have with loved ones. A calm and balanced mind communicates better and loves better. Health also prevents financial strain—poor health is costly physically, emotionally and financially. When health is strong, life feels stable. When health declines, everything else begins to shake.

What Health Truly Means

Health is a complete picture—not just the physical but the mental, emotional and lifestyle aspects of your life.

Physical health means strength, stamina, mobility, good sleep, strong immunity and proper nourishment. **Mental health** means clarity, focus, calmness and resilience.

Emotional health means balance, awareness and steady relationships. **Lifestyle health** means daily routines, mindful habits, rest and mindful living.

True wealth comes from taking care of *all* these dimensions, not just one.

Why People Ignore Health Until It Fails

Modern living subtly pushes people into habits that weaken well-being—irregular schedules, fast food, digital overload, lack of sleep, constant stress and long periods without movement. People postpone self-care, telling themselves "I'll start tomorrow." But health listens only to actions, not promises. Ignoring your health is like ignoring the foundation of your home—the structure above becomes shaky, no matter how impressive it looks.

How to Treat Health as Your Wealth

Good health doesn't require extreme effort; it requires gentle and consistent care. Guard your sleep as if it's your most precious currency, because a rested mind solves problems a tired mind creates. Eat with awareness instead of rushing; food becomes medicine when consumed mindfully. Move your body daily—even 20 minutes changes your energy. Drink water often; hydration improves clarity, digestion and mood. Protect your mind from noise by reducing unnecessary screens and setting emotional boundaries. Create simple wellness rituals: morning sunlight, an evening walk, stretching, breathing or gratitude. Listen to your body and respond early; health improves when habits improve.

Real-Life Examples:

- **Kael — Realizing Strength Comes Before Success** - Kael worked hard, earned well and was rising quickly in his career—but his health was collapsing quietly. Late nights, skipped meals and constant stress finally caught up to him when he felt faint during an important meeting. That moment changed everything. He rearranged his routine: morning walks, proper meals, earlier sleep and reduced screen time. Within weeks, his energy returned and his mind sharpened. He understood that success rests on the foundation of health—not the other way around.
- **Daria — Rebuilding Her Life Through Simple Daily Habits** - Daria often felt tired, anxious and disconnected. She assumed something was wrong with her life but it was her health that needed attention. She began sleeping earlier, drinking more water, eating simple nourishing foods and practicing deep breathing before bed. Slowly, her mood stabilized and her energy returned. She realised that when the body heals, life heals with it.

Your body is your home, your mind is your engine and your habits are the builders of your future. Money and achievements lose meaning when the body is weak or the mind is tired. But when you are healthy, everything becomes easier—your relationships, your work, your dreams and your daily experiences. Health is not a cost; it is an investment. It is not optional; it is foundational. Protect your strength, honor your body and choose a lifestyle where health supports your happiness every single day.

Your Body Is a Temple - Protect It with Respect and Discipline

"You live in your body every moment of your life. Treat it like the sacred space it is."

Your body is more than a physical form — it is the home of your mind, your emotions, your energy, your dreams and your spirit. It carries you through every season of your life: your joys, your struggles, your victories and your healing. Yet many people treat their bodies casually — eating without thought, drinking without limits, consuming disturbing content, ignoring the body's signals and allowing habits that quietly weaken health and clarity.

But when you begin to see your body as a **temple**, everything changes. You naturally become mindful of what you eat, drink, watch, listen to, speak and tolerate. A temple is kept clean, peaceful and pure — not because of rules but because its purpose deserves respect.

Your body deserves the same honor.
Your mind deserves the same protection.
Your inner world deserves the same purity.

What "Body Is a Temple" Really Means

This principle is simple: everything you allow inside — through your mouth, your eyes, your ears, your thoughts and your habits — becomes part of you. Good inputs elevate your energy; poor inputs drain it.

Healthy food strengthens the body.
Clean drinks preserve clarity.
Uplifting words soothe emotions.
Peaceful sounds calm the mind.
Positive images nourish the subconscious.
Good habits build your future.

A temple is protected from within — not from outside forces but by the choices we make every day.

The Subtle Ways We Harm Our Inner Temple

People often damage their body and mind without realizing it. Mindless junk food, late-night eating, sugary drinks and artificial stimulants weaken the system slowly. Disturbing videos, negative conversations, gossip and emotional chaos pollute the mind. Harsh speech, uncontrolled anger and living in constant noise disturb inner balance. Stress, irregular routines and ignoring the body's signals deepen the impact. Each negative input leaves a mark — small at first, then deeper over time. When your inner space becomes polluted, clarity fades, peace disappears and motivation weakens.

How to Honor Your Body as a Sacred Space

Honoring your body does not require perfection — only awareness.

- Choose cleaner food and calming drinks.
- Consume content that lifts your mind, not content that leaves it anxious.
- Surround yourself with uplifting conversations.
- Speak gently.
- Reduce noise.
- Disconnect from negativity.
- Protect your peace with intention.
- A clean body creates a clean mind.
- A clean mind creates a clean life.
  When your inner world is light, your outer life becomes beautiful.

Real-Life Examples:

- **Aarav — Transforming His Life by Respecting His Body** - Aarav had unknowingly slipped into unhealthy routines — late-night eating, sugary drinks, endless news cycles and occasional weekend drinking. His body felt heavy, his mind dull. One night he reflected deeply: he was demanding so much from his body while giving so little in return. He made small but consistent changes — cleaner meals, peaceful music, mindful content and gentle speech. Within weeks, his energy lifted, stress reduced and clarity returned. He realised the body responds like a temple: it shines when you treat it with respect.
- **Elina — Protecting Her Mind From Emotional Noise** - Elina ate well but consumed emotional pollution daily — overthinking, arguing, gossip, negative influencers and disturbing videos. Her mind felt crowded even when nothing was wrong. She began choosing positive content, distancing herself from negative circles and practicing silence before sleep. Slowly, her inner world softened. Her confidence grew. She felt lighter. She learned that the quality of your thoughts becomes the quality of your life.

You have only one body and one mind for your entire lifetime. Treat them with dignity. Fill your life with clean food, clean thoughts, clean content and clean habits. When you honor your body like a temple, you protect your peace, strengthen your health and elevate your happiness. Respect your inner space — and life will reward you with clarity, energy and joy.

PART V — Relationships, Family & Community

Understand how clarity, compassion and boundaries transform relationships

Chapter 12: Family Harmony & Home Peace

Clarity Within Family - Avoiding Clashes and Living in Harmony

"Families don't break because of problems; they break because of silence around problems."

Families may love deeply yet misunderstandings can arise quietly. Conflicts rarely start with one big incident — they grow slowly through unspoken expectations, unclear responsibilities, emotional assumptions, generational differences, ego clashes, money confusion, parenting disagreements and outside influences. Most family tension is not intentional; it is the result of **missing clarity**.

Clarity brings transparency.
Clarity reduces assumptions.
Clarity protects peace.

When families speak openly and listen without ego, problems dissolve before they become wounds. Clarity turns emotional chaos into emotional safety.

Why Clashes Really Happen

Family conflicts usually begin in small, unnoticed ways — a misunderstood comment, a financial assumption, someone feeling unappreciated or a decision made without discussion. Over time, these small emotional threads become tight knots. Different personalities, generational beliefs and daily stress add friction. Without clarity, even a minor issue becomes a battle of interpretations.

When expectations, boundaries or feelings are not expressed clearly, people start imagining the worst, even when no harm was intended. Silence becomes noise. Distance grows without anyone meaning to cause hurt.

How Clarity Creates Harmony

Clarity brings order into relationships. When everyone understands their roles, responsibilities, money matters and decision-making processes, emotional pressure instantly reduces. People feel respected when they are informed, safe when their boundaries are honored and valued when their opinions are heard.

Clarity strengthens trust by eliminating guesswork. It transforms interactions from reactive to calm, from defensive to understanding. When everyone knows where they stand, the home becomes a place of comfort rather than tension.

Simple Ways to Maintain Clarity at Home

Clarity thrives on small daily practices. Talk before assuming. Share feelings calmly instead of silently collecting hurt. Listen without preparing your defence. Discuss money openly and early. Make decisions together when they affect everyone. Respect differences, knowing every family member has a unique personality and perspective.

Quick repairs matter — a gentle apology, a clarifying conversation or a moment of understanding can prevent days of emotional distance. Clear boundaries, honest communication and timely discussions create peace. And when unsure, choose kindness — it calms situations more effectively than logic.

Real-Life Examples:

- **Leander — Resolving Tension Through Simple Transparency -** Leander lived with his parents in a joint household where monthly expenses created silent stress. No one spoke openly and misunderstandings kept growing. One weekend, the family sat together and created a simple list dividing responsibilities. The moment clarity arrived, the tension disappeared. Leander realised that families don't break because of money — they break because no one talks about it.

- **Sorrel — Turning Arguments Into Teamwork** - Sorrel and her husband disagreed frequently about decisions for their child. Both cared deeply but both assumed the other "should understand." She introduced a weekly 10-minute discussion to align decisions calmly. Within weeks, arguments reduced and cooperation grew. They discovered that clarity transforms two individuals into a team.

Family conflict is rarely a sign of weak relationships — it is a sign of unclear communication. When you express openly, listen respectfully and set simple boundaries, misunderstandings fade naturally. Clarity turns tension into teamwork and creates a home where everyone feels safe, respected and understood. A clear family is a peaceful family — and peace at home is the foundation of a happy life.

Family Rituals - The Heartbeat of Togetherness

"Families grow closer not by chance but by the small rituals repeated with love."

In today's fast-moving world, families often live together physically but drift apart emotionally. Everyone is present at home yet mentally pulled into work, screens, deadlines and routines. Relationships weaken not because love is missing but because **shared time is missing**. This is where **family rituals** make all the difference.

Family rituals are the small, steady moments that create belonging — a daily dinner, a shared walk, a Sunday outing, an evening tea break, a weekly family night or even 30 minutes of genuine conversation. These rituals don't require perfect timing, expensive plans or dramatic effort. They simply require presence, intention and consistency.

When families practice rituals, a house transforms into a home — a place to bond, laugh, heal and grow together.

Why Family Rituals Matter So Much

Rituals bring warmth, stability and emotional security into daily life. They reduce misunderstandings, lower stress and create shared memories that stay for years. Parents understand children better. Children feel emotionally safe. Couples stay connected. Elders feel included and valued.

Rituals create predictability — and predictability creates peace. Even 15–30 minutes of shared time each day can completely shift the emotional atmosphere of a home.

Daily Rituals That Strengthen Bonds

Daily rituals don't have to be long — they only need sincerity. Dinner together builds closeness through stories, conversations and laughter. A short window of togetherness — after dinner, before bed or early morning — brings calm connection. Even simple acts like sharing tea, folding laundry together, taking a small walk or helping with homework create strong emotional foundations. Daily rituals tell your family: ***"You matter. Our time together matters."***

Weekly Rituals That Build Connection

Weekly rituals give families something to look forward to. A small outing — a park visit, a café breakfast, a nature walk, a movie or a temple visit — refreshes the entire family. A weekly family night with games, music or storytelling deepens bonding. A short weekly planning circle reduces conflict and helps everyone feel involved. These rituals become emotional anchors that children remember even as adults.

Real-Life Examples:

- **Rafael — Rebuilding Connection Through Simple Rituals** - Rafael's home was full of activity but everyone stayed in their own digital bubble. He introduced one small ritual: dinner together every night. Within days, emotional distance began to fade. Conversations restarted. Laughter returned. Even his quiet teenage daughter began opening up.

He realised that family bonds grow strongest around the dinner table — not around screens.

- **Meera — Finding Balance Through Weekly Family Time** - As a working mother, Meera often felt guilty about not spending enough time with her family. Instead of trying to be perfect, she started a Saturday morning ritual — a simple homemade breakfast followed by a short outdoor walk. Those two hours became the brightest part of their week. Her children felt seen, her husband felt connected and she felt emotionally renewed. She learned that even one consistent ritual can turn a busy home into a loving one.

Family rituals may look small but their impact is deep. They turn houses into homes, relatives into companions and ordinary days into meaningful memories. When families commit to simple rituals — daily meals, shared conversations, weekly outings and small acts of togetherness — they build trust, warmth and connection that last a lifetime. Keep your rituals simple, practice them with heart and your family will feel the love long after the moment has passed.

Clean Surroundings for a Happy & Healthy Life

"A clean space creates a clean mind. When your environment is light, your heart becomes light too."

Your surroundings influence your emotions more than you realise. A clean home, a tidy desk, an organized room or a well-maintained outdoor area carries an invisible power — it calms the mind, reduces stress, improves focus and lifts your mood. Clutter, on the other hand, creates mental noise. It drains your energy, scatters your attention and makes even simple tasks feel heavier.

Cleanliness is not just about hygiene; it is about **clarity order, peace and mental freshness**. When your environment is clean, your inner world becomes cleaner too. A clean space is a quiet form of self-respect.

How Clean Surroundings Influence Your Life

Your environment is constantly talking to your mind. A clean desk improves concentration. A neat room brings emotional comfort. A fresh home reduces anxiety. An organized kitchen encourages healthier choices. A tidy workspace increases productivity. A clean outdoor space invites movement and positivity. Small acts of cleanliness create big shifts inside you — your mind becomes quieter, your body feels lighter and your day feels more manageable.

Why Many People Struggle With Cleanliness

Modern life keeps people busy and distracted. Clutter builds slowly: papers piling on tables, clothes left on chairs, dishes waiting in the sink, files crowding digital screens and notifications filling the phone. Before you notice, mess becomes the "new normal."

But clutter isn't harmless. It drains mental energy, slows your work, disrupts your routines and quietly increases stress. Even visual mess — a crowded shelf, a chaotic desk, an unmade bed — triggers emotional tension. Cleaning is not just a household chore; it is **emotional maintenance**.

How to Keep Your Surroundings Clean (Without Stress)

Cleanliness doesn't require hours of effort — it requires small, consistent actions. Put things back where they belong. Clear your desk before sleeping. Begin mornings with a simple five-minute tidy-up. Keep only what you actually use. Don't allow small messes to grow into big clutter. In shared spaces, involve everyone because a peaceful environment is everyone's responsibility.
A clean environment is created through routine, not pressure.

Real-Life Examples:

- **Jovan — A Clear Desk, A Clear Mind** - Jovan often felt overwhelmed at work. His desk was piled with old notes, cables and unnecessary items. One afternoon, he decided to declutter — keeping only what he truly needed. The change was immediate. His thoughts felt sharper, his attention steadier and his productivity smoother. He realised a clean desk is more than physical order — it is **mental order**.
- **Priya — Discovering Peace Through a Clean Home** - Priya lived in a busy household where clutter slowly accumulated. She introduced a simple ritual: ten minutes of tidying one small corner every evening. In a week, her home felt brighter. In a month, her stress softened. She found joy returning to her daily life — not because her home became perfect but because it became peaceful. She learned that a clean home creates a **clean mind**.

Your surroundings shape your thoughts, your emotions and your energy. A clean space invites clarity and calmness, while clutter creates noise and confusion. When you care for your environment — your home, your desk, your open spaces — you protect your inner world from unnecessary stress. Cleanliness may look small but its impact on happiness and health is profound. Keep your surroundings light and your life will feel lighter too.

The Peaceful Home - A Sanctuary for the Mind and Heart

"A peaceful home is not defined by how it looks but by how it feels."

Creating a peaceful home means transforming your living space into a sanctuary—one that calms your mind, comforts your heart and supports your daily well-being. A peaceful home doesn't need luxury or perfection. It requires intention. When your surroundings feel balanced, your thoughts settle, your stress reduces and your energy becomes lighter. Your home becomes a reflection of your inner world—and a space where healing, clarity and joy can grow.

Why a Peaceful Home Matters

In today's fast-paced life, your home should be a place where you can breathe freely, disconnect from noise and reconnect with yourself. Yet clutter, chaos, screens and constant activity silently drain your mental energy. Research shows that organized, restful spaces lower stress levels, improve sleep and enhance emotional stability. A peaceful home supports healthier relationships, better focus and a happier state of mind.

Key Elements of a Peaceful Home

- **Clutter-Free Spaces:** A clean environment creates a clear mind and reduces emotional heaviness.
- **Soft Lighting & Natural Air:** Warm light and fresh air bring calmness into every corner.
- **Nature Elements:** Plants, sunlight and natural textures ground your emotions.
- **Quiet Corners:** A small space for reflection, reading or meditation nurtures inner peace.
- **Mindful Use of Screens:** Reducing noise and digital distractions brings harmony into the home.

Real-Life Examples:

- **The Couple Who Reduced Stress by Decluttering Their Living Room** – Their home looked full yet felt heavy. After removing unused items, adding plants and choosing warm lighting, the room felt lighter, calmer and more welcoming. **Lesson:** A peaceful home begins with what you choose to remove.
- **The Working Mother Who Created a 'Calm Corner'** – With a small mat, a candle and a journal, she created a space where she spent five quiet minutes each morning. These moments improved her patience, emotional

stability and daily happiness. **Lesson:** Even a small peaceful space can change the energy of your entire home.

A peaceful home is created through intention—not expense. When you design your space with care, your home becomes a sanctuary where your mind rests, your heart heals and your life feels aligned. In a peaceful home, you rediscover clarity, comfort and the joy of simply being.

Effective Parenting - Guiding with Love, Wisdom and Presence

"Children don't need perfect parents—they need present, patient and emotionally grounded ones."

Effective parenting is not about control, perfection or strict rules. It is about guiding your child with love, understanding and mindful presence. Children learn more from what you *are* than from what you *say*. They watch your tone, your habits, your reactions and your values—and that becomes their emotional blueprint. Parenting is a journey of shaping young minds while also growing yourself. When you parent with awareness, you raise confident, secure and emotionally balanced children.

Why Effective Parenting Matters

The emotional environment in which a child grows becomes the foundation of their entire life. A supportive home builds self-esteem; a harsh home builds fear. A peaceful home builds stability; a chaotic home builds insecurity. Research in child psychology shows that children develop stronger emotional intelligence, better behaviour and healthier relationships when parents are patient, emotionally stable and communicative. You are not just raising a child—you are raising the adult they will become.

Key Principles of Effective Parenting

- **Listen Deeply:** Children open up when they feel heard, not judged.
- **Guide, Don't Control:** Give direction, not domination—let them learn through choices.
- **Be a Role Model:** Your behaviour teaches more than your words.
- **Show Unconditional Love:** A child must feel loved even when they make mistakes.
- **Set Healthy Boundaries:** Structure gives security; discipline gives direction.
- **Value Effort, Not Just Results:** This builds confidence and resilience.

Real-Life Examples:

- **The Parent Who Built Trust Through Calm Communication** – Rishi's son often threw tantrums. Instead of reacting with anger, Rishi practiced calm conversations, explaining emotions and offering choices. Over time, the tantrums decreased and the child felt more understood. **Lesson:** Connection reduces conflict.
- **The Mother Who Helped Her Daughter Grow with Encouragement** – Rina's daughter feared trying new activities. By appreciating effort rather than success, Rina slowly built her daughter's confidence. The child began participating more and enjoying new experiences. **Lesson:** Encouragement creates courage.

Effective parenting is a blend of love, patience, boundaries and presence. When you guide children with empathy and wisdom, you shape strong minds and gentle hearts. Your child will not remember every instruction—but they will remember how you made them feel. Create a home where they feel safe, valued and loved. In that environment, children grow—not just taller but happier and wiser.

Chapter 13: Friendship, Participation & Social Joy

Cultivate a Close Friends Group - Your Circle of Strength

"Happiness multiplies when shared and sadness becomes lighter when someone stands beside you."

Friends are the family we choose. In a world filled with busyness, distraction and endless responsibilities, having a small circle of close friends becomes one of life's greatest emotional supports. These are the people who celebrate your victories without envy and sit with you in silence when words are not enough. They don't need explanations, they don't wait for perfect timing — they show up because they care.

A strong friendship circle is not about quantity; it is about depth. Even two or three genuine friends can transform your emotional well-being. When you nurture such friendships intentionally, you are never alone — not in joy, not in grief, not in change and not in uncertainty. You carry a support system that makes life feel lighter, warmer and more meaningful.

Why a Close Friends Group Matters

Close friendships offer emotional support during difficult phases. Sometimes a simple conversation with a trusted friend can calm anxiety, bring clarity and make a heavy day feel manageable. Happiness also expands when shared — victories feel brighter and celebrations feel deeper when friends are part of them. Strong friendships reduce loneliness, even when life gets busy, because one message or one call can uplift the entire day.

Friends who accept your flaws, dreams and fears create a safe emotional space where you can be your true self. These bonds strengthen mental health, reduce stress and improve emotional stability. A close group of friends becomes an emotional safety net — invisible but always there.

What Makes a Friendship Deep and Reliable

Depth grows through consistency — not talking daily but showing up when it matters. Loyalty strengthens trust; keeping confidence and standing by each other builds emotional safety. Honesty, shared gently, keeps the bond authentic. Mutual effort — checking in, forgiving, supporting — ensures balance. And presence in both joy and pain turns friendships into lifelong connections. Real friendship is not measured by years but by sincerity.

How to Cultivate Your Close Friends Group

Strong friendships require intention. Invest time, not just messages — meet occasionally, call unexpectedly, plan simple moments. Be the friend you want to have: warm, reliable, honest and empathetic. Create shared rituals — maybe a monthly dinner, a weekend walk or a festival evening together. Offer help without being asked; true support is proactive. Celebrate their successes with full heart and stay connected without conditions. Friendships grow when nurtured consistently — not when taken for granted.

Real-Life Examples

- **Arlo and His Two Steady Friends — Connection Across Distance** - When Arlo moved abroad for work, he feared losing touch with the friends who mattered most. Instead, they created a simple ritual: a Sunday video call where they shared highlights, challenges and jokes from the week. This ritual kept their bond alive. Even though miles separated them, the friendship kept Arlo emotionally grounded. He felt lighter knowing he had two people who truly held space for him.
- **Mireya's Support Circle During Her Hardest Season** - When Mireya faced a sudden health challenge, her three close friends formed a quiet circle of care around her. They joined her for appointments, brought meals, handled small errands and kept her spirits high. Their presence didn't cure her illness but it healed her loneliness and fear. She realised that life becomes manageable when you have people who don't wait to be asked — they simply show up.

A close group of friends is not a luxury — it is emotional nourishment. You don't need many; you only need a few who understand you, care for you and stand beside you in every season. These friendships create joy in ordinary moments and strength in difficult ones. Build the circle that builds you — nurture your friendships, invest in them and let them grow with you. A happy life is never built alone; it is built together with the people who lift your spirit and lighten your heart.

Involve Yourself - The Happiness of Participation

"Joy blooms when you stop standing at the edge of life and start stepping into it."

Many people move through life as observers—attending events, visiting gatherings, joining celebrations—yet never truly participating. They smile politely, remain on the sidelines and behave like guests even in spaces where they belong.

But happiness grows not in watching life happen; it grows in **joining, engaging, helping and contributing**. The moment you involve yourself, you break the invisible wall between you and the world. You shift from "*I am here*" to "*I am part of this*" and that single shift invites belonging, emotional warmth, connection, confidence and the quiet joy that comes from contribution. Ordinary moments turn into memories. Gatherings become community. Community becomes happiness.

Why Participation Matters for a Happy Life

Modern routines often leave people feeling isolated even in crowds. Work pressure, digital distraction and busyness make it easy to attend a wedding, festival, birthday or community function and still stay emotionally distant. Involvement is where joy lives. When you take part, you feel useful; when you contribute, you feel connected; when you help, you feel valued. Participation transforms the mindset from "*guest" to "family*," from "*outsider" to "one of us.*" That shift nourishes happiness because meaning is created through **shared effort**, not mere presence.

The Reality of Staying on the Sidelines

Standing apart looks comfortable but slowly empties the heart. You are there physically yet your emotions stand at a distance. Others bond over shared tasks while you only observe; the event passes and you are not part of the story. Afterward, regret arrives—you could have interacted more, contributed more, felt more alive. Non-participation quietly erodes social ease and confidence shrinks each time you choose distance over presence.

What It Means to Involve Yourself

Involvement is simple: **help without being asked, join what's happening and treat every event as your own**. Offer a hand at a family function, carry chairs at a community meet, greet people warmly, appreciate someone's effort, suggest an idea or simply start a small conversation with kindness. Participation is rarely about special skill; it is about **showing up with heart**. When you include yourself, you feel included.

Real-Life Examples:

- **Pavel — Finding Joy Through Small Acts** - Pavel had long attended family functions quietly—eat, smile, leave. One holiday, he offered to set up lights and organize a quick game for the children. The house filled with laughter, the elders smiled, the kids cheered—and something shifted inside him. For the first time, he felt **part** of the celebration, not just present in it. Joy arrived the moment he stopped observing and started participating.
- **Nia — Choosing Involvement Over Distance** - At neighborhood gatherings, Nia often stood alone, scrolling her phone. One evening she

stepped in to plate the desserts and welcome guests at the door. Conversations opened, warmth followed and she left with new friends. The event felt different because she was different. Her happiness grew the moment she chose involvement over distance.

Life doesn't reward spectators; it rewards participants. When you involve yourself—serve, help, laugh and engage—you feel emotionally alive. You are not a guest in your own life; you are the host. The more you join, the more you belong; the more you contribute, the richer your happiness becomes. Participation is not just an action—it is a doorway to a joyful life.

Social Gathering for Happiness

"Human hearts light up when they meet. Joy grows in places where people come together."

Social gatherings—whether big or small, formal or casual—carry a quiet magic. They remind us that life is not meant to be lived alone. When people come together with warmth, openness and shared intention, happiness rises naturally. It doesn't need to be a grand event; even simple moments—tea with neighbors, dinner with friends, a family evening, a community meet or an office celebration—can nourish the heart.

In a world where digital conversations often replace real presence, gatherings reconnect us to something ancient and essential: **belonging**. Being with people—laughing, talking, helping, sharing—softens the heart, reduces stress, strengthens relationships and adds colour to life. Happiness grows when you allow yourself to be part of something bigger than your routine.

Why Social Gatherings Matter for Happiness

Human beings are built for companionship. We thrive in shared experiences, collective laughter and emotional support. But modern life often creates distance—packed schedules, screen habits, introverted routines and the fear of "disturbing others."Yet joy lives in involvement.

When you join the circle, you feel connected.
When you contribute, you feel valued.
When you participate, you feel alive.

Gatherings give a sense of belonging, keep the mind active, deepen relationships and create shared memories that stay long after the event ends. They show us that life becomes richer when we show up with presence, not just attendance.

How Social Gatherings Bring Joy

Shared moments create emotional warmth—happiness multiplies when experiences are shared, not stored. Laughter reduces stress and resets the mind. Participation builds confidence because contributing makes you feel meaningful. A supportive community creates safety, reminding you that you are not alone. Exposure to different cultures, stories and personalities expands your mind. And togetherness reduces loneliness, offering emotional stability and comfort.

How to Be an Active Part of Social Gatherings

Participation is simple: offer help, join conversations and be present instead of self-conscious. Appreciate others openly. Include someone who seems alone. Contribute your energy to the atmosphere—arrange something, support someone or simply listen with interest. Good gatherings don't require perfection; they require presence. When you join with heart, you become part of the memory instead of watching it pass by.

Real-Life Examples:

- **Milan — Finding Happiness Through Involvement** - Milan attended office gatherings for years but always stayed in the corner, observing rather than engaging. One celebration, he offered to manage the music and welcome people at the door. That small act changed everything. Conversations opened, colleagues warmed up to him and he felt surprisingly lighter. His joy came not from attending—but from becoming part of the moment.
- **Reina — Rebuilding Confidence Through Community** - Reina moved to a new city and felt isolated. She attended neighborhood events but remained quiet out of fear of judgment. One day, she helped arrange chairs and serve tea. That simple participation created warmth—people approached her, conversations flowed and invitations increased. Slowly, her confidence returned. She realised that involvement creates happiness faster than waiting for others to notice you.

Social gatherings are emotional anchors—reminders that joy is shared, not solitary. You don't need to be the center of attention; you only need to be present with an open heart. When you involve yourself instead of standing apart, you find community. When you find community, you find joy. And in these shared moments, you often find yourself.

Chapter 14: Communication, Compassion & Boundaries

Emotional Intimacy - A Path to Happiness and Health

"Closeness is not created by words alone; it is built by presence, care and trust."

Emotional intimacy is the quiet strength behind every fulfilling relationship. It is the comfort of being seen, understood and accepted—not because you are perfect but because you feel safe to be yourself. This intimacy grows when two people choose respect instead of ego, listening instead of winning and presence instead of distraction. In a fast-moving world, emotional closeness slows us down just enough to feel human again.

True intimacy is simple and gentle. It lives in small acts: warmth in your tone, kindness in daily routines, attention when someone speaks, forgiveness when tension rises and generosity when interpreting each other's words. When emotional intimacy is strong, happiness deepens, health stabilizes and life feels lighter—even in difficult seasons.

Why Emotional Intimacy Matters Today

Modern life often confuses connection with contact. We communicate constantly but feel understood rarely. Emotional intimacy bridges this gap. It turns partners into companions, families into supportive teams and homes into places of safety and peace. It encourages honest conversations, patient listening and a sense of belonging that reduces anxiety and softens frustration.

Intimacy simplifies life. When trust is high, there is less overthinking, fewer misunderstandings and less need to defend or perform. Decisions become easier, priorities clearer and the smallest shared moments start to feel meaningful. A relationship rich in intimacy becomes a basecamp for growth—both people feel supported enough to pursue their purpose without emotional fear.

The Foundations of Emotional Intimacy

Emotional intimacy grows through consistent presence. Giving full attention during meals, walks or evening conversations turns small moments into meaningful ones. Respectful honesty—speaking truth kindly and receiving feedback calmly—builds trust that survives pressure. Assuming goodwill prevents unnecessary hurt, as most pain comes from stress rather than intention. Repairing conflicts quickly keeps emotional distance from forming. And simple shared rituals—a morning check-in, an evening walk, reading together for a few minutes—create anchors that protect warmth and connection.

How Emotional Intimacy Supports Happiness and Health

When a relationship is emotionally safe, the mind becomes calmer and overthinking reduces. Kind communication stabilizes emotions, trust improves decision-making and companionship strengthens resilience during stressful periods. Even ordinary moments—tea together, a shared chore, light laughter—begin to feel soothing and joyful. Emotional intimacy turns everyday life into something gentler and more meaningful.

Real-Life Examples:

- **Rafael & Mira — Rebuilding Connection Through Presence** - Rafael and Mira often ended their evenings tired, distracted by screens and unaware of each other's feelings. They decided to create a simple ritual: a 20-minute phone-free conversation every night. One speaks, the other listens, then they switch. No judging, no fixing—just attention. Within weeks, their home felt warmer. Arguments reduced, understanding grew and even stressful days ended with a sense of closeness. Their relationship changed not through big efforts but through consistent presence.
- **Jonah & Elise — Strengthening Their Bond Through Gentle Repair** - Jonah and Elise found themselves caught in recurring small conflicts. Instead of letting tension build, they agreed to pause whenever emotions rose and return calmly to share one feeling and one need. This small habit changed their dynamic. Conflicts ended sooner, empathy deepened and both felt emotionally safe. They learned that intimacy grows when repair matters more than being right.

Emotional intimacy is created not by dramatic gestures but by daily presence, gentle honesty and small moments of warmth. When two people choose to connect rather than compete, listen rather than react and repair rather than blame, their relationship becomes a place of peace. Intimacy turns a house into a refuge and life into a shared journey. When closeness is nurtured, happiness rises and health finds a place to rest.

Do Not Think Too Much About Anyone

"Overthinking about people drains peace, energy and clarity"

Life becomes unnecessarily difficult when your mind keeps circling around someone—what they said, what they didn't say, why they behaved a certain way, why they didn't respond, whether they care, whether they don't. Overthinking about people is one of the most silent and exhausting sources of stress. It steals

your peace, distracts your mind and creates stories that might not even be true. Often, you are thinking day and night about someone… while that person is simply busy living their life. This imbalance creates emotional heaviness—not because of what they did but because of what your mind keeps imagining.

Over analysis Creates Unnecessary Pain

The mind loves to analyze everything—tone, words, pauses, expressions, delays, changes. But the problem is not the situation; the problem is *the overthinking that grows around it*.

When you focus too much on:

- someone's behaviour
- their mood
- their reply
- their silence
- their words or tone

…you create interpretations that may not match reality.

People say things casually.
People behave differently on different days.
People get busy.
People forget.
People have their own struggles.

But over analysis makes you take everything personally.

What was random becomes meaningful.

What was small becomes huge.

What was normal becomes hurtful.

This is how peace gets disturbed—**not by the world but by the thoughts you attach to it.**

Do Not Build Stories in Your Head

When you think too much about someone, you start creating stories:

- "Maybe he ignored me."
- "Maybe she is upset."
- "Maybe I did something wrong."
- "Maybe they don't care anymore."

Most of these stories are built from assumptions, not truth. Your mind fills the gaps with imagination, not facts. This leads to disappointment, emotional dependency and unnecessary stress. People's behaviour often has nothing to do with you. They may be busy, tired, distracted, preoccupied or handling something privately. But your mind creates a narrative that punishes you.

Do Not Focus Beyond One Point on What Someone Says

People speak based on their mood, not your reality. Sometimes words are careless. Sometimes tone is rough. Sometimes reactions are quick. If you keep replaying their words in your head, you give them more power than they had.

A simple rule for peace: **Take the message. Leave the emotional weight. Move on.** Thinking beyond one point drains energy that you could invest in your own growth, health, goals and happiness.

Free Yourself from the Critical Point

If someone's action, silence or behaviour is repeatedly disturbing your mind, it means you are placing your peace in someone else's hands. That is a dangerous place to live.

Free yourself by remembering:

- Their priorities are different.
- Their life is different.
- Their schedule is different.
- Their thinking is different.

Your mind is over-focused but their mind may not even be aware. Why carry emotional load for someone who isn't even thinking about it?

Choose Yourself. Choose Your Peace.

The moment you stop overthinking about others, your life becomes lighter. You sleep better. You think clearer. You feel calmer. You regain your energy. Your confidence increases. A peaceful mind is a powerful mind.

Real-Life Examples:

- **Arjun** spent weeks replaying a brief conversation with a colleague, analysing every word and pause, convinced he had been subtly criticised and excluded, until one day he chose to stop rehearsing the scene in his head, sent a calm follow-up message for clarity and discovered the colleague had been dealing with a family emergency and hadn't even registered the tone Arjun was worried about; the moment Arjun shifted from assumption to action—and from rumination to reality—his mind felt lighter, his sleep improved and his work regained focus.

Do not surrender your peace to passing moments or other people's moods; return your attention to what nourishes you, allow space for imperfect communication, choose clarity over stories and let your energy serve your growth rather than your worries.

Think less about anyone—and live more as yourself.

Romance: A Path to Happiness and Health

"Romance is not about grand gestures—it is about keeping the heart alive in everyday life."

Romance is often misunderstood as something reserved for relationships, celebrations or special moments. In reality, **romance is a way of living**—a way of feeling, expressing and connecting with life itself. A romantic life is one where warmth, appreciation and emotional presence flow naturally into daily routines. It is not dramatic or unrealistic; it is gentle, sincere and deeply human.

When romance is present, life feels lighter and more meaningful. When it disappears, life can become efficient but emotionally dry. Responsibilities get done yet joy reduces. Health remains yet emotional richness fades. Living a romantic life keeps the heart open—and an open heart supports both happiness and health.

Why Romance Matters for Happiness and Health

Romance nourishes the emotional system. It reduces stress, calms the nervous system and strengthens relationships—one of the strongest predictors of long-term well-being. Psychological and health studies consistently show that people who experience emotional warmth, affection and connection tend to have better mental balance, lower stress levels and improved physical health.

Romance slows us down just enough to feel life again. It brings softness into a fast world and warmth into rigid routines. Without romance, people may function well but feel internally tired. With romance, even ordinary days carry meaning and emotional nourishment.

Key Principles to Live a Romantic Life

- **Practice Presence:** Be emotionally available—listen fully, look attentively and slow down when connecting.
- **Express Warmth Openly:** Appreciate, compliment and show affection without waiting for special occasions.
- **Value Emotional Moments:** Small gestures often matter more than big plans.
- **Be Romantic With Yourself:** Care for yourself with gentleness, beauty and self-respect.
- **Bring Softness into Routine:** Romance lives in ordinary moments when lived consciously.

Real-Life Examples:

- **The Man Who Treated Life Only as Responsibility – Marco** Marco was disciplined, hardworking and reliable but emotionally distant. Life felt stable yet joyless. When he consciously brought romance back—shared meals without phones, gentle words, music and simple affection—his stress reduced and sleep improved. **Lesson:** Romance softens the body and mind without needing to change life's responsibilities.
- **The Woman Who Forgot to Be Romantic with Herself – Leena** Leena cared deeply for everyone but neglected her own emotional needs. She lived efficiently but felt drained. When she began treating herself with romance—slowing her pace, dressing with care, enjoying silence and beauty—her emotional balance improved and anxiety reduced. **Lesson:** A romantic relationship with yourself is the foundation of health and happiness.

Without romance, life slowly becomes mechanical. With romance, life regains colour, warmth and emotional depth. You do not need to do more or achieve more—only **feel more and connect more**.

Be gentle where life is harsh. Be warm where routine is cold.
Be romantic—not to impress others but to keep your heart alive.

Because a romantic life is not careless— it is **emotionally healthy, deeply fulfilling and quietly joyful**.

The Power of Unseen Kindness: Quiet Acts That Make Life Better

"Not all goodness needs an audience—some of the most powerful kindness is never seen."

Kindness is often imagined as something big, planned or dramatic. In reality, **the kindness that changes lives most deeply is often small, quiet and unnoticed**. A gentle word, a patient pause, a thoughtful gesture done without expectation—these moments rarely make headlines yet they shape the emotional quality of daily life. Small, unseen kindness is not about recognition. It is about intention. When kindness is offered silently and without reward, it carries a purity that touches both the giver and the receiver. These simple acts soften stress, restore faith in people and quietly improve emotional and physical well-being.

Why Small Acts of Unseen Kindness Matter

Everyday life is filled with pressure, hurry and mental noise. Small acts of kindness interrupt this tension. A brief moment of human warmth can calm the nervous system, lift emotional weight and remind someone that they are not alone. Psychological research shows that both giving and receiving kindness reduce stress, elevate mood and strengthen emotional resilience.

Unseen kindness is especially powerful because it is free from ego. When no one is watching, kindness becomes a reflection of inner values rather than a performance. Over time, these moments shape character, relationships and inner peace. A kind society is not built by grand gestures—but by **thousands of small, quiet ones**.

Key Principles of Everyday Kindness

- **Give Without Expectation:** Let kindness exist for its own sake.
- **Notice Small Opportunities:** Everyday moments offer chances to help or uplift.
- **Act Silently When Possible:** Unseen acts keep kindness pure.
- **Trust the Ripple Effect:** One gentle act often inspires many more.
- **Make Kindness a Habit:** Small daily actions shape a compassionate life.

Real-Life Examples:

- **The Stranger Who Chose Patience – Daniel** - Daniel noticed a tired cashier struggling during a busy shift. Instead of showing impatience, he spoke gently and waited quietly. The moment passed unnoticed by others but the cashier's relief was visible. **Lesson:** Kindness does not need words—it often appears as patience.

- **The Woman Who Lightened an Invisible Burden – Farah** - Farah noticed a colleague overwhelmed at work. Without announcing it, she completed a small task on that colleague's list. Nothing was said but the stress eased. **Lesson:** Helping without claiming credit strengthens trust and connection.

Small, unseen kindness may look ordinary—but it leaves a lasting emotional imprint. These gestures do not change the whole world yet they make the world **softer, calmer and more human**—one moment at a time.

Offer kindness when it is easy.
Offer it especially when it is unnoticed.
Let goodness move quietly through your day.

Because every small, unseen act of kindness adds warmth to life—and makes both giver and receiver **a little healthier, a little lighter and a little happier**.

Why You Must Cut Off Toxic People and Environments

"Your environment shapes your energy—choose wisely."

Toxic people drain your mental energy, spread negativity and block your growth. They criticize, manipulate, gossip or constantly pull you into drama. Similarly toxic surroundings—chaotic workplaces, unhealthy social circles—create stress and anxiety. Staying in such environments costs you peace, productivity and happiness. Cutting off toxicity isn't selfish—it's self-care.

Signs of Toxic People

- Constant negativity and complaints.
- Disrespecting boundaries.
- Manipulation or guilt-tripping.
- Lack of support for your goals.
- Draining conversations that leave you exhausted.

Real-Life Examples:

- **Anjali**, a young professional, had a friend who always belittled her achievements and pushed her into unnecessary spending. Every meeting left her stressed and doubting herself. Anjali decided to limit contact—she stopped responding to negative messages and focused on supportive friends. Within weeks:

- Her confidence improved.
- She saved money and time.
- She felt lighter and more positive.

How to Cut Off Toxicity

- **Identify patterns**: Notice who drains your energy.
- **Set boundaries**: Limit calls, meetings and social media interactions.
- **Replace negativity**: Surround yourself with positive, growth-oriented people.
- **Create safe spaces**: Spend time in nature, hobbies or with supportive communities.

Your mental health is priceless. Protect it by removing what poisons it. Distance from toxicity is not isolation—it's liberation.

Your Circle, Your Energy - Designing Relationships to Grow

"Your environment shapes your energy and your people shape your growth."

Designing your social circle means choosing relationships that uplift, support and inspire you. The people around you influence how you think, feel and live. When your circle is healthy, you feel encouraged, valued and emotionally secure. When it is chaotic or negative, even your best days feel heavy. A consciously designed social circle helps you grow with confidence, protects your peace and strengthens your emotional well-being. The right people don't change you—they help you become more of who you truly are.

Why Your Social Circle Matters

Humans are deeply influenced by the energy and behaviour of those around them. From motivation to habits, from emotional state to long-term success—your circle impacts every area of your life. Research consistently shows that supportive relationships reduce stress, increase resilience and improve overall happiness. Meanwhile, draining or toxic connections create emotional fatigue, self-doubt and unnecessary complexity. You cannot always choose life's situations—but you can choose the people who walk with you.

Key Principles for Designing a Healthy Social Circle

- **Choose Uplifting Minds:** Surround yourself with people who inspire growth, kindness and positivity.
- **Set Clear Boundaries:** Protect your time and emotional space from negativity or over-demanding relationships.
- **Prioritize Quality Over Quantity:** A few genuine connections are more powerful than many superficial ones.
- **Seek Mutual Respect:** Healthy relationships are balanced—both give, both receive, both grow.
- **Let Go of Draining Connections:** Releasing unhealthy ties creates room for healthier ones to enter.

Real-Life Examples:

- **The Young Professional Who Flourished with Better Company** – Arjun often felt discouraged because his friends dismissed his ambitions. He gradually shifted toward colleagues who shared similar goals and values. His motivation increased, he grew more confident and his habits improved. **Lesson:** Your circle can pull you down—or lift you higher.
- **The Homemaker Who Created Her Supportive Tribe** – Meera felt lonely and overwhelmed. She joined a small women's group focused on learning and self-care. Their support made her feel understood, lighter and emotionally stronger. **Lesson:** A supportive circle becomes emotional strength.

Designing your social circle is an act of self-respect. When you consciously choose people who reflect your values, support your dreams and honor your peace, your life becomes calmer and more meaningful. You grow when your circle grows with you. Choose wisely, connect deeply and protect the relationships that bring light to your life.

Seva: The Joy of Helping Others

"True happiness begins when we serve beyond ourselves."

The Spirit of Seva

Seva, the act of selfless service, is one of the most profound ways to live a happy and healthy life. It is not charity done out of obligation but love expressed through action. When we help others, we step beyond the boundaries of self and connect with the larger rhythm of humanity. In giving, we receive; in serving, we grow.

Helping as Healing

Modern life often teaches us to focus inward—on our goals, our possessions, our success. Yet true well-being blossoms when we look outward. Helping others reduces stress, nurtures compassion and strengthens community. Science confirms what wisdom traditions have long taught: acts of kindness release joy within us, improving both mental and physical health. Seva heals not only those we serve but also ourselves.

Simplicity in Service

Seva does not require grand gestures. It can be as simple as listening to someone in pain, sharing a meal or offering time to a cause. The essence lies in intention—doing something without expectation of reward. In simplicity, service becomes pure. A smile given freely, a hand extended in support or a word of encouragement can transform lives in ways we may never see.

Building Connection

Helping others strengthens the invisible threads that bind us together. Communities thrive when service is shared. Families grow closer when kindness is practiced. Even strangers become companions when touched by generosity. Seva reminds us that happiness is not an individual pursuit—it is a collective experience. By lifting others, we rise together.

The Health of the Heart

Serving others nourishes the heart. It cultivates gratitude, reduces loneliness and brings meaning to daily life. When we live with a spirit of seva, we shift focus from what we lack to what we can give. This shift creates resilience, peace and joy. Helping others is not a distraction from our own happiness—it is the very path to it.

Real-Life Examples:

The Story of Ramesh

Ramesh was a young professional living in Mumbai. His days were filled with deadlines, meetings and the constant rush of city life. Yet every Sunday morning, he dedicated two hours to volunteering at a local community kitchen that served free meals to underprivileged children.

At first, he thought of it as a small gesture—just helping to chop vegetables or serve food. But over time, he noticed something profound. The children greeted him with smiles, their laughter filled the room and their gratitude was unspoken yet deeply felt. Ramesh realised that those two hours gave him more joy and peace than any shopping trip or weekend outing.

His act of seva didn't stop at the kitchen. Inspired by his experience, Ramesh began encouraging his colleagues to join him. Soon, the kitchen had more volunteers, more meals and more children being fed. What started as one man's small act of service became a ripple of kindness that touched many lives.

The Lesson - Ramesh's story shows that seva is not about grand gestures—it is about consistency, intention and love. Helping others nourished his own mental health, reduced his stress and gave him a sense of purpose. In serving others, he discovered a deeper happiness and a healthier way of living.

Seva is not something reserved for saints or philanthropists—it is available to all of us, in everyday acts. Whether it is feeding the hungry, listening to someone in pain or simply offering time, seva transforms both the giver and the receiver. Real happiness and health are found not in what we keep but in what we share.

The Story of Kavita

Kavita was a corporate trainer in Bengaluru, constantly juggling deadlines and travel. Despite her success, she often felt disconnected and exhausted. One weekend, she visited a nearby old-age home through a friend's suggestion. What began as a casual visit turned into a profound experience. She spent time listening to the elderly share stories of their youth—their laughter, regrets, memories and wisdom.

What surprised her was how much *she* received from those conversations. One elderly woman told her, *"You coming here made my week. Someone remembered me."* Those words stayed with Kavita. She returned the following week, this time helping with reading sessions and basic activities. Slowly, the residents eagerly waited for her visits; her presence brought lightness to their days.

In the process, Kavita noticed her own stress melt away. Her weekends felt meaningful, her outlook softened and her gratitude deepened. By giving her time, she received emotional clarity she didn't even know she needed.

The Lesson: Seva fills the heart of the giver just as much as the one who receives.

Seva is not a grand performance; it is a quiet practice. In serving, we remember who we are and why we are here. Give a little time, a little attention, a little love—consistently. You will find that what you offer the world returns as peace, meaning and joy. Seva is the art of living beyond the self. It is the practice of turning compassion into action, of transforming kindness into health and of discovering joy in giving. To live well is to serve well. In helping others, we find the secret to a happy and healthy life: that true success is measured not by what we keep but by what we share.

Touching Human Lives - The Gentle Power of Making a Difference

"One kind word, one small gesture, one moment of understanding can change someone's entire day—or their entire life."

Touching human lives is the art of bringing warmth, compassion and support into the lives of others. It is not about doing grand things—it is about showing care in simple moments. A smile, a listening ear, a helping hand or a few encouraging words can heal hearts more deeply than we realise. When you touch someone's life with kindness, you create a ripple of positivity that travels much farther than you can see. You may forget the moment but the person you helped will remember it forever.

Why Touching Lives Matters

In a world filled with speed, stress and silent struggles, human hearts crave understanding and connection. Many people walk around feeling unseen, unheard or overwhelmed. A single act of genuine kindness can bring hope, strength and emotional relief. Research shows that kindness boosts serotonin, reduces stress, strengthens relationships and improves overall happiness—for both the giver and the receiver. Touching lives is not a duty—it is a blessing. It lifts others and uplifts you at the same time.

Ways to Touch Human Lives

- **Listen Without Interrupting:** Sometimes people don't need advice—they just need a safe space.
- **Offer Encouragement:** A few sincere words can reignite someone's belief in themselves.
- **Help Without Being Asked:** Small acts of service lighten emotional and physical burdens.
- **Show Appreciation:** Saying "thank you" or acknowledging someone's efforts makes them feel valued.
- **Be Present:** Your presence during someone's difficult moment can be more powerful than solutions.

Real-Life Examples:

- **The Stranger Who Lifted Someone Out of Loneliness** – A simple smile and a friendly greeting from a neighbor made an elderly man feel seen and appreciated after weeks of isolation. That small gesture became a turning point in his emotional well-being. **Lesson:** Tiny gestures can heal deeply.
- **The Teacher Who Believed in a Silent Child** – A quiet student lacked confidence and rarely spoke. The teacher began encouraging him with small, consistent words of belief. Over time, the child opened up, participated more and rediscovered his potential. **Lesson:** Belief can be the spark that transforms a life.

Touching human lives is not about doing more—it is about caring more. When you lift others with kindness, patience and compassion, you bring purpose to your life and comfort to theirs. A gentle word can heal. A small act can inspire. A sincere connection can transform someone's path. Touch lives wherever you go and you'll find that your own life becomes richer, warmer and more meaningful.

The Law of Connection - The Energy That Flows Between Hearts

"Connection is not built by words or presence—it is built by understanding, empathy and shared energy."

The Law of Connection teaches that every human interaction carries energy—and this energy shapes relationships, trust and emotional well-being. When you truly connect with someone, you create a bond that brings comfort, strength and belonging. Connection is not about talking more; it is about feeling heard, valued and understood. Whether with family, friends, colleagues or strangers—the quality of connection determines the quality of life. A deep connection doesn't need perfect communication; it needs genuine intention.

Why the Law of Connection Matters

In today's fast world, people often feel isolated despite being surrounded by others. Digital interactions have replaced genuine conversations. Stress has replaced presence. And schedules have replaced connection. Research shows that meaningful human connection reduces anxiety, increases happiness, boosts immunity and enhances emotional resilience. When you connect deeply, you feel supported. When you disconnect, even a room full of people can feel lonely.
Connection is not a luxury—it is a human need.

Key Principles of the Law of Connection

Be Present: True connection happens when your mind is where your body is.
Listen to Understand, Not to Reply: Listening is the doorway to bonding.
Show Empathy: Feeling someone's emotions creates trust and openness.
Share Authenticity: Honest and vulnerable conversations deepen connection.
Value People: Appreciation makes relationships safe, warm and lasting.

Real-Life Examples:

- **The Manager Who Transformed His Team Through Connection** – Rohan noticed his team was disengaged. Instead of pushing harder, he began listening more—checking in personally, understanding challenges and celebrating small wins. The team became more united, motivated and confident. **Lesson:** People work better for someone who truly connects with them.
- **The Parent Who Rebuilt Their Bond Through Presence** – Meena realised she spent time with her children but was rarely mentally present. She began giving undivided attention—putting away her phone, listening deeply and being emotionally available. Her relationship with her children strengthened beautifully. **Lesson:** Presence creates connection; distraction destroys it.

The Law of Connection reminds you that relationships thrive not through perfection but through presence, empathy and genuine care. When you connect with others from the heart, you build bonds that uplift, inspire and heal. Connection is the thread that weaves meaning into life. Nurture it. Protect it. And let it guide you toward deeper happiness.

PART VI: Practical Living: Daily Balance & Personal Growth

Create order and calm in everyday life through simple systems and routines.

Chapter 15: Order, Focus & Everyday Systems

Simplifying Life - Creating Space for What Truly Matters

"Simplicity is not about having less—it is about making space for what truly matters."

Reducing life complexity means consciously removing the unnecessary so your time, energy and mind can focus on what adds meaning, joy and clarity to your life. In a world filled with endless choices, constant notifications, multitasking and mental clutter, simplicity becomes a source of strength. When you reduce complexity, stress decreases, clarity increases and your daily life becomes lighter and more intentional. Simplicity is not deprivation—it is liberation.

Why Reducing Complexity Matters

Modern life often overwhelms people with options, obligations, distractions and constant comparison. This overload silently drains mental energy, increases stress and leaves little room for rest or reflection. Research shows that reducing complexity—through minimalism, clear priorities and structured routines—improves focus, emotional well-being and decision-making. A simpler life gives you more time for what nourishes your heart and strengthens your purpose.

Key Principles to Reduce Life Complexity

- **Prioritize What Truly Matters:** Identify your top values and focus your time around them.
- **Declutter Your Physical Space:** A simpler environment clears mental noise.
- **Limit Digital Overload:** Reduce screen time, mute distractions and set boundaries with technology.
- **Simplify Decisions:** Create routines that reduce daily decision fatigue.
- **Say "No" More Often:** Protect your time from unnecessary commitments.

Real-Life Examples:

- **The Professional Who Simplified His Schedule** – Raghav used to say "yes" to every task. His days were chaotic and his mind constantly restless. By streamlining his priorities and declining non-essential meetings, he regained focus and felt less overwhelmed. **Lesson:** Simplicity brings back clarity.

- **The Homemaker Who Found Peace Through Minimalism** – Padmini felt stressed by clutter and constant chores. After donating unused items and organizing her home, she felt lighter, calmer and more in control of her days. **Lesson:** When your surroundings are simple, your mind feels spacious.

Reducing life complexity is an act of self-care. When you let go of what overwhelms you, you create room for what nourishes you. In simplicity you discover freedom and in freedom you rediscover yourself. A simpler life is not a smaller life—it's a richer, more meaningful one.

Define Your Orbit

"Know where you belong, choose what you revolve around and your life gains direction."

Every person functions within an orbit—a space of routines, values, relationships, habits and priorities that guide their life. If you do not define your orbit, the world will define it for you. You may start revolving around other people's goals, expectations and pressures without realising it. Defining your orbit means taking control of **what influences you, what you focus on** and what **you allow to shape your life**. It is the art of choosing the right center so your life moves with purpose instead of drifting. When your orbit is clear, your actions align, your mind stabilizes and your destiny becomes predictable.

Why Defining Your Orbit Matters

- **Gives Direction:** A clear orbit tells you where to go and what to avoid.
- **Protects Your Energy:** You stop wasting time on unimportant people, tasks and distractions.
- **Strengthens Identity:** You know who you are and what you stand for.
- **Improves Decision-Making:** Choices become simpler because your priorities are defined.
- **Attracts the Right Opportunities:** When your orbit is strong, the right people and paths gravitate toward you.

How to Define Your Orbit

1. **Choose Your Center:** Decide what your life revolves around—purpose, family, health, growth, service, peace. Your center shapes your destiny.
2. **Identify Your Influences:** List the people, habits and environments that currently affect you. Keep what helps your orbit; remove what disturbs it.

3. **Set Clear Boundaries:** Protect your time, emotions and focus. Boundaries keep your orbit pure and prevent chaos.
4. **Simplify Your Priorities:** Pick 3–5 priorities that will define this stage of your life. Let everything else rotate outside your core.
5. **Review Your Orbit Often:** Life changes, seasons change, you change. Re-shape your orbit as needed so it continues to serve your growth.

Real-Life Examples:

- **Professional:** A manager defines his orbit around discipline, learning and leadership—this clarity guides his behaviour at work and accelerates growth.
- **Personal:** A parent centers life around family and wellness, thus designing routines and boundaries that support harmony.
- **Students:** When students define their orbit around learning and improvement, distractions naturally decrease.
- **Entrepreneurs:** Successful founders protect their orbit fiercely fewer people, focused work, clear priority systems.

Your orbit determines your movement. Your movement determines your progress. Your progress determines your destiny.

When you define your orbit, you control your direction. You choose what you revolve around, what you grow toward and what you ignore.

Do not drift in someone else's orbit. Define your own. Protect it. Strengthen it. And let it guide you to a life of purpose, clarity and meaning.

Once you define what your life revolves around, build a single command centre to run it—*one place, one diary.*

One Place, One Diary: Your Life's Command Centre

"When everything is everywhere, clarity is nowhere."

In today's fast-paced world, information is scattered—notes on your phone, reminders in apps, bills in emails, ideas on sticky notes. This fragmentation creates stress and inefficiency. The solution? **One diary, one place for everything.** A single organized hub for your thoughts, tasks, goals and records. When your mind knows where to find things, it feels lighter, focused and in control.

Why It Matters

- **Reduces mental clutter**: No more hunting for scraps of paper or random files.
- **Boosts productivity**: Everything is accessible in seconds.

- **Improves planning**: See your goals, finances and priorities in one view.
- **Enhances peace of mind**: A clear system means less stress.

Real-Life Examples:

- Rajesh, a senior executive, used to juggle multiple notebooks, apps and sticky notes. Meeting points were lost, bills missed and ideas forgotten. He switched to one diary system:
    - **Sections**: Daily tasks, monthly goals, expenses, health notes, ideas.
    - **Routine**: Every morning, he updates tasks; every evening, he logs expenses and reflections. Result? Rajesh feels organized, meets deadlines and even finds time for hobbies—because his brain isn't busy remembering where things are.

How to Implement

- Choose a **physical diary** or a **digital notebook app** (Evernote, Notion, OneNote).
- Create **sections**: Tasks, Goals, Finance, Health, Ideas.
- Update daily; review weekly.
- Keep it **accessible and simple**—don't overcomplicate.

Scattered information scatters your mind. One diary brings unity, clarity and control. It's not just a notebook—it's your **life dashboard**.

One place, one diary—because simplicity is power.

The Power of Place: Choosing a Right Location

"Your surroundings shape your habits, health, happiness—and even your finances."

Where you live is more than an address — it is the background of your lifestyle. Your environment influences your physical health, mental peace, opportunities and even financial stability. A supportive location helps you grow with ease, while a stressful one drains energy and limits progress.

Why Your Location Matters

1. **Health & Well-Being -** Clean air, access to nature, safety and quiet surroundings improve physical and emotional health. Living in a peaceful environment naturally encourages better habits and reduces stress.
2. **Opportunities & Growth -** Your location affects access to jobs, education, networks and learning. Being close to the right opportunities can accelerate success.

3. **Financial Freedom -** Cost of living changes everything. Moving from an expensive urban centre to a smaller city or suburb can lower rent, reduce commuting costs and make daily life more affordable. This financial breathing room allows more saving, investing and long-term stability.

What to Consider When Choosing a Place to Live

- Does this environment support my health?
- Does it give me a sense of peace and safety?
- Does it offer opportunities for career or personal growth?
- Can I comfortably live within my means here?
- Will this place help me build the lifestyle I desire?

A location should support your goals — not work against them.

Real-Life Examples:

- **A Life Transformed -** A high-pressure executive living in a congested city struggled with traffic, pollution and high expenses. Daily stress and rising costs affected his health and mood. He decided to move to a smaller, cleaner city. Within months, his stress reduced, his health improved and his monthly expenses dropped by nearly 30%. With shorter commutes and a calmer environment, he had more time for family, hobbies and rest. The location didn't just change his surroundings — it changed the quality of his life.

Your surroundings influence your habits, mindset and financial stability. Choose a location that supports your **health**, **happiness**, **success** and **freedom**. A peaceful environment is not a luxury — it is a foundation for a better life

Small Stuff, Big Happiness

"Life becomes lighter when joy is found in the little things."

People often chase happiness in big achievements or milestones. But real, lasting happiness rarely comes from grand moments — it comes from the small, everyday experiences that are easy to overlook. A warm cup of tea, a kind word, a clean corner at home, a quiet walk, a moment of gratitude — these tiny touches create emotional balance and everyday joy. Over time, small joys become the real foundation of a peaceful, meaningful life.

Real-Life Examples of Small Happiness

1. **Morning Calm -** A few minutes of stretching, breathing or sipping tea can shape your entire day with calm and clarity.
2. **A Clean Corner** - Tidying a desk or room reduces stress and brings instant mental clarity — a small action with big relief.
3. **Simple Kindness** - Smiling, holding the door or offering a compliment builds warmth for both giver and receiver.
4. **Short Breaks** - A two-minute walk, slow breaths or a sip of water refreshes the mind and prevents burnout.
5. **Everyday Gratitude** - Sunsets, good food, laughter, a friendly message — noticing these moments deepens contentment.
6. **Celebrating Tiny Wins** - Finishing a small task or maintaining a habit boosts motivation and self-confidence.
7. **Touch of Nature -** A brief step outdoors — sunlight, trees, birds — instantly lifts the mood.

Why Small Things Matter

- Easy to practice daily
- Their effects compound over time
- Shift attention from stress to appreciation
- Reduce overthinking
- Create natural, quiet joy without effort or cost

Small joys are like drops of water — tiny alone, powerful together.

How to Grow Big Happiness from Small Moments

1. **Slow Down -** Small joys appear only when life isn't rushed.
2. **Practice Micro-Gratitude** - Appreciate everyday blessings — food, comfort, health, messages from loved ones.
3. **Create Tiny Rituals** - Morning reflection, evening tea, a short walk, a small prayer — repeated daily.

4. **Reduce Noise** - Simplify your routine and cut distractions so joy has space to appear.
5. **Celebrate Progress** - Appreciate every small step toward your goals.
6. **Build Mini-Habits** - Even 1% daily improvement creates transformation.
7. **Connect in Simple Ways** - Send a message, share a smile, express appreciation — small gestures multiply happiness.

A joyful life isn't built only on big achievements — it's built on small, meaningful moments repeated every day. When you begin noticing and valuing the simple pleasures around you, happiness stops being something to chase and becomes something you naturally experience.

Living Green - Bringing Nature into Your Daily Life

"Nature doesn't ask for much—yet it gives you peace, energy and healing in return."

Green Living is the practice of surrounding yourself with nature—plants, sunlight, fresh air and natural elements—to create a life that feels calm, grounded and emotionally balanced. Plants purify the air, soothe the mind and refresh your environment. Even a little greenery can transform your mood, reduce stress and bring a sense of harmony into your home. Nature has a way of slowing you down without stopping your progress. It invites you to breathe, pause and reconnect with the simplicity of life.

Why Green Living Matters

Modern life pulls people indoors—towards screens, artificial lighting and closed spaces that often feel draining. Yet research shows that being around plants, natural light and outdoor spaces reduces anxiety, boosts mood and enhances overall well-being. Nature improves concentration, regulates emotions and increases creativity. It is one of the most effortless ways to create peace in your daily environment. Green living is not about big gardens—it's about small, meaningful touches of nature in everyday life.

Key Benefits of Green Living

- **Cleaner Air & Better Health:** Plants absorb toxins and release oxygen, improving indoor air quality.
- **Reduced Stress & Anxiety:** Greenery naturally relaxes the mind and lowers stress levels.
- **Enhanced Focus & Productivity:** Nature elements improve attention and mental clarity.

- **Better Sleep & Mood:** Natural light regulates your circadian rhythm, influencing sleep and emotional balance.
- **Sense of Connection:** Plants create a living environment that feels warm, nurturing and alive.

Real-Life Examples:

- **The Professional Who Recharged Through Indoor Plants** – Anita worked long hours in front of screens. She added a few low-maintenance plants—snake plant, money plant and peace lily—around her desk. The greenery made her workspace feel peaceful, improved her mood and reduced her mid-day stress. **Lesson:** A few plants can bring life to even the busiest spaces.
- **The Family Who Found Calm Through Evening Outdoor Time** – After feeling mentally exhausted each day, Ramesh and his family began taking a short walk in a nearby garden every evening. The fresh air, open space and greenery improved their conversations, lifted their mood and strengthened family bonding. **Lesson:** Time in nature restores emotional balance.

Green Living is a gentle reminder that nature is always ready to support you—whether through a small plant, a walk under the sky or a quiet moment near trees. When you surround yourself with nature, you surround yourself with peace. Greenery heals, grounds and energizes you—one leaf, one breath, one moment at a time. In nature, you rediscover balance, clarity and the quiet joy of simply being alive.

Journeys That Shape You - Travel as a Path to Inner Growth

"Travel doesn't just show you new places—it reveals new parts of yourself."

Travel for Growth is not about sightseeing or ticking destinations off a list. It is about stepping outside your comfort zone, expanding your perspective and experiencing life with fresh eyes. When you travel, you break routine, meet new ideas, observe new cultures and discover new versions of yourself. Every journey—short or long, within your city or across the world—teaches humility, openness and courage. Travel reminds you how big the world is and how much more you can grow.

Why Travel Matters for Personal Growth

Daily routines can limit your thinking, narrow your experiences and keep you stuck in old patterns. Travel disrupts that autopilot mode. It allows you to pause, breathe

and see life from different angles. Research shows that travel enhances creativity, reduces stress, builds resilience and increases emotional flexibility. New experiences activate new parts of the brain, boosting learning and self-awareness. When you travel, you don't just move across places—you move forward in life.

Key Benefits of Travelling for Growth

- **New Perspectives:** Seeing different lifestyles and cultures broadens your worldview.
- **Emotional Renewal:** A change of environment restores mental clarity and reduces emotional overload.
- **Increased Confidence:** Managing new situations builds independence and inner strength.
- **Creativity Boost:** New sights, sounds and experiences spark fresh ideas and inspiration.
- **Deeper Appreciation:** Travel makes you value your home, relationships and routines more deeply.

Real-Life Examples:

- **The Corporate Professional Who Found Clarity Through Solo Travel** – After months of burnout, Shantanu took a weekend trip to the hills. Away from screens and deadlines, he journaled, walked in nature and reflected. He returned with renewed purpose and a clearer vision of what he wanted next in his career. **Lesson:** Sometimes distance brings the clarity that routine hides.
- **The Homemaker Who Regained Joy Through Family Travel** – Priya felt drained by repetitive days. A short family trip brought laughter, bonding and a sense of lightness she had been missing. The change of

environment revived her emotional energy. **Lesson:** Travel refreshes both the heart and the relationships we value.

Travel is not an escape—it is a return. A return to curiosity, wonder and the deeper parts of yourself that daily life often overshadows. When you travel, you open your mind, lighten your heart and expand your spirit. Every journey becomes a lesson and every destination becomes a doorway to growth. Travel far when you can. Travel near when you must. But always travel with the intention to grow.

Joyful Living - Hobbies That Nurture Happiness

"Hobbies are not a waste of time—they are a way to reclaim your time, your joy and your inner light."

Hobbies that build happiness are the activities that bring you alive—things you do not for achievement or applause but for pure joy, expression and emotional nourishment. They remind you who you are beyond roles, responsibilities and routines. In a fast-paced world where people often feel drained, hobbies become a source of energy, creativity and emotional renewal. They help you reconnect with your interests, explore your potential and experience moments of genuine presence and flow.

Why Hobbies Matter for Happiness

Many adults stop engaging in hobbies because life becomes busy, demanding or structured around productivity. But the absence of play, creativity and exploration slowly dims emotional well-being. Research shows that engaging in meaningful hobbies reduces stress, enhances positive emotions, improves mental resilience and strengthens overall life satisfaction. Hobbies create space for joy—without goals, deadlines or pressure.

Key Benefits of Happiness-Building Hobbies

- **Stress Relief:** Hobbies shift your mind away from pressure and bring relaxation.
- **Creativity & Flow:** Activities you love stimulate imagination and focused concentration.
- **Emotional Balance:** Hobbies provide a healthy outlet for feelings and unprocessed emotions.
- **Identity & Confidence:** Doing what you enjoy helps you reconnect with your authentic self.
- **Social Connection:** Group hobbies build friendships and shared joy.

Real-Life Examples:

- **The Banker Who Found Calm Through Gardening** – Surrounded by numbers and deadlines, Suresh felt mentally exhausted. He began spending 10 minutes each morning with his plants—watering, trimming and simply observing. This simple hobby brought calmness, patience and a sense of grounding into his life. **Lesson:** Nurturing nature often nurtures you.
- **The Teacher Who Rediscovered Joy Through Painting** – Mira felt emotionally drained after work. She picked up her childhood hobby—painting—just once a week. The colors, creativity and silence helped her unwind and brought back a spark she thought she had lost. **Lesson:** Hobbies awaken forgotten parts of your soul.

Hobbies are not a luxury—they are a necessity for emotional well-being. They remind you to slow down, explore and express the joy that already exists within. When you make time for hobbies, you make time for happiness. Through these small moments of joy, you rediscover creativity, balance and the simple pleasure of being yourself.

The One-Page Protector: Keep Your Family Safe When You're Away

"Prepare in calm so your family can act in chaos."

Life has its own timing. Phones die, meetings run long, flights get delayed and emergencies don't wait until you are reachable. In those first frantic minutes, what your family needs is not a long manual or a half-remembered number—they need a single, clear page that tells them exactly what to do next.

Emergencies at home don't announce themselves. A sudden fall in the bathroom, a gas leak in the kitchen, a midnight water burst or an elderly family member struggling to breathe—uncertainty quickly turns into panic when the right information isn't within reach. The first few minutes decide whether the situation escalates or comes under control. The simplest and most powerful protection any family can create is a ***one-page emergency contact sheet***—visible, accessible and complete. It turns chaos into a clear plan of action: who to call, where to go and what to do next. Pair this with calm communication and basic awareness and your home becomes not just safer—but more confident and resilient.

This topic gives you a simple system: one page that turns confusion into steps and steps into safety. It combines two ideas—**a household emergency plan** and **an**

"I'm-not-home" information sheet—into a single, minimalist tool your family, elders, children and helpers can use without hesitation. Create it once, keep it visible and review it on a routine. The result is a calmer home, quicker decisions and fewer mistakes when time is precious.

Real-Life Examples: (How One Page Changes Outcomes)

- **Dev & Asha—The midnight leak.** A pipe burst when Dev was out of town. Asha opened the "One-Page Protector," found the **main valve note** and the **plumber's number**, shut the water within minutes, called for help and prevented major damage. No guessing, no scrolling through messages.
- **Mira & her mother—Medical clarity.** Mira's mother felt dizzy in the afternoon. The sheet listed **the preferred hospital**, **doctor's line** and **current medicines**. With everything at hand, the cab was booked in seconds, the file was ready at the door and admission was smooth.
- **Omar—Teaching independence.** Omar lives with his younger brother. During a brief power fault, his brother used the sheet to call **building maintenance**, found the **torch location** and kept calm. A small success built big confidence.
- **Lina—Helper support.** Lina's caregiver used the sheet to contact **two neighbours** and **a family decision-maker** when the door lock jammed and a delivery arrived early. What could have become stress turned into simple coordination.
- **Kabir—Travel without worry.** Kabir travels frequently. His spouse knows where to find **insurance papers**, **emergency cash** and **the passbook** because the sheet says "**Documents folder in top study drawer—green file**." No frantic calls, no scattered files.
- **"Seconds matter."** Lakshmi, 68, slipped in the bathroom at dawn. Her daughter, calling from Pune, couldn't find their family doctor's number. Ten minutes were lost searching old messages. Afterward, they printed a one-page sheet and pinned it near the kitchen and main door—now everyone knows exactly whom to call.
- **"Contacts shouldn't live in one phone."** Ahmed and Sofia faced a midnight water leak. The trusted plumber's number was saved only on an old device. They spent two anxious hours containing the flood. The next day, they created a visible list: building maintenance, security desk, plumber and electrician—placed on the fridge.
- **"Helpers need access too."** Ten-year-old Mehul and the domestic helper panicked when his grandmother had breathing difficulty. The helper didn't know the ambulance number or hospital address. A clearly printed sheet

would have cut the delay and stress. They now keep a laminated copy by the entrance.

ONE-PAGE FAMILY INFORMATION SUMMARY

Essential information if I am unrreacchable.

1) PRIMARY CONTACTS

- Primary Contact (Decision): ____________ Phone: ____________
- Secondary Contact: ____________ Phone: ____________
- Out-of-Town Relative (backup): ____________ Phone: ____________

2) MEDICAL ESSENTIALS

- Doctor / Clinic: ____________ Phone: ____________
- Hospital / ER: ____________ Phone: ____________
- Current Medications: ____________
- Allergies / Special Notes: ____________

3) HOME BASICS

- Full Address + Landmark: ____________
- Main Keys Kept At: ____________
- First-Aid Kit: ____________ Torch/Power Bank: ____________
- Gas Shutoff: ____________ Water Valve: ____________
- Router/Internet Reset (if needed): ____________

4) IMPORTANT NUMBERS

- Security / Reception: ____________ Phone: ____________
- Maintenance / Supervisor: ____________ Phone: ____________
- Plumber (Trusted): ____________ Phone: ____________
- Electrician (Trusted): ____________ Phone: ____________
- Transport / Driver: ____________ Phone: ____________
- Two Trusted Neighbors: ____________ Phone: ____________

5) FINANCIAL BASICS (EMERGENCY-ONLY)

- Insurance Support / Agent: ____________ Phone: ____________
- Bank Relationship Contact: ____________ Phone: ____________
- Where to find: Insurance papers ____________ Passbook / Cheque: ____________
- Emergency Cash Kept At: ____________

Last updated: ________ Next review date: ________ Prepared by: ________

- **"Children can act if guided."** Twins Aarav and Aanya were home with their tutor when there was a small electrical short. Because a simple emergency sheet listed the building security, electrician and fire helpline, the tutor acted quickly and avoided a larger incident.

- **"Medical notes save minutes."** Priya's father is diabetic and allergic to a medication. During a late-night episode, the ER team used the printed sheet that listed his **blood group, allergies and current medications**—speeding up safe treatment.

How to use these templates:

1. Print the **Quick Card** (A5 or A6) for the fridge/entrance.
2. Print the **Full Summary** (A4/Letter) for the family file.
3. Save a photo/PDF in a shared family folder.
4. Do a 2-minute drill with everyone at home.

Templates – Follow below sample template. Customize it as per your need.

A one-page summary may seem simple but during an emergency it becomes priceless. It gives your family direction when stress clouds judgment… It saves time when every minute matters…And it offers peace of mind long before it is ever needed.

Create it once. Update it occasionally. Your family will always be thankful.

Chapter 16: Inner Growth & Life Management

One Life. Live It Well

"This life is your only chance. Don't live it carelessly—live it consciously."

Life is a one-time gift. There is no second version, no replay button, no chance to start again from zero. Yet many people treat life as if it is endless—postponing happiness, delaying health, neglecting peace, carrying stress for years and wasting precious time on conflicts, comparisons and meaningless distractions.
We often protect our belongings more than we protect our life. We maintain our vehicles, fix our homes, save our money— but forget to maintain our body, mind and inner world.

Your life is the only place you will ever live. If you don't take care of it, no one else can do it for you.

Why This One Life Deserves Your Best Attention

Life is fragile, unpredictable and incredibly precious. Every day you get is a day you will never receive again. Every sunrise is one less you will see in this lifetime. Your time, your energy, your body, your relationships, your peace, your dreams—everything you value flows from one source: **your life**.

When you neglect your health, ignore your happiness or suppress your peace, you are not just harming your present—you are sacrificing your future

You get only one mind—protect its clarity.
You get only one body—protect its strength.
You get only one soul—protect its peace.
You get only one lifetime—protect its meaning.

How People Often Lose Sight of This One Life

Life's responsibilities—career, family, finances, expectations—slowly consume attention. People begin to survive instead of live. The body sends signals of exhaustion but they ignore it. The mind feels heavy but they push through. Happiness feels distant but they postpone it. Many people spend years pleasing others, competing unnecessarily, chasing perfection or living according to someone else's script. In the process, they forget that **their own well-being is their first responsibility**.
Life is not meant to be lived in stress, noise or pressure. It is meant to be lived with presence, purpose and joy.

What Taking Care of Your One Life Really Means

Taking care of life is not selfish—it is essential. It means listening to your body, protecting your mental health, choosing healthy habits, maintaining meaningful relationships, leaving toxic environments, learning continuously, resting deeply and living with gratitude.

It means setting boundaries to protect your peace.
It means saying "no" when necessary.
It means choosing joy without guilt.
It means giving your future self a better life by improving your present self.

This life is yours. Treat it with respect.

Real-Life Examples:

- **Jack:** Jack spent years working endlessly, sleeping late, eating poorly and pushing through stress. One day, he felt a sharp pain and ended up in the hospital. That moment changed him. He reorganized his life—better routines, healthier habits, meaningful breaks, family time. He realised he had nearly lost the very life he was trying to improve. **His success began the moment he started valuing his life more than his workload.**
- **Sophia:** Sophia always put others first—her family, colleagues, friends. She never said no, even when she felt exhausted. Slowly her emotional health declined. When she finally paused and reflected, she understood that she had ignored herself for too long. She started setting gentle boundaries, practicing self-care, taking small holidays and reconnecting with her hobbies. **She discovered that caring for herself made her a better person for everyone else.**

You have only one life—one body, one mind, one chance to create joy, peace and meaning. Don't wait for pain to remind you of its value. Don't rush through your days without noticing the beauty in them. Don't live for others so much that you forget to live for yourself. Take care of your life with love, gratitude and intention. When you honor your life, your life honors you back—with happiness, health and purpose.

Fill Life into Your Years

"A long life means nothing if it isn't lived well. Joy is measured in moments, not in calendars."

Many people spend years collecting responsibilities, achievements and possessions — yet forget to actually **live**. They repeat the same days, carry the same stress, follow the same routines and soon time passes quietly while the heart stays untouched. They count years but the years don't count.

*Life is not about how long you live; it is about **how deeply, joyfully and consciously you live**.*

A meaningful life is built from moments — moments of connection, gratitude, wonder, learning, laughter and presence. You don't need more years; you need more **life** in the years you already have.

Why People Forget to Live Fully

Modern life moves fast. Responsibilities multiply. Pressures grow. Happiness is postponed endlessly with promises like:
"I'll enjoy after retirement… I'll relax when work gets easier… I'll travel when I have time… I'll take care of myself someday." But "someday" never arrives unless you create it.

- Daily routines take over.
- Worries dominate thoughts.
- The future overshadows the present.
- And the heart quietly hungers for joy.

Life cannot be lived later. Life is always happening **now**.

What It Means to Fill Life Into Your Years

Living fully is not about excitement — it is about **intention**. It means noticing beauty in ordinary moments, nurturing relationships, doing things that energize you, investing in your health, exploring new experiences, showing gratitude, laughing more, simplifying your lifestyle and letting go of unnecessary comparison. When you enrich your days with meaning, your years automatically become richer. Quality matters more than quantity. Meaning matters more than measurement.

Daily Ways to Bring Life Into Your Years

You don't need grand adventures to feel alive. Small, simple choices are enough — spending time with uplifting people, taking short pauses to breathe, enjoying music, books and creativity, attending social or cultural gatherings, maintaining your physical and emotional well-being, trying something new occasionally, celebrating small wins, expressing love freely, smiling often and simplifying whatever feels heavy.

A meaningful life is built gently, one choice at a time.

Real-Life Examples:

- **Kaiden — Realizing He Was Surviving, Not Living** - Kaiden worked hard, earned well and achieved milestones yet his days felt lifeless. A quiet moment of reflection made him realise he had been moving but not truly living. He made small changes — reconnecting with friends, attending gatherings, exploring nature, practicing gratitude and improving his health habits. Within months, life felt lighter, richer and more joyful. He discovered that fullness comes from intention, not income.
- **Elowen — Bringing Color Back Into Ordinary Days** - Elowen spent years caring for her family but forgot to care for herself. A friend invited her to a cultural event and that single experience awakened a sense of joy she had forgotten. Slowly, she added simple pleasures to her week — music, reading, evening walks, laughter. Her days brightened and her happiness returned. She realised she didn't need a new life — she needed to **live her current life more deeply**.

You may not control how many years you receive but you fully control how much life you bring into each of them. Fill your days with joy, presence, gratitude, health and meaningful moments. Let your life be rich in experience, not just in duration. When you fill your years with moments that matter, you don't just live longer — you live *better*.

Free to Be You: Rising Above Social Expectations

"Break free from expectations—live life on your own terms."

Social expectations are subtle forces that shape how people think, choose and live. Over time, these pressures—family norms, cultural rules, societal definitions of success—can push individuals away from their true values. Choosing simplicity means choosing authenticity. It means living by **your** priorities instead of society's script.

1. Recognize the Pressures - Expectations about "success," "normal life," or "acceptable choices" begin early and often go unquestioned. Becoming aware of what's influencing you—family, peers, media, culture—is the first step toward freedom.

2. Choose What Aligns with You - Many people follow expected paths—career, marriage, lifestyle—without asking what genuinely fulfils them. Intentional living encourages choices based on values, not approval. When actions align with your truth, life feels lighter.

3. Reject Material Pressures - Society links status to possessions, pushing people to constantly buy and compare. This cycle creates stress and insecurity. Minimalist thinking shifts attention to experiences, purpose and relationships instead of accumulation.

4. Balance Family Expectations - Family influence is powerful but shouldn't replace your inner voice. Open, respectful communication and setting boundaries help you honour both family bonds and your own aspirations.

5. Question Cultural Norms - Cultural traditions give identity but not all norms fit every person. When expectations restrict your growth, you can honour your roots while choosing a path that feels authentic.

6. Reduce Social Comparison - Comparing your life to others creates unnecessary pressure. Replace comparison with self-reflection. Focus on your progress, your values and your direction.

7. Embrace Your Individuality - Trying to please everyone often buries your unique strengths. Simplicity encourages embracing what sets you apart—your preferences, talents and perspective.

8. Seek Internal, Not External, Validation - External approval fades quickly. Confidence grows from living by your own standards of success—ones that reflect who you are, not who others expect you to be.

9. Set Boundaries with Confidence - You gain freedom when you say "no" to obligations that don't fit your life. Prioritize relationships that respect your choices and distance yourself from those driven only by expectation or obligation.

10. Practical Ways to Break Free

- Clarify your values and check if your choices match them
- Limit exposure to media that promotes unrealistic standards
- Say "no" to activities, purchases or commitments that don't align with your priorities
- Surround yourself with people who respect your path
- Invest time in growth, self-care and genuine interests

11. The Reward of Authentic Living - Living authentically may disappoint some people—but it will satisfy your soul. When you stop performing for others and start choosing for yourself, life becomes calmer, simpler and more meaningful.

12. Courage to Create Your Own Path - Choosing your own way in a world built on conformity requires courage. But each authentic choice you make encourages others to question expectations and embrace their own truth.

Real-Life Examples:

- **The Engineer Who Chose Passion Over Pressure -** Rajat came from a family where "success" meant becoming a doctor or engineer. Although he completed engineering, his real interest was filmmaking. After years of living under expectation, he finally chose his own path—taking weekend film courses, creating short videos and eventually switching careers. Today, he works in a creative agency and feels more fulfilled than ever before. **Lesson:** When you stop following society's script, you start living your own story.

- **The Woman Who Redefined Success Beyond Marriage Timelines -** Ananya faced constant pressure from relatives to "settle down" by a certain age. Instead of giving in, she focused on her career, health and travel goals. She communicated her boundaries clearly and chose relationships based on compatibility, not deadlines. With time, she found a partner who respected her values and ambition. **Lesson:** Freedom comes when you choose your own timing, not society's expectations.

Social expectations will always exist—but they don't have to define your life. Simplicity gives you space to hear your own voice. Authenticity gives you the strength to follow it.

Live with clarity. Choose with intention. Your life belongs to you.

Break Free from the Comparison Trap

"You lose yourself the moment you start measuring your life with someone else's ruler."

Comparison is one of the quietest thieves of happiness. It slips into life almost unnoticed—when you scroll through social media, hear about someone's achievement, see a lifestyle you don't have or watch someone progressing faster than you. Suddenly, your peaceful life feels small. Your pace feels slow. Your confidence begins to shake.

But comparison is an illusion. You see only the polished surface of someone else's life, never their struggles, tears or timing. Every life is a unique journey. Every person carries battles you cannot see. Yet comparison convinces you that you're behind—even when you are exactly where you need to be.

Happiness grows when you stop competing with others and start connecting with your own path.

Why Comparison Lowers Happiness

Comparison shifts your attention from what you have to what you lack. Your own achievements begin to feel small when placed next to someone else's highlight reel. It creates pressure—you rush your life, push yourself beyond healthy limits or chase goals that aren't even yours. Slowly, self-esteem drops, doubt grows and your true identity begins to blur.

Comparison offers nothing but anxiety, restlessness and dissatisfaction. It disconnects you from your strengths and blinds you to your progress.

Why People Fall Into the Comparison Trap

Modern life exposes you to filtered lives, perfect photos, curated success and constant updates about others. Social pressure to "match up" grows louder. Childhood conditioning around competition lingers. And during difficult seasons, insecurity makes comparison feel unavoidable. People begin to believe that success is limited, forgetting that life is not a race—it's a personal journey with its own timing. Someone else's success is not your failure. Your path is your own. Your pace is your own.

Signs You Are Stuck in the Comparison Trap

Comparison shows up in subtle ways: Feeling "not enough" without reason. Feeling jealous instead of inspired. Pursuing goals you don't even want. Feeling drained after social media scrolling. Whispering to yourself, "I should have been there by now." Measuring your life by achievements instead of values.
Recognizing these signs is the first step to breaking free.

How to Come Out of the Comparison Trap

Start by shifting your focus from others to your own progress. Compare today with who you were last year—not with someone else. Limit digital triggers because most comparison begins on screens, not in real life. Identify your core values; when you live by them, other people's lives stop distracting you. Celebrate your small wins—they are the building blocks of big change. Practice gratitude daily; it brings your attention back to what is present, not what is missing. Most importantly, trust your pace. Life unfolds differently for everyone. Your timing is personal, not competitive.

Real-Life Examples:

- **Harlan — Finding Peace Through His Own Progress** - Harlan constantly compared himself to colleagues who moved faster in their careers. Each promotion announcement felt like a personal failure. One day, he paused and looked at his own journey. He noticed strengths others didn't have—patience, consistency and deep knowledge. When he shifted attention inward, his anxiety dropped and his work began to feel meaningful again. Peace returned the moment he stopped racing others.
- **Elara — Reclaiming Joy From Social Media Pressure** - Elara admired her friends' vacations, homes and achievements online. Slowly, she began feeling inadequate. She reduced her screen time, set simple personal goals and practiced gratitude at night. Within weeks, her emotional heaviness

eased. Her life didn't need to look like anyone else's—it only needed to feel meaningful to her.

Comparison steals joy and blinds you to your own path. Freedom arrives when you stop competing with the world and begin understanding yourself. You're not late. You're not behind. You're not in a race. Your only competition is the person you were yesterday. When you step out of the comparison trap, life becomes lighter, calmer and beautifully your own.

Live Your Life Without Regret – Choosing Truth Over Fear

"Regret is not about what went wrong—it is about what was never lived."

Regret is one of the quietest yet heaviest emotions a person can carry. It does not arise only from mistakes but from **unexpressed feelings, delayed decisions and ignored inner truths**. Many people live carefully and responsibly, doing what is expected of them yet deep inside they feel incomplete. That incompleteness often comes from moments when the heart knew the right direction but fear, comfort or social pressure made them choose otherwise.

Living without regret does not mean living impulsively or taking unnecessary risks. It means living **honestly and consciously**, making choices aligned with who you truly are. A regret-free life is not perfect—it is sincere. It is the peace of knowing that even when outcomes were uncertain, you lived with courage and integrity.

Why You Must Let Go of Regret

Regret keeps the mind anchored in the past. It drains emotional energy, creates mental restlessness and quietly steals joy from the present moment. Psychological studies show that unresolved regret contributes to stress, anxiety, emotional fatigue and dissatisfaction with life. When people constantly replay old decisions, missed chances or unspoken words, their ability to live fully today weakens.

Most regret does not come from failure—it comes from **inaction**. From not speaking when the heart wanted to speak. From not choosing oneself when it mattered. You cannot change what has already happened but you can stop repeating the same pattern. The moment you begin living aligned with your inner truth, regret starts losing its grip.

Key Principles to Live Without Regret

- **Choose Alignment Over Approval:** Living to satisfy others often creates inner conflict.

- **Express What Matters:** Speak honestly and kindly—unfinished words create lasting regret.
- **Act Despite Uncertainty:** Courage grows only through action, not overthinking.
- **Accept Imperfection:** Growth comes from experience, not flawless decisions.
- **Make Peace With the Past:** Learn from it but do not live inside it.

Real-Life Examples:

- **The Professional Who Ignored His Inner Calling** – Lukas followed a career path chosen for security and social approval. On the outside, he looked successful but inside he felt disconnected. His deepest regret was not hard work—it was never trying what truly mattered to him. When he finally took a step toward his passion, even with uncertainty, he felt lightness return. **Lesson:** Regret fades when you choose authenticity over fear.
- **The Woman Who Stayed Silent to Avoid Conflict** – Amara avoided expressing her feelings to keep relationships calm. Over time, silence turned into emotional distance and inner heaviness. When she finally spoke her truth respectfully, relationships improved and her emotional burden lifted. **Lesson:** Honest expression may feel uncomfortable for a moment but silence creates regret that lasts much longer.

Do not let regret become your silent companion—it weakens the present and steals peace from the future. When you live consciously, express your truth and choose alignment over fear, life feels complete, even with imperfections.

Live carefully but not fearfully.
Live wisely but not hesitantly.
Live true—so that when you look back, your heart feels peaceful, not heavy.

Because a life lived with courage is never perfect— but it is always **free from regret**.

Take Expert Help for a Happy and Peaceful Life

"Asking for help is not weakness — it is wisdom."

Life becomes complicated not because challenges are too big but because we try to handle everything alone. In today's fast and demanding world, no one can master every area — health, emotions, finances, relationships, career, parenting, home management or personal growth. When you attempt to carry all of it by yourself, stress grows, clarity disappears and emotional burnout begins to form quietly.

Sometimes, the most powerful step toward a peaceful and happy life is simple: **take expert help.**

An expert — whether a doctor, therapist, nutritionist, financial advisor, fitness trainer, mentor, teacher or skilled professional — brings experience that saves you time, protects you from mistakes and gives you clarity you may not reach alone. Experts see patterns you can't and their guidance can help you solve challenges that would otherwise take years to understand.

Asking for help doesn't mean you are weak. It means you value your time, your peace and your personal growth.

Why Expert Help Matters

Expert guidance shortens learning curves. Years of their experience become your shortcut. Mistakes that could cost time, health or relationships can be prevented through one conversation. Stress reduces immediately when a knowledgeable person explains the path forward. Clarity replaces confusion. You stop guessing and start progressing. Wise guidance also builds confidence — when you know someone capable is helping you, your decisions feel stronger and your mind feels calmer. You don't need to know everything. You just need to know **whom to ask**.

Where Expert Help Improves Life

Expert support enhances all areas of living. Health professionals help you understand your body, prevent problems and build better routines. Emotional and mental well-being improve when counselors, mentors or coaches help you navigate stress, relationships or self-doubt. Financial experts protect you from avoidable mistakes and teach you long-term stability. Professional mentors accelerate your career and skill development. Relationship experts improve communication. Home and lifestyle experts bring ease, structure and order.
Expert help is not a luxury — it is a tool for peace.

Why People Avoid Asking for Help

Many people hesitate out of fear of judgment, ego or the belief that they should manage everything themselves. Some worry about cost or feel unsure whom to approach. In certain cultures, emotional or mental health support is misunderstood, causing unnecessary hesitation. But struggling alone often costs far more — mentally, emotionally and financially.
Asking for help is not surrender — it is choosing wisdom over pride.

Real-Life Examples:

- **Rohan — Finding Peace Through Professional Support** - Rohan often felt anxious and overwhelmed at work. Instead of continuing alone, he reached out to a counselor who taught him simple tools for emotional balance. In a few months, his stress eased, confidence grew and relationships improved. He realised that one hour of expert guidance saved him years of internal struggle.

- **Elena — Transforming Her Health Through Expert Advice** - Elena tried countless online tips and diets but continued feeling tired and confused. She finally met a nutrition expert who simplified her routine — mindful eating, water intake, regular meals and small lifestyle changes. Her energy improved, her mood stabilized and she felt lighter. She understood that expertise brings clarity guesswork never can.

How to Take Expert Help Wisely

Identify your challenge clearly. Choose genuine, qualified experts. Ask openly and listen without defensiveness. Apply the advice consistently and review your progress regularly. Seek a second opinion when needed and invest in your growth without guilt. The right guidance turns complexity into simplicity.

You don't need to fight every battle alone. Expert help brings clarity when you feel confused, strength when you feel stuck and direction when life feels overwhelming. When you allow knowledgeable people to guide you, your life becomes lighter, calmer and far more meaningful. Asking for help is not a weakness — it is the smartest investment you can make in your peace and well-being.

A Guide for Every Stage of Life

"When the mind feels lost, even one guiding voice can bring you back to yourself."

No one becomes wise, grounded or successful alone. Behind every steady human being, there is someone — sometimes one person, sometimes many — who offered clarity, direction or inspiration at exactly the right moment. A guru or role model is not someone you worship; it is someone who helps you see your own potential more clearly. They open doors inside you. They show you what is possible. They help you navigate moments of confusion, doubt or emotional fog.

A guide can be anyone — a spiritual teacher, a mentor at work, a senior in your community, an author whose words stayed with you or even a distant figure whose life inspires you. And just as you grow, your guides will change. Life has seasons; each season asks for a different kind of wisdom. What matters is not the number of guides you have but the **direction** they bring into your life.

Why Having a Guru or Role Model Matters

A good guide provides clarity when emotions cloud judgment. Their presence helps you see truth instead of reacting blindly to stress or fear. They challenge you to grow but also support you with compassion. A role model teaches through action — discipline, humility, simplicity, kindness, resilience. You naturally begin adopting the qualities you admire in them. Guidance shortens learning curves. It prevents unnecessary mistakes, strengthens character and makes the journey smoother. A person with the right guide walks with direction instead of confusion.

How Guides Influence Your Growth

A genuine guide helps you think clearly. Their words reduce emotional noise. By simply observing how they live, your habits rise. Their discipline inspires consistency; their humility keeps your ego grounded. In difficult moments, their wisdom gives courage; in confusing moments, their perspective gives direction. A good guide doesn't pull you forward — they walk beside you until you find your own path.

You Can Have More Than One Guide

Life is not one subject, so one teacher is rarely enough. You might learn discipline from one person, compassion from another, wisdom from a mentor, creative courage from a leader and emotional steadiness from a spiritual guide.
Your guides change as you change — childhood role models, teachers who appear in difficult phases, elders who offer life lessons, colleagues who give direction, authors who shape your thinking, friends who bring emotional grounding.

Each guide adds a piece to who you become.

Real-Life Examples:

- **Nikolai — Finding Direction in a Clouded Career Phase** - Nikolai worked hard but felt lost. A senior colleague began guiding him — helping him set priorities, understand long-term thinking and stay calm under pressure. Slowly, Nikolai found clarity. His mentor didn't push him; he walked with him until the path became visible. He learned that one guiding voice can save years of wandering.
- **Samira — Different Guides for Different Seasons** - Samira grew through many guides. As a child, her grandmother taught her kindness. In school, a teacher encouraged her confidence. Later, a spiritual mentor taught her silence and presence. Each guide shaped a different layer of her character. She realised she didn't need one guru forever — she needed the right wisdom for each stage of life.

How to Choose the Right Guru or Role Model

Choose someone whose values match the person you want to become. Look for people who inspire peace, not pressure. Follow those who teach through their actions, not their ego. Let your admiration be natural, not forced. And allow your guides to evolve as you evolve. A true guide expands your life — they do not control it.

A guide brings clarity to confusion, courage to fear and direction to your journey. You don't need to walk through life alone. When you allow someone's wisdom to touch your path — even briefly — you grow faster, think clearer and live more purposefully. Different guides appear at different times and each one leaves you stronger. Let inspiration shape you gently and let wisdom — wherever it comes from — become a quiet light on your path.

PART VII —Smart Money, Simple Living

Develop a peaceful relationship with money through clarity and intention.

Chapter 17: Financial Peace & Wise Choices

Smart Money, Peaceful Life

"Money is not happiness but poor money habits silently steal it."

Money plays a powerful role in life — not because it guarantees happiness but because it protects peace. When money is used wisely, life becomes simple, stable and stress-free. When used carelessly, it brings tension, arguments, insecurity and emotional pressure. Money habits shape the emotional climate of your life. Good habits create clarity and comfort; poor habits create confusion and chaos. You don't need great wealth to live happily — you simply need to handle your money with wisdom and intention.

Why Good Money Habits Matter

Money influences every part of life — your health, your home environment, your relationships, your decisions and your peace of mind. When your money habits are strong, you live without fear of emergencies, you feel in control, you buy without guilt and you avoid unnecessary stress. Good money habits prevent financial conflicts in relationships and help you move through life with stability and confidence. Money itself is neutral — but your habits around it create your emotional reality.

Spend on Needs, Control Your Wants

Needs keep life functional; wants keep life distracted. Wants grow endlessly — faster than income, faster than progress and faster than satisfaction. When your wants control you, happiness quietly disappears. A simple formula for peace: **fulfill your needs first**, then consider your wants — slowly, thoughtfully, rarely. Buying sometimes brings joy; buying constantly becomes an emotional trap.

Make an Emergency Plan

Life surprises everyone. Job changes, health issues, sudden expenses — they arrive without notice. An emergency fund protects your confidence. It prevents panic, debt and emotional breakdown during difficult times. Even a small monthly contribution builds a safety net. Peace comes from knowing, *"If something unexpected happens, I am prepared."*

Have the Right Insurance Plans

Insurance is emotional protection, not a financial burden. It shields your family from financial shocks and prevents a small crisis from becoming a large disaster.

Health insurance, life insurance and essential safety plans create strong security — and secure people are calmer, kinder and more stable.

Earn Smartly, Spend Wisely

Earning money is hard; wasting it is easy. Saving money is discipline; growing money is intelligence. Earning smartly means using your strengths wisely, upgrading your skills, choosing meaningful work and avoiding unnecessary job stress caused by comparison. Spending wisely means thoughtful decisions, planning expenses and valuing long-term peace over short-term excitement.
Smart earning + wise spending = peaceful living.

Invest Heavily in Your Future

Investment is not limited to stocks or property — it includes everything that strengthens your future. Your skills, your health, your knowledge, your savings, your retirement plans and your long-term financial strategy. Money invested wisely is not money lost — it is **security gained**. Even small, consistent investments grow into powerful results over time.

Real-Life Examples:

- **Ilan — Finding Peace Through Smart Habits** - Ilan lived month to month, spending freely on wants and ignoring planning. Every time an emergency arose, stress followed. One day, he decided to change — he separated needs from wants, built a small emergency fund and created a simple spending plan. Within months, his financial anxiety reduced and his confidence grew. He realised peace doesn't come from income — it comes from habits.
- **Reva — Building Stability Through Discipline** - Reva earned well but saved very little. She enjoyed shopping and dining out until a sudden medical expense shook her stability. That moment became her turning point. She started budgeting, investing regularly and controlling impulsive spending. Within a year, her financial life felt lighter, calmer and safer. She learned that strong money habits build the foundation for long-term peace.

Money cannot create happiness but wise money habits protect it. When you spend mindfully, save consistently, plan for emergencies, insure your risks and invest in your future, life becomes stable, calm and emotionally secure. Good money habits don't require high income — they require clarity, discipline and intention. Take care of your money and your money will take care of your peace.

Money Clarity for Peaceful Relationships

"Relationships break not because of money but because of silence around it."

Money is one of the most sensitive areas in close relationships. Lending, borrowing, gifting, contributing or sharing expenses may look simple on the surface but without clarity they create emotional undercurrents that quietly strain even strong bonds. Most conflicts around money do not arise from selfishness or bad intentions — they arise from **unspoken expectations**, unclear agreements, forgotten conversations, delayed communication and emotional hesitation.

People feel awkward discussing money with those they love. They avoid the topic to keep the peace, not realizing that silence creates more damage than the money ever could. When financial matters are handled with honesty and openness, relationships feel lighter and trust grows naturally. Money clarity is not about strictness — it is about keeping things simple, clean and respectful so relationships stay warm and healthy.

Why Money Creates Tension in Close Relationships

Money conversations feel uncomfortable, so people avoid them until misunderstandings grow. What one person sees as help, the other may view as a loan. When expectations are not spoken clearly, assumptions fill the space. Over time, memory fades — who paid what, who agreed to what, what the intention was — and this silence turns into emotional discomfort.

Delays in repayment create awkwardness; ego and guilt interfere; borrowers hesitate to update and lenders hesitate to remind. This creates friction that has nothing to do with money and everything to do with unclear communication. Clarity prevents tension. Openness protects the relationship.

Principles for Healthy Money Relationships

Before any financial exchange, clarity is kindness. Define the amount, purpose and timeline. Keep a simple written note or message so nothing is forgotten. Respect agreements and update early if circumstances change. Never mix ego with money — both lending and borrowing require humility. Treat family and friends with the same respect you'd offer a professional — delays and silence hurt more when relationships are close. And keep gifts, loans and support clearly separate so no one feels burdened later. Relationships should not feel like accounting books. Clarity keeps love at the center.

What Clarity Looks Like in Everyday Life

A few simple sentences can prevent months of discomfort —

- "I can help with this amount; just return it next month."

- "Let's split the bill and settle it today."
- "This is a gift — no need to return it."
- "I'll update you about the payment on Friday."
- "Let me write it down so there's no confusion later."

These small gestures remove emotional weight and protect mutual respect.

Real-Life Examples:

- **Arden — Saving a Friendship Through Clear Communication** - Arden lent a small amount to his friend but avoided reminding him out of discomfort. Months passed, frustration grew and distance formed. One day, Arden sent a gentle message explaining the situation honestly. His friend immediately apologized — he had simply forgotten. The amount was settled and the tension dissolved. Arden realised that silence creates distance but clarity brings peace.
- **Mira — Keeping Family Harmony Through Transparency** - When Mira helped her cousin financially during a difficult season, she clearly said, "This is support, not a loan. You don't need to return it." Her cousin felt relieved and their relationship stayed warm instead of strained. A year later, the same cousin supported her through a personal challenge. Mira understood that generosity feels lighter when expectations are clear.

How Clarity Protects Both Sides

Clarity protects the lender from resentment, awkwardness and misunderstandings. It protects the borrower from guilt, stress and confusion. When both sides know the truth from the beginning, the relationship remains emotionally balanced. Money becomes a tool — not a tension.

Money does not harm relationships — silence does. Clear communication, respectful agreements and timely updates keep financial matters simple and relationships peaceful. When money is handled with honesty and clarity, it becomes an expression of care, not a source of conflict. Keep money simple, keep relationships clean and let clarity protect the love you share.

Own Less, Access More: Go Digital

"Free your space. Free your mind. Let the cloud carry the weight."

We often buy and keep physical things out of habit—documents we print "just in case," board games that gather dust, cash we queue to withdraw, DVDs we rarely play. Each item takes space, money and attention. **Digital alternatives** compress these burdens into a few taps: files live in secure cloud folders, games are on apps, payments happen instantly and movies stream anywhere. Going digital isn't about denying joy; it's about **removing friction**—no printing, no storage boxes, no device clutter, no maintenance. The payoff is immediate: **lighter homes, quicker workflows and more time** for what truly matters.

Real-Life Examples:

- **Meera**, a 34-year-old project lead, used to spend Mondays fighting paper: **Checking paper prints**: She printed 60–80 pages to mark corrections with a pen. **Digital switch**: She began using a PDF annotation app on her tablet. Now she highlights, comments and signs digitally—no queues at the printer, no cartridges, no file cabinets.
- **Indoor games at home**: Chess boards and Snakes & Ladders lay scattered; pieces went missing after every weekend. **Digital switch**: Family game night moved to mobile/TV apps. Same fun, zero cleanup, no broken dice, no missing pawns.
- **Housie (Tambola) with friends**: Ticket books, pens and shouting numbers across a hall. **Digital switch**: She hosts housie on an app with auto-tickets and random draws. The group plays from anywhere; results are tracked and shared instantly.
- **Money payment**: Cash withdrawals, small change and bill queues ate evenings. **Digital switch**: UPI and online banking replaced cash. Bill reminders trigger one-tap payments; receipts are auto-saved to a cloud "Finance" folder.

Practical Digital Replacements (quick bullets you can include in the chapter)

- **Checking paper prints** → PDF/Word annotation + e-signature tools.
- **Chess / Snakes & Ladders / Housie** → Mobile/TV apps; invite friends online.
- **Money payment** → UPI/mobile wallets/online banking; receipts auto-saved to cloud.
- **Docs & records** → Paperless filing in cloud folders with shared access.
- **Movies & music** → Streaming libraries; no discs, no shelves.
- **Photos** → Cloud albums with automatic backup and smart search.

Physical stuff promises convenience but often **demands maintenance**—space, cleaning, sorting and replacements. Digital choices convert ownership into **access**: lighter rooms, faster workflows, fewer errands and calmer days. It's not about having less; it's about **freeing capacity** for health, relationships and meaningful work.

PART VIII — Happiness: Joy Beyond Possessions

Redefine happiness beyond achievement and material success.

Chapter 18: Redefining Happiness

"Happiness is not a destination—it's a way of living in the present.

The True Pursuit of Happiness

"Happiness is not something you chase—it's something you create in the present."

Happiness isn't found in the future or the past — it exists only here and now. When you detach from what you cannot control, release unnecessary emotional weight and engage fully in the present, life starts to feel light, peaceful and meaningful.

True happiness grows from perspective, not possessions.

1. Detach and Let Go - Holding on to past hurts, failed plans or unrealistic expectations drains joy. Detachment is not indifference — it is choosing peace over emotional baggage. Example: The Buddha taught that letting go is the doorway to inner freedom.

2. Focus Only on What You Can Control - Trying to control people or circumstances creates frustration. What you *can* control is your mindset, your choices and your response. Example: Stoic philosopher Epictetus taught that your reactions define your freedom.

3. Balance Emotions and Take Things Lightly - Overreacting to small problems steals happiness. Respond, don't explode. Example: Gandhi's calmness allowed him to lead with clarity even under pressure.

4. Move Beyond Fear - Fear restricts growth. Happiness expands when you act despite uncertainty. Example: Malala continued her mission for girls' education despite immense danger.

5. Stop Living in the Past or Future - Regret and worry are happiness thieves. Life unfolds only in the present. Example: Eckhart Tolle's work reminds people to return to "the now."

6. Forgive and Free Yourself - Forgiveness empties the heart of bitterness. Happiness cannot coexist with resentment. Example: Nelson Mandela chose reconciliation over revenge after decades of imprisonment.

7. Give More Than You Take - Contribution creates purpose. Happiness grows when you help others rise. Example: Mother Teresa found joy in serving the poorest communities.

8. Enjoy the Small Moments - Happiness is built from ordinary joys — a conversation, a meal, a small task done well. Example: The Japanese idea of *Ikigai* encourages finding meaning in simple routines.

9. Slow Down and Live One Day at a Time - Rushing through life blinds you to its beauty. Slowing down brings awareness. Example: Mindfulness teaches presence — savour meals, walks and conversations.

10. Stop Overthinking - Thinking endlessly about outcomes, mistakes or hypotheticals drains energy. Simplicity brings relief. Example: Steve Jobs removed distractions, so his focus stayed on creation, not clutter.

11. One Task at a Time - Multitasking splits attention and increases errors. Single-tasking builds calm and mastery. Example: Serena Williams excels by focusing fully on each drill, one moment at a time.

Happiness isn't a destination reached through achievements — it is a daily practice of presence, forgiveness, contribution and simplicity. When you stop chasing what's outside and start nurturing what's inside, joy becomes your natural state.

The secret is simple: be here now.

Progress as the Ultimate Source of Happiness

Advancement is the Heartbeat of Happiness."

The Essence of Progress

Tony Robbins often emphasizes that *"Progress equals happiness."* This statement *captures* a universal truth: human beings thrive not simply when they achieve but when they grow. Happiness is not found in comfort or stagnation; it is found in movement, in becoming more than we were yesterday.

Progress is the invisible fuel of fulfilment. Even small steps — learning a new skill, improving health, deepening relationships — create momentum. That momentum reassures us that life is not static but evolving and this sense of forward motion is what generates joy.

Why Progress Matters More Than Achievement

Many people believe happiness comes from reaching a destination: earning wealth, buying a house or achieving recognition. Yet, once the goal is reached, the joy often fades quickly. The trophy gathers dust, the promotion becomes routine and the new car loses its shine. What sustains happiness is not the achievement itself but the journey of growth that led to it.

Achievement Without Progress: Winning a prize feels good for a moment but without continued growth, emptiness follows.

Progress Without Achievement: Even if the final goal is far away, steady improvement brings satisfaction and hope.

Example: A person trying to lose weight may not reach their ideal number immediately but noticing small changes — more energy, better sleep, healthier habits — creates happiness long before the final result.

The Psychology of Progress

Progress creates happiness because it aligns with three fundamental human needs:

- **Growth:** We are wired to expand beyond our current limits. Stagnation feels unnatural, while growth feels energizing.
- **Contribution:** Progress allows us to give more to others — whether through skills, resources or wisdom.
- **Meaning:** Moving forward gives life a sense of purpose. Without progress, even abundance feels empty.

This is why people often feel restless when stuck in routines. The absence of growth creates dissatisfaction, while even small improvements restore hope and vitality.

Modern Life and the Hunger for Progress

In today's fast-paced world, people often confuse consumption with progress. Buying new gadgets or chasing trends gives temporary pleasure but not lasting fulfilment. True progress is internal: developing discipline, emotional intelligence and purpose.

Real-Life Examples:

- **Workplace Example**: An employee feels stuck in routine tasks. When they learn a new skill or take on a challenge, their motivation rises.
- **Family Example**: Parents who consciously improve communication with their children feel joy in the progress of deeper bonds.
- **Personal Example**: Someone practicing meditation daily notices gradual calmness. This progress, though subtle, becomes a source of lasting happiness.

The Marathon Runner

Arjun, a 40-year-old businessman, decided to run a marathon. At first, he struggled to jog even two kilometres. But he committed to daily training, gradually increasing his distance. Each week, he noticed progress — stronger stamina, better breathing, more confidence. By the time he completed the marathon, the medal was a symbol but the real joy had already been experienced in the months of progress. His happiness came not from the finish line but from the journey of becoming stronger and more disciplined. **Lesson**: Progress transforms identity. It makes us proud not of what we have but of who we are becoming.

Parable: The Climber's Joy

A climber sets out to reach the mountain peak. Halfway up, storms slow him down. He hasn't reached the summit yet but every step upward fills him with pride and energy. The joy is not only in standing at the top but in knowing he is climbing. **Lesson**: Happiness is not at the destination; it is in the progress of the climb.

Progress is the ultimate source of happiness because it assures us that life is evolving. Achievements fade, possessions lose their shine but growth remains a constant source of joy. When we commit to progress — in health, relationships, work and spirit — we discover that happiness is not something to be found at the end of the road but something created along the way.

Happiness and Longevity: The Science Behind It

"A joyful heart is the secret to a longer life."

Happiness isn't just a feeling—it's a powerful force that influences health, resilience and even lifespan. Science shows that joy and optimism can add years to life, while stress and negativity shorten it. Let's explore why happiness matters and how you can cultivate it for a longer, healthier life.

What Research Reveals

- **Optimism and Longevity** - A Harvard study found that people with higher levels of optimism were significantly more likely to live past age 85.
- **Happiness and Health** - Research in Singapore showed that older adults with higher happiness scores had lower risks of death from all causes.
- **Relationships Matter** - The 85-year Harvard Study of Adult Development revealed that strong, positive relationships are the single biggest predictor of happiness and long life.

Why Happiness Extends Life

- **Reduced Stress** - Joy lowers stress hormones, protecting the heart and immune system.
- **Healthier Habits** - Happy people tend to exercise more, eat better and avoid harmful behaviours.
- **Social Connection** -Joyful individuals maintain stronger relationships, which are linked to longevity.

- **Resilience**
  Optimism helps people recover faster from illness and cope better with challenges.

Real-Life Examples:

- Imagine two people of the same age and health. One maintains a positive outlook, nurtures friendships and enjoys daily pleasures. The other isolates themselves and focuses on negativity. Over time, the first person's emotional resilience and healthier lifestyle contribute to a longer, more fulfilling life.

Happiness is more than a mood—it's a protective factor for health and longevity. By cultivating optimism, nurturing relationships and finding joy in everyday life, you not only live better but also live longer.

Culture Is King - The Foundation of a Happy Life

"Culture shapes behaviour, behaviour shapes habits and habits shape destiny."

Culture is the invisible force that guides how we think, act, communicate and live. It is the set of values, beliefs, principles and practices that shape our identity and influence every decision we make. Whether in families, workplaces or societies, a strong and healthy culture builds trust, unity, respect and happiness. When people live in an environment that reflects positive culture—gratitude, kindness, discipline, respect, honesty and collaboration—they feel safe, supported and inspired. A good culture is not just a 'nice to have'—it is the king that rules happiness and long-term well-being.

Why Culture Matters in Creating a Happy Life

In families, culture becomes the emotional environment where children grow and adults feel anchored. In workplaces, culture determines motivation, teamwork and satisfaction. In society, culture shapes harmony, responsibility and collective peace. Research in behavioural science shows that strong cultures reduce stress, improve relationships, increase resilience and foster a deeper sense of belonging. Culture doesn't just define the environment—it defines the experience.

Key Elements of a Happiness-Driven Culture

- **Respect as a Foundation:** When people feel valued, trust and harmony naturally grow.
- **Kindness & Empathy:** A culture of compassion strengthens emotional bonds.
- **Integrity & Responsibility:** Honest behaviour creates reliability and emotional safety.

- **Gratitude & Appreciation:** Small words of thanks transform the energy of any environment.
- **Support & Unity:** People thrive when they know they are not alone.

Real-Life Examples:

- **The Family That Built Happiness Through Rituals** – The Shah family created a habit of having dinner together, expressing gratitude and celebrating even small achievements. Over time, these simple rituals built emotional closeness and a peaceful, joyful home. **Lesson:** Culture is built in the small daily practices, not grand gestures.
- **The Company That Grew Because of Good Culture** – A small firm adopted values like transparency, appreciation and collaboration. Employees felt respected and supported. Productivity increased, conflicts decreased and the company became known for its positive environment. **Lesson:** Culture shapes results even before strategies do.

Culture is the silent king that rules happiness. When you build a culture based on respect, compassion, gratitude and integrity, life becomes lighter, relationships become richer and challenges become easier to face. A strong culture doesn't happen by chance—it is built consciously, lived consistently and passed lovingly to others. Create the right culture and happiness will naturally follow.

Embracing Slow Living

"Slow down. Life is not a race; it's a rhythm."

Life today moves fast—too fast. Slow living is not about doing less; it's about doing what truly matters with clarity, intention and presence. These principles offer a simple, sustainable way to slow down without disconnecting from the world.

Why Slow Living Matters

- **Presence:** You savour the moment instead of rushing through it.
- **Meaningful Choices:** You prioritise what brings joy and purpose.
- **Better Relationships:** Quality time strengthens emotional bonds.
- **Inner Calm:** Letting go of unnecessary busyness restores balance.
- **Self-Care:** Health and well-being become natural priorities.
- **Memories:** Life feels richer when you're fully present for it.

How to Live Slowly – Living one day at a time. Begin each morning by consciously noticing the date. It is a simple practice yet it reconnects you with the flow of time. When you look at the date before your day begins, you become aware of where you stand in the month, the week and your

own life's rhythm. This awareness brings clarity, helps you plan with intention and gently trains your mind to live in the present moment. When you value time, you naturally begin to value the way you spend it. Following shall be put in practice.

1. **Slow Down & Create Stillness -** Stillness is the doorway to clarity. A few minutes of quiet reflection, meditation or prayer helps calm the mind and resets your inner pace. When you pause, you start hearing what life has been trying to tell you.
2. **Know Your Values & Let Them Lead -** Simplicity begins with clarity. Identify what matters most and say yes only to what aligns with your values. This removes confusion and brings direction to your days.
4. **Begin Your Day with Purpose -** Rise early and start gently. A short routine—movement, journaling, mindfulness or reading—sets a calm rhythm and boosts focus for the rest of the day.
5. **Prioritise What Truly Matters -** Do the most important tasks first. Label them by urgency and impact. Release unnecessary tasks and simplify your to-do list so your energy goes where it matters.
6. **Set Boundaries & Protect Your Time -** Saying "no" is a slow-living superpower. Decline obligations that drain your energy or add clutter to your schedule. Each "no" creates space for what nourishes you.
7. **Declutter Your Space & Your Life -** Physical clutter creates mental clutter. Clear your home, donate unused items and avoid impulse shopping. Minimal space leads to a calmer mind.
8. **Practice Gratitude & Mindfulness -** Gratitude shifts your focus from lack to abundance. Slow down enough to notice small joys. Eat slowly, breathe deeply, walk mindfully—presence brings peace.

9. **Live Within Your Means** - Simplify finances by reducing unnecessary expenses, ending unused subscriptions and avoiding lifestyle comparison. Track where your time and money go to gain clarity and control.
10. **Care for Health: Body, Mind & Rest** - Nourish yourself with wholesome food, movement and good sleep. Choose activities that energise and restore you. A healthy body makes life naturally simpler.
11. **Reconnect with Nature** - Nature slows the mind naturally. Walk outdoors, listen to birds, feel the breeze, watch the sky. Even 10 minutes outdoors can reset your mood and perspective.
12. **Nurture Meaningful Relationships** - Invest in genuine friendships and let go of draining connections. Practice kindness, empathy and generosity. Support others—and allow others to support you.
13. **Reduce Digital Overload** - Limit unnecessary screen time and constant scrolling. Reduce media consumption and protect your attention. Use your time for what enriches you, not what empties you.
14. **Create Simple Routines** - Daily routines reduce mental load. Establish simple rhythms for mornings, meals, work, rest and winding down—small rituals bring stability and ease.
15. **Embrace Solitude & Silence** - Quiet time strengthens clarity. Spend moments alone to reflect, recharge and reconnect with yourself. Solitude isn't loneliness—it's self-connection.
16. **Be Present & Enjoy the Moment** - Stop rushing. Eat slowly, drive calmly, breathe deeply. Let go of past regrets and future worries. Life becomes fuller when lived one moment at a time.

Real-Life Examples:

- **The Overworked Professional Who Found Peace in Slowing Down** - Rhea spent years racing through her mornings—skipping breakfast, checking emails in bed and rushing to work. After feeling constantly exhausted, she experimented with "slow mornings": a quiet cup of tea, a short stretch and five minutes of journaling. Within weeks, her stress reduced, her thinking became clearer and she felt more present throughout the day. **Lesson:** Slowing down the first hour of the day can elevate the next fourteen.
- **The Young Couple Who Simplified Weekends for Joy** - Vikram and Aditi realised their weekends were filled with errands, social pressure and endless screen time. They created a simple slow-living ritual: morning walks, phone-free brunch and an evening spent cooking together. These small, intentional moments strengthened their bond and turned ordinary

weekends into meaningful memories. **Lesson:** When you slow down, life becomes richer—not smaller.

- **Imagine starting your day without rushing**. You enjoy a mindful breakfast, take a short walk and spend time on one meaningful task instead of juggling ten. Later, you share dinner with loved ones, free from distractions. Each moment feels richer because you are fully present.

Slow living is not about doing less—it is about doing what matters most. By living slowly, you find balance, create lasting memories and discover peace in the present moment. It is a path to a more intentional, fulfilling and joyful life.

Slow living isn't about escaping life; it's about returning to it. By slowing down, simplifying, choosing mindfully and living intentionally, you reclaim your peace, energy and joy. A slow life is not a small life—it's a deeply lived one.

Discovering Your Ikigai

"Find your reason for being—the bridge between joy and purpose."

Your ikigai is your ***"reason for being"*** *— the unique blend of what you love, what you're good at, what the world needs and what you can be paid for*. It's a Japanese concept that helps people find purpose and fulfilment in life.

Ikigai is a Japanese word that combines *iki* (life) and *gai* (worth or benefit). Together, it means *"a reason for living"* or *"what makes life worth it."* It's like the French idea of *raison d'être*—your reason for being.

Rather than chasing success or happiness as separate goals, ikigai encourages you to align your passions, talents and contributions to the world. When these elements overlap, you find a life that feels both meaningful and joyful.

Ikigai sits at the intersection of four key questions:
When all four overlap, you discover your ikigai—the sweet spot where purpose and fulfilment meet.

The Four Elements of Ikigai

Element	Question	Outcome
Passion	What do you love?	Brings joy and excitement
Mission	What does the world need?	Creates impact and meaning
Vocation	What can you be paid for?	Ensures sustainability
Profession	What are you good at?	Builds confidence and mastery

How to Find Your Ikigai

1. **Reflect Deeply:** Write down answers to the four questions above.
2. **Look for Overlaps:** Notice where your passions, skills and opportunities intersect.
3. **Experiment:** Try small steps toward activities that feel aligned.
4. **Adjust Over Time:** Ikigai is not fixed—it evolves as you grow.
5. **Live Intentionally:** Use your ikigai as a compass for decisions, big and small.

Real-Life Examples:

- A chef may love cooking (*passion*), be skilled at it (*profession*), serve communities that need nourishing food (*mission*) and earn a living from it (*vocation*). Their ikigai is not just cooking—it's creating joy and health through food.

Your ikigai is the bridge between personal joy and collective good. It's not about chasing endless goals but about aligning your life with what truly matters. When you live your ikigai, every day feels purposeful, balanced and deeply fulfilling.

Ikigai isn't found by searching outside — it's revealed by listening within.

Your Happiness, Your Responsibility - The Path to Inner Freedom

"Happiness grows the moment you stop handing its keys to other people."

Your happiness is not determined by what someone says, what someone does, what someone gives or what someone withholds. It does not depend on possessions, praise, status, wealth or circumstances. True happiness begins the moment you take full ownership of your internal world. When you realise *"I am responsible for my happiness"*, you stop waiting for others to make you feel good and you stop blaming others for making you feel bad. You become emotionally self-reliant. You choose your response, your meaning and your state of mind.
Happiness is not given—it is created.

Why This Realisation Matters

Most unhappiness comes from expecting others to behave a certain way. When they don't, our emotions collapse. We hand our peace to situations, moods, opinions and events outside our control. But joy that depends on people is fragile. Joy that depends on possessions is temporary. Joy that depends on outcomes is unstable. Psychological research shows that long-term happiness is shaped more by **inner habits** than external conditions.

When you take responsibility for your happiness, you gain emotional freedom:
Less reacting.
Less blaming.
More choosing.
More living.
Happiness becomes steady when it comes from within.

How to Take Responsibility for Your Happiness

Begin by shifting one belief:

"No one can make me unhappy without my participation."

This does not mean ignoring emotions; it means owning them. It means understanding that your response is your choice. It means recognising that your peace comes from your perspective, not people.

Focus on what you can control—your thoughts, your reactions, your habits, your boundaries, your routines. Practise gratitude for what you already have. Choose good inputs for your mind. Detach from over-expectation. Remind yourself that people act from their nature, not your preferences. When you stop tying your happiness to others' behaviour, your emotional life becomes calmer and more stable.

Being responsible for your happiness is not selfish—it is self-respect.

Real-Life Examples:

- **The Professional Who Stopped Giving Others Power -** Neev felt upset every time his boss spoke harshly or a colleague ignored him. He realised he had outsourced his mood to other people's behaviour. He shifted his mindset: *"Their behaviour is theirs; my happiness is mine."* He began focusing on his work, his self-talk and his emotional boundaries. Gradually, external comments lost their power. He became more confident and peaceful at work. **Lesson:** When you stop taking things personally, happiness becomes steady.
- **The Homemaker Who Took Back Control of Her Joy -** For years, Isha believed her happiness depended on how her family treated her. If her day wasn't appreciated, she felt invisible. One day she decided: *"My joy comes from my heart, not from others' reactions."* She created her own morning routine, started reading, walking and investing in herself. She became calmer, more cheerful and more fulfilled—without depending on anyone's approval. **Lesson:** Happiness grows when you nurture it from within.

You are the creator of your joy, the keeper of your peace and the owner of your emotions. Others may influence your day but they do not define your happiness unless you allow them to.

Choose thoughts that strengthen you.
Choose habits that nourish you.
Choose responses that respect your inner peace.

Because when you take responsibility for your happiness, **you take responsibility for your life.**

You Are Enough - Letting Go of Inferiority

"You are not less than anyone—you are simply different and your differences hold your unique power."

An inferiority complex is a heavy burden many people carry silently. It grows when you compare yourself with others, judge yourself harshly or believe that your worth depends on external approval. This inner belief of "I am not good enough" weakens confidence, limits potential and clouds your ability to see your own strengths. Letting go of the inferiority complex is not about proving anything to others—it is about rediscovering your own value, embracing your uniqueness and standing tall in your truth.

Why You Must Let Go of Inferiority

Inferiority creates emotional pressure, fear and self-doubt. It makes you shrink when you should rise, stay quiet when you should speak and hesitate when you should move forward. Psychological studies show that inferiority impacts mental well-being, relationships, decision-making and personal growth. When you constantly compare, you drain your confidence and disconnect from your inner strengths. You are not inferior—you are evolving.

Key Principles to Overcome Inferiority

- **Stop Comparison:** Every life has a different journey; comparison hides your gifts.
- **Recognize Your Strengths:** List your natural talents—these are your foundations of confidence.
- **Accept Your Imperfections:** Imperfection is part of being human, not a sign of being "less."
- **Celebrate Progress:** Notice every small improvement; growth is built step by step.
- **Affirm Your Worth:** Speak to yourself with kindness—your words shape your identity.

Real-Life Examples:

- **The Student Who Always Felt "Not Smart Enough"** – Aarav constantly compared his grades with others. His confidence dropped and he avoided challenges. When he shifted focus to his strengths—visual learning and creativity—his performance improved and his self-esteem grew. **Lesson:** You become strong when you stop measuring yourself by someone else's scale.
- **The Homemaker Who Believed She Was Not Important** – Sunita often felt inferior because she wasn't earning an income. Through reflection and acknowledgment of her contributions—managing the home, caring for the family—she realised her worth was far greater than she thought. **Lesson:** Your role never defines your value—your essence does.

Do not carry the weight of inferiority—it dims your spirit and hides your brilliance. When you embrace your strengths, accept your imperfections and trust your journey, you rise with authenticity and confidence. You are enough, you are capable and you are worthy—exactly as you are. When you stop seeing yourself as "less," you open the door to becoming your best.

The Sense of Humour - Lightness That Heals the Mind

"A good sense of humour doesn't change life—it changes the way you carry life."

A sense of humour is one of the greatest gifts you can give yourself. It helps you stay light in heavy moments, find joy in ordinary situations and handle challenges with grace instead of stress. Humour doesn't mean ignoring problems—it means facing them with a calmer heart and a lighter mind. When you laugh, tension melts, perspective widens and hope returns. Humour brings warmth to relationships, ease to conversations and resilience to your spirit. It reminds you that life doesn't always have to be serious to be meaningful.

Why Sense of Humour Matters

In today's fast, stressful world, people often forget to smile. Responsibilities increase, expectations rise and emotional pressure builds up. Without humour, life becomes heavier than it needs to be. Research shows that laughter reduces stress hormones, strengthens immunity, improves mood and boosts emotional resilience. It creates connection, lightens the atmosphere and helps people bond more deeply. Humour is not entertainment—it is emotional medicine.

How a Sense of Humour Improves Life

- **Reduces Stress & Anxiety:** Laughter relaxes the body and eases mental tension.
- **Strengthens Relationships:** Sharing a smile or a joke builds closeness and warmth.
- **Improves Emotional Balance:** Humour helps you step back and see situations more clearly.
- **Boosts Resilience:** People with humour bounce back faster from challenges.
- **Enhances Communication:** A light tone can resolve conflicts and improve understanding.

Real-Life Examples:

- **The Leader Who Used Humour to Build Team Spirit** – Amit's team was often stressed during deadlines. He gently added humour to meetings—light jokes, funny examples, tiny moments of laughter. This simple shift made the team feel more relaxed, connected and productive. **Lesson:** Humour builds trust and breaks tension.
- **The Homemaker Who Used Laughter to Handle Tough Days** – Kavita often felt overwhelmed by household responsibilities. Instead of complaining, she began turning stressful moments into humorous stories with her family. This brought joy, reduced arguments and made the home environment lighter. **Lesson:** Humour transforms pressure into playfulness.

A sense of humour does not remove life's problems—but it removes their power over you. It helps you breathe, recover and move forward with optimism. Laugh often. Smile freely. Lighten your heart. Humour is not just an emotion—it is strength disguised as joy. It reminds you that even in difficult times, there is always room for light.

Stay Active - Never Retire from Life

"Retirement is the end of a job, not the end of purpose."

Staying active is one of the strongest foundations of a happy, healthy and meaningful life. While professional retirement is natural, *life retirement*—where people stop learning, stop contributing, stop challenging themselves—leads to emotional decline, physical slowing and loss of meaning. A long, fulfilling life is built by remaining mentally engaged, socially connected and physically active. You may retire from a role but you must never retire from growth, service, learning and movement. Activity keeps your mind sharp, your body strong and your spirit alive.

Why Staying Active Matters

Life becomes hollow when routine disappears, when contribution stops and when days have no purpose. Many people decline rapidly after retirement—not because of age but because of *inactivity*. Research across cultures shows that people who remain active—working in some form, volunteering, learning, travelling, teaching, mentoring, exercising—live longer, stay healthier and feel happier. Activity gives structure to your day, meaning to your actions and direction to your identity. The heart stays young when the mind stays engaged.

How to Stay Active for a Meaningful Life

Remaining active doesn't mean rushing or overworking. It means intentionally staying connected to life. Continue doing work you enjoy, even if not for money. Build routines that include walking, learning, reading, gardening, teaching, helping, creating or mentoring. Stay curious—learn new skills, explore new places, meet new people. Keep your brain challenged with problem-solving, conversations and simple creativity. Give yourself goals—fitness, community service, family projects, personal learning targets. Activity is not just movement—it is purpose in motion.

Real-Life Examples:

- **The Engineer Who "Retired" but Never Stopped Being Useful -** After 35 years in industry, Sunil retired formally. But instead of slowing down, he began helping young engineers with interview preparation and project guidance. His days became full of purpose, conversations and contribution. His health improved because his mind stayed sharp and his routine stayed active. **Lesson:** When you stay useful, you stay youthful.
- **The Homemaker Who Found New Joy Through New Activity -** After her children moved out, Meena felt empty. But she refused to retire from life. She joined a yoga group, learned classical music, travelled with friends and volunteered at a local school. Within months, she felt emotionally brighter, physically energetic and socially connected. **Lesson:** New activity brings new life.

Stay active, stay curious, stay involved. Do not retire from movement, learning or contribution. When you wake up with a purpose, your body gains energy and your mind finds peace. You may retire from a job—but never retire from life. Keep moving, keep growing, keep giving. Because an active life is not just longer—it is richer, happier and deeply meaningful.

Bonus Tips to achieve Happy and Healthy life

1. Home & Surroundings

Home Interior

A peaceful interior supports a peaceful mind. Clean lines, calm colors, natural light and minimal décor cultivate clarity. When visual noise reduces, emotional noise reduces. Organized storage keeps daily life light. A beautiful home is not luxury—it's balance, comfort and energy that supports you.

Plan Your Day and Week

Planning turns chaos into calm. A short daily note and a brief weekly review help you see priorities clearly. When you know what matters, your attention softens and productivity rises. Planning protects your energy from constant firefighting. A planned life feels balanced and purposeful.

2. Money & Shared Costs

Money Sharing Within Group (Travel, Eating Out, etc.)

Clarity keeps friendships clean. Discuss budgets beforehand, split transparently and settle promptly. When expectations are spoken, outings feel lighter. Avoid assumptions—one short message prevents long discomfort. Shared experiences stay joyful when money is handled simply.

Avoid Lifestyle Inflation

As income grows, don't let spending outrun wisdom. Choose comfort over show, stability over status. Extra money deserves a plan—savings, learning, health and meaningful experiences. Peace comes from margins, not from more bills. A simple lifestyle is long-term wealth.

3. One-Option Living (Across All Items, Not Just Gadgets)

One Option in Life — One Mobile, One Laptop, One of Each Essential

Duplication breeds clutter and decision fatigue. Choose **one** reliable item per category—one phone, one laptop, one watch, one bag, one set of tools—and maintain it well. Fewer things mean fewer repairs, fewer choices and more focus. This isn't deprivation; it's design. When tools are intentional, life feels ordered.

Buy Best Quality Items for Your Daily Needs

Quality reduces replacement, frustration and hidden costs. A few reliable essentials beat cupboards of breakables. Good cookware, sturdy shoes, a supportive chair—small upgrades, daily relief. Quality is not about price; it's about lifespan and experience. Fewer, better things = a calmer day.

4. Digital Simplicity & Real Connection

Reduce Social Media Consumption

Social media is loud, persuasive, endless. Reducing it protects clarity and stops pointless comparison. Keep it intentional: check on purpose, not on impulse. The mind rests when inputs are fewer. Choose reality more often than the feed.

Sometimes Go Out Without Your Mobile

A phone-free walk is a reset. Your senses return—light, wind, voices, your own thoughts. Disconnection reduces anxiety and restores presence. Not every moment must be captured. Life feels more real when you meet it with empty hands.

Spend Time With Humans More Than Digital Tools

Joy travels through eye contact and laughter, not notifications. Choose conversations over scrolling, shared meals over shared links. People regulate our emotions in ways screens never will. Technology should support bonding—not replace it. The more human your day, the warmer it feels.

5. Children & Parenting

Kids Away From Mobile

Childhood is built by mud, books, puzzles and play—not by screens. Reduce device time to protect attention, sleep and creativity. Offer alternatives: games, outdoor time, craft corners and chores with praise. Children copy you—model the habits you want to see. Their memories should be experiences, not episodes.

Spend Time With Children to Become Happy and Young

Children return you to wonder. Join their games, answer their "why," take short walks, read aloud, laugh freely. Presence beats presents. Their curiosity will soften your stress and renew your spirit. Time with them is time back to yourself.

6. Relationships & Community

Respect Others

Respect is the simplest gift and the hardest to fake. It sounds like patient listening and looks like gentle behaviour. Honor differences without trying to win every point. Respect builds emotional safety; safety builds trust. Where there is respect, relationships flourish.

Meet Old Friends You Spent Time With in the Past

Old friends carry your unfiltered history. Meeting them resets your emotional compass. Stories, jokes and shared silence remind you who you are underneath roles. A short reunion can refill the heart. Some bonds are roots—return to them.

Celebrate Festivals for Joy

Festivals are pauses that say, "Life is meant to be felt." Decorations, rituals, music and food renew connection. Keep them simple and sincere; joy doesn't need grandeur. Festivals create family memory and cultural continuity. Celebration is gratitude in motion.

Attend Events for Recreation — Fuel Your Joy and Energy

Plays, concerts, talks and community shows refresh the spirit. They interrupt routine, spark ideas and lighten mood. Go with friends or go alone—just go. Recreation isn't escape; it's maintenance for joy. Schedule it the way you schedule work.

7. Personal Boundaries & Growth

The Art of Saying NO

A clear "no" is a gift to your future self. It protects time, energy and focus. Say no kindly, early and without essays. Boundaries reduce resentment and increase respect. Every "no" to noise is a "yes" to what matters.

Reduce Over-Commitment

Busy isn't noble if it empties you. Choose fewer duties and do them well. Align commitments with your values; decline the rest. Over-commitment breeds errors and irritability. A lighter calendar creates a kinder you.

Believe in Consistency Over Perfection

Perfection delays; consistency delivers. Small daily steps outperform rare heroic sprints. Track effort, not ego. When you show up steadily, confidence compounds. Progress loves routine.

Reflection Journaling

Put thoughts on paper to clear the head. Note one feeling, one win, one lesson—five minutes is enough. Writing slows the mind and reveals patterns. Journaling turns confusion into direction. The page is a gentle mirror.

8. Health & Safety

Regular Health Check-ups (Especially After a Certain Age)

Health issues often grow silently. Regular check-ups help you detect problems early, prevent complications and stay in control of your well-being. After a certain age, screenings become essential — they act as long-term protection for your body. Early awareness saves time, stress and suffering. Check-ups are not fear — they are responsibility.

Chapter 19: Icons of Simplicity: Great Lives, Simple Choices

Real-Life Stories of People Who Embraced Simplicity

Simplicity isn't less—it's leverage.

Throughout history and into our own time, many remarkable individuals have lived with a simplicity that magnified—not reduced—their power, clarity and contribution. Their lives show that simplicity is not an aesthetic; it is a discipline. It is a deliberate reduction of noise so the essential can rise to the surface. Below are portraits of people who lived lightly, thought deeply and acted with uncommon focus—revealing how simplicity scales success and how we can translate their choices into our own lives.

Mahatma Gandhi — Simplicity as Strength

Gandhi lived in a way that made his message visible through every detail of his day. Hand-spun khadi, modest possessions, unadorned travel and simple meals were not symbols of poverty but intentional alignment. He reduced wants to reduce distraction. His simplicity was a strategy for moral clarity—closing the gap between what he preached and how he lived. The quieter his life became, the louder his influence grew; the more he shed, the more he could serve.

Dr. A. P. J. Abdul Kalam — Frugal Mind, Abundant Mission

Kalam carried his brilliance lightly. Whether in a laboratory, a classroom or the President's office, his life remained grounded in modest routines and minimal possessions. Books, ideas and teaching filled his world—not display. He protected long blocks of uninterrupted work and carved out time for students even on his busiest days. His simplicity was not accidental; it was the architecture that allowed an enormous mission to fit inside an ordinary life.

Steve Jobs — Minimalism for Creative Focus

Jobs stripped away the unnecessary so imagination could breathe. His uniform outfits, uncluttered spaces and habit of relentless editing all served a single purpose: protect attention. The fewer decisions he made about trivial things, the more bandwidth he had for design, storytelling and product vision. Simplicity for Jobs was cognitive conservation—preserving the mental sharpness required to reshape entire industries.

Warren Buffett — Grounded Wealth, Clear Routine

Buffett's billions were built on a life remarkably free from excess. He stayed in the same home, kept predictable routines and embraced long stretches of quiet reading and reflection. He avoided lifestyle inflation because he understood that noise destroys judgment. Simplicity kept him consistent, patient and rational—qualities that compounded into historic success.

Nelson Mandela — Humility Beyond Power

After years of imprisonment, Mandela reentered the world with grace instead of grandeur. He cooked simple meals, tended gardens and took long walks—rituals that preserved his humanity in the midst of political turbulence. He led a nation through forgiveness rather than force. His simplicity came from humility: the awareness that personal grounding is the only safeguard against the distortions of power.

Mother Teresa — Service Over Possessions

Mother Teresa lived with barely anything yet gave everything. By shedding material needs, she freed her time, presence and heart for service. Simplicity kept her close to the people she served and prevented the ego from slipping into performance. Her influence flowed from a life that demanded little for herself and poured much into others.

The Dalai Lama — Joy in Fewer Attachments

The Dalai Lama's simplicity radiates through gentle routines, spiritual study, laughter and compassion. He teaches that when attachment decreases, inner peace expands. His days—built around reflection, silence and kindness—embody a life where joy arises not from accumulation but from emotional lightness.

Mark Zuckerberg — Defaults that Protect Focus

Zuckerberg simplified by pre-deciding the small things. A uniform wardrobe, predictable mornings and structured work blocks reduced decision friction, allowing him to conserve energy for high-leverage thinking. Simplicity, for him, was a system—a way of ensuring that attention stayed on building rather than browsing.

J. K. Rowling — Grounded After Greatness

Rowling's global success never pulled her into spectacle. She guarded quiet writing windows, gave generously and kept her life anchored in privacy and purpose. Her craft thrived because her world remained simpler than her fame. She knew that protecting the essential was more important than performing it.

Leonardo da Vinci — Elegance in Essentialism

Leonardo lived with simple tools, direct questions and an obsession with clarity. His notebooks reveal a mind that pursued precision over noise, function over flair. He stripped complexity until patterns appeared. Essentialism was not a restriction for Leonardo—it was a gateway to genius.

Nikola Tesla — Spartan Life, Singular Focus

Tesla lived sparsely so his inventions could live abundantly. A hotel room doubled as his laboratory; long solitary walks became engines of insight. He captured ideas instantly, guarding the spark before it faded. His simplicity was a force multiplier: the fewer distractions he kept, the more breakthroughs he produced.

Albert Einstein — Simplify to See the Pattern

Einstein favoured repeatable days, simple clothes and long thinking walks so his mind could stay devoted to higher questions. His genius came from distilling complexity into elegant truths. He believed the universe itself was simple at its core and his lifestyle mirrored that conviction—remove what is unnecessary and the pattern becomes visible.

The Pattern Behind Their Power

Across centuries and fields, these icons reveal the same equation:
Fewer wants → fewer distractions → more focus → deeper work → greater impact.
Simplicity does not shrink capacity—it concentrates it.
Clarity strengthens when non-essentials fall away.
Character stabilizes when the lifestyle is grounded.
Contribution expands when ego's demands stay low.
Calm becomes natural when life is light.

Principles → Micro Moves

- **Alignment (Gandhi):** Audit one habit to match your values.
- **Service (Kalam):** Keep a weekly "teacher's hour."
- **Focus (Jobs):** Start the day with one device-free deep task.
- **Discipline (Buffett):** Read and think for 30–60 minutes daily.
- **Humility (Mandela):** Maintain a grounding ritual under pressure.
- **Compassion (Mother Teresa):** Perform one silent service weekly.
- **Detachment (Dalai Lama):** Sit in silence for 15 minutes.
- **Defaults (Zuckerberg):** Pre-decide outfits, meals or work blocks.
- **Craft (Rowling):** Guard one sacred hour for core work.
- **Essentialism (Leonardo):** Use fewer tools; ask sharper questions.
- **Flow Protection (Tesla):** Keep a capture log for sparks.
- **Elegant Reduction (Einstein):** Remove one assumption from every plan.

These individuals could afford everything—and yet they chose only what served their purpose. In choosing *enough*, they found more: more clarity, more peace, more influence and more inner freedom. Their lives show that simplicity is not the absence of wealth or ambition; it is the presence of intention.

Part IX: Embracing Minimalism – The Joy of Less

Understand minimalism as a philosophy of freedom, not sacrifice.

Minimalism is more than a trend — it is a philosophy that challenges the way we see possessions, success and happiness. In a world that constantly tells us to want more, minimalism invites us to pause and ask: What truly adds value to my life? By stripping away excess, we create space for clarity, freedom and deeper joy. This part of the book explores the foundations of minimalism, defines what it really means and shows why living with less can lead to more fulfilment. Through stories, benefits and even common misconceptions, you'll discover how minimalism reshapes not only our homes and habits but also our identities and the way we connect with the world.

Chapter 20: Minimalism — The Philosophy of Living with Less

Defining Minimalism

"Minimalism is not about having less—it's about making room for more of what matters."

Minimalism is a philosophy of **intentional living**. It invites you to remove the excess—physical, mental and emotional—so your time, attention and energy can flow to what truly matters. It challenges the quiet belief that happiness arrives through more—more possessions, more achievements, more experiences—and replaces it with clarity, purpose and deliberate choice.

Minimalism is often mistaken for owning very few items or keeping sparse rooms. Those are possible expressions, not the essence. The true spirit is **discernment**—clearing what distracts, so your best effort, your best presence and your best love meet the places that deserve them most. It is not deprivation; it is deciding with care what you own, how you spend your hours and how you relate to others—so that life feels lighter, calmer and more aligned.

The Myth of More

We live in a culture that gently repeats, "more is better." More things, more status, more activity. Yet the more we accumulate—objects, obligations, even goals—the more scattered we can feel. In the chase for "more," attention fragments, rooms fill, schedules tighten and peace slips quietly to the edges. Minimalism begins by questioning that script.

Less Is More: The Power of Subtraction

Subtraction is not loss; it is liberation. By releasing what is unnecessary—unused items, non-essential commitments, noise you no longer need—you create space for what is essential: health, relationships, meaningful work and a settled mind. The first moments of subtraction can feel uncomfortable but what follows is significant: more time, more focus, more calm, more joy.

The Minimalist Mindset

Minimalism starts on the inside—how you evaluate and decide. Instead of operating on autopilot, you ask honest questions and let the answers guide you:

- Do I truly need this?
- Does this add value to my life now?
- What improves if I remove what drains my energy and attention?

These questions do not police your choices; they **clarify** them. As clarity grows, your actions begin to match your values.

Minimalism as Freedom

Letting go of excess frees you from maintaining what does not serve you—keeping up with trends, managing clutter, filling every spare moment with activity. The result is not a smaller life but a truer one: more room for authenticity, for deep work, for unhurried rest, for the people you love. Minimalism returns your hours and your headspace to where they can do the most good.

Minimalism Is Personal

There is no single minimalist look. For some, it's a modest home; for others, it's a well-used family space with intentional belongings. Some begin with digital decluttering; others simplify their calendar. Expression varies by need and season but the essence is constant: **simplify to make room for what truly matters.**

A Few Core Principles

- **Clarity and Focus:** As the noise reduces, your real priorities come into view. Energy gathers around what brings joy and growth.
- **Intentionality:** Possessions, habits and commitments are chosen because they fit your values. You decide what to bring in, what to continue and what to release.
- **Quality Over Quantity:** Appreciation replaces accumulation. You choose fewer, better things—and give them space to serve you well.
- **Freedom from Excess:** The more you own, the more you must maintain; the more you promise, the more you must perform. Minimalism loosens these bindings and returns peace of mind.
- **Simplicity Supports Sustainability:** Buying less and buying wisely reduces waste and honours durability, repair and care.

Inner Work That Changes the Outer World

Minimalism is as much emotional as it is practical. Letting go applies to objects—and to old stories, resentments and roles that quietly tire the spirit. As attachments loosen, gratitude and calm find room to grow. Your time becomes something you steward, not a storage room for other people's urgencies. Consumption becomes mindful: fewer impulses, more nourishment. And success, slowly, is measured by peace, presence and contribution—not by comparison or applause.

Everyday Expressions

You will see minimalism in many small ways: spending that slows and aligns with your values; rooms that breathe; a calendar with buffers and anchors; technology used with boundaries; deeper conversations; steadier routines; simpler, kinder choices for the planet. When there is less to manage and maintain, there is more room to think, create and truly live.

Why It Works

As you simplify, cause and effect become visible. Rooms clear and thoughts follow. Decisions get lighter because options are fewer and better. With less to maintain, you have more to give—to your health, your craft, your relationships and your rest. Minimalism does not shrink life; it **concentrates** it. What remains is stronger, kinder and unmistakably your own.

Begin Small

Minimalism is a direction, not a destination. Start where you are: one drawer, one routine, one decision. Let each small act of clarity ripple outward. Over time you will notice a pattern—less rush, more presence; less clutter, more ease; less proving, more living. This is the heart of minimalism: not an aesthetic but a way of seeing and choosing that brings you back to what matters most.

How Minimalism Challenges Conventional Thinking

"Breaking the Myth: Why Less Can Achieve More."

Minimalism is more than a lifestyle choice; it is a direct challenge to the way modern society teaches us to live. It questions long-held beliefs about success, happiness and fulfilment. In a world built on the idea that **more means better**, minimalism asks a quieter but far more powerful question: **"What if less is actually enough—and sometimes even more?"**

We grow up surrounded by messages that encourage accumulation—own more, earn more, achieve more, experience more. This constant pursuit creates a life crowded with possessions, obligations and expectations. Minimalism disrupts this pattern by turning the focus inward. It asks us to pause, reconsider our assumptions and realign our choices with what truly matters.

Less Is More

Conventional thinking links success with addition: more assets, more achievements, more comfort. Yet this mindset fuels constant consumption, leaving many people overstimulated, overextended and overwhelmed. Minimalism flips this idea. It reminds us that the **value** of life is not in the volume of things we have but in the **meaning** they bring. When we remove the unnecessary—items we don't use, commitments that drain us, obligations we no longer believe in—we uncover space for clarity, purpose and peace. "Less" becomes a pathway to "more": more time, more joy, more focus, more freedom. Minimalism is not about restriction. It is about **intentionality**—choosing what supports the life you want and releasing what does not.

Happiness Isn't Found in Material Possessions

Culture teaches us to chase happiness through purchases: the newest phone, the bigger car, the nicer wardrobe, the next vacation. Advertisements whisper that fulfilment is only one acquisition away. But the thrill fades quickly and the cycle repeats. Minimalism challenges this illusion. It suggests that happiness lives not in things but in **experiences, relationships and appreciation**. When we stop looking outward for satisfaction, we start noticing the richness of what we already have. Joy shifts from consumption to presence, from the next purchase to the current moment. This perspective calls us to redefine happiness—less as ownership, more as gratitude.

The Weight of the Backpack

Ravi and Aditya's mountain hike reveals the essence of minimalism. Ravi carried only what he truly needed. Aditya, fearing lack, packed everything "just in case." As the trail steepened, Aditya's heavy backpack slowed him down. His focus shifted from the journey to the burden he carried. Ravi, with his lighter load, moved freely enjoying the breeze, the scenery and the moment.

By evening, Aditya realised he didn't need half the items he brought. The next morning, he left behind the excess. Suddenly, the hike felt lighter. His attention returned to the beauty around him. At the summit he said, "Less isn't a disadvantage—it's freedom."

The story mirrors life. Often, we carry too much—not just physically but emotionally and mentally. We assume more will keep us safe. Instead, it makes the journey harder. Minimalism helps us release what weighs us down so we can enjoy the path we are on.

The Coffee Cart Revolution

Ramesh's simple coffee cart challenged the conventional belief that success requires scale, variety and complexity. While big cafés offered long menus, he focused on three high-quality drinks.

No frills. No noise. Just great coffee.

People loved it. They didn't have to choose from dozens of options. They didn't feel rushed or overwhelmed. His simplicity became his strength. Low costs, focused effort, consistent quality—his small cart thrived while larger cafés struggled under complexity.

When asked the secret behind his success, Ramesh said, "Businesses fail when they try to do too much. Simplicity builds sustainability." Minimalism in action shows that clarity and focus often outperform excess and complication.

Success Isn't Measured by External Achievements

Society often ties success to numbers: income, titles, awards, status. This creates a race with no finish line—people endlessly striving for more, even at the cost of peace, health and relationships.
Minimalism questions this definition. It suggests success is **living aligned with your values**—not impressing others. It shifts attention from what you achieve to how you live. For many, success becomes time with loved ones, meaningful work, personal growth or simply waking up with a calm mind.

Minimalism replaces pressure with purpose.

Consumerism Isn't the Path to Fulfilment

The global economy thrives on constant consumption. Buy, use, discard—repeat. Minimalism interrupts this cycle by teaching contentment. It guides us toward mindful choices and appreciation of what we already own. Instead of chasing novelty, minimalists focus on quality. Instead of accumulating more, they nurture what matters. Fulfilment grows from intention, not indulgence.

Freedom Isn't Found in Having More—but in Carrying Less

Conventional thinking equates freedom with abundance. Minimalism reveals a deeper truth: **the more we carry, the more we are bound to maintain.** Less clutter, fewer obligations and simpler choices open the door to emotional, financial and mental freedom. Freedom is not about endless options—it is about clarity and ease.

Relationships Matter More Than Status

Traditional thinking encourages social climbing, networking and expanding circles to gain influence. Minimalism gently questions this. It places value on **authentic connections**, not strategic ones. Deep, honest relationships nourish far more than wide, superficial networks. When we stop seeking approval, we find belonging. When we stop collecting contacts, we start building community. Minimalism brings relationships back to the heart.

Minimalism challenges the deeply rooted belief that "more" leads to happiness, success or fulfilment. It invites us to question societal norms, consumer pressures and the constant push to accumulate. It offers a quieter, clearer alternative: **Live intentionally. Keep what matters. Release what doesn't.**

Benefits of Minimalism

"Less isn't lack—it's liberation."

Minimalism is much more than simplifying your space; it is a shift in how you live, think and choose. When you remove what is unnecessary, you make room for clarity, peace and meaningful living. Whether it is mental calm, financial freedom or stronger relationships, minimalism enhances almost every area of life.

Mental Clarity and Focus

A cluttered environment creates a cluttered mind. When physical space is overloaded, your thoughts mirror that chaos. By decluttering, you reduce mental noise and restore focus. With fewer distractions, your mind feels lighter and more creative, decision-making becomes easier and your daily rhythm becomes calmer.

Reduced Stress and Anxiety

Modern life pushes us to constantly achieve, acquire and compare. This pressure builds stress, anxiety and burnout. Minimalism softens this burden by removing excess commitments and possessions. When you release what doesn't serve you, you create space for peace, rest and emotional balance. Less to manage means less to worry about.

More Time and Energy
Every possession requires attention: cleaning organising, maintaining or thinking about it. By simplifying what you own and do, you regain time and energy. You can invest this time in relationships, rest, hobbies or meaningful work. With less on your plate, your days become smoother and more intentional.

Financial Freedom
Minimalism transforms your relationship with money. Instead of buying on impulse, you purchase with intention. You naturally spend less, avoid unnecessary debt and save more for experiences or long-term goals. Financial stress reduces and you gain freedom to live without the weight of constant consumption.

Improved Relationships
When life is not dominated by possessions or performance, relationships move to the centre. Minimalism encourages presence—listening, connecting and spending quality time. It also helps you release relationships that drain your energy, making space for those that uplift and support you. Simplicity strengthens connection.

Greater Self-Awareness and Personal Growth
Minimalism requires introspection: What matters? What aligns with my values? What can I release? This process deepens self-awareness and reveals what truly fulfils you. With less distraction, you grow more mindful, confident and purpose-driven. Your inner world becomes clearer and stronger.

A Sense of Purpose and Fulfilment
By removing noise, you can focus on what genuinely matters—purpose, passions, family and meaningful goals. You stop chasing what doesn't align with your values and start building a life that feels true to you. This alignment creates lasting fulfilment and inner contentment.

Improved Productivity
A simpler environment means fewer interruptions and smoother workflow. Whether at home or at work, minimalism helps you focus on priorities and eliminate distractions. When your surroundings support clarity, your productivity naturally rises.

Increased Happiness
Minimalism shifts happiness from "more things" to "more meaning." When you stop relying on external possessions for satisfaction, your attention moves to experiences, growth, relationships and gratitude. Happiness becomes internal and stable.

Simplicity in Design and Aesthetics

Minimalist design—clear lines, open spaces, calm colours—creates an atmosphere of peace. A simple home feels breathable organised and easy to maintain. This clarity often extends to digital spaces as well, reducing overwhelm and supporting mental calm.

Environmental Impact

Consuming less automatically reduces waste, clutter and environmental harm. By choosing fewer, better and more sustainable items, you contribute to a healthier planet and a more conscious way of living.

Holistic Well-Being

Minimalism nurtures physical, mental and emotional health. With less clutter and more intentional routines, sleep improves, stress reduces and healthier habits take root. Simplicity supports long-term balance and well-being.

Simplicity as Freedom

Minimalism liberates you from the weight of excess—too many things too much pressure too many obligations. When you own less and commit less, you gain more freedom to live on your terms, with clarity and independence.

Personal Growth Through Letting Go

Letting go is emotional work. Releasing objects, old roles or draining relationships teaches resilience and builds inner strength. You learn to detach from what no longer supports your growth, creating space for renewal and change.

Redefining Success

Minimalism encourages you to measure success by peace, purpose and authenticity—not by accumulation, status or comparison. This shift creates a healthier, more grounded sense of fulfilment.

Living in the Present Moment

With fewer distractions and less mental clutter, you return naturally to the present. You notice small joys—a slow morning, a conversation, a quiet walk—and appreciate the richness of now.

Intentional Relationships

Minimalism helps you invest deeply in relationships that matter. Instead of maintaining many superficial connections, you build genuine bonds grounded in mutual respect and shared values.

Sustainable and Ethical Consumption

Minimalism encourages conscious purchasing—fewer items, better quality, ethical sourcing and reduced waste. This supports both personal integrity and planetary well-being.

Creative and Innovative Thinking

When distractions fall away, mental space expands. Creativity grows, ideas flow more freely and innovation becomes a natural part of your life. Minimalism creates room for imagination.

Simplicity in Technology

Digital simplicity—fewer apps, fewer notifications organised devices—reduces overwhelm and allows technology to support your life instead of controlling it. Intentional tech use increases focus and peace.

Mindful Parenting

Minimalism supports parenting by emphasising time, attention and experiences over material goods. It helps children learn gratitude, creativity and presence through simple, meaningful moments.

The Joy of Empty Spaces

Empty spaces are not empty—they are calming. A clear countertop or an uncluttered shelf gives your mind a moment of rest. Space becomes a source of peace.

Living with Purpose Over Perfection

Minimalism removes the pressure to meet external standards. Instead of chasing perfection, you focus on what feels true, meaningful and aligned with your values.

Minimalism in Travel

Travel becomes lighter and richer. With fewer belongings and fewer expectations, you immerse yourself in new places more fully, enjoying the experience rather than the checklist.

Holistic Living

Minimalism promotes balance across all areas—mental, physical, emotional and spiritual. It guides you toward a lifestyle grounded in healthy choices and intentional rhythms.

Empowerment through Simplicity

Each time you choose simplicity over excess, you take control of your life. The more clarity you create, the more empowered and purposeful you feel.

Emotional Clarity
Minimalism helps you release emotional baggage—old hurts, unhealthy patterns, draining relationships—making space for peace, gratitude and healing.

Cultivating Gratitude
When you stop chasing more, you begin appreciating what you already have. Gratitude becomes natural, grounding your life in contentment rather than comparison.

In Summary
Minimalism clears the excess and amplifies what matters. You gain clarity, reduce stress, free time and energy, strengthen relationships and rediscover purpose. Minimalism is not deprivation—it is **making room for a richer, calmer and more meaningful life.**

It is always Quality over Quantity
Less indeed a way more than you think

Common Misconceptions About Minimalism

"It's Not About Less—It's About What Matters."

Minimalism is often misunderstood. These misconceptions prevent people from experiencing its real benefits. Here are the most common misunderstandings—simplified and clarified.

1. Minimalism Means Owning Very Few Things
Misconception: You must live with the bare minimum.
Reality: Minimalism is about keeping only what adds value—guided by needs and priorities, not a specific number of items.

2. Minimalism Is Only About Decluttering
Misconception: It's just cleaning your home.
Reality: Minimalism extends to your schedule, relationships, commitments, digital life and mindset.

3. Minimalists Don't Enjoy Life or Have Fun
Misconception: Minimalism removes joy, entertainment and social life.
Reality: It frees time, energy and money for meaningful relationships and richer experiences.

4. Minimalists Are Extreme or Rigid
Misconception: There are strict rules you must follow.
Reality: Minimalism is personal and flexible—your version should match your values.

5. Minimalism Is Only for Certain Types of People
Misconception: Only the wealthy, young or specific lifestyle groups can practice it.
Reality: Minimalism works for anyone who wants to live intentionally at any age or income.

6. Minimalist Spaces Must Be Empty or Tiny
Misconception: Minimalism equals empty rooms or small houses.
Reality: Minimalist spaces are simple and purposeful—not bare and not dependent on size.

7. Minimalism Is Just About Physical Items
Misconception: It only applies to possessions.
Reality: It reduces mental clutter, digital overload, social pressure and emotional baggage too.

8. Minimalists Never Buy Anything
Misconception: You must avoid all purchases.
Reality: Minimalists buy intentionally—fewer, better and only what adds value.

9. Minimalism Removes Comfort, Luxury or Quality
Misconception: You must sacrifice comfort and live without nice things.
Reality: You keep comfort—just without excess or clutter that doesn't serve your well-being.

10. Minimalism Is a Trend
Misconception: It's just another lifestyle fad.
Reality: Minimalism is a timeless philosophy practiced for centuries across cultures.

11. Minimalism Equals Buying Less, So It's Deprivation
Misconception: It means restricting yourself.
Reality: It creates space for relationships, time, peace and personal growth—not deprivation.

12. Minimalism Isn't Sustainable Long-Term
Misconception: It's a temporary phase or one-time decluttering session.
Reality: It becomes a natural, ongoing lifestyle of intentional choices.

13. Minimalism Rejects Technology
Misconception: You must avoid digital tools.
Reality: Minimalists use technology intentionally—not mindlessly.

14. Minimalists Don't Keep Sentimental Items
Misconception: You must discard all memories.
Reality: Minimalists keep meaningful sentimental items intentionally—not everything by default.

15. Minimalism Must Look Perfect
Misconception: Homes must always be spotless and organized.
Reality: Minimalists still experience mess; the focus is manageable simplicity, not perfection.

Minimalism is **not** a rigid lifestyle. It is a personal philosophy built on **intentional choices**, **clear values** and **a focus on what truly matters**. It fits any home, income, age or stage of life. It removes what drains you so you can live lighter, clearer and more joyfully.

Minimalism is not about less. It's about **more life in your life**.

Why You Don't Need More Stuff

"You Already Have Enough."

Here are several reasons why you don't need more stuff, which can help guide your thinking towards embracing a simpler, more minimalist lifestyle:

You already have what you need

Believe it or not, we need very little to survive. You really do not need too many shoes, suits and clothes to survive. What you need is toothpaste toothbrush, bath soap, shampoo and minimum pair of clothes. We should not go up to that level of minimalism. But fact is, we are not using 80% of the items in our house are in daily routine. We have many duplicate items. Today there are many businesses who worked on shared resources like bicycle, sports instruments etc., Because one does not need many things. Also, if something required, occasionally, it can be taken on rent. If you need ambulance in emergency, you hire it, you will never purchase it. Same things applicable for all personal stuff. There is no reason to own everything. So before you start purchasing anything, take a look at you stuff and you will surprise to find you already have what are you are going to buy.

1. **The Diderot Effect**
   The Diderot Effect describes how one new purchase triggers a chain of more purchases. You upgrade one item and suddenly everything else looks outdated,

pushing you to buy more. This cycle drains money and creates endless dissatisfaction. Recognizing this pattern helps you stop unnecessary consumption. *Example:* You buy a new sofa, then feel your curtains, carpet and décor all need replacing.

2. **You Already Have What You Need**
   Most people already own far more than they use. Many items sit untouched for months or years yet we still feel the urge to buy more. When you take inventory, you realise your needs are already met. This awareness builds contentment and reduces impulse buying. *Example:* You think you need new workout clothes but you already have five sets in perfect condition.

3. **Less Stuff Creates More Space**
   Every item you own takes up physical space and cluttered spaces create mental clutter. When you reduce possessions, your home feels lighter, cleaner and more peaceful. A spacious environment improves focus and creativity. *Example:* Clearing your desk of unnecessary items instantly makes it easier to work.

4. **Stuff Takes Time**
   More possessions mean more cleaning organizing, repairing and decision making. Time spent managing things is time taken away from meaningful activities. Simplifying your belongings frees up hours every week. *Example:* Owning 20 shirts means more laundry, more folding and more decisions every morning

5. **If You Don't Own It, You Don't Stress About It**
   Ownership brings responsibility — maintenance, repairs and worry. When you avoid unnecessary possessions, you avoid unnecessary stress. Renting or borrowing occasionally is often more practical. *Example:* A home swimming pool requires constant cleaning, chemicals and repairs; visiting a resort twice a year gives the same joy without the burden.

6. **Less Stuff Builds Gratitude**
   When you own fewer things, you appreciate each one more deeply. Gratitude increases happiness and reduces the constant desire for more. You begin to value quality over quantity. *Example:* With only two pairs of shoes, you take better care of them and feel thankful for what you have.

7. **Your Stuff Can Own You**
   Possessions demand time, money and emotional energy. Instead of serving you, they often become your masters. The more you own, the more you feel

tied to maintaining and protecting it. *Example:* A luxury car brings pride but also insurance, servicing, fear of scratches and constant worry.

8. **Decluttering Prevents Backsliding**
   Once you declutter and feel the benefits, you naturally avoid accumulating again. You become more mindful and intentional with purchases. This awareness protects you from falling back into old habits. *Example:* After reducing your wardrobe from 50 items to 15, you think twice before buying another shirt.

9. **Less Stuff Increases Mobility**
   Fewer belongings make it easier to move homes, travel or relocate for opportunities. You're not tied down by heavy possessions. Mobility gives you freedom and flexibility. *Example:* A person with two suitcases can move cities in a day; someone with a full house needs weeks.

10. **Liquidity Equals Freedom**
    Money locked in unused items cannot help you. Cash savings give you choices — travel, education, career changes or emergencies. Financial freedom is more valuable than material possessions. *Example:* Selling unused gadgets can fund a weekend trip or reduce debt.

11. **Clutter Increases Stress**
    A cluttered environment overwhelms the senses and increases anxiety. Your brain constantly processes visual information, even when you're not aware of it. A clean space promotes calm and focus. *Example:* A messy kitchen makes cooking stressful; a tidy one feels inviting.

12. **Possessions Don't Create Lasting Happiness**
    Buying something gives a short burst of excitement but the feeling fades quickly. Experiences and relationships bring deeper, longer-lasting joy. Stuff cannot fill emotional gaps. *Example:* A new phone feels exciting for a week; a meaningful trip creates memories for life.

13. **Material Items Are Temporary**
    Most things wear out, break or go out of style. They require maintenance and eventually become waste. Investing in experiences or skills lasts longer. *Example:* A trendy jacket becomes outdated in a year; learning a skill stays with you forever.

14. **More Stuff Means More Maintenance**
    Every item adds cleaning, repairs, storage and mental load. More things = more responsibilities. Simplifying reduces daily chores and stress. *Example:*

Owning 10 kitchen appliances means more cleaning and storage; using 2 essentials is easier.

15. **Possessions Can Distract You from Your Purpose**
Focusing on things pulls attention away from your goals, passions and personal growth. Simplicity helps you stay aligned with your values. *Example:* Spending weekends shopping leaves no time for hobbies or self-improvement.

16. **Too Much Stuff Reduces Functionality**
Cluttered spaces are harder to use and navigate. Simplifying your environment increases efficiency and comfort. *Example:* A kitchen counter full of gadgets leaves no space to cook.

17. **More Stuff Hurts the Environment**
Every purchase has an environmental cost — production, packaging, transport and disposal. Consuming less protects the planet. *Example:* Buying fewer clothes reduces textile waste and carbon emissions.

18. **You Can't Take It with You**
Material possessions don't follow you beyond life. What remains is how you lived, not what you owned. *Example:* People remember your kindness, not your furniture.

19. **True Wealth Is Time and Freedom**
Less stuff frees time for relationships, passions and rest. Freedom is worth more than any object. Example: Owning fewer things means fewer chores and more time for family.

20. **Overconsumption Leads to Debt**
Buying more than you need creates financial stress. Living within your means builds long-term security. *Example:* Credit card shopping sprees lead to months of repayment.

21. **Fewer Things = Greater Focus**
A clean environment helps you concentrate on what matters. Less visual noise means more mental clarity. *Example:* A minimalist workspace boosts productivity.

22. **Buying More Doesn't Solve Emotional Problems**
Shopping can temporarily distract from stress or loneliness but it never solves the root issue. Emotional well-being comes from inner work. *Example:* Retail therapy feels good for an hour but the problem remains.

23. **You Can Be Creative with What You Already Have**
    Resourcefulness grows when you repurpose or innovate instead of buying new. Creativity thrives in simplicity. *Example:* Using old jars as storage instead of buying new containers.

24. **Simplicity Promotes Freedom**
    Owning less frees you from clutter, debt and pressure to keep up with others. It allows flexibility and spontaneous living. *Example:* With fewer commitments, you can take a last minute trip without stress.

25. **More Stuff Can Lower Self Esteem**
    Comparing your possessions to others can create insecurity. Minimalism helps you value yourself beyond material things. *Example:* Feeling inferior because someone has a newer car.

26. **Excess Items Cause Decision Fatigue**
    More choices drain mental energy. Fewer options simplify daily routines and reduce stress. *Example:* Choosing from 20 shirts every morning is exhausting; choosing from 5 is easy.

27. **You Don't Need to Follow Trends**
    Trends change constantly. Simplicity frees you from the pressure to buy the latest gadgets or fashion. *Example:* Not upgrading your phone every year saves money and stress.

28. **Possessions Can Limit Experiences**
    Large or numerous items tie you down and reduce flexibility. Owning less opens space for new experiences. *Example:* A house full of stuff makes hosting guests difficult.

29. **Minimalism Encourages Generosity**
    When you stop hoarding, you naturally share more — time, energy and resources. Giving becomes easier. *Example:* Donating unused clothes to someone who needs them.

30. **Simplicity Builds Better Habits**
    A minimalist lifestyle encourages intentional choices and healthier routines. Less distraction = better discipline. *Example:* A clean kitchen encourages healthy cooking.

31. **You Spend Less Time Shopping**
    Minimalism reduces browsing, comparing and buying. That time can be used for meaningful activities. *Example:* Instead of spending weekends at the mall, you spend them with family.

32. **Material Things Create a False Sense of Security**
    Objects can't guarantee safety or stability. True security comes from skills, relationships and financial health. *Example:* Owning expensive jewelry doesn't make you safer; having savings does.

33. **Your Value Isn't Defined by What You Own**
    Self-worth comes from character, not possessions. Minimalism helps you focus on who you are, not what you have. *Example:* A kind person with few belongings is more respected than a rude person with many.

34. **Less Stuff Helps You Live in the Present**
    You stop waiting for the next purchase to feel happy. You start enjoying the moment. *Example:* Instead of thinking about your next phone, you enjoy the one you have.

Closing note - By adopting the mindset of minimalism and simplifying your life, you're able to let go of the pressure to acquire more and instead focus on what truly adds value to your well-being, relationships and long-term happiness.

Minimalism in Action - Stories That Inspire

The Little House on the Hill

There was a man named Arun who lived in a bustling city. He worked tirelessly, earning promotions, buying the latest gadgets and upgrading his lifestyle. Yet, deep down, he felt empty and restless, as though he was chasing something he couldn't define.

One day, while cleaning out his late grandfather's belongings, Arun found a letter addressed to him. It read:

"My dearest Arun,
Happiness is not in having everything but in needing little. If life feels heavy, visit the little house on the hill."

Arun remembered the old countryside home his grandfather had built. Curious, he decided to visit it.

The house was small, with a clay roof and wooden walls. It stood in the middle of a green field surrounded by wildflowers. No Wi-Fi, no noise, just the chirping of birds and the rustling of leaves in the wind. For the first time in years, Arun felt at peace.

He spent a week there, doing simple things: brewing tea in the morning, reading a dusty book he found on a shelf and tending to the small garden out back. As he slowed down, he noticed the little things—the way the sun painted the sky pink at dusk, the soothing rhythm of raindrops on the roof and the joy of eating food he had grown himself.

The simplicity of the place changed him. He realised he didn't need endless possessions or achievements to be happy. Happiness, he discovered, was in living mindfully, nurturing relationships and being grateful for the small joys of life.

When Arun returned to the city, he didn't quit his job or sell his belongings. But he began making small changes. He decluttered his home, prioritized time with loved ones and adopted a slower, more intentional routine. Every few months, he returned to the little house on the hill to remind himself of what truly mattered.

In the end, Arun didn't become richer or more powerful but he became something far more important.

Lesson: Simplicity is not about abandoning life—it's about embracing what makes life beautiful. In slowing down, Arun found peace, purpose and joy.

Buddha and the Farmer

"True happiness begins when we let go of what weighs us down."

One serene afternoon, Buddha sat under the shade of a large tree, surrounded by forty monks. They had just finished a simple meal and were enjoying the quiet harmony of nature. The air was calm, filled with the gentle rustle of leaves and the distant chirping of birds.

Suddenly, a distressed farmer approached, his face etched with worry. His clothes were dusty and his voice trembled as he spoke: *"Have you seen my cows? I had twelve and they've all run away! And my sesame fields... insects have destroyed everything. I'm suffering so much I feel like ending my life."*

Buddha looked at him with compassion and replied softly:
"My friend, we haven't seen any cows. You may want to search in another direction." The farmer nodded hurriedly and left, still burdened by his troubles.

The Teaching
Buddha then turned to his monks and said: "My dear friends, you are the happiest people in the world—because you have no cows to lose." He continued: "When a person has too many cows—too many possessions, responsibilities and attachments—they spend their whole life worrying, protecting and chasing after them. To be truly happy, you must learn the art of releasing. At first, you believe

your cows are essential to your happiness. You try to collect more and more. But eventually, you realise these cows are not conditions for happiness—they are obstacles to it."

"So you begin to let them go, one by one. This doesn't mean you must live without material things. But remember: the more you have, the more you worry. The more you possess, the more you fear losing it. The only possessions you can never lose are the ones you keep in your heart."

Lesson: The story of the farmer and his cows is a timeless reminder: happiness is not about adding more but about letting go of what weighs us down. Our "cows" may be possessions, ambitions or even relationships that drain our peace. When we release the excess, we create space for freedom, clarity and joy.

Minimalism Story: Bodh Saint

"True wealth is not in what you own but in what you can live without."

In a quiet, lush valley nestled between towering mountains, there lived a sage named Bodh, known to all as Bodh Saint. His name was whispered with reverence, not because of his great miracles but because of his extraordinary way of living. Unlike the powerful kings and merchants in the nearby villages who filled their homes with treasures and trinkets, Bodh lived a life of radical simplicity.

Bodh had once been a rich merchant, surrounded by luxuries—glistening jewels, fine silks and countless possessions. His house had been grand, with servants attending to his every need. Yet, despite his wealth, Bodh found little peace. He felt burdened by the weight of his possessions, constantly managing, protecting and desiring more. His heart ached and his mind was in turmoil, never at rest, always chasing after something that seemed just out of reach.

One day, tired of the constant noise of his life, Bodh walked away from his mansion, leaving behind his family, his riches and everything he had known. He ventured into the forest, seeking solitude and answers. It was in the quiet of nature that he discovered a profound truth—the more he owned, the more he was owned. The weight of his possessions had weighed down his spirit, preventing him from being free.

Bodh soon became a wanderer, living with nothing but the bare essentials: a simple robe, a staff and the food he could find in nature. Each day, he woke with the sun, meditated on the present moment and shared his wisdom with anyone he met. He realised that minimalism wasn't just about getting rid of things but about releasing attachments—attachments to both material possessions and the labels people placed on him.

The villagers who heard about Bodh's transformation were curious. "What does it mean to live with so little?" they asked. So, Bodh began to teach them:

Lesson 1: Freedom from Attachment

One day, a young farmer came to Bodh, asking, "I have many animals, fields and tools. How can I be free if I must care for so much?"

Bodh smiled and replied, "You have what you need but do not let these things define you. Care for them but do not cling to them. The moment you let go of attachment to what you own, you will discover a freedom that goes beyond your fields and animals."

The farmer spent the next several weeks simplifying his life, giving away unnecessary tools and focusing only on the essentials. He found peace in the simplicity, realizing that his true self was not defined by the wealth of his land but by his actions and heart.

Lesson 2: The Joy of Less

One evening, an elderly woman approached Bodh with a basket full of gold coins. "I wish to give this to you," she said. "You live so humbly and I admire your way of life."
Bodh looked at the gold and gently replied, "I do not need these coins, for they are a heavy burden. The true treasures of life are found in the simplicity of the moment, in kindness and in peace. Leave this basket with me and you will feel the weight lift from your heart."

The woman hesitated but decided to follow his advice. She left the coins behind and found that she had not only lightened her load but had also found a sense of joy and fulfilment in giving up what she thought she needed. In doing so, she discovered that the real riches of life were not found in material wealth but in love, compassion and simplicity.

Lesson 3: Be Present

Bodh's teachings spread and soon many came to him, seeking wisdom. A young warrior, weary from endless battles and the pursuit of glory, asked, "How can I find peace when my life has been so filled with violence and ambition?"
Bodh spoke softly, "The past is gone and the future is unknown. Peace is found in the present moment. Let go of your battles, your need for recognition and embrace the now. In that space, you will find everything you need."

The warrior, confused at first, began to practice stillness, meditating daily, focusing on the present instead of his past glories or future wars. Gradually, his heart became calm and his mind free from the incessant urge for validation. He realised that true peace did not come from external victories but from within.

The Final Lesson

Years passed and Bodh continued to live his simple life in the forest, teaching those who came seeking answers. One day, a grand procession passed through the valley—kings, merchants and dignitaries from far-off lands came to pay their respects to Bodh, bringing treasures beyond imagination.

Bodh received them not with grandeur or ceremony but with a simple greeting and a warm smile. "The greatest treasure," he said, "is the freedom that comes with letting go. Nothing you bring will enrich me, for I am already rich with simplicity and peace."

The kings, who had spent their lives amassing kingdoms and wealth, suddenly realised the truth in Bodh's words. They had spent their entire lives pursuing more, never stopping to consider that what they had was already enough.

The Final Transformation

In the quiet of the forest, Bodh sat under a tree, his mind clear, his heart at peace. The valley had changed in the years since he first walked away from his riches. Many of the villagers had embraced simplicity, leaving behind their attachments to things that no longer served them. Bodh Saint had become more than just a teacher; he had become a symbol of the freedom that comes with living with less. He died one evening as the sun set, surrounded by the people whose lives he had transformed. His legacy was not one of grand monuments or riches but of simplicity, peace and the deep wisdom that less is often more.

The Lesson of Bodh Saint Bodh Saint's life teaches us that minimalism is not just about what we remove from our lives but about what we choose to focus on. When we free ourselves from the weight of possessions, external validation and attachment to the past, we open ourselves to the beauty of the present moment. We find peace, clarity and, most importantly, freedom.

By living simply, we can create a life that reflects our true values, not the expectations of others. In doing so, we can discover the richness of life that is not measured by what we have but by who we are.

Part X: Applying Minimalism to Life

See how minimalism can transform personal, professional, financial and digital aspects of living.

Chapter 21: Minimalist Living — Small Shifts, Big Impact

Minimalism in Personal Life

"Simplify to amplify what truly matters."

Minimalism can be applied to various aspects of personal life, helping to simplify, declutter and focus on what truly matters. Here are key areas where you can apply minimalism to make a positive impact:

1. Home and Living Space

Declutter and Simplify Possessions: Keep only what adds value or joy to your life. Go room by room, deciding which items are essential and meaningful and let go of things you don't use or love.
Choose Multipurpose and High-Quality Items: Instead of accumulating multiple items for different tasks, invest in versatile, high-quality pieces that serve multiple purposes, which will reduce clutter and increase longevity.
Create a Calming Environment: Arrange your living space to feel open, airy and peaceful, with a focus on functionality. Simple spaces with fewer items can bring calmness and make cleaning easier.

2. Digital Life

Limit Social Media Usage: Be intentional with your digital time. Unfollow accounts that don't inspire or uplift you and set boundaries around how much time you spend online to avoid information overload.

Declutter Digital Files: Regularly clean up files, photos and apps on your devices. Organize only the files you actually use or need and delete duplicates or unnecessary documents to create a streamlined digital experience.

Practice Email Minimalism: Unsubscribe from promotional emails, reduce notifications and clear your inbox regularly. Use folders or labels to organize important emails, keeping your inbox manageable and reducing digital stress.

3. Wardrobe and Personal Style

Curate a Capsule Wardrobe: Select a small number of versatile, high-quality pieces that match well together and reflect your style. This reduces decision fatigue and makes getting dressed a more enjoyable experience.

Prioritize Quality Over Quantity: Invest in fewer, high-quality clothing items that last, instead of frequently buying new, trendy pieces. This approach supports sustainability and reduces clutter.

Let Go of Unworn Clothing: Donate or sell clothes you haven't worn in the past year or that don't fit your style. By simplifying your wardrobe, you make space for only the pieces that you love and feel confident in.

4. Relationships and Social Life

Focus on Meaningful Relationships: Spend more time with people who uplift, inspire and support you, rather than trying to maintain superficial relationships. This leads to deeper connections and more fulfilling interactions.

Set Boundaries and Say No When Necessary: Don't overcommit socially; focus on activities and gatherings that bring you joy or align with your values. This way, you preserve time and energy for what matters most.

Be Present in Interactions: Practice mindful listening and engaging in conversations without distractions. Focusing on quality over quantity in your social life can lead to more meaningful relationships and stronger bonds.

6. Finances and Spending

Practice Intentional Spending: Reflect on your purchases, focusing on items that add long-term value. This can reduce impulsive buying, prevent clutter and lead to better financial health.

Create a Budget and Prioritize Saving: Align your spending with your priorities, reducing expenses that don't contribute to your goals. By being intentional with your finances, you can save more and reduce financial stress.

Avoid Lifestyle Inflation: As your income increases, resist the urge to upgrade your lifestyle unnecessarily. Instead, invest in experiences, savings or causes that resonate with you, maintaining simplicity in material possessions.

7. Health and Well-being

Simplify Your Diet: Focus on wholesome, nourishing foods that support your health rather than complicated diets or excess indulgences. Preparing simple, balanced meals can streamline your diet and improve overall well-being.

Prioritize Sleep and Rest: Embrace minimalism in your sleep routine by creating a relaxing environment, reducing nighttime screen time and establishing a simple bedtime ritual. Quality rest leads to a more focused, energetic day.

Exercise Consistently and Enjoyably: Find simple, enjoyable forms of movement that you can incorporate regularly, whether it's walking, yoga or at-home workouts. Choose activities that you genuinely enjoy and can commit to sustainably.

8. Work and Career

Focus on High-Impact Tasks: Prioritize the most impactful and essential tasks over busy work. Simplifying your approach to work can improve productivity and lead to a better work-life balance.

Minimize Distractions: Reduce distractions in your workspace by creating an organized environment, limiting notifications and setting dedicated focus times. A clear workspace and focused mind make for more efficient, meaningful work.

Set Clear Professional Boundaries: Know when to disconnect from work, especially outside work hours. Simplifying your approach to work-life boundaries can help protect your mental health and ensure a well-rounded personal life.

9. Time Management

Prioritize and Say No to Nonessential Commitments: Reflect on what truly aligns with your goals and values and don't be afraid to decline obligations that don't serve those. This gives you more time for activities that genuinely enrich your life.

Limit Screen Time and Media Consumption: Practice intentional media consumption by choosing quality content over quantity and setting limits on time spent watching TV, browsing the internet or using apps.

Schedule Time for Rest and Reflection: Protect time for self-care, reflection and activities that bring you joy. This intentional approach allows you to recharge and fosters a balanced, purposeful life.

10. Hobbies and Personal Interests

Choose a Few Fulfilling Hobbies: Instead of pursuing multiple hobbies at once, focus on a few that you genuinely enjoy and find rewarding. This approach allows you to develop your skills and gain deeper satisfaction from your interests.

Reduce Hobby-Related Clutter: Clear out supplies, materials or equipment for hobbies you no longer pursue. A simpler approach to hobbies encourages you to focus on activities you're passionate about, without unnecessary clutter.

Be Intentional with New Hobbies: Before trying a new hobby, consider if it aligns with your values and lifestyle. By being selective, you can ensure your hobbies are truly meaningful rather than fleeting interests.

11. Mindset and Emotional Health

Practice Gratitude Daily: Focusing on gratitude allows you to appreciate what you have rather than constantly seeking more. Journaling or reflecting on positive moments each day can foster a contented, peaceful mindset.

Let Go of Negative Thoughts and Judgments: Minimalism applies to your mental landscape too. Regularly let go of grudges, judgments and self-criticism to cultivate inner peace and a more positive outlook.

Embrace Mindful Consumption: Be mindful of the information, relationships and items you allow into your life. By focusing on the things that uplift you and align with your values, you can cultivate a more peaceful, fulfilling life.

12. Decision-Making

Simplify Choices: Limit the options you consider for everyday decisions, such as what to wear, what to eat or how to spend your free time. Fewer choices reduce decision fatigue and free up mental energy for more important matters.

Adopt Principles for Quick Decisions: Establish clear principles (like "always choose quality over quantity" or "opt for the simpler option") to help make decisions faster and more confidently, rather than overthinking every choice.

Focus on Intentional Living: Instead of making decisions based on impulse, practice aligning your choices with your values. This fosters a clearer sense of direction and purpose in life.

13. Family Life and Parenting

Minimize Toys and Child Gadgets: Focus on quality, open-ended toys that encourage creativity, rather than accumulating lots of toys that may quickly lose their appeal. A minimalist approach to children's belongings can promote imagination and reduce clutter.

Model a Simple, Purposeful Lifestyle: Children often adopt habits from their parents. Demonstrating minimalism by prioritizing meaningful activities and avoiding excessive purchases can instill valuable life lessons on contentment and gratitude.

Prioritize Time Over Things: Instead of filling your family life with possessions, focus on creating memories through experiences. Regular family activities or quality time together fosters stronger connections and lasting memories.

14. Personal Growth and Learning

Focus on Selective Learning: With so much information available, it's easy to feel overwhelmed by endless courses, books and tutorials. Choose a few key areas for personal development, focusing on in-depth mastery rather than broad, shallow learning.

Let Go of Old Beliefs That Don't Serve You: Minimalism applies to beliefs and assumptions too. Reflect on outdated beliefs or mindsets that may hold you back and embrace perspectives that align with your personal growth journey.

Streamline Your Goals: Avoid setting too many goals at once, as it can dilute your focus and energy. Instead, prioritize a few meaningful goals that align with your values and vision for life, which allows you to make consistent progress.

15. Food and Nutrition

Adopt a Simple Meal Plan: Choose a few balanced, healthy meals that you enjoy and can easily prepare. This reduces the stress of meal planning and grocery shopping while promoting a healthier diet.

Buy Fresh, Whole Foods in Limited Quantities: Instead of stocking up on processed foods and snacks, focus on fresh produce and whole foods. A simpler, natural diet can boost energy levels, promote health and reduce unnecessary waste.

Practice Mindful Eating: Eating without distractions allows you to enjoy your food fully, recognize your hunger and fullness cues and make healthier, more satisfying choices. This minimal approach to eating fosters a positive relationship with food.

16. Communication and Information Consumption

Limit Your News Intake: In today's 24/7 news cycle, it's easy to feel overwhelmed. Limit news consumption to reliable sources and set aside a specific time to stay updated. This reduces anxiety and helps focus on actionable information.

Practice Minimalist Communication: Be intentional with your conversations and digital communications. Focus on clear, meaningful exchanges and avoid excessive messaging or emails, which can be time-consuming and distracting.

Unsubscribe from Unnecessary Notifications: Reduce digital interruptions by unsubscribing from newsletters, alerts or app notifications that don't serve you. Fewer notifications allow you to stay focused and reduce digital stress.

17. Mindfulness and Meditation

Simplify Meditation Practices: Instead of adopting complex meditation routines, focus on simple practices like mindful breathing, a body scan or silent reflection. Practicing minimalistic meditation helps you cultivate inner peace without needing elaborate rituals.

Be Present in Daily Life: Minimalism in mindfulness involves focusing on the present moment, whether it's during mundane tasks like washing dishes or during conversations. This presence reduces stress and enhances the quality of each experience.

Let Go of Unnecessary Thoughts: Practice recognizing and releasing unnecessary thoughts, judgments or worries. Mindfulness exercises can help you stay present and let go of mental clutter that doesn't serve you.

18. Energy Use and Sustainability

Reduce Energy Consumption at Home: Use minimal energy by turning off lights when not needed, unplugging devices and opting for energy-efficient appliances. These small efforts conserve resources and reduce environmental impact.

Adopt Eco-Friendly Habits: Minimalism can encourage eco-conscious choices, such as reducing single-use plastics, recycling, composting and choosing sustainable products. This approach benefits both your well-being and the environment.

Minimize Waste: Aim for a zero-waste lifestyle by reusing, repurposing and buying only what you need. Avoiding excess packaging and waste helps simplify your life and reduces your ecological footprint.

19. Travel and Leisure

Pack Light When Traveling: Adopting a minimalist approach to travel by packing only essentials can make your journey less stressful, freeing you to enjoy experiences rather than being burdened by possessions.

Focus on Experiences Over Souvenirs: While traveling, prioritize meaningful experiences over buying material souvenirs. Document memories through photos or journaling rather than accumulating items that add clutter.

Opt for Simple, Slow Travel: Minimalist travel encourages slowing down to experience a place fully, focusing on quality experiences over quantity. This way, you can savor the culture, scenery and ambiance of each destination.

20. Spirituality and Purpose

Strip Away Unnecessary Rituals: Instead of complex rituals or practices, focus on the core of your spiritual beliefs, fostering a deeper and more personal connection to your faith or inner self.

Focus on Inner Peace and Growth: Minimalism in spirituality encourages practices that promote inner calm, self-awareness and peace, rather than getting caught up in external expectations or excessive rituals.
Align Actions with Core Values: Living a minimalist spiritual life involves aligning actions with your highest values. Instead of outward expressions, focus on how your beliefs translate into kindness, compassion and authenticity in your everyday interactions.

21. Entertainment and Leisure Activities

Prioritize Quality Over Quantity in Entertainment: Instead of binge-watching shows or mindlessly scrolling, choose high-quality content that aligns with your interests. Focusing on intentional entertainment can reduce overstimulation and create a more fulfilling leisure time.
Enjoy Simple Activities: Find joy in simple activities like reading, walking, journaling or spending time in nature. These low-cost, low-stress forms of entertainment promote relaxation and contribute to a balanced, peaceful life.
Limit Unnecessary Screen Time: Apply minimalism by setting boundaries around screen time, especially for passive consumption. This frees up time for more intentional, enriching activities that contribute to personal growth and relaxation.

Applying minimalism across various areas of personal life encourages a shift from materialism and superficiality toward intention, purpose and depth. By stripping away what is unnecessary, you gain clarity and create room for the relationships, experiences and activities that truly enrich your life. Minimalism is about finding freedom in simplicity, embracing what genuinely brings value and building a life of contentment, peace and fulfilment.

Chapter 22: Minimalism at Work & Business

Minimalism at Work

"Work smarter, not busier."

Minimalism can be transformative in a professional setting, allowing you to focus on meaningful work, streamline tasks and reduce stress. Here's a breakdown of how to apply minimalism across various aspects of professional life:

1. Workspace Organization

Declutter Your Desk and Workspace: Remove items that don't serve a purpose or contribute to productivity. A clear desk promotes focus, reduces distractions and fosters a calm, efficient work environment.

Go Paperless Where Possible: Minimize physical files by digitizing documents, using cloud storage and organizing files digitally. This approach saves space, improves access to information and aligns with sustainable practices.

Simplify Tools and Equipment: Use only essential tools and software that enhance productivity. Avoid using redundant tools or equipment, which can add to mental clutter and complexity.

Decluttered Work Environment (Example/Result): Keeping a clean organized workspace with only essential tools and materials improves focus and reduces distractions. **Result:** Increased productivity, clearer thinking and reduced stress from clutter.

2. Time Management

Prioritize High-Impact Tasks: Focus on tasks that have the most significant impact on your work or contribute to major goals. Applying the Pareto Principle (80/20 rule) can help identify the 20% of tasks that yield 80% of results, allowing you to work smarter.

Adopt a Single Tasking Approach: Rather than juggling multiple tasks, focus on completing one task at a time. Single tasking helps increase efficiency, reduce errors and ensure high-quality work.

Limit Meetings: Avoid unnecessary meetings or keep them brief and focused. Establish clear agendas and stick to essential points to save time and increase productivity for everyone involved.

Fewer Meetings (Example/Result): Reduce number or length of meetings; use collaborative tools for updates. **Result:** Less time in meetings, more time for actual work and higher efficiency.

Fewer Work Hours for Greater Productivity (Example/Result): Adopt focused schedules (e.g., four-day workweek trials) to maintain output with fewer hours. **Result:** Better focus, work-life balance and improved morale and creativity.

Limiting Work Interruptions (Example/Result): Set boundaries for notifications, email checks and calls to reduce context switching. **Result:** Increased concentration, higher productivity and improved mental well-being.

3. Email and Communication

Practice Inbox Minimalism: Unsubscribe from irrelevant newsletters, sort important emails with folders or labels and aim for an organized, low-stress inbox. Schedule specific times to check emails instead of constantly reacting to notifications.

Use Concise Language: Be direct and to the point in emails and messages. Avoid lengthy explanations unless necessary; clear and concise communication saves time and ensures that information is easily understood.

Limit Communication Channels: Stick to a few essential communication tools rather than juggling multiple platforms. This minimizes distractions and allows you to focus on high-quality communication without spreading yourself thin.

Simplified Communication (Example/Result): Communicate only what's necessary; keep messages clear and actionable. **Result:** Reduced misunderstandings, quicker decisions and less wasted time.

4. Project and Task Management

Define Clear Goals and Objectives: Establish clear goals for each project, focusing on what truly matters rather than adding unnecessary layers. Clear objectives help reduce scope creep and ensure a focused, effective project path.

Use Simple Project Management Tools: Rather than overloading with complex software, choose a tool that meets your basic needs without unnecessary features. A simple tool keeps the process streamlined and easy to manage.

Eliminate Redundant Tasks: Regularly assess and cut out tasks that don't contribute to overall goals. This ensures that each task has a clear purpose and contributes to productivity rather than creating busy work.

Fewer Project Deliverables (Example/Result): Combine multiple small reports into a single comprehensive deliverable. **Result:** Higher-quality output and clearer communication.

5. Decision-Making

Set Guiding Principles: Use principles or criteria to streamline decisions, like prioritizing customer satisfaction, profitability or sustainability. This helps make decisions faster, reduces overthinking and builds consistency.

Limit Options: When making choices, narrow down your options to a few core ones. Simplifying options prevents decision fatigue, allowing you to make informed decisions more quickly.

Delegate or Automate: Where possible, delegate tasks or automate repetitive decisions. This frees up mental bandwidth for strategic thinking and high-priority tasks.

Simplified Decision-Making (Example/Result): Create simple guidelines for autonomy. **Result:** Reduced decision fatigue, faster turnaround and greater empowerment.

Fewer Stakeholders in Decision-Making (Example/Result): Involve a core decision team. **Result:** More agility, faster delivery and fewer conflicting opinions.

6. Relationships and Networking

Cultivate Quality Relationships: Instead of connecting with everyone, focus on building meaningful relationships with people who share your values or goals. Quality over quantity leads to stronger professional bonds and more effective collaboration.

Set Boundaries: Establish clear boundaries with colleagues and clients regarding availability and communication times. Boundaries protect your time and allow you to focus on meaningful interactions.

Network with Purpose: Attend only networking events or engagements that align with your professional goals or personal growth. This selective approach prevents burnout and allows you to foster connections that genuinely matter.

Minimalist Personal Branding (Example/Result): Emphasize unique expertise and story rather than a broad image. **Result:** A clearer, stronger brand that resonates.

7. Work-Life Balance

Create a Work-Free Zone at Home: If you work from home, designate a specific workspace and avoid bringing work into personal spaces. This separation helps maintain a balanced lifestyle and prevents work from consuming your home life.
Define Clear Work Hours: Set boundaries around your work hours and resist checking work emails or messages outside of these times. This creates a healthier balance, enabling you to recharge and stay productive during work hours.
Prioritize Health and Well-Being: Minimalism in professional life means not overcommitting and recognizing when rest is needed. Prioritize time for exercise, healthy meals and breaks, which ultimately improve both your professional output and personal satisfaction.

8. Digital Minimalism

Streamline Digital Tools and Applications: Use only essential apps and software for work, reducing the number of platforms you need to check or manage. Keeping digital tools to a minimum prevents overload and optimizes productivity.
Organize Digital Files and Folders: Set up a simple and consistent folder structure, so you can easily find what you need without clutter. Regularly delete outdated files, ensuring your digital workspace stays organized.
Limit Social Media Use: If social media isn't essential to your job, set limits on its use during work hours. Removing distractions from social media helps maintain focus and reduce unnecessary interruptions.
Fewer Tools and Systems (Example/Result): Use a single platform for communication, file sharing and task tracking where possible. **Result:** Less tool-hopping, reduced confusion and easier integration.

9. Professional Growth and Skill Development

Focus on Core Skills: Instead of learning every new skill or tool, concentrate on a few high-impact skills relevant to your role or long-term career goals. This approach allows for deeper mastery and avoids overwhelm.
Adopt Just-in-Time Learning: Learn new skills or tools only when you need them for a project. This method keeps you focused and prevents wasting time on unnecessary skills that may not be immediately useful.
Prioritize Learning from Experiences: Instead of chasing multiple certifications or courses, look for on-the-job learning opportunities, mentorship and real-life applications that foster practical, valuable skills.
Shorter Job Training Programs (Example/Result): Use concise, targeted training and self-paced tools. **Result:** Faster onboarding, better retention and more time to apply learning.

10. Leadership and Team Management

Lead with Clarity and Focus: When managing a team, provide clear and focused guidance, reducing ambiguity and unnecessary complexity. Minimalist communication as a leader promotes efficiency and reduces misunderstandings.

Foster a Culture of Essentialism: Encourage team members to focus on essential tasks that drive results rather than spreading themselves too thin. This approach enhances productivity and team satisfaction.

Practice Delegation Wisely: Delegate responsibilities strategically, allowing each team member to focus on tasks that match their strengths. Effective delegation prevents micromanagement and empowers the team, promoting a healthy, minimalist work culture.

Reduced Workload and Delegation (Example/Result): Empower ownership to reduce micromanagement. **Result:** Higher autonomy, faster decisions and leadership focus on strategy.

11. Goal Setting and Performance Review

Set Fewer, Clearer Goals: Establish a few key goals that drive impact instead of overloading with too many objectives. Focusing on a few impactful goals enables more focused, effective work.

Avoid Overly Complex Performance Metrics: Use a small set of clear metrics to measure success. Streamlined, meaningful metrics keep team members focused on what truly matters and eliminate unnecessary reporting.

Emphasize Continuous Improvement Over Perfection: Encourage growth and gradual improvement rather than perfectionism. This minimalist approach reduces stress and fosters a culture of learning and adaptability.

Clearer, More Focused Goals (Example/Result): Align on one or two key objectives per quarter. **Result:** Higher clarity, faster execution and better alignment.

12. Personal Productivity Techniques

Apply the 2-Minute Rule: If a task takes less than two minutes, complete it right away to prevent small tasks from piling up. This keeps your workload manageable and prevents clutter in your task list.

Use a Simple To-Do List: Organize tasks using a straightforward to-do list rather than complex task management systems. A simple list keeps tasks visible and encourages prioritization without becoming overwhelming.

Practice the "One-In, One-Out" Rule for Tasks: For each new task you take on, aim to complete or delegate an existing one. This keeps your task list balanced and prevents overcommitment.

Single Task Focus (Deep Work) (Example/Result): Schedule undistracted blocks for important tasks. **Result:** Better quality, fewer mistakes and higher satisfaction.

13. Streamlining Processes and Workflows

Simplify Repetitive Processes: Identify repetitive tasks and streamline them. For instance, create templates for frequently used documents or emails. This approach saves time and ensures consistency without reinventing the wheel each time.

Optimize Cross-Department Communication: Reduce the number of steps involved in inter-departmental communication by establishing a clear and efficient process. This cuts down on time spent clarifying tasks and ensures smoother collaboration.

Eliminate Unnecessary Approvals: Avoid bottlenecks by reducing the number of approvals required for routine actions. Empower team members with the autonomy to make decisions within their areas, allowing work to flow more efficiently.

Streamlined Processes (Example/Result): Automate routine steps (e.g., inventory, status). **Result:** Greater efficiency, fewer errors and more time for high-priority work.

9. Information Management

Organize Knowledge Resources: Centralize important documents and resources in a single, well-organized location where team members can easily access what they need. This reduces time spent searching for information and ensures everyone has the tools they need.

Limit Information Intake: Instead of consuming all industry news, choose a few trusted sources for staying informed. Too much information can be overwhelming; curating sources allows for a focused, high-quality knowledge base.

Use a "Knowledge Hub": Create a go-to hub for frequently asked questions, resources and guidelines. This prevents repetitive inquiries and empowers team members to find answers independently.

Minimize Information Overload (Example/Result): Provide concise dashboards, charts or summaries instead of lengthy reports. **Result:** Reduced cognitive load, faster decisions and higher retention.

10. Data and Metrics Minimalism

Track Only Key Performance Indicators (KPIs): Focus on a few essential metrics that directly reflect the company's health and goals. Too many metrics can dilute focus and make performance harder to evaluate.

Simplify Reports and Presentations: When preparing reports or presentations, focus on clear, essential insights instead of adding every possible detail. This minimalist approach to data presentation enables more effective, decision-driven discussions.

Adopt a Quarterly Metrics Review: Avoid constant metric evaluation and opt for quarterly reviews to see the bigger picture. This allows for reflection on meaningful changes and prevents unnecessary adjustments based on short-term fluctuations.

Eliminate Unnecessary Reports (Example/Result): Use automated dashboards to replace manual reporting. **Result:** Clarity in tracking, less admin and more time for value-adding work.

11. Client and Stakeholder Management

Set Realistic Expectations: Practice minimalism by managing expectations clearly from the start, reducing the need for constant updates and adjustments. This builds trust and allows you to focus on delivering quality rather than constant revisions.

Limit Project Scope with Clients: Avoid over-promising by defining a clear project scope with clients and stakeholders. Minimalism here means focusing on the core objectives of each project rather than overloading it with extra features.

Streamline Client Communication: Schedule regular check-ins with clients rather than frequent back-and-forth. A structured communication approach ensures that updates are efficient and avoids excessive client requests.

Simplifying Client Contracts and Agreements: Use standardized, concise contracts focusing on key terms. **Result:** Reduced legal fees, faster execution and less confusion.

Reduced Client Interaction Frequency: Prioritize key milestones and periodic reports/automated updates. **Result:** More time to deliver value and better time use for clients.

12. Talent and Team Development

Focus on Core Skills for Growth: Encourage team members to develop key skills that align with organizational needs rather than pushing them to take on unrelated skills. This promotes depth and mastery in relevant areas.

Limit the Number of Training Programs: Rather than offering many training sessions, focus on high-impact ones that align with team goals. Quality over quantity in professional development ensures time and energy are used effectively.

Mentorship Instead of Large Group Training: For skills that need nurturing, offer one-on-one mentorship or small-group sessions. Personalized guidance often leads to better results than large, generalized training sessions.

Simplified Onboarding Process: Emphasize culture, key tools and job responsibilities without overwhelming documentation. **Result:** Faster integration and smoother transitions.

Minimized Employee Roles: Define roles around a few key strengths to ensure mastery and efficiency. **Result:** Higher satisfaction, performance and clarity.

13. Simplified Goal Setting and Performance Tracking

Set Quarterly Goals Instead of Annual Goals: Focusing on shorter-term, actionable goals allows for quicker adjustments and reduces the pressure of large, year-long projects. Quarterly goals help maintain momentum and make it easier to stay aligned.

Use a Simple Performance Tracking System: Choose a straightforward performance-tracking method, such as a monthly checklist or a simple scorecard. This allows team members to monitor their progress without becoming overwhelmed.

Encourage Progress Reflection: Minimalism in performance tracking also means focusing on improvement rather than perfection. Encourage regular, brief reflections on what's working and what isn't to foster a growth mindset.

14. Financial and Budgetary Minimalism

Prioritize Essential Expenses: Focus on budget essentials that directly support core activities and goals. Avoid allocating funds to unnecessary tools, subscriptions or "nice-to-haves" that don't add value.

Implement Simple Financial Tracking: Rather than complex accounting systems, consider using a basic budgeting approach that keeps spending visible and transparent, especially for smaller teams.

Cut Costs through Outsourcing: Where possible, outsource non-core tasks. This not only saves costs but also allows internal resources to focus on the organization's primary objectives.

Minimized Travel Costs: Travel only for critical meetings; use virtual conferencing otherwise. **Result:** Savings, fewer logistics and better time management.

Minimalist Budgeting and Financial Management (Example/Result): Focus on operational costs, marketing ROI and core investments. **Result:** More financial clarity and better resource allocation.

15. Innovation and Continuous Improvement

Focus on Incremental Improvements: Instead of constantly aiming for large, disruptive innovations, look for small changes that lead to consistent improvement.

This minimalist approach to innovation reduces risk and can yield compounding benefits over time.

Encourage Minimalist Brainstorming Sessions: Hold brief, focused brainstorming sessions to generate ideas without losing momentum. Define clear problem statements, set time limits and focus on actionable solutions.

Limit New Initiatives to a Few at a Time: Instead of launching multiple initiatives at once, prioritize a small number of impactful projects. This allows for concentrated effort and greater success in achieving meaningful results.

Lean Innovation Processes: Focus on iterative improvements or small, manageable innovations to move faster and pivot with feedback. **Result:** Faster development and reduced risk.

16. Ethics and Corporate Responsibility

Reduce Waste in Office Practices: Apply minimalism by reducing waste in daily office operations. Encourage sustainable practices like recycling, energy conservation and reducing unnecessary printouts.

Focus on Core Social Responsibility Efforts: Instead of a broad approach to corporate social responsibility, concentrate on one or two causes that align closely with the company's values and mission. This focused impact can be more meaningful and sustainable.

Simplify Corporate Ethics Policies: Develop clear, straightforward guidelines that are easy for employees to follow. Simple ethics policies reduce ambiguity and ensure everyone understands the standards of conduct.

Simplified Product Packaging: Reduce excess materials, unnecessary layers or complicated designs for clarity and sustainability. **Result:** Lower costs and clearer value communication.

17. Task and Priority Filtering

Adopt a "Most Important Task" Approach: Begin each day by identifying the single most important task and complete it first. This creates a strong foundation for productivity and prevents less important tasks from taking over.

Use the "No List": Keep a list of tasks, responsibilities or requests that you intentionally decide to avoid. The "No List" helps you stay focused on core priorities and resist activities that don't add value.

Batch Similar Tasks Together: Group similar tasks, such as responding to emails, administrative work or phone calls to handle them all at once. Task batching is an effective minimalist approach that minimizes interruptions and saves time.

18. Feedback and Evaluation

Streamline Feedback Systems: Instead of exhaustive feedback processes, encourage concise, constructive and actionable feedback sessions. Simplified feedback helps employees focus on what matters most and facilitates real improvement.

Limit the Frequency of Formal Reviews: Rather than holding constant performance reviews, conduct them periodically with an emphasis on growth areas. This prevents review fatigue and allows team members to focus on implementing feedback.

Encourage Self-Assessment: Give employees tools for self-assessment rather than relying solely on managerial reviews. Self-assessment fosters personal accountability and aligns with minimalist values by encouraging independent growth.

19. Client and Customer Experience

Offer Simple, Transparent Solutions: Avoid overwhelming customers with too many choices. Offering a few straightforward, high-quality options can improve customer satisfaction and foster trust.

Simplify Service Processes: Streamline service processes so that customer interactions are smooth and efficient. A minimalist approach to customer service focuses on resolving issues with minimal back-and-forth.

Focus on Quality Over Quantity of Services: Rather than providing an exhaustive list of services, concentrate on delivering a few core services exceptionally well. This allows the company to allocate resources more effectively and maintain a strong reputation.

Minimized Customer Support Channels: Focus on the most effective channels for both customers and support teams. **Result:** Reduced confusion and smoother service.

Simplify Customer Feedback Loops: Ask fewer, focused questions that yield actionable insights. **Result:** Better understanding and higher response rates.

Focus on a Single High-Impact Marketing Channel: Concentrate on one or two channels that best reach your target audience. **Result:** More focused efforts, higher engagement and stronger brand presence.

Fewer Products and Services in Marketing: Run fewer, targeted campaigns with clearer messages. **Result:** Better ROI.

20. Vendor and External Dependencies

Minimize Vendor Relationships: Consolidate to a smaller group of trusted, high-performing vendors to reduce complexity and strengthen partnerships. **Result:** Lower transaction costs and simplified supply chains.

Fewer Dependencies on External Resources: Build internal capabilities and upskill employees to reduce reliance on external agencies or consultants. **Result:** Greater control, cost savings and internal expertise.

21. Product and Service Focus

Minimalist Product or Service Offerings: Reduce product lines to core offerings that deliver the most value. **Result:** Less overhead and greater focus and profitability.

Focus on Core Competencies: Specialize deeply rather than spreading resources thin across many offerings. **Result:** Increased brand clarity, expertise and market strength.

Simplified Product Packaging: Use functional, minimal packaging that communicates core purpose. **Result:** Lower costs and environmental benefits.

22. Administrative Simplification

Less Administrative Overhead: Simplify paperwork, approvals and compliance through automation or clear delegation. **Result:** More time for value-creating activities and faster workflows.

Reduced Documentation: Provide concise, easy-to-understand guides or templates. **Result:** Faster access to information and less time lost in reading.

23. Travel and Meetings Efficiency

Reducing Business Travel: Use video calls or virtual meetings in place of frequent travel and reserve travel for critical in-person meetings. **Result:** Reduced costs and time savings.

Fewer, More Effective Meetings: Replace daily check-ins with collaborative tools; keep meetings short and focused on decisions. **Result:** Higher efficiency and more time for deep work.

24. Mindfulness and Stress Reduction

Practice Mindful Transitions: Take a few moments between tasks to reset mentally, promoting focus and reducing stress.

Avoid Over-Working: A minimalist approach includes knowing when to stop. Working excessive hours can reduce productivity and increase burnout. Set limits to ensure work is sustainable in the long term.

Encourage Short Breaks for Recharging: Short breaks improve concentration and reduce mental fatigue. Focus on quality rest, like quick walks or mindfulness exercises, instead of browsing devices.

25. Organizational Simplicity

Eliminating Unnecessary Hierarchy: Flatten organizational structures by eliminating redundant levels of management to allow quicker decision-making and foster an environment of trust and autonomy. **Result:** Faster communication, improved collaboration and agility.

Consolidated Work Teams: Instead of multiple teams on similar projects, create cross-functional teams. **Result:** Improved collaboration, faster decisions and reduced redundancies.

By applying the "Less is More" philosophy in these areas, businesses and professionals can continue to simplify, prioritize and focus on what truly drives value. Whether it's reducing complexity in communication, streamlining processes or focusing on high-impact projects, adopting this mindset can lead to more efficient, effective and fulfilling professional experiences. The key is to continuously evaluate where simplification can yield positive outcomes, allowing time and resources to be focused on what truly matters.

Embracing Minimalism in Professional Growth

By integrating minimalist principles into your professional life, you gain clarity, reduce unnecessary complexity and can better focus on what truly matters. Minimalism encourages a disciplined approach, where each decision and action align with the broader purpose and goals of both personal and organizational success. It leads to a workplace that values well-being, simplicity and intentional productivity, benefiting not only individual professionals but also entire teams and organizations.

Minimalism in Business

"Efficiency thrives in simplicity."

Minimalism in business is about focusing on the essentials—eliminating waste, simplifying processes and cutting out anything that doesn't add value to the core mission or operations of the company. It is a philosophy that encourages businesses to operate with less complexity, lower costs and greater focus, ultimately driving efficiency, productivity and sustainability. By applying minimalist principles, businesses can reduce clutter—whether in their products, services or internal processes—and align resources more effectively to meet customer needs and company goals.

Key Principles of Minimalism in Business

1. Simplified Operations

Streamline Processes: Remove unnecessary steps, outdated forms and repetitive approvals that slow work. A simplified workflow ensures teams move faster and maintain consistency. Regularly map processes end-to-end and ask, *"What can we eliminate, standardize or automate?"* Continuous pruning keeps operations lean as you scale.
Automate Repetitive Work: Use automation tools wherever possible to eliminate manual repetition in data entry, approvals and reporting. Automation reduces errors and frees employees for strategic, high-impact activities. Start with high-volume, low-variation tasks and measure time saved to reinvest in innovation.
Integrate Systems: Replace scattered tools with unified platforms to improve information flow and reduce confusion. Integration minimizes duplicate efforts and lowers long-term costs. A single source of truth ensures decisions are made quickly and accurately.

Simple operations also create transparency—everyone knows what to do, how to do it and where to find what they need. Clear ownership and fewer handoffs reduce delays and accountability gaps.

Simplified Operations (Example/Result): Streamlining approvals and unifying tools reduces delays and improves coordination. **Result:** Faster execution, fewer mistakes, lower overhead and happier teams.

2. Focusing on Core Competencies

Identify What You Do Best: Determine the strengths that truly set your business apart and quantify their impact. Focus energy on activities that create the highest value. Protect these core strengths through training, systems and leadership clarity.
Eliminate Non-Core Activities: Let go of services, features or markets that consume time but add little value. Saying "no" to distractions strengthens your strategic position and frees resources for excellence.
Align Teams with Core Strengths: Ensure hiring, training tools and investments support the company's core capabilities. Encourage depth rather than spreading teams thin.

When a business sharpens its focus, customers clearly understand its value—making the brand stronger and more trusted. Focus also boosts team morale because people see how their work directly contributes to success.

Core Competency Focus (Example/Result): Doubling down on customer excellence or a signature product improves brand recognition.
Result: Higher loyalty, clearer identity, better ROI and focused growth.

3. Lean Product Development

Avoid Feature Overload: Build only what customers truly need. Unnecessary features increase cost, slow development and confuse users. Treat every new feature as a deliberate choice, not an automatic addition.
Use Rapid Prototyping: Test early and refine frequently. User feedback ensures you build the right thing instead of the expensive thing. Keep cycles short and kill weak ideas quickly.
Iterate Continuously: Small, frequent improvements reduce risk and increase relevance. A transparent roadmap aligns teams and prevents bloated releases.
Lean development not only lowers cost—it boosts innovation because teams stay flexible and open to fresh ideas. Simple products are easier to maintain, easier to scale and easier for customers to love.
Lean Development (Example/Result): Launching with essential features allows quicker customer validation. **Result:** Faster market entry, improved adoption, reduced cost and better product–market fit.

4. Clear and Direct Communication

Use Simple Language: Avoid jargon and complex explanations. Clear, plain communication saves time and improves understanding across all levels of the business.
Keep It Concise: Short, structured messages enable faster decisions. Distinguish between urgent, essential and optional information and communicate accordingly.

Standardize Channels: Limit tools to a few essential platforms to reduce fragmentation. Establish norms for what belongs where so everyone communicates consistently.

Clear communication builds trust—teams feel informed, aligned and confident about expectations. It reduces conflict, prevents misunderstandings and creates a culture of transparency.

Simplified Communication (Example/Result): Use weekly summaries and decision logs for alignment. **Result:** Fewer misunderstandings, faster decisions and more productive workdays.

5. Waste Reduction

Cut Unnecessary Costs: Identify areas with repeated loss—idle inventory, long wait times, frequent rework or unproductive labor—and eliminate them. Evaluate every cost using the lens: *"Does this produce visible value?"*

Optimize Resource Efficiency: Lean systems reduce material waste, energy usage and time wastage. Smart scheduling and better planning increase flow and reduce operational variability.

Improve Supply Chains: Remove bottlenecks and reduce overstocking. Strong partnerships with fewer suppliers improve reliability and reduce waste across the chain.

Reducing waste increases profits and supports environmental sustainability. Customers and employees increasingly prefer companies that balance efficiency with responsibility.

Waste Reduction (Example/Result): Lean practices reduce rework, dead inventory and resource leakage. **Result:** Lower costs, higher sustainability, improved margins and resilient operations.

6. Minimalist Design and Branding

Adopt Clean, Simple Designs: Clarity in design enhances brand recognition. Use white space effectively and remove unnecessary visual noise to let your message shine.

Focus on One Core Message: Make your value proposition obvious at first glance. Minimalist marketing communicates powerfully because customers understand quickly.

Use Intuitive Layouts: Design digital interfaces and packaging that guide users naturally. Fewer choices reduce confusion and increase customer satisfaction.

Minimalist brands appear premium, timeless and trustworthy. Customers appreciate clarity and emotional ease—and associate simple design with higher quality.

Minimalist Branding (Example/Result):
Simple logos, clean visuals and focused messaging elevate perception. **Result:** Stronger recall, improved engagement, better conversion and lower branding costs.

7. Prioritize Profitability Over Endless Growth

Strengthen Profit Margins: Focus on high-value offerings and customers. Adopt disciplined pricing and avoid discount traps that erode profit.
Avoid Overexpansion: Expand only after building a strong core foundation. Test new markets with small experiments before scaling aggressively.
Improve Core Markets First: Double down on retention, service quality and efficiency improvements before diversifying into new territories.
Sustainable success comes from financial stability, not overextension. Profit-first simplicity creates healthier companies that survive downturns and thrive long-term.

Profit-First Focus (Example/Result): Ending low-margin ventures frees resources for high-impact initiatives. **Result:** Stronger finances, healthier growth, better cash flow and long-term resilience.

Benefits of Minimalism in Business

1. **Improved Efficiency -** With fewer steps and simplified processes, businesses can operate more efficiently. By eliminating unnecessary complexity, tasks get done faster and with fewer mistakes, improving overall productivity.
2. **Cost Savings -** By cutting out waste—whether in resources, processes or products—businesses can significantly reduce costs. Leaner operations lead to higher margins and better use of company resources.
3. **Better Customer Experience -** Minimalism often leads to clearer communication, more user-friendly products and faster, more responsive customer service—all of which improve the customer experience and foster loyalty.
4. **Increased Agility -** Businesses that embrace minimalism can adapt more quickly to changing market conditions. With less bureaucracy and fewer layers of complexity, decisions can be made more swiftly and changes can be implemented with less resistance.
5. **Stronger Focus on What Matters -** A minimalist business strategy allows the company to stay laser-focused on its core values, strengths and customer needs. This focus prevents distractions and encourages the company to invest in what truly drives value, whether in products, services or customer relationships.

6. **Sustainability -** Minimalism promotes more sustainable business practices by reducing waste and focusing on long-term value creation. By operating with fewer resources and adopting eco-friendly practices, businesses can reduce their environmental impact.

How to Implement Minimalism in Business

1. **Simplify Your Product Line -** Instead of offering a wide range of products or services, focus on your top-performing ones. Eliminate anything that isn't generating strong demand or contributing meaningfully to your business's bottom line.
2. **Streamline Internal Processes -** Map out your business processes and identify areas where steps can be eliminated, automated or simplified. Consider adopting Agile methodologies or lean principles to continuously improve processes and cut unnecessary steps.
3. **Embrace Technology and Automation -** Use technology to automate repetitive tasks, reduce human error and increase efficiency. Software tools for project management, customer service (e.g., chatbots) and data analysis can help streamline operations and free up time for more valuable tasks.
4. **Outsource Non-Core Tasks -** Consider outsourcing tasks that are important but not central to your business operations (such as accounting, IT support or HR). This allows your internal team to focus on what they do best while keeping overhead costs lower.
5. **Refine Your Brand Message -** Keep your branding simple and focused. Avoid overloading customers with information or too many product options. A minimalist approach to your brand identity can help you stand out by being clear, direct and memorable.
6. **Create a Lean Marketing Strategy -** Focus on the most effective marketing channels rather than trying to be everywhere. Invest in quality content, word-of-mouth referrals and targeted campaigns that resonate with your specific audience.
7. **Build Strong Relationships with Customers -** Instead of constantly seeking new customers, focus on building long-term relationships with existing ones. Simplifying customer interactions, offering exceptional service and maintaining open communication can help foster loyalty and repeat business.

Examples of Minimalism in Business

1. **Apple -** Apple's minimalist approach is evident in its product design, branding and marketing strategies. Their products are known for their simple, clean lines, easy-to-use interfaces and a focus on essential features. The company

also simplifies its product range, offering only a few select options that focus on quality and functionality rather than quantity.

2. **IKEA -** IKEA embraces minimalism in its design, packaging and product offerings. The company's flat-pack furniture, clean and simple aesthetic and focus on providing value through affordable, functional designs reflect minimalist principles. The company also keeps its store layout simple, guiding customers directly to the most essential products.

3. **Tesla -** Tesla's approach to business is focused on innovation with simplicity. Their vehicles have a minimalist design, with fewer buttons and complicated interfaces. Tesla's strategy revolves around offering a limited but high-quality product range that focuses on the essentials of electric mobility, helping the company stay focused on its mission of sustainable transportation.

4. **Dropbox -** Dropbox's user interface is famously simple and minimalist. By focusing solely on the core functionality of file storage and sharing, it has been able to simplify the user experience, making it easy for users to understand and navigate.

Minimalism in business is about cutting through the clutter and focusing on what truly matters—whether that's creating valuable products, simplifying processes or enhancing customer experience. By adopting minimalist principles, businesses can operate more efficiently, save costs and achieve greater impact. It's not about doing less but about doing more with less, ensuring that every action, decision and resource aligns with the company's core mission and delivers the highest value to its customers and stakeholders.

Expanding Minimalism in Business: A Comprehensive Approach

1. Minimalist Leadership and Decision-Making

Why: Leadership plays a critical role in steering the business toward efficiency. When leaders adopt a minimalist mindset, it encourages simplicity in decision-making and clarity in vision, which can significantly enhance organizational coherence and speed.

How: Leaders should focus on clear and simple decision-making frameworks, avoiding over-complication or micromanagement. Empower teams to make decisions and trust their judgment while maintaining clear goals and guidelines. Leadership should be accessible, transparent and focused on empowering employees to act decisively and independently.

2. Cutting Down on Meetings

Why: Excessive meetings waste time and resources, often without yielding meaningful results. By reducing meetings to only the essential ones, businesses can create more time for employees to focus on actual work and productivity.

How: Streamline meetings by establishing clear agendas and specific objectives for each one. Avoid unnecessary check-ins or long discussions that don't add value. Instead, encourage asynchronous communication through collaborative tools that allow teams to work together without requiring constant meetings.

3. Simplifying Your Supply Chain

Why: A complex and overextended supply chain can lead to inefficiencies, higher costs and delays. Streamlining the supply chain can help businesses become more agile and cost-effective.

How: Assess the supply chain to identify bottlenecks and areas of over-complication. Reduce the number of suppliers, eliminate intermediaries and establish direct relationships where possible. Focus on building strong, reliable partnerships with fewer but more trusted suppliers who can deliver quality on time and at a competitive price.

4. Eliminating Unnecessary Products or Services

Why: Sometimes businesses fall into the trap of offering too many products or services, just to expand their portfolio. This can lead to confusion, diluted focus and higher operational costs.

How: Periodically evaluate your product or service portfolio to determine which items are driving the most value for your business and your customers. Discontinue products or services that no longer align with the company's goals, customer needs or profitability. This allows businesses to concentrate their resources on the offerings that truly matter.

5. Customer-Centric Minimalism

Why: Customers are increasingly seeking simpler, more streamlined experiences. A business that focuses on providing just the right amount of value—without overwhelming customers with too many options or complex features—will build stronger loyalty and satisfaction.

How: Understand your customers' needs deeply and avoid overloading them with choices or complexity. Focus on providing simple solutions that solve their problems effectively. For instance, simplify pricing models, optimize customer journeys and create clear, straightforward product instructions and support channels.

6. Adopting Agile Practices

Why: Minimalism in business often goes hand-in-hand with agility. Agile methodologies emphasize flexibility, speed and iterative progress, making it easier for companies to adapt to changing demands or unforeseen challenges.

How: Incorporate Agile principles into your development cycles, project management and team collaboration. Use short, focused sprints to execute tasks, allow for rapid testing and feedback and make quick adjustments as needed. This approach minimizes wasted effort and ensures constant alignment with core business goals.

7. Sustainability and Ethical Minimalism

Why: In today's market, sustainability is more than just a buzzword—it's a business imperative. Minimizing waste and focusing on ethical practices not only align with minimalist principles but also appeal to increasingly conscious consumers.

How: Businesses can incorporate sustainability by reducing packaging, sourcing materials responsibly and minimizing their carbon footprint. Ethical minimalism also includes fostering fair labour practices, promoting diversity and inclusion and supporting social causes that align with the company's values. Being transparent about sustainability efforts can attract customers who value ethical and responsible businesses.

8. Streamlined Technology and Tools

Why: Many businesses invest in an array of software and tools, often overlapping in functionality and creating unnecessary complexity. By streamlining technology use, businesses can save time, reduce costs and make it easier for teams to collaborate.

How: Evaluate the current technology stack and eliminate redundant tools or software. Choose tools that consolidate functions (e.g., project management, time tracking, communication) into one platform to reduce fragmentation. Ensure that employees are well-trained on the tools they use, so they can maximize their efficiency with minimal effort.

9. Employee-Centric Minimalism

Why: Overloading employees with tasks, expectations or resources can lead to burnout and decreased productivity. A minimalist approach to workforce management can improve morale, foster creativity and reduce turnover.

How: Focus on creating a work environment that prioritizes employee well-being, offering clear goals, manageable workloads and opportunities for autonomy. Encourage employees to focus on meaningful work rather than getting bogged down by unnecessary tasks or distractions. Offer flexibility and trust your team to manage their work efficiently.

10. Smart Financial Management

Why: Financial minimalism ensures that the company's resources are allocated to the most important and impactful areas. It also fosters better cash flow management and reduces the strain of carrying debt or unnecessary liabilities.

How: Review your company's finances regularly and trim unnecessary expenses. Invest only in areas that will drive growth and productivity. Adopt a lean approach to budgeting, focusing on maximizing ROI rather than just expanding for the sake of growth. Look for opportunities to renegotiate contracts, reduce fixed costs and manage cash flow effectively.

Real-Life Examples of Business Minimalism

1. **Basecamp -** Basecamp, a project management software company, embodies minimalist principles in its products and company operations. Its software is intentionally simple, with a focus on core features that prioritize user experience over complexity. Basecamp's approach also extends to the company's internal culture, where the team is intentionally kept small and efficient to maintain focus and productivity.

2. **Zara -** Zara's business model is a great example of minimalist efficiency in the fashion industry. By focusing on a lean supply chain and a limited but frequently updated product range, Zara ensures fast delivery of high-demand products while avoiding overstocking or unnecessary inventory. The company's ability to design, manufacture and distribute new styles quickly has been a key factor in its global success.

3. **Amazon's Prime Day -** Amazon embraces minimalism in its sales strategy with events like Prime Day, focusing on exclusive offers for Prime members, cutting out unnecessary deals and promotions. The minimalistic approach to the event is highly streamlined, concentrating on a small set of deals, which drives customer urgency and satisfaction.

4. **Patagonia -** Patagonia has committed to both minimalist production practices and a focus on sustainability. By reducing waste in manufacturing, offering durable products and encouraging customers to buy less, Patagonia has managed to build a brand that appeals to ethical consumers while staying profitable.

5. **Muji** - The Japanese retail company Muji is a prime example of minimalist branding and product design. It focuses on simple, functional products without unnecessary decoration, with an emphasis on quality and sustainability. The store layout and advertising are also minimalist, creating a calm, straightforward shopping experience.

Conclusion: The Future of Minimalism in Business

Embracing minimalism in business is about focusing on value, efficiency and sustainability while eliminating excess and inefficiency. In a world that increasingly values simplicity and clarity, businesses that adopt minimalist strategies can achieve more with fewer resources, offering high-quality products and services while reducing waste and complexity. The key is to continuously evaluate every aspect of the business—from product design to leadership practices—to ensure that everything serves a purpose and adds value.

By adopting minimalism across all facets of a business, companies can achieve better profitability, improve customer satisfaction, foster innovation and create a more sustainable future. Whether you're a small startup or a large enterprise, embracing minimalist principles can be a transformative approach to achieving long-term success.

Chapter 23: Digital and Financial Minimalism

Digital Minimalism: Decluttering Your Online World

"Digital Minimalism: Reclaim Your Time, Focus and Freedom."

A Digital minimalism is about building a mindful, intentional relationship with technology—using it to support your goals instead of consuming your attention. By simplifying your digital environment, reducing online noise and creating boundaries, you regain clarity, focus and control over your time.

1. Clarify Your Goals with Technology

Identify Your Purpose for Using Technology: Determine how technology supports your life—productivity, communication or learning. Understanding this purpose helps you avoid mindless scrolling and choose apps that truly matter.
Align Apps and Devices with Your Intentions: Keep only the tools that genuinely contribute to your goals and remove those that don't. This alignment ensures every digital tool has a purpose, reducing clutter and distractions.

2. Audit Your Digital Usage

Track Your Time Online: Review your average screen time and app usage patterns to understand where your attention goes each day. This awareness highlights habits you didn't realise were draining your time.
Identify Areas to Reduce: Highlight apps, websites or digital habits that consume energy but offer little value. Gradually reduce usage and replace these habits with more meaningful activities.

3. Declutter Your Digital Space

Organize and Clean Your Devices: Remove unused apps, old files, screenshots and photos. This frees storage, reduces visual noise and speeds up your device's performance.

Create a Minimal Home Screen: Keep only essential apps visible; categorize others into purposeful folders. A clean, simple home screen reduces the temptation to open distracting apps.

5. Set Boundaries and Limit Screen Time

Create Time Limits for Non-Essential Apps: Reduce time spent on social media, browsing or gaming by setting daily limits. This prevents overuse caused by impulse and habit.

Use Scheduled Tech Windows: Allocate specific periods for checking emails or social media to avoid constant checking. This helps you stay more present and focused.

5. Turn Off Non-Essential Notifications

Silence Distracting Alerts: Disable notifications for apps that do not require immediate attention, helping protect your focus from constant interruptions.

Retain Only Critical Alerts: Keep essential notifications such as calls, messages or urgent work updates. This ensures you stay informed without being overwhelmed.

6. Adopt a "One Screen at a Time" Policy

Focus on a Single Device: Avoid using multiple screens simultaneously, such as scrolling your phone while watching TV. Multitasking scatters attention and reduces enjoyment of both activities.

Stay Present During Each Activity: Keep devices aside while working, relaxing or spending time with others. Single tasking improves productivity and enhances quality of life.

6. Use Your Phone with Intent

Pick Up Your Phone with a Clear Purpose: Decide what you intend to do before unlocking your device, so your actions remain intentional, not habitual.

Keep Your Phone Out of Immediate Reach: Store it in a drawer, bag or another room when you need uninterrupted focus. Reducing proximity reduces temptation.

7. Engage in Regular Digital Detoxes

Schedule Tech-Free Moments: Introduce daily or weekly periods away from screens to rest your mind and recharge your energy.
Dedicate Extended Offline Time: Plan monthly digital-free days to reset habits, break dependency and reconnect with real-world experiences.

8. Optimize Your Social Media Usage

Reduce the Number of Platforms You Use: Keep only platforms that genuinely add value or align with your goals. Fewer platforms mean fewer distractions.
Curate Your Feed: Unfollow accounts that add noise, negativity or unnecessary comparison.
Set Daily Usage Limits: Prevent overuse by defining boundaries for how long and how often you scroll.

9. Establish Digital-Free Zones

Create Spaces Without Devices: Avoid using technology in areas such as the bedroom, dining table or living room. These spaces become restful, connected zones.
Encourage Present-Moment Interaction: Strengthen personal connections and reduce dependency by keeping devices physically out of sight.

10. Create a Morning and Evening Routine Without Tech

Start Your Day Screen-Free: Use the first 30 minutes for stretching prayer, meditation or journaling. This sets a calm tone for the day.
End Your Day Without Screens: Set a nightly tech cut-off point to improve relaxation and sleep quality. Blue light exposure before bed disrupts rest and overstimulates the mind.

11. Replace Digital Habits with Offline Alternatives

Choose Enriching Non-Digital Activities: Replace scrolling with reading, music or meaningful hobbies that bring joy and personal growth.
Build Meaningful Offline Routines: Engage in gardening, walking, cooking or playing with children. These moments strengthen bonds and nurture wellbeing.

12. Embrace "Slow Tech"

Use Technology Intentionally: Engage deeply with digital content instead of skimming or multitasking. This enhances understanding and enjoyment.
Capture Meaningful Moments: Take fewer, more thoughtful photos rather than dozens without intention. Slow tech helps you be more present.

13. Streamline Your Online Accounts and Subscriptions

Reduce Digital Commitments: Unsubscribe from newsletters and cancel unused services to cut digital clutter.
Regularly Review Your Subscriptions: Keep only those that genuinely add value or support your goals. This avoids wasted money and attention.

14. Reflect Regularly on Your Digital Habits

Review Your Relationship with Technology: Assess what's working and what needs adjustment so your habits stay healthy.
Maintain Alignment with Your Goals: Ensure your digital habits support—rather than distract from—your personal and professional priorities.

Digital minimalism encourages a healthier, more balanced relationship with technology. By simplifying your digital world, reducing distractions and using devices with intention, you regain control of your time, sharpen your focus and create space for what truly matters in life. It is a path to deeper presence, stronger clarity and more meaningful living in a digitally crowded world.

Financial Minimalism: Spending with Purpose

"Intentional Spending for a Stress-Free Future."

In an age where consumerism often dictates our choices, it's easy to get caught in the trap of constantly wanting more. We are constantly bombarded by advertisements, peer pressure and societal expectations to accumulate wealth, possessions and experiences that promise happiness. However, financial minimalism offers a refreshing approach—an intentional way of living that emphasizes reducing excess, simplifying your finances and focusing on what truly adds value to your life.

What is Financial Minimalism?

At its core, financial minimalism is about simplifying your relationship with money. It's about intentionally choosing to spend, save and invest in ways that align with your personal values, goals and long-term happiness. Unlike traditional approaches to wealth-building, which often encourage more consumption and accumulation, financial minimalism focuses on doing more with less. It's about freeing yourself from the burdens of excessive spending, consumer debt and clutter, allowing you to live a more peaceful and financially secure life.
Financial minimalism is the art of simplifying your financial life—reducing excess, eliminating waste and choosing money habits that support peace,

clarity and long-term well-being. It shifts your relationship with money from unconscious spending to intentional living, helping you focus on what truly adds value.

I make myself rich by making my wants FEW.

At its heart, financial minimalism is about needing less, wanting wisely and building a life of freedom rather than financial pressure.

The Pillars of Financial Minimalism

1. Intentional Spending

Spend with Purpose: Choose purchases that genuinely improve your life. Skip impulse buying and let every purchase align with your values.
Quality Over Quantity: Prefer fewer, durable and meaningful items instead of frequent low-quality purchases that cost more in the long run.
Remove Impulse Purchases: Practice pausing before buying anything. Ask yourself if it adds real value to your life.
Focus on Meaningful Expenditures: Direct money toward experiences, health, learning and well-being rather than clutter or trends.

2. Debt-Free Living

Reduce Financial Burden: Pay down existing debts to regain control of your finances.

Avoid New Debt: Make mindful choices that prevent unnecessary EMIs or loans.

Choose Freedom Over Pressure: A debt-free life reduces stress and creates mental clarity.

Use Simple Repayment Systems: Follow structured methods like snowball or avalanche to eliminate debt gradually and consistently.

3. Simplified Budgeting

Create a Minimal Budget: Focus on essentials—housing, food, health, education, savings.

Track Only What Matters: Keep your budget simple, clear and easy to maintain.

Focus on Long-Term Stability: Let your spending habits align with your future goals, not temporary desires.

4. Quality Over Quantity

Invest in Things That Last: Choose high-quality essentials that reduce the need for replacements.

Reduce Clutter: Keep only the items you truly use.

Focus on Value, Not Volume: Each purchase should serve a purpose, not fill a space.

Enjoy Fewer, Better Things: A smaller wardrobe or fewer gadgets can still offer great satisfaction when chosen wisely.

5. Automating Finances

Automate Bill Payments: Avoid missed payments and late fees.

Automate Investments: SIPs, recurring deposits and passive investment channels simplify wealth building.

Automate Savings: Set a monthly fixed amount for emergency funds, retirement and goals.

Simplify Money Flow: Let automation reduce stress and decision-making fatigue.

6. Purposeful Investments

Invest for the Long Term: Choose simple, low-risk investment vehicles that grow steadily over time.

Prefer Index Funds & ETFs: Build wealth with minimal monitoring or complexity.
Avoid Trend Chasing: Stick to investment strategies that match your goals and risk comfort.
Let Investments Support Your Future: Invest with intention, not excitement or fear.

7. Adopt a Minimalist Mindset & Lifestyle

Live with Fewer Wants: Reduce dependence on material possessions and focus on meaningful experiences.
Declutter Regularly: Keep only what you genuinely use and appreciate.
Consider Alternatives: Before buying, think if you can borrow, reuse or rent.
Choose Satisfaction Over Consumption: Contentment builds financial stability effortlessly.

8. Avoid Lifestyle Inflation

Maintain Simplicity as Income Grows: Let increased income improve savings, not expenses.
Protect Long-Term Goals: Direct extra earnings toward investments and emergency funds.
Stay Grounded: Avoid unnecessary upgrades driven by comparison or social pressure.
Live Within Your Means: Let your lifestyle reflect your values, not external expectations.

9. Invest in Yourself

Learn Meaningful Skills: Education, creativity and personal growth offer lifelong returns.
Use Free & Low-Cost Resources: Books, courses, workshops and mentorship build your competency.
Increase Your Earning Potential: Skills often deliver better outcomes than possessions.
Choose Growth Over Consumption: Invest in what expands your mind and future opportunities.

Financial minimalism is not about restriction—it's about clarity. It helps you control money instead of letting money control you. When you reduce unnecessary spending, avoid debt, buy intentionally and invest wisely, your life shifts from stress to stability, from clutter to clarity and from pressure to purpose.

The goal is simple: Spend on what matters. Save for what's important. Release what weighs you down. Live with freedom, security and peace.

How to Get Started with Financial Minimalism

- **Audit Your Finances**: Start by reviewing your current financial situation. List all income sources, debts, subscriptions, expenses and savings. This will give you a clear picture of where you stand and help identify areas where you can cut back.
- **Set Clear Financial Goals**: Define what you want to achieve financially. Whether it's paying off debt, saving for a home or building a retirement fund, having clear goals helps you focus your efforts and make more intentional financial decisions.
- **Declutter Your Financial Life**: Eliminate any unnecessary subscriptions, financial products or excess possessions that are draining your resources. Streamline your accounts, consolidate debt where possible and stop spending on things you don't truly need.
- **Embrace Simplicity in Spending**: Evaluate your spending habits and make conscious decisions to cut back on unnecessary expenses. Focus on buying only what adds true value to your life and what serves your long-term goals.
- **Automate Your Finances**: Set up automatic transfers for savings and bill payments to reduce the amount of time you spend managing money. Automating savings ensures that you consistently build wealth, regardless of your current spending patterns.
- **Invest in What Matters**: Shift your mindset from consumerism to investing in assets and experiences that align with your values. This could mean investing in low-cost index funds, spending money on experiences that build lasting memories or putting resources into personal development.

Financial minimalism is about more than just cutting back on expenses—it's about creating a financial life that is aligned with your deepest values and long-term goals. By simplifying your finances, reducing debt and focusing on what truly matters, you can build a life that is financially secure, free from stress and full of purpose. Achieving more with less isn't just a financial strategy; it's a philosophy for living a richer, more fulfilling life.

Chapter 24: Minimalism in Communication

Minimalism in Communication Skills

"Minimalism in Communication: The Art of Saying More with Less"

Minimalism in communication involves expressing ideas clearly, concisely and effectively by eliminating unnecessary words and focusing on what truly matters. It's about distilling complex thoughts into simple, direct messages that resonate and engage the audience without overwhelming them with excessive information. Whether in writing, speaking or non-verbal communication, minimalist principles help create more impactful, efficient and meaningful exchanges.

Key Principles of Minimalism in Communication

1. Clarity and Simplicity

Use Simple, Everyday Words: Communicate with language that is easy for anyone to understand, ensuring your message reaches your audience without effort.
Keep Sentences Short and Direct: Express your point in a straightforward manner so listeners follow your message without confusion.
Avoid Complex Phrasing: Reduce jargon and complicated expressions so your communication stays clean, natural and accessible.

2. Precision and Focus

Center on One Main Idea: Stick to the core message so the listener clearly understands your intention.
Remove Unnecessary Details: Keep only what adds value and let go of information that distracts from the message.

Choose Words with Purpose: Use accurate, meaningful vocabulary that delivers your point effectively.

3. Conciseness

Say Only What Matters: Express your thoughts in fewer words to keep your message sharp and easy to remember.
Eliminate Repetition and Fillers: Remove redundant lines and avoid fillers that add no meaning.
End When the Point Is Made: Stop once the core message is delivered to maintain clarity and impact.

4. Active Listening

Listen Completely Before Responding: Pay full attention so you understand the speaker's message clearly.
Respond Only to What Is Relevant: Focus your reply on key points to keep the conversation meaningful.
Use Pauses Thoughtfully: Allow brief moments of silence to show understanding and give space for reflection.

5. Non-Verbal Communication

Maintain Confident Body Language: Keep a calm posture and steady presence to reinforce your words.
Use Controlled, Natural Gestures: Let your movements support your message without overpowering it.
Match Expression with Message: Ensure your facial expressions and tone align with the meaning you want to convey.

6. Strategic Use of Silence

Pause to Emphasize Key Points: Silence after important statements helps listeners absorb the message.
Take a Moment Before You Speak: Reflecting briefly creates thoughtful and confident responses.
Let Silence Strengthen Meaning: When used intentionally, quiet moments add depth and importance to your words.

7. Consistency

Maintain a Steady Tone Throughout: Keep your communication aligned from start to finish so the message feels cohesive.

Align Words and Actions: Make sure what you say matches what you do to build trust and reliability.
Repeat Key Messages Simply: Reinforce important points with consistency, not length, for better understanding.

Benefits of Minimalism in Communication

"Clarity Over Clutter: The Power of Minimalist Communication."

- **Improved Understanding -** Clear and concise messages are easier to understand, reducing the chances of misunderstandings and confusion. Your audience is more likely to absorb and retain what you're saying when you keep it simple.
- **Better Engagement -** In today's information-heavy world, people are more likely to engage with content that's brief and to the point. Minimalist communication cuts through the noise, keeping your audience's attention focused on what's important.
- **Time Efficiency -** With minimalism, you avoid wasting time on irrelevant details or excessive explanations. Whether you're having a quick conversation, sending an email or presenting, minimalist communication allows you to convey your message efficiently.
- **Enhanced Credibility -** Being able to express your ideas clearly and succinctly shows that you understand the topic well. This boosts your credibility and demonstrates respect for your audience's time and intelligence.
- **Improved Decision-Making -** When communication is focused and concise, it allows people to make decisions more quickly and effectively. By providing only the most relevant information, you help others evaluate situations and take action without unnecessary delays.
- **Reduced Miscommunication -** When you communicate with minimalism, the risk of misinterpretation decreases. Clarity and precision reduce the likelihood of confusion and ensure that your audience understands your message as intended.

How to Apply Minimalism in Communication

1. **Plan Ahead** - Before communicating, especially in writing or presentations, plan what you want to say. Identify the key message or main points and eliminate any distractions or irrelevant information. This helps you stay on topic and communicate more effectively.

2. **Avoid Over-Explaining** - Resist the urge to explain every detail. Trust that your audience can fill in the gaps where necessary. Provide enough information to make your point clear but leave room for them to think for themselves.

3. **Use Visuals When Necessary** - In presentations or written communication, visuals can enhance your message. A simple diagram or image can often convey a message more quickly and clearly than a block of text.

4. **Be Direct** - Whether you're speaking or writing, get to the point as quickly as possible. Avoid hedging your statements or using unnecessary qualifiers like "I think" or "I believe." Speak with confidence and assertiveness.

5. **Minimize Digital Overload** - In the age of emails and instant messaging, it's easy to overwhelm others with long threads or unnecessary notifications. Keep digital communication concise and purposeful. Limit the use of emojis, unnecessary attachments or excessive follow-ups unless absolutely necessary.

6. **Encourage Feedback** - After communicating, seek feedback to ensure that your message was received as intended. By listening and adjusting accordingly, you can refine your minimalist communication approach to better meet your audience's needs.

Real – Life Examples of Minimalism in Communication

- **Steve Jobs' Product Launches** - Steve Jobs was known for his minimalist communication style, particularly in his product launch presentations. He kept slides simple, with a single powerful image and a few words. His speeches were short, clear and impactful, with each word chosen carefully to resonate with the audience.
- **Warren Buffett's Interviews** - Warren Buffett is another example of minimalist communication. He's known for giving clear, direct responses that cut through the complexity of financial topics. His simple, straightforward style makes his advice accessible to a wide audience.
- **Short and Sweet Texts** - In the digital world, minimalism in communication is especially important. Text messages or emails that are short to the point and free from unnecessary fluff tend to be more effective. For instance, instead of writing "I just wanted to let you know that I have received your email and will get back to you as soon as I have more information," a minimalist response could be: "Received your email. I'll get back to you soon."

Minimalism in communication isn't about saying less but about saying more with less. It's about delivering your message efficiently and effectively, without unnecessary embellishments or distractions. By embracing clarity, precision and brevity, you can communicate in a way that respects your audience's time and attention while ensuring that your message is heard loud and clear. Minimalist communication not only fosters better understanding and engagement but it also strengthens your credibility and enhances your ability to influence and connect with others.

Minimalism in Writing: The Power of Simplicity and Clarity

"Minimal Words, Maximum Impact."

Minimalism in writing is a style that emphasizes brevity, clarity and directness. It involves stripping away unnecessary words, decorations and embellishments to deliver a message in the simplest and most effective way possible. Minimalist writers focus on what's essential, providing just enough detail to engage the reader and convey the core idea, without overwhelming them with excess.

Key Elements of Minimalism in Writing

1. **Concise Language -** The hallmark of minimalist writing is the use of concise, straightforward language. Every word, sentence and paragraph serves a purpose and nothing is included that doesn't directly contribute to the meaning or the atmosphere of the piece. Writers aim to avoid superfluous adjectives, adverbs and overly complex sentence structures. The goal is clarity, so the reader's attention is focused on the message, not the delivery.

2. **Simplicity in Sentence Structure -** Minimalist writing favours short, simple sentences rather than long, convoluted ones. Complex ideas are often broken down into digestible parts and the rhythm of the writing is kept smooth and easy to follow. Repetition is minimized and sentence structure is direct. The simplicity of the sentences allows the meaning to be conveyed efficiently and without distraction.

3. **Eliminating Unnecessary Detail -** Minimalist writers often leave much unsaid. Instead of providing exhaustive descriptions, they focus on what is essential to the scene or theme. The writing allows room for the reader's imagination to fill in the gaps. This approach emphasizes suggestion over explicitness, using economy of detail to create a sense of atmosphere or emotion without over-explaining.

4. **Focus on Action and Dialogue -** In minimalist fiction, action and dialogue often take center stage. The plot moves forward with sparse but purposeful details and characters' emotions or motivations are often conveyed through what they say and do, rather than lengthy internal monologues or descriptions.

The focus on what characters do and say keeps the story moving and allows the reader to interpret deeper meanings.

5. **Evoking Emotion with Simplicity** - Even though minimalist writing avoids excessive emotional detail, it can still convey deep feelings through small, poignant moments. A well-chosen word or a quiet gesture can evoke more emotion than an elaborate description. The absence of overt sentimentality often makes the emotional moments more powerful because they feel authentic and unforced.

6. **Economy of Words** - The minimalist writer is often as concerned with the words they leave out as with those they include. Each sentence is weighed for its necessity and relevance, ensuring that only the most vital parts of the narrative remain. This makes the writing more focused, efficient and impactful.

Benefits of Minimalism in Writing

1. **Clarity and Precision** - Minimalist writing is clear because it eliminates the clutter of unnecessary words or ideas. The writing's message is presented in a direct and efficient manner, which helps readers understand the central themes without distraction.

2. **Engagement through Suggestion** - Instead of telling the reader everything, minimalist writing allows the reader to fill in the gaps. This can be a more engaging experience, as readers are encouraged to interpret the subtext and contribute to the meaning of the story.

3. **Faster Reading** - Because minimalist writing uses fewer words, it can make for a quicker, more streamlined reading experience. Readers can consume the text at a faster pace without feeling bogged down by excessive details.

4. **Focus on What Matters** - By cutting away the excess, minimalist writing draws the reader's attention to the most important elements of the story—whether it's a character's actions, a plot twist or an emotional moment. The story becomes more focused, keeping the reader's attention where it matters most.

5. **Universality** - The simplicity of minimalist writing allows the themes and messages to feel universal. By stripping away cultural or historical markers that might tie a story to a specific place or time, minimalist writers can craft stories that resonate more widely.

Real – Life Examples of Minimalism in Writing

- **Ernest Hemingway** is often cited as a pioneer of minimalist writing. His "Iceberg Theory" suggests that the bulk of a story's meaning lies beneath the surface, with the visible text representing only a small portion of the total experience. In his stories, Hemingway's simple, sparse prose is filled with unspoken meaning. For example, in The Old Man and the Sea, much of the novel's deeper themes are conveyed through the actions and sparse dialogue of the protagonist, Santiago.
- **Raymond Carver**, another minimalist writer, often uses pared-down prose to explore complex emotional states. In stories like "Cathedral" and "What We Talk About When We Talk About Love," Carver's spare descriptions and dialogue focus on the raw, unsaid emotions between characters, leaving much to the reader's interpretation.

How to Implement Minimalism in Your Own Writing

1. **Trim the Fat -** After writing your first draft, go through your work and remove any words, sentences or paragraphs that don't serve a specific purpose. Look for redundancies, excessive adjectives or adverbs and long-winded descriptions.

2. **Focus on Essential Details -** Instead of trying to describe everything, focus on the most important, evocative details that help create mood or push the plot forward. Choose your words carefully to ensure that every detail adds something to the piece.

3. **Use Dialogue and Action -** Let characters speak for themselves. Show their emotions and motivations through what they do and say, rather than telling the reader how they feel. Dialogue should be purposeful and reveal more than just the surface meaning.

4. **Be Concise but Don't Lose Emotion -** Minimalism doesn't mean an absence of emotion, just that it is conveyed in a more subtle way. Use concise language to convey emotional moments with a few carefully chosen words or actions.

5. **Leave Room for Interpretation -** Avoid over-explaining. Trust the reader to fill in some of the gaps, allowing them to engage with the story and draw their own conclusions. Sometimes, less is more when it comes to meaning.

Minimalism in writing is about doing more with less. It's about creating a powerful, immersive experience for the reader through simplicity, precision and suggestion. By stripping away the unnecessary and focusing on what truly matters, minimalist writers create works that resonate on a deeper level. Whether you're writing fiction, poetry or non-fiction, embracing minimalist principles can help you communicate more effectively and with greater impact, allowing your message to shine through with clarity and beauty.

Minimalism in Speaking: The Power of Brevity and Clarity

"Clarity Over Complexity in Every Conversation."

Minimalism in speaking is about communicating your message in the simplest and most effective way possible. It involves focusing on the essentials, avoiding unnecessary words and using clear, direct language to get your point across. By speaking less but meaning more, minimalist speakers can engage their audience more effectively, ensuring that their words are impactful and memorable.

Key Principles of Minimalism in Speaking

1. Clarity and Precision

Use Clear, Simple Words: Speak with language that is easy for everyone to understand so your message connects instantly. Clear words remove confusion and help the listener follow your point effortlessly.
Get Straight to the Point: State your main message early to keep conversations sharp and purposeful. Beginning with clarity ensures your audience knows exactly where you are heading.
Avoid Complex Expressions: Skip jargon and roundabout explanations so your ideas stay clean and accessible.

2. Economy of Words

Say Only What Is Necessary: Focus on essential details so your message remains sharp and meaningful. Fewer words help listeners grasp your intention without effort.
Remove Verbal Fillers: Eliminate habits like "um," "like," "you know" and "basically," which dilute impact. Clean speech enhances confidence and authority.
Keep Sentences Purposeful: Each line should contribute to the conversation and move it forward.

3. Concise Sentences

Use Short, Direct Sentences: Deliver ideas in crisp statements that are easy to absorb. Short sentences help maintain the listener's attention.
Break Long Thoughts into Parts: Divide complex ideas into clear segments so the message stays organized. This keeps your communication steady and digestible.

Avoid Long Monologues: Stay focused so the listener never loses track of the key point.

4. Focus on Key Points

Highlight Only What Matters: Choose the most important idea and build around it, avoiding unnecessary backstory. This keeps the message meaningful and easy to follow.

Stick to One or Two Core Ideas: Concentrate the conversation on the essentials to prevent information overload. Limiting topics strengthens clarity.

Remove Extra Details: Let go of side information that does not support the main point.

5. Effective Pauses

Use Pauses to Add Impact: A short silence after key points helps the listener absorb the meaning. Pauses bring weight and rhythm to your message.

Avoid Rushing: Speaking slowly and leaving brief gaps improves clarity and reduces mistakes. Controlled pacing builds confidence and presence.

Let Silence Strengthen Your Words: A thoughtful pause often communicates more than continuous speech.

6. Engaging with Silence

Be Comfortable with Quiet Moments: Silence gives the listener space to reflect and understand. It also shows your confidence and composure.

Allow Space for Thought: Quiet gaps encourage deeper engagement and prevent rushed reactions. Silence can anchor a conversation with depth and meaning.

Use Stillness Wisely: Silence can often emphasize an idea better than extra words.

7. Non-Verbal Communication

Maintain Calm, Confident Body Language: Your posture, gestures and expressions should support your message naturally. Physical presence often communicates more than words.

Use Intentional Gestures: Simple, controlled gestures reinforce clarity while avoiding distraction.

Align Expressions with Tone: Make sure your facial expressions match what you are saying so the message feels authentic and trustworthy.

Benefits of Minimalism in Speaking

1. **Improved Focus and Clarity -** By reducing unnecessary information, you allow your listener to concentrate on the core message. The clearer and more

focused your message is, the better your audience will understand and remember it.

2. **Better Retention** - Short, impactful statements are easier for listeners to remember than long-winded speeches. When you speak with precision, your audience is more likely to retain the key points.

3. **Enhanced Impact** - Minimalism forces you to choose your words carefully, ensuring that each one carries weight. This makes your speech more compelling and impactful, as listeners will appreciate the thoughtfulness and intention behind your words.

4. **Avoiding Overload** - When you speak less, you avoid overwhelming your audience with too much information. In a world full of distractions, being concise helps maintain your listener's attention.

5. **Increased Credibility** - Speaking in a clear, minimalist manner can make you appear more confident and authoritative. When you speak with precision, people are more likely to trust your opinions and take you seriously.

How to Apply Minimalism in Speaking

1. **Know Your Purpose** - Before speaking, be clear about what you want to achieve. Are you informing, persuading or simply engaging? Having a clear purpose will help you stay focused on the essential parts of your message and avoid veering off track.

2. **Eliminate Unnecessary Details** - Ask yourself: Does this detail add to the core message? If not, leave it out. Trim any excess words that don't contribute meaningfully to the conversation or presentation.

3. **Use Simple Language** - Avoid the temptation to use complex vocabulary or technical terms unless necessary. Speak in a language that is easily understood by your audience.

4. **Practice Active Listening** - Being a minimalist speaker also means being an active listener. By listening carefully to others, you can respond more thoughtfully and directly, without the need for excess elaboration.

5. **Be Mindful of Your Audience** - Tailor your speech to the needs of your listeners. Consider their level of understanding, attention span and interests. Be brief and relevant to keep them engaged.

6. **Embrace the Power of Silence -** Don't rush to fill every moment with words. Use silence to emphasize your points, allow for reflection and create a sense of importance around your message.

Real-Life Examples of Minimalism in Speaking

- **The Doctor Who Spoke in Pictures**
  Dr. Meera noticed patients felt overwhelmed by medical jargon, so she simplified everything. She used **one clear sentence** to explain conditions, **simple analogies** instead of technical terms and gave **one actionable instruction** per visit. Her conversations became shorter but patients understood more, remembered more and followed through better. Her mantra: **"Say it simply so they can live it fully."**
- **Joshua Becker — A Leading Minimalist Speaker**
  Joshua Becker is known globally for a **clean, direct speaking style** that avoids unnecessary words. His talks at Google, Airbnb, Salesforce, Deloitte and major universities highlight his clarity-first approach.
  He exemplifies minimalist speaking by:
  Using **few but powerful stories**.
  Getting to the point quickly.
  Speaking with **warm precision** and no verbal clutter.
  Keeping talks **brief, structured and purposeful**.
  He embodies the core idea: **say less, mean more and let clarity lead.**

Minimalism in speaking is a powerful tool for communicating effectively and efficiently. By focusing on clarity, conciseness and precision, you can make a greater impact with fewer words. Whether you're speaking in a professional setting, delivering a presentation or having a personal conversation, embracing minimalism allows you to be more purposeful in your communication, ensuring that your message is both clear and memorable. The art of speaking with simplicity is not about saying less but about saying more with less.

Chapter 25: Minimalism in Design, Living Spaces & Mental Clarity

Minimalism in Product Design

"Less Complexity, More Usability."

Minimalism in product design focuses on creating products that are simple, functional and free from unnecessary elements. This approach emphasizes the essential functions of a product, striving for efficiency and clarity in design while removing any excess that could distract from the user experience.

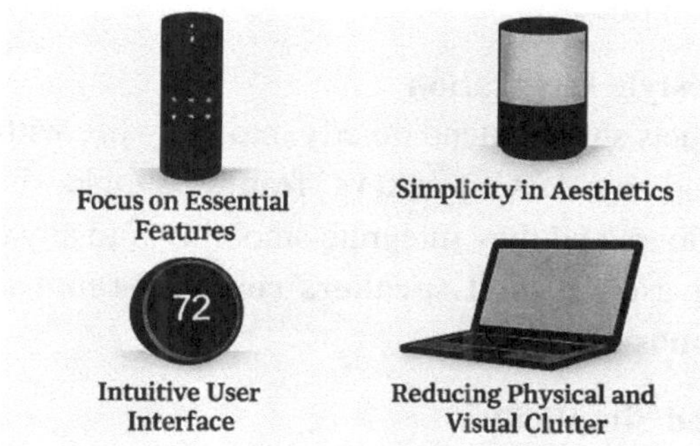

Here's how minimalism is applied in product design, along with examples to illustrate its impact:

1. Focus on Essential Features
Design only what the user truly needs so the product is instantly usable. **Example: Apple iPod (historic)** popularized stripped-down music navigation with the click wheel—few controls, clear purpose. *(General historical example—no current citation needed)*

2. Simple, Clean Aesthetics
Neutral colours, quiet forms and unobtrusive details make products timeless and easy to place anywhere. **Example: MUJI** stationery and home goods use unbranded, plain finishes to reduce visual noise and fit any setting

3. Functionality as Beauty
Every visible element should earn its place by improving use. **Example: Dyson** vacuums expose functional engineering (clear bin, cyclones) and emphasize performance over decoration.

4. Intuitive User Interfaces

Use clear displays, simple gestures and logical flows so anyone can operate the product fast. **Example: Google Nest Thermostat**—a simple circular control (turn or swipe) with a minimal display showing essentials.

5. Reduce Physical & Visual Clutter

Fewer buttons and consolidated controls enhance clarity. **Example: Apple MacBook**—seamless body and a large multi-gesture trackpad streamline input and cut hardware clutter.

6. Sustainable, Repairable by Design

Use fewer materials, extend life and enable fixes. **Example: Fairphone**—a modular smartphone with **user-replaceable** screen, battery, cameras and USB-C port; parts are sold directly.

7. Seamless Lifestyle Integration

Minimalist products should blend quietly into daily life without drawing attention. **Example: Sonos wireless speakers** feature simple, understated designs in monochrome colours and they integrate smoothly into any home. They work over **Wi-Fi**, allowing users to **add speakers room-by-room** and control everything from a **single Sonos ap**

8. User-Centered Simplicity

Design from real tasks outward; remove steps and friction. **Example: Moleskine Classic Notebook**—plain cover, elastic band, simple layouts; a minimal canvas for notes anywhere.

9. High-Quality, Durable Materials

Favour strong materials that look clean without ornament. **Example: Logitech MX Keys Mini**—a compact, minimalist keyboard focused on typing quality and ergonomics in a space-saving form.

10. Clear, Purposeful Branding

Let the product speak; keep labels restrained and informative. **Example: Aesop**—iconic **amber glass** bottles with quiet black-on-white labels; minimal packaging that serves protection and recognition.

In Essence

Minimalist product design delivers **function, clarity, durability and calm**. By stripping the non-essential, these globally used products show how "less" leads to **easier use, longer life and timeless appeal**

Minimalism in Home Design

"Simplify Your Space, Amplify Your Life."

Minimalism in house design emphasizes simplicity, functionality and a sense of calm by reducing visual clutter and focusing on essential elements. The minimalist home often combines clean lines, open spaces and a neutral colour palette to create an environment that feels both welcoming and spacious. Here's a look at how minimalism can transform a house into a space that is practical, aesthetically pleasing and peaceful:

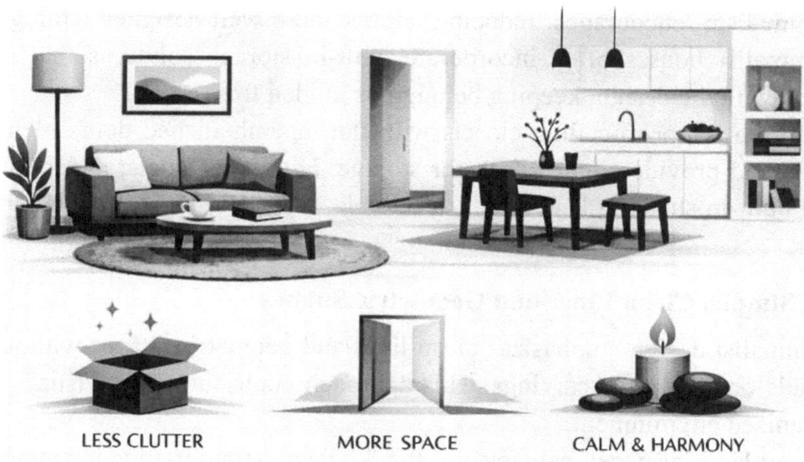

1. Open Floor Plans

Minimalist houses often feature open layouts that maximize space and allow light to flow freely. This approach makes the home feel larger, brighter and more inviting.

Example: A minimalist home may combine the kitchen, dining and living room into one open area. This creates a sense of unity and removes unnecessary walls or barriers that can make a space feel cramped.

2. Neutral and Monochromatic Colour Schemes

Minimalist homes typically use a neutral colour palette—white, beige, grey or earthy tones—paired with natural textures like wood or stone. These colours create a calm, cohesive look, making the space feel light and airy.

Example: Walls painted in a soft white with natural wood accents or furnishings add warmth without overwhelming the space. Light grey or beige floors create continuity and make rooms look larger and more cohesive.

3. Functional and Multi-Purpose Furniture

In minimalist design, each piece of furniture serves a clear purpose and often has a multifunctional use. This reduces clutter and ensures that only essential items are included.

Example: A minimalist living room might feature a sofa with hidden storage, a coffee table that can be expanded for dining and minimalist shelving for a sleek, clean look. Multi-purpose furniture maximizes space and keeps rooms free of excess.

6. Built-In Storage Solutions

Minimalism encourages reducing clutter and well-designed storage is key. Minimalist houses often incorporate built-in storage solutions that seamlessly blend with the design, keeping belongings hidden from view.

Example: Floor-to-ceiling closets with flat, unembellished doors blend into the walls and provide ample space for storage. Hidden cabinets, under-stair storage and built-in shelving keep items accessible but out of sight, maintaining a clean look.

7. Simple, Clean Lines and Geometric Shapes

Minimalist design emphasizes clean lines and geometric shapes without intricate details or decorative carvings. This approach contributes to a visually calm and organized environment.

Example: Flat-panel cabinets in the kitchen, straight-edged countertops and rectangular windows with no excessive mouldings create a sense of order. Simple, geometric furniture and décor follow the same principle, adding to the unified feel of the home.

6. Abundant Natural Light

Minimalist homes maximize natural light, creating a bright and open atmosphere that brings out the simplicity of the design. Large windows, glass walls or skylights are often used to bring light into the home and reduce the need for artificial lighting during the day.

Example: Floor-to-ceiling windows in a living room not only allow light to flood in but also connect the interior with the surrounding nature, enhancing the feeling of space and openness. Skylights in hallways or bathrooms bring light to otherwise dark areas.

7. Natural Materials and Textures

Minimalist interiors often include materials like wood, concrete, stone and metal to add warmth and texture without overwhelming the design. These materials offer visual interest and create a grounded, timeless aesthetic.

Example: A wood accent wall, polished concrete floors or a stone fireplace adds texture to the home while maintaining a natural look. The combination of neutral colours and organic materials creates a serene, earthy feel that's both simple and sophisticated.

8. Intentional Use of Art and Décor

Minimalist homes use art and décor sparingly, with each piece carefully selected for impact and meaning. Rather than filling the home with decorations, minimalist spaces use a few high-quality pieces to create focal points.

Example: A single large painting or a minimalist sculpture can make a strong statement in a living room without overwhelming the space. A few curated items, like a single potted plant or a tasteful vase, add character without clutter.

9. Seamless Indoor-Outdoor Connection

Minimalism often extends to the exterior of the home by creating a seamless connection between indoor and outdoor spaces. Large sliding doors or expansive windows allow easy access to patios, gardens or natural surroundings.

Example: A minimalist house might feature glass doors that open onto a garden, patio or pool area, blurring the boundary between the interior and the landscape. This connection enhances natural views and extends the living space.

10. Efficient Layout and Flow

Minimalist homes prioritize an efficient layout, where each area is well-defined yet flows naturally into the next. The design maximizes the usable area of the house, ensuring there's enough space for essential activities without redundancy.

Example: In a minimalist bedroom, the bed is positioned to face a window for natural light, with a simple wardrobe and nightstands for essential storage. An open bathroom nearby may feature clean, simple fixtures, creating a seamless flow from one space to the next.

11. Concealed Technology and Appliances

Minimalist homes often hide technology and appliances to maintain a streamlined look. Built-in or concealed appliances help to reduce visual noise, creating a clean, uninterrupted aesthetic.

Example: In a minimalist kitchen, the refrigerator, dishwasher and other appliances are built into cabinetry, so they blend with the overall design. Wall-mounted TVs in the living room or bedroom may be recessed to avoid disrupting the clean lines of the walls.

12. Minimal Outdoor Landscaping

Minimalist home design often extends to the outdoor space, where landscaping is simple and purposeful. The exterior design avoids over-decoration, focusing on a clean, harmonious connection with nature.

Example: A minimalist garden might use native plants, gravel or simple stone pathways, avoiding overly elaborate plants or decorations. A few trees or a well-placed seating area create a tranquil outdoor space that complements the minimalist house design.

Minimalism in house design creates an environment that is calm, clutter-free and centered on the essentials. By focusing on open spaces, natural light, functional furniture and simple, quality materials, minimalist homes offer a sense of peace and clarity that's conducive to modern living. This design approach can improve well-being by fostering a more organized, intentional and visually serene home environment.

Decluttering Thoughts and Mental Noise

"Mental Minimalism: Space for What Matters."

The Weight of Clutter

Clutter is not only physical. It exists in our minds, our thoughts, our obligations and even our relationships. Just as a messy room drains energy, a cluttered inner life creates stress, confusion and unhappiness. Decluttering is the art of removing what no longer serves us, so we can focus on what truly enhances our life.

Decluttering the Mind

The mind often carries unnecessary baggage — regrets of the past, worries about the future and endless mental chatter.

- **Practice Mindfulness**: Spend a few minutes daily in silence, focusing on breath or nature.
- **Let Go of Regrets**: Accept what cannot be changed and redirect energy toward growth.
- **Limit Information Overload**: Reduce constant news and social media consumption.

Example: Rohan realised his mind was always racing with "what ifs." By journaling daily, he released these thoughts onto paper, freeing his mind for clarity.

Decluttering Thoughts

Thoughts shape emotions and actions. Negative, repetitive thinking entangles us.

- **Replace Negativity with Positivity**: Consciously shift from “I can’t” to “I will try.”
- **Focus on Essentials**: Not every thought deserves attention. Prioritize what matters.
- **Create Mental Boundaries**: Avoid overthinking situations beyond your control.

Example: Anita constantly worried about others’ opinions. By practicing affirmations, she replaced self-doubt with confidence.

Decluttering Life Obligations

Modern life is full of commitments — work, social events, errands — many of which are unnecessary.

- **Say No**: Decluttering obligations means refusing what doesn’t align with your values.
- **Prioritize**: Focus on tasks that truly matter.
- **Simplify Routines**: Streamline daily habits to reduce stress.

Example: Meera attended every social gathering out of guilt. When she began saying no, she found more time for family and self-care.

Decluttering Relationships

Relationships should enhance life, not entangle it. Yet many people hold on to toxic or draining connections.

- **Identify Supportive Bonds**: Nurture relationships that bring joy and growth.

- **Release Toxic Ties**: Distance yourself from those who drain energy or spread negativity.
- **Communicate Clearly**: Honest conversations prevent misunderstandings and emotional clutter.

Example: Arjun realised a long-time friend constantly criticized him. By setting boundaries, he protected his peace and invested in healthier friendships.

Real-Life Examples:

- **Parable: The Heavy Backpack -** A traveller carried a backpack filled with stones. Each stone represented regrets, obligations and toxic ties. The weight slowed him down. When he began removing stones one by one, his journey became lighter and joyful.
  Lesson: Life becomes easier when we let go of what no longer serves us.

Decluttering is not about abandoning responsibilities or people. It is about consciously choosing what enhances life and releasing what entangles it. A decluttered mind, simplified obligations and healthier relationships create space for peace, clarity and joy. When we let go of what we don't need, we discover the freedom to live fully.

Chapter 26: Emotional Minimalism — Letting Go Gracefully

Emotional Minimalism

"Letting go doesn't erase the past—it frees your hands to hold the present."

Some things in our homes feel heavier than they look. A small letter, an old trophy, a scarf someone gave you years ago—these items hold memories, love and pieces of who you once were. Emotional minimalism is not about throwing everything away. It is about choosing what truly matters and releasing what quietly weighs on your heart. It helps you feel lighter, more present and more connected to the life you are living now.

This chapter guides you through five gentle areas:

1. Sentimental items
2. Memory vs. memorabilia
3. Guilt and inherited clutter
4. Past selves vs. your current identity
5. Self-compassion during decluttering

1. Sentimental Items — The "Few That Matter" Box

"Memories live in you, not in everything you own."

You don't need to keep every sentimental object to keep the feeling. Create one small box in your home—your **"Few That Matter"** box. This is the place where only your most meaningful pieces go.

Here's a simple way to choose:

1. Gather all sentimental things in one place.
2. Look at everything together—your heart will naturally sort what matters most.
3. Hold each item and ask:
    - *What moment does this remind me of?*
    - *Which value does it carry—love, courage, growth, gratitude?*
    - *Can a photo and a short note keep the same memory?*
4. Keep just **one item per memory or phase**—one letter, one medal, one memento.

When the box becomes full, your choosing is complete. If something new enters, something old leaves. This isn't about less—it is about deeper, clearer meaning.

2. Memory vs. Memorabilia — Keep the Story, Not the Stack

"A captured story weighs less than a stored object."
Often we keep things we never look at—projects, souvenirs, childhood crafts—because they remind us of earlier chapters. But the memory exists **in you**, not in the pile.

To lighten your load:

- Photograph bulky items.
- Make a small printed album or a simple digital folder called **"What Built Me."**
- Add one sentence under each picture to keep the emotion alive.
- Then choose **one physical item** from each stage of life to represent that time.

When the story is saved, the extra objects can let go.

3. Guilt & Inherited Clutter — Honour Without Hoarding

"You honour people best by living their values, not by storing their belongings." Gifts and inherited items can carry pressure. We keep them out of guilt, not love.

A kinder way:

- Keep only pieces that truly carry the person's spirit—a recipe card instead of a whole kitchen set, one shawl instead of a trunk of old fabric.
- Offer other items to family members with a short note explaining the story.
- Donate the rest where they can serve others—a school, library, shelter or vocational centre.

And remember: A gift completes its purpose the moment it expresses love. You're allowed to let it move on.

4. Past Selves & Current Identity — Closing Chapters with Respect

"You didn't fail when you moved on—you evolved." We all keep things from old versions of ourselves—sports gear, work files, instruments, hobbies we no longer practise.

Ask yourself gently:

- *Does this support the person I am becoming?*
- *Am I keeping this out of guilt or fear?*
- *If I ever need it again, could I borrow or rent it?*

Keep one symbolic item—a badge, a book, a small tool—and let the rest go to someone who can use it **now**. For each past-self item you release, add one future-self step: a course, a better tool or simply more free space in your life. This isn't loss—it's alignment.

5. Self-Compassion While Decluttering — Gentle Pace, No Shame

"Kindness to yourself is the shortest path to lasting change." Decluttering your emotions is delicate work. It should never feel like punishment.

- Move slowly and kindly.
- If an item hurts to decide on, put it in a box labelled **"Revisit in 90 days."**
- Aim for progress, not perfection—one drawer today, one shelf next week.
- Your "enough" is personal. Comparison is noise.
- When resistance appears, ask: *What part of this feels hard? What tiny step would help?*

Speak to yourself the way you would to a friend: "Letting go doesn't erase love. I can keep the memory and release the weight." Your home—and your heart—will feel softer and freer.

Real-Life Examples:

- **Aditi — Keeping Only What Still Sparks Joy -** Aditi had two shoeboxes full of college letters. She read them all, kept five that still touched her heart, photographed the rest and placed the five in her "Few That Matter" box. Now she revisits them on birthdays—not overwhelmed, just connected.
- **Ishaan — A Lighter Legacy -** After his grandfather passed away, Ishaan inherited cupboards full of tools. He kept just one—the hand plane they had used together. He digitised the old photos and donated the remaining tools to a vocational school. Legacy felt lighter because it continued serving others.

- **Riya — Respectfully Retiring a Past Self -** Riya hadn't played the violin in six years. She kept one annotated score and her rosin block, then gifted the violin to a student. She wrote a short note thanking her younger self for that beautiful chapter. The music didn't end—it simply found a new home.

How to Choose What Stays and What Goes

- Keep what **protects meaning**, not what takes space.
- If a photo and a sentence can capture the memory, let the object go.
- Keep what you use, what you love and what supports who you're becoming.
- Release what drains your space, your attention or your energy.

You're not reducing your life—you're concentrating it. When you keep the essence and release the excess, you don't lose your story. You finally make room for the chapter you're ready to live.

Let love stay. Let the weight go.

Chapter 27: Minimalism in Relationships & Family Life

Relationships & Family Life

"A simpler home is not the work of one person—it is the agreement of many hearts."

Minimalism at home is more than having fewer things. It is about having fewer arguments, fewer stress points and more room for kindness. When the people we love move with us—slowly, imperfectly, willingly—life at home becomes lighter and more connected.

This chapter offers gentle, practical ways to live simply **together**:

- with a partner who isn't minimalist,
- with children who treasure everything,
- with calendars that stay too full,
- and with shared habits that protect peace at home.

1. Partner Not Minimalist? — Shared Spaces & Opt-In Zones

"Respect creates more space than rules ever will."
If your partner doesn't love decluttering as much as you do, start with kindness, not pressure. You don't need to convince them. You only need gentle agreements.

How to Simplify Without Conflict

- **Shared Zones vs. Private Zones** - Keep common areas—like the kitchen, living room and hallways—calm and clutter-free. Let bedrooms, desks or hobby spaces be "opt-in zones" where your partner chooses their own style, even if it's not minimalist.

- **The Floor–Counter–Table Rule** - Agree on one simple guideline:
    - Floors clear
    - Counters mostly clear
    - Dining table reset daily
    - One sentence. Easy to remember. Fewer arguments.
- **One Shared Win at a Time** - Pick one small shared space—the entry table, the coffee table—and keep it neat together for one week. Tiny victories build trust and teamwork.
- **Trade, Don't Tug-of-War** - "I'll maintain the living room; you design your hobby shelf." Compromise isn't losing—it's designing peace.

2. Minimalism with Kids — Rotation, Experiences & Simple Routines

"Children don't need everything; they need enough—and our attention."
Minimalism with children doesn't mean saying "no" all the time. It means giving them **clear, calm choices** and a home they can manage.

Make Play Simple and Joyful

- **Toy Rotation** - Keep only a small set of toys out. Store the rest. Rotate every 2–4 weeks. Kids feel the excitement of "new" toys and clean-ups become fast.
- **Experience Gifts Over Stuff** - Replace piles of plastic toys with:
  picnics
  nature walks
  library trips
  sports passes
  cooking nights together
  Memories last longer than batteries.
- **The 5-Minute Reset** - Before meals or bedtime, play one song and everyone puts things back. Short, shared routines build responsibility without nagging.
- **Keep What Teaches or Delights** - Choose toys that spark imagination—blocks, art supplies, books, instruments—over gadgets that entertain for minutes and clutter for months.

3. Social Minimalism — Time, Boundaries & Emotional Energy

"A full calendar can still leave an empty heart."
Minimalism also means creating space in your schedule for what truly nourishes you and your relationships.

Protect Your Time Together

- **The "Two Yes" Rule** - If both partners don't feel a genuine yes to a plan, it's a no—or a shorter visit. This avoids resentment later.
- **Capacity Before Commitment** - Decide your weekly "energy budget": two evenings out or one big outing per weekend. When the energy is used, you rest—without guilt.
- **Quarterly Calendar Cleanse** - Review your recurring events, chats, subscriptions and social groups every three months. Keep the ones that feed you; pause the rest for 90 days.
- **Default Togetherness** - Protect simple anchors at home: unrushed dinners, device-free walks, quiet Sunday hours. Presence is the real minimalism.

4. Shared Decisions — Money, Stuff & Screens

"Peace at home is built from agreed, repeatable choices." A few light, clear agreements can make daily life smoother.

Money (Spend)

- **The Purchase Pause:** - Wait 24 hours for wants and 7 days for anything expensive. If you still want it later, revisit together.
- **Values Spending:** - Decide what matters most—family, learning, travel, giving—and assign a small percentage to each. When values lead, impulse shrinks.

Stuff (Keep)

- **One-In One-Out:** If something new enters, something old leaves. Keep a donation box near the door.
- **Every Item Has a Story:** Anything you keep should have:
    - a use,
    - a home,
    - and a reason both agree on. If not, it's a guest—time to say goodbye.

Screens (See)

- **Phones Parked at Meals:** - Devices go in a basket; conversation stays at the table.
- **Evening Wind-Down:** - Agree on a nightly off-time (60–90 minutes before bed).
- **Kids' Screen Clarity:** - Set time blocks, safe content and a weekend "create / learn" swap for passive scrolling.

5. Community & Giving — More Sharing, Less Owning

"When a neighbourhood shares, every home needs less."
Minimalism becomes richer when it expands beyond your home.

- **Lend, Don't Duplicate** - Create a micro-lending circle with neighbours—tools, cake tins, party decor, camping gear.
- **Skill Swaps** - Exchange abilities instead of outsourcing: bike repair, tutoring, cooking lessons, story time.
- **Give with Purpose** - Donate items to places where they will be used immediately—schools, shelters, libraries, makerspaces. Passing things on with intention gives them a second life.

Real-Life Examples:

- **Meera & Kunal — Peace Through Zones -** Meera loved clear counters; Kunal loved visible gadgets. They agreed on "shared-calm" spaces—kitchen and living room—and Kunal kept his study as his creative zone. A weekly 20-minute reset and a donation box near the exit changed the home. Fewer arguments. More dinners together.
- **Anita's Family — Rotation Changed Everything**
  Anita labelled four toy bins and kept only one out. Every second Saturday was "new old toys day." The kids felt joy instead of overwhelm and cleanup became quick. For birthdays, the grandparents gifted zoo passes and "bake with Nani" days. Memories replaced clutter.

How to Choose What Your Family Keeps (and Does)

Keep what supports daily peace and shared values.
If a purchase needs persuading, wait.
If an item needs constant managing, let it go.
If an event drains more than it gives, decline kindly.
Minimalism in relationships isn't about control—it's about cooperation and care.

When your family chooses fewer frictions and more presence, love finally has room to breathe.

Protect the moments. The moments will protect the bond.

Part XI: Your Minimalist Transformation — A Step-by-Step Roadmap

Explore how daily discipline and simple rules create lasting success and productivity.

Chapter 28: Begin Your Minimalist Journey

An Invitation to Begin

"Your Path to Freedom Starts Here."

Are you ready to begin a journey that will transform not only your surroundings but your mindset, your habits and your entire way of living? Minimalism is not just about decluttering your home; it's about simplifying your life in a way that allows you to focus on what truly matters. It's an invitation to let go of the unnecessary and embrace what brings you true joy, peace and fulfilment.

The road to minimalism may seem daunting at first. The idea of letting go of things, commitments or even long-held beliefs can be uncomfortable. But know this: the journey toward simplicity is not a path of deprivation. Rather, it is one of liberation — liberation from the clutter that overwhelms your mind, your home and your life. It's a journey of making room for the things that truly matter, things that bring you happiness and align with your values.

You don't need to make radical changes all at once. This process is about taking small, intentional steps — gradually shedding the excess in your life and creating space for more meaningful experiences, relationships and opportunities. Each small action is a step toward a more peaceful, focused and intentional way of living.

The First Step

Take a moment to reflect on what truly brings you joy. What are the things in your life that add value? What are the relationships, experiences or possessions that enhance your well-being? Now think about what is weighing you down. What do you have that doesn't serve you? What is taking up space in your mind or home that you no longer need?

The first step is simple: start small. Begin by decluttering one area of your life. It could be as simple as clearing out a drawer or a closet. Or it could mean saying no to a commitment that doesn't align with your values. Each step, no matter how small, is a victory in the journey toward minimalism.

Be Kind to Yourself

It's important to remember that minimalism is a personal journey. There is no "right" or "wrong" way to approach it. Some people may choose to live with fewer possessions, while others may focus on simplifying their schedule or their mental clutter. What matters is that you take the time to understand what works for you and what truly contributes to your happiness.

There will be challenges along the way — moments of doubt, moments when you question whether letting go of something is the right choice. But trust the process. Each step you take toward a simpler life will bring clarity, peace and freedom. And as you embrace minimalism, you'll begin to see that happiness doesn't come from what you have but from how you live and what you value.

The Journey Is Yours

This is your invitation to start the journey toward a simpler, more intentional life. The beauty of minimalism is that it's not a destination but an ongoing process — a journey of discovery, growth and transformation. As you simplify your life, you'll begin to make room for the things that bring you true joy and fulfilment. You'll discover that living with less allows you to live with more — more time, more peace, more freedom and more purpose.

So, take the first step today. Embrace the journey of minimalism and watch how it transforms your life, one mindful decision at a time.

Finding Your Version of Minimalism

"Your Minimalism, Your Rules."

You don't have to copy anyone's version of a simple life. The most powerful minimalism is **personal** built around your values, rhythms and season of life. This is a **practical, do-it-now chapter** to help you design a version that fits you (and keeps fitting you as you grow).

1) Start with One Clear Reason

Finish this sentence, out loud if you can:

"I want a simpler life so that I can ________."

Maybe it's to sleep better, be present with your family, make space for health or focus on meaningful work. Write it on a small card and place it where you'll see it daily. This reason will guide your choices when motivation dips.

2) Choose a Micro-Arena (One Week Focus)

Don't simplify everything. Simplify **one small arena** for seven days:

- **One space:** bedside table, one kitchen shelf, your work bag.
- **One routine:** the first 20 minutes after waking, the last 20 before sleep.
- **One decision loop:** purchases, screens or social commitments.

Pick only one. Name it. Commit to a week.

3) The 7-Day Personalization Plan

- **Day 1 — See it as it is.** Stand in your chosen arena. Ask: *What helps my best day? What pulls me off course?* Remove the obvious "no's." Five minutes is enough.
- **Day 2 — Set one boundary.** Examples: phone outside the bedroom; 24-hour pause before non-essential buys; one-tab rule at work; devices off during dinner.
- **Day 3 — Keep the few that matter.** Choose the best of the category (the mug you always grab, the app you truly use). Box or delete the rest—no guilt, just clarity.
- **Day 4 — Swap one habit.** Replace a draining micro-habit with a nourishing one: doom-scroll → 10 calm breaths; late snack → herbal tea; impulse add-to-cart → add-to-list.
- **Day 5 — Add a tiny anchor.** A 2–10 minute ritual you can't fail: reset the surface before bed, a short walk, one page of journaling.
- **Day 6 — One brave "No."** Say a clear, kind no to a non-essential request. Spend the saved energy on your reason from Step 1.
- **Day 7 — Review & renew.** Keep what worked, drop what didn't and choose your next micro-arena.

Your version emerges through iteration, not inspiration. The plan is simple by design so you can actually do it.

4) Create Your Personal Guardrails (Write 3)

Guardrails make good choices automatic. Draft three that suit your life right now:

- **Purchases:** "I use it weekly, I love it tomorrow after a pause and it replaces something—otherwise I pass."
- **Screens:** "No phones at meals; last 60 minutes of the day are device-free."
- **Time:** "Two evenings out max per week; Sundays are slow."

Keep them visible for a month. Adjust as needed—guardrails are living, not rigid.

5) Design for Friction & Ease

Make the right thing easy and the wrong thing awkward.

- Place the **helpful** in your path (water bottle on desk, book on pillow, shoes by the door).
- Put **distractions** out of reach (snacks on the top shelf, social apps off the home screen, TV remote in a drawer). Small placements change daily outcomes without willpower.

6) Invent Your "Few That Matter" Sets

Your life runs on a few high-impact essentials. Name them—**your few that matter**:

- **Health set:** sleep window, simple meals, daily movement.
- **Focus set:** one priority before messages, a quiet start, a clean desk.
- **Connection set:** daily check-in with a loved one, device-free dinners.
- **Recovery set:** a walk, music, prayer/meditation, early lights-out.

Write the sets that suit **you**. Revisit monthly.

7) Personal Pace, Personal Rules

- **Rule of One:** one shelf, one habit, one loop at a time. Concentrated effort beats scattered effort.
- **80/20 Fit:** if a change works 80% of the time, it's working. Perfection is often a delay tactic.
- **Seasonal Edits:** review with the seasons—what stays, what goes, what shifts for this phase of life.

8) When You Hit Resistance

- If it feels **overwhelming** → shrink the target to **five minutes** or **five items**.
- If it feels **emotional** → photo + one-line caption, then release.
- If you fear **needing it later** → note where to borrow/rent; 90% of items are reacquirable.
- If you **relapse** → reset tonight. Minimalism is practice, not performance.

9) What *Your* Minimalism Might Look Like (Examples to Spark Ideas)

- A lively family home with **fewer, better toys** and a weekly "reset song."
- An intense work season anchored by **one quiet hour** every morning.
- A creative life with **more open time** and fewer commitments.
- A digital-light month: **messages in batches**, socials on weekends only.
- A travel-ready lifestyle: **carry-on only**, memories over merchandise.

No single "look" is required; only **fit** is required.

10) Your One-Page Starter

On one page, write:

1. **My reason:** "I want a simpler life so that I can ________."
2. **This week's arena:** space/routine/decision loop.

3. **Three guardrails:** purchases, screens, time (or your custom set).
4. **My few that matter:** 3–5 essentials for health, focus, connection, recovery.
5. **Review date:** seven days from today.

Sign it. Put it where you'll see it. Begin today.
You're not chasing an aesthetic—you're building a life that fits. Your version of minimalism will appear as you act, adjust and act again. Keep it small. Keep it kind. Keep it yours.

Tricks to Eliminate Unnecessary Purchases

"Buy Less, Live More."

Eliminating unnecessary purchases is a crucial aspect of adopting minimalism and building a more intentional life. Here are some practical tips to help you avoid impulse buying and make smarter financial decisions:

1. Create a Budget and Stick to It

Set Spending Limits: Define clear categories for your monthly expenses (e.g., groceries, entertainment etc.) and set a budget for each. Make sure you're only purchasing what's necessary within these limits.
Track Your Spending: Keep track of your daily and weekly expenses. Use budgeting apps or spreadsheets to ensure you're sticking to your limits and avoid overspending.

2. Adopt the 30-Day Rule

Delay Gratification: If you're tempted by a non-essential purchase, commit to waiting for 30 days before buying it. This gives you time to reflect on whether the item is truly necessary and whether it adds lasting value to your life.

3. Prioritize Needs Over Wants

Assess Necessity: Before making a purchase, ask yourself: "Do I truly need this or is it something I want impulsively?" Focus on buying things that solve problems or fulfill real needs rather than giving in to momentary desires.

4. Avoid Shopping When Emotional

Don't Shop to Cope: Many people shop when they're bored, stressed or emotional. Try to recognize these triggers and find healthier alternatives for coping with emotions, like exercise or journaling.

Mindful Shopping: If you're feeling emotional, avoid shopping altogether. Wait for a calm moment to reflect on whether your purchase is a thoughtful decision or an impulse.

5. Unsubscribe from Marketing Emails

Reduce Temptation: Unsubscribe from email lists or marketing newsletters that bombard you with promotions. This minimizes the chances of receiving tempting offers for unnecessary products.

Unfollow Social Media Ads: On social platforms, unfollow or mute accounts that regularly promote products you don't need.

6. Set Long-Term Financial Goals

Focus on Financial Independence: Align your purchasing decisions with your long-term financial goals, such as saving for a home, building an emergency fund or investing for retirement. Every unnecessary purchase delays your progress toward these goals.

Save for Big Purchases: Rather than making spontaneous buys, save up for larger purchases and make them intentional. This ensures you're getting the most value out of your spending.

7. Practice Mindful Consumption

Think Before You Buy: Ask yourself: "Will this improve my life or simply add clutter?" If you're uncertain, walk away and revisit the purchase later with a clearer perspective.

Quality Over Quantity: Opt for fewer, high-quality items that will last longer rather than cheap, disposable products that require frequent replacement.

8. Develop a "One In, One Out" Rule

Maintain Balance: For every new item you bring into your life, commit to getting rid of one. This helps keep your home uncluttered and ensures you're only acquiring what truly adds value.

9. Stick to a Shopping List

Plan Your Purchases: Before going shopping, make a list of the things you actually need. Stick to this list and avoid impulse purchases. This works for grocery shopping, clothing or even online shopping.

10. Avoid Shopping in Bulk (Unless Necessary)

Avoid Overbuying: While buying in bulk can save money, it often leads to buying more than necessary. Only purchase bulk items that have a long shelf life and are things you regularly use.
Buy What You Can Use: Focus on buying quantities that you can realistically consume or use within a short period.

11. Evaluate the True Cost of Ownership

Factor in Maintenance Costs: When buying big-ticket items (like gadgets, furniture or vehicles), consider the ongoing costs of maintenance, repairs and storage. This will help you decide if the item is worth the total cost in the long run.
Environmental Impact: Consider the environmental cost of the product—how it's made, how long it lasts and how it's disposed of. If the item's environmental impact outweighs its usefulness, it may not be worth purchasing.

12. Limit Exposure to Shopping Triggers

Avoid Tempting Locations: Don't frequent malls, online stores or apps that tempt you to buy things you don't need. The less you expose yourself to these environments, the less likely you are to make unnecessary purchases.
Practice Gratitude: Focus on appreciating what you already have. A mindset of contentment makes it easier to resist the temptation to buy new items that don't truly add value to your life.

13. Use the "Do I Really Need This?" Checklist

Before purchasing anything, ask yourself the following:

- Do I already have something like this?
- Will this improve my life in a meaningful way?
- Can I afford it without affecting my financial goals?
- Will this item bring lasting happiness or will the excitement wear off?
- Do I have a clear purpose for this purchase or is it just a passing fancy?

14. Practice the 24-Hour Rule for Online Shopping

Wait Before Clicking Buy: When shopping online, wait 24 hours before making a purchase. This delay allows you to reflect on the necessity of the item and gives you time to reconsider whether it's worth buying.

15. Buy Second-Hand or Rent

Consider Used Items: Buying second-hand items from thrift stores or online marketplaces can be a sustainable and cost-effective alternative to buying new.
Rent Rather Than Buy: For items that are used infrequently (e.g., equipment for a hobby or special occasion), consider renting instead of purchasing.

16. Embrace Experiences Over Possessions

Prioritize Experiences: Rather than spending money on material possessions, focus on spending your resources on meaningful experiences, such as travel, learning or creating memories with loved ones.
Create Lasting Memories: Experiences often bring more joy and fulfilment than things and they don't clutter your home or require maintenance.

17. Review Your Purchases Regularly

Track and Assess: At the end of each month, review your purchases and evaluate whether they were necessary or impulsive. This reflection will help you identify patterns and triggers, allowing you to make better purchasing decisions in the future.

To eliminate unnecessary purchases, focus on mindfulness, intentionality and long-term financial and emotional well-being. The key is to stop living reactively to marketing pressures and societal expectations. By being proactive, evaluating your purchases critically and aligning your choices with your values and goals, you can avoid impulsive spending and simplify your life.

Asking the Right Questions

"Questioning is beginning of intelligence"

That's a great way to apply minimalism in a simple and effective manner! Asking the right questions is a powerful way to determine what truly adds value to your life. Here's how you can incorporate this approach into your daily life:

The Question Method:

- "Does this item or possession bring me joy or serve a meaningful purpose?"
- Have I used this item in last one year?
- If you lost this item, will you buy again?

If your answer is **YES**, then keep it. It adds value to your life, whether it's through utility, emotional connection or enjoyment.

If your answer is **NO**, then it's time to consider decluttering. Let go of items that no longer serve you or contribute to your happiness.

Why This Works:

- **Intentionality**: By constantly evaluating the purpose and value of your belongings, you align your possessions with your values and needs, reducing unnecessary clutter.
- **Emotional Clarity**: It helps you differentiate between items that spark joy or serve a functional role and those that are just filling space. This process can be liberating and refreshing.
- **Simplifies Decision Making**: Rather than being overwhelmed by a pile of stuff, asking yourself this question simplifies the process of letting go. Each item is evaluated individually for its worth in your life.
- **Encourages Mindfulness**: It helps cultivate a mindful approach to consumption—whether it's in the shopping process or in organizing your space. You'll begin to make more thoughtful choices about what you bring into your life.

This mindset works for all areas of your life, from your home and wardrobe to relationships and commitments. By regularly asking this question, you can maintain a lifestyle that is free from unnecessary clutter and focused on the things that truly matter.

How Can I Achieve More in Less Time?

"Efficiency is doing things right; effectiveness is doing the right things."

Asking the question *"How can I achieve more in less time?"* is a great approach to increasing productivity, focusing on efficiency and adopting a minimalist mindset in your personal and professional life. Here are strategies you can apply to achieve more in less time:

1. **Prioritize Effectively -** Focus on high-impact tasks that contribute the most to your goals. Use frameworks like the Eisenhower Matrix (urgent vs. important) to identify what truly needs your attention and what can be delegated or deferred.
   80/20 Rule (Pareto Principle): Identify the 20% of tasks that will yield 80% of the results and focus your energy there.

2. **Time Blocking -** Time blocking involves dividing your day into blocks of time dedicated to specific tasks or types of work. This method helps you stay focused and ensures that you work on the most important tasks without distractions.

3. **Eliminate Distractions** - Reduce distractions by creating a focused work environment. Turn off non-essential notifications, declutter your workspace and set specific times for checking emails and social media.
   Deep Work: Practice periods of deep, uninterrupted work, where you immerse yourself fully in tasks without distractions.

4. **Use the Pomodoro Technique** - Break your work into 25-minute focused intervals (Pomodoros), followed by a 5-minute break. After four Pomodoros, take a longer break. This technique helps maintain energy levels and prevents burnout.

5. **Delegate and Outsource** - Identify tasks that others can do and delegate them. This could be at work or in personal life (e.g., hiring help for cleaning or administrative tasks). Delegating frees up your time for more important responsibilities. Use tools like virtual assistants or task management apps to outsource routine tasks.

6. **Batch Similar Tasks** - Group similar tasks together and complete them in one go to save time and reduce decision fatigue. For example, schedule all phone calls for one block of time or answer emails during a specific part of your day

7. **Automate Repetitive Tasks** - Identify tasks that can be automated, such as setting up email filters, scheduling social media posts or using finance apps to track spending.
   Use tools like Zapier or IFTTT to automate workflows and save time on repetitive actions.

8. **Simplify Decision-Making** - Simplify your decisions by having clear goals and guidelines. Reduce the number of choices you make in a day to conserve your mental energy (e.g., following a set routine or meal plan).

9. **Set Boundaries** - Set boundaries for when and where you work. By defining your working hours and ensuring that you can focus on work without constant interruptions, you ensure that your time is used efficiently.

10. **Use Technology Wisely** - Use productivity tools like Trello, Asana or Notion to organize tasks and projects. These tools help you keep track of what needs to be done, manage deadlines and ensure nothing falls through the cracks.
    Invest in apps or tools that automate or streamline repetitive tasks, such as time tracking apps or task managers.

11. **Avoid Perfectionism** - Strive for "good enough" instead of perfection. Spending too much time perfecting every detail can lead to inefficiency. Recognize when something is complete and move on to the next task.

12. **Take Care of Your Health -** A healthy body leads to a productive mind. Make time for regular exercise, eat nutritious food and get enough sleep. When your body and mind are well-rested and energized, you can accomplish tasks faster and with greater focus.

13. **Simplify Processes -** Look at your work or personal processes and see where you can simplify. For example, if you regularly prepare reports or presentations, create templates or standardized processes that reduce the time you spend on these tasks.
    Minimalist Approach: Avoid overcomplicating things. The more streamlined your processes are, the faster and more efficiently you can get things done.

14. **Learn to Say "NO"** - Saying "NO" to tasks or commitments that don't align with your goals or that will drain your energy is essential for saving time and maintaining focus on your priorities.
    Limit Commitments: Be selective about the projects you take on to ensure you're not overburdened with low-priority tasks.

15. **Master the Art of Focused Work -** Train yourself to focus deeply on one task at a time, rather than multi-tasking, which can reduce productivity. Studies show that switching between tasks can lower efficiency by up to 40%.
    Practice techniques like meditation or mindfulness to strengthen your ability to stay focused.

16. **Create Habits for Efficiency** - Develop habits that help you work more efficiently. For example, setting up a morning routine that prepares you mentally for the day or a nightly routine that helps you wind down effectively. Create habits like meal prepping for the week to save time or having a designated time for planning to ensure your day is organized.

17. **Use Shortcuts -** In both your professional and personal life, find ways to use shortcuts to save time. This could be using keyboard shortcuts, quick templates for emails or pre-made reports or documents.
    Streamline your communication by using concise language, minimizing meetings and focusing on key points.

18. **Review and Adjust Regularly** - Regularly review your goals, routines and systems to identify areas where you could improve. Adjust your strategies as needed to maintain efficiency and productivity over time.

19. **Leverage Others' Time -** Collaborate effectively with others to get more done in less time. Teamwork allows you to delegate tasks, share knowledge and pool resources for faster results.

20. **Focus on Progress, Not Perfection**
    Perfectionism can slow you down. Aim to make consistent progress toward your goals, even if it's not always perfect. Embrace the idea of "done is better than perfect."

By consistently asking the question *"How can I achieve more in less time?"* and applying these strategies, you'll be able to increase your productivity and achieve your goals faster while maintaining balance and simplicity in your life.

Identity Investment and Loss Aversion

"You Are More Than What You Own."

Identity Investment and Loss Aversion are psychological concepts that can play a significant role in the way we approach minimalism and make decisions, particularly when it comes to decluttering our lives—whether that involves possessions, habits or even relationships.

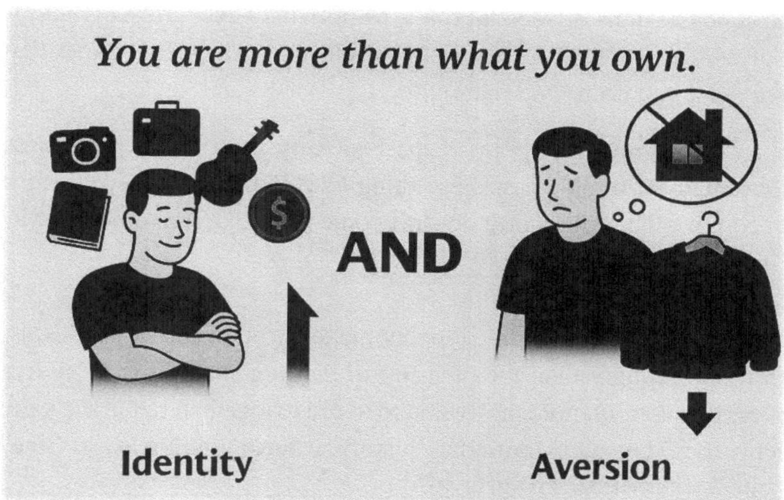

Identity investment

Identity investment refers to the degree to which we tie our sense of self to certain possessions, beliefs or roles in our lives. When we invest in something—be it a career, a hobby, a brand or even a collection of physical items—we often tie that investment to our identity. We start to believe that "I am what I own" or "I am what I do."

This investment can become deeply entrenched in our self-image, making it difficult to let go of things, even if they no longer serve us.

Real-Life Examples:

- **Possessions:** If you've spent a lot of money on items like clothes, gadgets or luxury goods, your sense of value may be tied to them. Getting rid of those things can feel like you're losing a part of yourself.
- **Career:** A person who has spent decades building their career may find it difficult to let go of that identity when contemplating a career change or stepping away from their professional life.
- **Hobbies or Roles:** If you define yourself as a "runner," "gardener," or "chef," it might be hard to part with items associated with those activities, even if they're no longer a source of joy or fulfilment.

Minimalism challenges this attachment by encouraging us to evaluate what really reflects our true identity and what is simply an external manifestation of something we feel obligated to maintain.

Why It's Important for Minimalism: When you adopt a minimalist mindset, you start to challenge those aspects of your identity that are too heavily reliant on material possessions or societal roles. Minimalism encourages you to focus on the core of who you are—your values, passions and priorities—rather than what you own or what you do for validation.

How to Overcome It: To move past identity investment, ask yourself, "What would remain of me if I lost these things?" Reconnect with your intrinsic values and recognize that your worth doesn't come from external objects or labels.

Loss Aversion

Loss aversion is a psychological phenomenon where the pain of losing something is felt more strongly than the pleasure of gaining something of equivalent value. People are generally more motivated to avoid losses than to pursue gains. This bias is deeply rooted in our evolutionary history, where avoiding losses (like losing food or shelter) was critical for survival.

When it comes to minimalism, loss aversion can be a significant barrier. We may feel a stronger emotional attachment to our things because we fear the loss of their utility, perceived value or the memories attached to them. Even if we know that downsizing might make us happier, the discomfort of parting with possessions or habits often outweighs the rational benefits.

Real-Life Examples:

- **Physical Possessions:** You might resist letting go of clothes you no longer wear because you think you "might need them someday" or because they represent past milestones in your life. The thought of losing them creates more discomfort than the imagined benefits of decluttering.

- **Habits:** You might be reluctant to change a routine or lifestyle habit—even if it's no longer serving you—because it feels like a loss of control or comfort.

Minimalism forces you to confront loss aversion by challenging the emotional attachment to things that no longer serve a purpose or add value to your life.

Why It's Important for Minimalism: Loss aversion can prevent progress when trying to simplify your life. Minimalism asks you to shift your perspective: focus not on what you'll lose but on what you'll gain in terms of time, clarity and mental peace.

How to Overcome It: The key to overcoming loss aversion is reframing your mindset. Instead of focusing on the loss, think about the potential gains, such as freedom, reduced stress and emotional space. Recognize that by releasing items, you create room for new experiences, relationships or even personal growth. Ask yourself: What would I gain by letting this go?

How Identity Investment and Loss Aversion Affect Minimalism

These psychological factors are intertwined and can make the minimalist journey more challenging. For instance: **Identity Investment** may cause you to resist letting go of possessions, activities or roles that define you, even when they no longer align with your true self or goals. **Loss Aversion** makes the process of decluttering feel like a painful loss, even though the actual benefits of minimalism (e.g., clarity, freedom, peace) may be far greater.

To switch to minimalism, it's important to address these underlying psychological challenges:

- **Self-Reflection:** Regularly check in with yourself about why you're holding onto certain possessions, habits or roles. Are they truly serving your current goals and identity or are they remnants of a past version of yourself that no longer fit?
- **Gradual Letting Go:** If you're facing resistance due to loss aversion, start small. Begin by decluttering non-sentimental items and gradually move on to things that are harder to part with. This will help you build confidence in the process and reduce the emotional burden of loss.
- **Shift Your Focus to Gains:** Focus on the positive aspects of minimalism—less mental clutter, more time, fewer distractions and a deeper connection with the things that matter most.

How to Apply These Concepts in Your Life:

- **Reframe the Loss:** When you're hesitant to get rid of something, reframe it by focusing on the emotional and practical benefits you'll gain. Ask yourself, What am I freeing up by letting go of this?
- **Declutter in Stages:** Instead of tackling everything at once, break the process down into manageable steps. Start with less emotionally charged items and build confidence to address more difficult areas, like sentimental possessions.
- **Reevaluate Your Identity:** Regularly reassess your identity and how it's tied to external factors like material possessions, career roles or past accomplishments. Understand that your true identity is more resilient than the things you own or the labels you wear.
- **Practice Mindful Decision-Making:** When deciding whether to keep or discard something, take time to reflect on whether it aligns with your current values and long-term vision. This helps you avoid holding onto things simply because of past emotional investment or fear of loss.

By understanding and addressing identity investment and loss aversion, you can approach minimalism with a greater sense of clarity and purpose, making the process more manageable and rewarding.

Taking more than what we need without exploring ourselves will lead to emotional bankruptcy

Chapter 29: Decluttering Experiments — What Truly Works

How to Get Rid of Excess Stuff

"Clear the Clutter, Create Space for Life."

Getting rid of excess stuff can be an overwhelming process but it's a crucial step towards embracing a minimalist lifestyle. Here's a step-by-step guide to help you declutter effectively and make your environment simpler and more intentional:

1. Start Small

Choose one area to focus on, such as a single drawer, closet or room. Starting small will prevent you from feeling overwhelmed and allow you to build momentum as you go.

Set a timer for 30 minutes to 1 hour, so you don't get distracted or tired during the process. Small, focused bursts will help keep you energized.

2. The "Does It Spark Joy?" Method

Take each item in your space and ask yourself, "Does this bring me joy or serve a purpose?" If the answer is **yes**, keep it. If **no**, put it in the discard pile.

Focus on emotional value and utility—if something doesn't have one of these qualities, let it go.

3. Sort Into Categories

Set up 3 categories: Keep, Donate/Sell and Trash.
Keep: Only keep what adds value or joy to your life.
Donate/Sell: Items in good condition that could be used by others.
Trash: Items that are broken, outdated or no longer useful.

4. Be Ruthless

Challenge Sentimental Attachments: Letting go of sentimental items can be tough but if they don't serve a purpose, consider alternatives like taking photos or keeping one special item.
Avoid "Just in Case" Thinking: If you haven't used it in the last year or don't need it for a specific purpose, it's time to let go.

5. One-In, One-Out Rule

To prevent the accumulation of excess items, adopt the "One-In, One-Out" rule: for every new item you bring into your home, let go of one item you already own. This will help you maintain balance.

6. Organize What's Left

Once you've sorted your items, focus on organizing what remains. Keep things accessible and easy to maintain. Consider using boxes, baskets or drawer organizers for a tidy, decluttered space.

7. Sell or Donate

Items in good condition can be sold or donated to others. You can use online platforms like eBay, Facebook Marketplace or local charity stores to sell or give away things that no longer serve you. This not only clears space but also benefits others.

8. Dispose Responsibly

Recycle or dispose of things responsibly, especially electronics, hazardous materials or large furniture. Check local guidelines for the proper disposal or recycling methods.

9. Review Regularly

After your initial decluttering, make it a habit to review your belongings regularly. Decluttering is an ongoing process and even once you've simplified your life, you can periodically assess what you own.

10. Change Your Shopping Habits

To prevent accumulating more stuff, be more intentional with purchases moving forward:

Ask yourself if you really need it.

Think long-term: Choose items that will last, have practical value and serve a specific purpose.

Avoid impulse buying: Stop and assess whether it truly adds value to your life before making a purchase.

11. Maintain the Simplicity

Simplify your mindset: Let go of the need for constant consumerism and focus on experiences, relationships and personal growth instead of material goods.

Stay mindful of what you bring into your life and how it fits with your minimalist values.

12. Set Clear Goals and Intentions

Why are you decluttering? Set a clear reason for why you want to simplify your space. Whether it's to create more mental clarity, reduce stress or make room for more meaningful possessions, having a purpose behind your decluttering will help keep you focused.

Visualize the Outcome: Picture how you want your space to look and feel once you've finished the process. This vision will motivate you to stay on track and help you make decisions with confidence.

13. Tackle One Category at a Time

Instead of decluttering room by room, consider focusing on categories of items, such as:

Clothing: Go through your closet, removing anything you don't wear regularly or that doesn't bring you joy.

Books: Only keep books that you love, will read again or are essential. Donate or sell others.

Kitchen Items: Declutter duplicates (extra mugs, unused gadgets) and only keep essentials.

Electronics: Get rid of outdated gadgets or accessories that no longer serve you.

Sentimental Items: Slowly sift through photos, keepsakes and mementos and keep only what is truly meaningful.

14. Use the "Four-Box Method"

For each area or category you're decluttering, use four boxes:

Keep – Items you truly need or love.

Donate/Sell – Items that can be passed on to others.

Trash – Broken or useless items.

Undecided – Items you're unsure about, which you can revisit later.

The goal is to quickly sort items into one of these categories to avoid overthinking.

15. Declutter with a Friend or Family Member

Sometimes, having a second opinion can help you be more objective about what you should keep or let go. Ask a trusted friend or family member to help you. They can provide a fresh perspective and help keep you on track.

16. Digitally Declutter

Digital clutter can be just as overwhelming as physical clutter. Clean up your digital space by:

Deleting old files, you no longer need (photos, documents, apps).

Unsubscribing from email lists that don't serve you.

Organizing your inbox with folders and filters.

Limiting social media accounts or apps to those that truly add value to your life.

Cleaning up your desktop by creating organized folders and eliminating unused shortcuts.

17. Practice the "One Week" Rule

If you're unsure whether you should keep something, put it in a box or drawer and leave it for a week. If you haven't used it or thought about it in that time, it's a clear sign it might not be necessary. Let it go without regret.

18. Adopt the "Minimalist Mindset" in Everyday Life

Avoid accumulating things by adopting a minimalist mindset in your everyday life:

Be mindful of your purchases: Avoid impulse buying by carefully considering every new purchase before making it.

Reduce the need for new things: Repair, reuse and recycle items whenever possible instead of replacing them.

Appreciate non-material things: Focus more on experiences, relationships and personal growth, which don't require physical possessions.

Embrace "good enough": You don't need the latest model or a perfect version of everything. Aim for functionality and simplicity.

19. Take Before-and-After Photos

Document the process by taking before-and-after photos. Not only will this help you see the progress you've made but it'll also motivate you to continue decluttering. You'll be amazed at how much lighter and more spacious your environment becomes.

20. Celebrate Small Wins

Decluttering can feel like a big task, so celebrate your small victories along the way. Whether you finish clearing out a closet or organize your kitchen drawers, give yourself credit for every step forward. These small wins add up and will keep you motivated.

21. Stay Accountable

Set deadlines for your decluttering tasks and share your goals with someone you trust. This will help keep you accountable and ensure that you stay on track. You can even create a decluttering challenge with a friend to make the process more fun and motivating.

22. Understand the Emotional Attachment

Sometimes, we hold on to things because of emotional reasons. Acknowledge the attachment and ask yourself if keeping it still adds value to your life today. If it's an object with sentimental value, consider taking a photo of it to keep the memory and then let go of the physical item.

23. Make Decluttering a Regular Habit

Make decluttering a regular part of your routine. Aim to do a small declutter session every month or quarter to ensure your space remains minimal and organized. It's better to tackle small tasks consistently than to let clutter pile up over time.

24. The "90/90 Rule"

If you haven't used an item in the past 90 days and you don't plan to use it in the next 90 days, then it's a strong indicator that you don't need it. Follow this rule to help you identify and remove unnecessary items.

25. Donate to Causes You Care About

When donating or selling items, choose causes or charities that resonate with you. Knowing that your unwanted items will benefit others can make the process feel more fulfilling and purposeful.

26. One Year Challenge

Try the "one-year challenge" to help you gauge what you really need. If you haven't used or worn an item in the past year, it's probably time to part with it. This method helps you eliminate things that may have accumulated over time but no longer serve a meaningful purpose.

27. Avoid Sentimental Hoarding

It's easy to hold onto items because of sentimental value but ask yourself if keeping everything is truly helpful. Keep the most meaningful items that carry the deepest emotional connection and consider letting go of others.

28. Use a Decluttering Checklist

Create a checklist with specific areas of your home (kitchen, living room, bedroom etc.) and mark off each area as you declutter it. A checklist gives you a clear roadmap to follow and makes the process less overwhelming.

29. Practice Gratitude

Shift your focus from material possessions to experiences and personal growth. Practice gratitude for the things that really matter, such as your health, relationships and opportunities. This mindset can help reduce the desire to acquire more unnecessary items.

30. Challenge Yourself to a "No-Buy" Period

Commit to a "no-buy" challenge for a set period of time, such as a month or three months. During this time, avoid buying anything that isn't essential. This will force you to examine your consumption habits and develop more thoughtful approaches to purchasing.

31. Be Aware of Emotional Spending

Often, people buy things to fill emotional voids or to cope with stress. Identify if you tend to accumulate things when you're feeling bored, stressed or sad and instead find healthier ways to cope, such as exercise, journaling or meditation.

32. Avoid the "Keeping Up with the Joneses" Mentality

Social comparison can lead us to accumulate unnecessary items. Resist the urge to buy things just because others have them. Focus on what aligns with your values rather than external pressures or societal trends.

33. Limit Your "Wish List"

Create a Wishlist but don't act on it impulsively. If you're considering purchasing something, put it on the list and revisit it in 30 days. After a month, you may find you don't need or desire the item anymore.

34. Quality Over Quantity

When you do purchase new items, prioritize quality over quantity. Choose items that are durable, long-lasting and versatile, even if they cost more upfront. This reduces the need for constant replacement and ultimately saves you money.

35. Use Multi-Functional Items

Opt for items that serve multiple purposes. For example, choose a sofa bed instead of a separate bed and couch or a phone that replaces several gadgets. Multi-functional items reduce clutter and help simplify your space.

36. Apply Minimalism to Social Media

Apply minimalist principles to your digital life, not just your physical space. Unfollow accounts that no longer add value to your life, remove apps that waste your time and keep your social media use intentional and meaningful.

37. Declutter by Sentimentality, Not Guilt

When you're letting go of sentimental items, don't keep them out of guilt or obligation. If you don't feel a strong emotional connection to something anymore, it's okay to part with it. Remember that memories are not tied to objects; they live within you.

38. Use the "30-Day Rule" for New Purchases

Before making any new purchases, wait 30 days. If, after 30 days, you still feel that the item is necessary or important, then go ahead and buy it. This delay will help you distinguish between genuine needs and passing desires.

39. Focus on Experience over Possessions

Shift your focus from accumulating things to creating memories. Travel, spend time with loved ones, take part in activities that enrich your life and foster personal growth. This will help you appreciate life's simpler pleasures rather than material possessions.

40. Simplify Your Wardrobe (Capsule Wardrobe)

Build a capsule wardrobe with timeless, versatile pieces that can be mixed and matched to create multiple outfits. This reduces the need for excessive clothing and makes getting dressed easier and more efficient.

41. Consider Minimalist Living Spaces

If possible, consider downsizing your living space or adopting minimalist architecture. Smaller, more efficient spaces encourage less clutter and make it easier to keep only the essentials.

42. Do a "Reverse Declutter" (Add Meaning)

In some cases, adding a few meaningful items that bring value or spark joy can help shift your perspective on minimalism. Whether it's a beautiful piece of art or a cherished heirloom, sometimes adding intentional items can elevate your space.

43. Stop Buying Temporary Items

Avoid purchasing cheap or temporary solutions that don't last long, such as fast fashion or disposable items. Instead, invest in higher-quality items that will stand the test of time, making you less likely to acquire more clutter.

44. Practice "The 5-Minute Rule"

If an item doesn't have a designated place or hasn't been used in a while, spend five minutes organizing or disposing of it. Little regular maintenance will keep your space from accumulating unnecessary items.

45. Simplify Your Meal Prep

Cut down on excess kitchen tools, ingredients and unnecessary appliances. Stick to a few key tools, such as a sharp knife, a cutting board and a few pots and pans and prepare simple meals with fresh, whole ingredients.

46. Give Yourself Permission to Let Go

Many people hold on to things because they feel guilty or worry about what others will think if they give things away. Give yourself permission to let go of items that no longer serve you, even if they were gifts or once had sentimental value.

47. Focus on Digital Minimalism

Reduce the amount of digital content you consume. Unsubscribe from newsletters and emails that don't serve your interests and clear your devices of unnecessary apps and files. This digital decluttering will give you more time to focus on what matters.

48. Create a "Memory Box"

If you have many sentimental items, designate a small memory box where you keep only the most meaningful objects. This helps reduce the number of sentimental items you keep while preserving memories.

49. Incorporate Daily Decluttering Habits

Make decluttering part of your daily routine. Spend just 5–10 minutes a day organizing or removing items that no longer serve you. Small, consistent efforts can lead to long-term minimalism without feeling overwhelmed.

50. Don't Wait for the Perfect Time

A common misconception is that decluttering needs to happen in one large, perfect session. The reality is that it's an ongoing process that can be done in bits and pieces. Start today and you'll see progress over time.

51. Start with a Clean Slate

If you're overwhelmed by the clutter, sometimes it's helpful to start with a clean slate. Set aside a day to remove everything from a room, clean it and then only add back what's absolutely necessary or meaningful. This method can give you a sense of freedom and control.

52. Ask Yourself: "Do I Use This Daily?"
If you haven't used something in your home or workspace on a daily or weekly basis, consider whether it's worth keeping. Items that are used rarely can often be donated, sold or thrown away.

53. Create a Vision of Your Ideal Life
Visualizing your ideal lifestyle and environment will help you make decisions about what to keep and what to eliminate. Ask yourself: *What do I want my life and space to look like? What can I remove to align my reality with that vision?*
By consistently applying these strategies, you'll be able to eliminate excess stuff in your life and create space for things that are truly meaningful. Minimalism isn't about deprivation; it's about intentional living and making room for what truly adds value to your life.

The 30-Day Packing Party

"Declutter in 30 Days: One Step at a Time."

Day 1: Start With the Closet
Begin with your closet. Pack up 5 items (clothes, shoes or accessories) that you haven't worn in the last 6 months or that no longer fit.
Keep only those pieces that you absolutely love and wear frequently.

Day 2: The Bedroom
Pack up 5 items from your bedroom, such as extra bedding, old pillows or books that are collecting dust.
Keep your essentials and anything that contributes to a restful environment.

Day 3: Shoes & Accessories
Pack 3 pairs of shoes that you never wear or that are in poor condition.
Consider if accessories like jewelry, bags or scarves bring joy or serve a functional purpose.

Day 4: Kitchenware
Pack up 5 kitchen items (mugs, gadgets or utensils) you don't use regularly.
Focus on eliminating duplicates or tools that have been sitting unused for a while.

Day 5: Bathroom Items
Pack 5 beauty products, old medications or unused toiletries.
Evaluate each item for expiration dates, excess or products you don't enjoy using.

Day 6: Books
Pack up 3 books that you no longer have an interest in reading or those you haven't touched in months. Keep only the books that truly inspire, educate or entertain you.

Day 7: Digital Declutter (Emails and Files)
Pack up 10 old emails or documents you no longer need. Delete files that are cluttering your digital life.
Organize your folders so you can find what you need easily.

Day 8: Personal Papers
Pack 5 personal documents (old tax forms, receipts or papers) that are no longer needed. Go paperless where possible or store only the essential documents.

Day 9: Sentimental Items
Pack 5 sentimental items that you've been holding onto but don't bring you happiness. Consider keeping only the items that have a strong, positive emotional connection.

Day 10: Extra Furniture
Pack up 1 piece of furniture (a table, chair or decoration) that's no longer needed or doesn't fit in with your lifestyle. Choose items that contribute to your home's simplicity.

Day 11: Electronics and Cables
Pack 5 electronics or cables that are outdated or no longer used.
Donate or recycle old gadgets like phones, chargers or random cords.

Day 12: Children's Items
If you have kids, pack up 5 toys, clothes or items they've outgrown or no longer use.Encourage them to make choices on what they truly enjoy playing with.

Day 13: Office Supplies
Pack up 5 office supplies or desk items that you don't use anymore.
Focus on simplifying your workspace by keeping only essential tools.

Day 14: Gifts & Memorabilia
Pack 3 gifts or memorabilia items that no longer hold meaning for you.
Let go of the pressure to keep gifts out of obligation.

Day 15: Music & Movies
Pack 3 CDs, DVDs or music collections that you no longer listen to or watch. Opt for digital streaming services or minimalist media collections.

Day 16: Collectibles
If you collect items (coins, figurines, memorabilia), pack 3 items that no longer bring you joy or have become burdensome to store. Keep only those collections that are meaningful to you.

Day 17: Old Bills or Unused Subscriptions
Pack 5 old bills, subscriptions or services that you don't use anymore. Unsubscribe from magazines, memberships or services that add clutter to your life.

Day 18: Travel Accessories
Pack 3 unused travel accessories (bags, shoes or gadgets). Streamline your travel essentials to include only what's necessary for your trips.

Day 19: Cleaning Supplies
Pack 3 cleaning products that you no longer use or that you've replaced with more eco-friendly alternatives. Simplify your cleaning routine with multipurpose products.

Day 20: Unworn Clothing
Pack 5 items of clothing that still have tags on them or that you haven't worn in the last year. Let go of items that were impulse buys or no longer fit your personal style.

Day 21: Leftover Craft Supplies
Pack up 3 craft supplies or materials that you've been holding onto without ever using. Keep only the items you regularly use for hobbies and projects.

Day 22: Miscellaneous Gadgets
Pack up 3 miscellaneous gadgets that you've acquired but never use. Streamline your collection of tech or home tools.

Day 23: Magazines, Papers and Notes
Pack up magazines or papers that you haven't read or referenced in months. Recycle old articles, notes or projects that are just taking up space.

Day 24: Gifts You Don't Need

Pack up any gifts you've received but don't have any use for or don't resonate with you.

Donate them to others who might appreciate them more.

Day 25: Tupperware & Containers

Pack 5 pieces of Tupperware or food containers that are mismatched or that you have too many of. Keep only the containers you use regularly.

Day 26: Seasonal Items

Pack up 5 seasonal items that you don't use year-round (like winter coats, decorations etc.). Rotate and declutter your seasonal items based on your needs.

Day 27: Workout Gear

Pack 3 pieces of exercise equipment or sports gear that you no longer use.

Focus on keeping gear that aligns with your current fitness routine.

Day 28: Kitchen Pantry

Pack 5 food items from your pantry that are expired, unopened or that you no longer use. Be mindful of what's in your pantry to avoid waste.

Day 29: Decor Items

Pack up 5 decor items (vases, candles, frames etc.) that don't add value to your living space. Keep only the pieces that make you feel relaxed and inspired.

Day 30: Final Sweep

Do a final sweep of your entire home and pack up any remaining items that don't serve you. Evaluate your home and see how far you've come with the decluttering process.

At the end of the 30 days, you will have packed up many items and simplified your space. Take some time to reflect on how the process felt—did you feel lighter? Did you gain a better understanding of what truly matters to you? Let go of anything that you didn't feel a deep connection to and enjoy the benefits of living with less.

This challenge not only clears physical clutter but can also be a liberating mental exercise that helps you embrace minimalism in other areas of life.

The Joy of Giving and Sharing

"Kindness Multiplies When Shared."

This is a powerful and fulfilling experience that transcends material possessions. It create a ripple effect that makes the world a kinder, more connected place.

Minimalism teaches that life feels lighter when we release what no longer serves us. Giving and sharing are natural extensions of this philosophy. When we pass on items, space or resources we no longer need, we reduce our own burden and increase someone else's ease. The joy comes not from the object itself but from the freedom and connection created in the process.

Why Giving Matters in Minimalism

1. **Letting Go Becomes Easier**
   Releasing possessions can be emotionally difficult, especially when items carry identity, memories or past investments. Giving transforms letting go into something meaningful. You are not "losing" an item — you are allowing it to live a useful second life.

2. **Creates Physical and Mental Space**
   Every donated item reduces visual noise, maintenance work and mental load. Giving clears space in both your home and your mind, making room for clarity, calmness and intentional living.

3. **Prevents Waste and Extends Usefulness**
   Minimalism values sustainability. When you donate functional items—clothes, appliances, books, furniture—you return them to circulation instead of letting them stagnate in storage or end up in landfills.

4. **Shifts Focus From "Having More" to "Needing Less"**
   Giving reminds you that your worth is not tied to what you own. It strengthens the mindset that **enough** is better than **excess**.

5. **Builds a Sense of Connection**
   Even simple acts—passing on a toy, sharing kitchenware, donating clothes—create invisible threads of connection. Minimalism is not just personal; it strengthens community through shared responsibility.

The Minimalist Joy of Sharing

- **Sharing Reduces the Need to Own Everything -** When people share tools, appliances, decor or equipment, fewer items sit unused in individual homes. A drill used twice a year doesn't need ten permanent homes — one shared item saves space for everyone.

- **Shared Use Reduces Clutter -** Borrowing instead of buying keeps unnecessary items out of your home. Sharing seasonal, occasional or bulky items (luggage, party supplies, camping gear) prevents long-term accumulation.
- **Sharing Reinforces "People Over Possessions" -** When you share what you can spare—food, resources, household items—you affirm that relationships matter more than ownership.
- **Sharing Aligns With Intentional Living -** Instead of stockpiling "just in case," minimalism encourages trust, cooperation and resourcefulness. A shared community needs fewer things, less space and less waste.

Practical Minimalist Ways to Give and Share

- **Donate What You Don't Use -** Clothes, décor, gadgets, linens, books, kitchen items—if it hasn't been used in months, someone else can benefit from it.
- **Create a Regular Donation Routine -** A monthly "release cycle" keeps clutter from building up again. A box near the door or in the wardrobe makes letting go effortless.
- **Share Items Instead of Owning Extras -** Trade or borrow tools, appliances, festive décor or outdoor gear with neighbours, family or colleagues.
- **Offer Useful Items Thoughtfully -** Give things people actually need — not things you simply want to get rid of. Intentional giving prevents your clutter from becoming someone else's burden.
- **Celebrate Experiences, Not Objects -** Share meals, time and simple moments. These create lasting joy without adding physical clutter.
- **Support Local Needs -** Donate directly to shelters, schools, community centers or individuals who can use items immediately. This ensures your things go where they matter most.

The Essence of Minimalist Giving

Minimalism helps you recognize what truly adds value. You gain:

- more space
- more clarity

- more emotional ease
- more connection
- more freedom

And others gain something useful that you no longer needed. Giving is not the loss of a possession — it is the gain of peace, purpose and generosity.

Life After Eight Weeks

"From Chaos to Clarity in Just Two Months."

Life after 8 weeks of living a more minimalist, simplified or intentional lifestyle can feel transformative. It's a time where you begin to see the tangible and intangible benefits of the choices you've made during this period. Whether you've spent the last two months focusing on decluttering, adopting a healthier routine or practicing minimalism in various areas of life, you'll likely experience a shift in your mindset and daily habits.

Here's what life might look like **after 8 weeks** of intentionally focusing on simplicity, clarity and self-awareness:

1. Greater Clarity and Mental Calmness

Less mental clutter: After eliminating distractions, excess possessions and unnecessary commitments, your mind feels clearer and less overwhelmed. With fewer things to manage, you have more space to focus on what truly matters to you. **More focus**: You may find it easier to concentrate on long-term goals, work or personal projects, as your mind is no longer bogged down by the distractions of excess stuff or endless to-do lists.

2. A More Intentional Life

Mindful decision-making: With the practice of intentional living, you'll be more conscious of your choices. Whether it's what you buy, how you spend your time or how you interact with others, you'll be making decisions that align with your core values and goals.

Purposeful living: You've gained a deeper understanding of what truly brings you joy, satisfaction and fulfilment. As a result, you've likely prioritized activities and relationships that add meaning to your life.

3. Simplified Space and Environment

Organized living space: If you've decluttered, your home will likely feel more spacious organized and peaceful. The act of reducing possessions not only makes it easier to maintain your space but also fosters a sense of calmness and order.

Decluttered digital space: If you've also streamlined your digital life (such as inbox management or organizing files), you might feel less overwhelmed by technology and better able to focus on the essentials.

4. Improved Emotional Well-Being

Less stress: By prioritizing what's most important to you and eliminating unnecessary distractions, you may find yourself feeling less stressed and anxious. Your emotional health has benefited from not having to manage excess.

Increased gratitude: As you've let go of non-essentials, you likely have gained a greater sense of gratitude for the things and people that truly matter in your life. You may find joy in simple moments, whether it's spending time with loved ones or enjoying quiet personal time.

5. Financial Benefits

Financial freedom: By practicing mindful spending and cutting back on impulse purchases, you've likely saved money or reduced unnecessary expenses. This could provide you with more financial freedom, less debt and a stronger ability to save for the future.

More savings: With fewer material possessions, fewer purchases are required, leading to potential savings. You might now focus on purchasing only what you truly need or want, contributing to a healthier financial situation.

6. Improved Health and Energy

Healthier routine: If you've adopted healthier habits (such as exercise, mindful eating or proper sleep), you may notice increased energy, improved physical health and better sleep quality. Your new routines will likely become more automatic, helping you maintain balance in your physical well-being.

More time for self-care: With fewer distractions, you may have more time to invest in your mental and physical health. You might find yourself more consistent with workouts, meditation, hobbies and other activities that promote well-being.

7. More Time and Space for Meaningful Relationships

Closer connections: By simplifying your schedule, you've created more time for meaningful relationships. You might find that you're more present with family and friends and have more quality time to spend with them.

Stronger social circles: With your focus on quality over quantity, you may notice that your social circles are smaller but more meaningful, with connections that truly align with your values.

8. Increased Productivity and Creativity

Better work-life balance: With fewer distractions and a clearer mind, you're likely more productive at work or in your personal projects. You've created a schedule and work environment that fosters efficiency and focus.

Creative space: By removing excess clutter (both physical and mental), you may find that your creativity has increased. Whether through artistic expression, problem-solving at work or generating new ideas, minimalism often frees up space for innovation.

9. A Stronger Sense of Purpose

Living with intention: After 8 weeks of simplifying your life, you may feel a stronger sense of direction and purpose. You've likely identified your core values and the things that bring you joy and fulfilment and you're now aligning your actions with those priorities.

Clearer goals: With fewer distractions, you may find that you are clearer about your long-term goals and more motivated to pursue them. Your life may feel more directed and purposeful, as you now understand what's worth your time and energy.

10. Reduced Environmental Impact

Sustainability: If part of your minimalist journey involved reducing your consumption, you may notice a positive impact on the environment. Less waste, fewer products that harm the planet and more sustainable choices might be part of your daily life.

Living more sustainably: By consuming less, you've embraced a simpler lifestyle that has a smaller environmental footprint. You might feel good knowing that your choices align with your values of sustainability and responsible living.

11. Increased Resilience and Adaptability

Better handling of challenges: The practice of minimalism often leads to greater mental clarity and a deeper sense of emotional resilience. With fewer distractions and more control over your environment, you may find it easier to adapt to challenges and navigate difficult situations with a calmer, more composed mindset.
Less emotional attachment to material possessions: After simplifying your life, you may have let go of emotional attachments to material things, which means you're less likely to feel overwhelmed when circumstances change. This adaptability makes it easier to cope with unexpected events.

12. A Greater Sense of Freedom

Freedom from consumerism: One of the most significant benefits of minimalism is the freedom it provides from the constant pull of consumerism. After 8 weeks of focusing on only the essentials, you're likely to feel less pressured by advertising, social media or societal expectations to accumulate more stuff. This sense of freedom allows you to pursue life on your terms, rather than being driven by the need to acquire things.
More space to travel or explore: With fewer possessions and responsibilities, you might feel freer to travel, experience new cultures or explore new hobbies. This freedom gives you more flexibility in how you spend your time, which can be especially fulfilling if you've prioritized meaningful experiences over accumulating material wealth.

13. Improved Financial Independence

Prioritizing financial goals: With less focus on spending money on things you don't need, your finances may begin to stabilize. You're likely putting more emphasis on saving, investing and paying off debt, which gives you a greater sense of financial freedom and security.
Living within your means: By adopting a minimalist mindset, you're learning to live more within your means, reducing impulsive spending and focusing on what truly adds value to your life. This financial discipline may lead to more sustainable wealth-building in the future.

14. Developing Healthy and Long-Term Habits

More consistent routines: With a clearer sense of purpose and less distraction, your daily routines have become more structured and consistent. Whether it's waking up earlier, exercising regularly or practicing mindfulness, these habits are becoming second nature and contributing to a healthier, more balanced lifestyle.
Focus on long-term health: Minimalism doesn't just apply to physical possessions—it also extends to habits that improve your well-being. After 8 weeks,

you may find yourself more focused on long-term health goals, such as improving your mental health, practicing mindfulness or taking better care of your body.

15. Stronger Sense of Community

Building supportive networks: With your focus shifted toward what really matters, you may be fostering deeper, more meaningful relationships with friends, family and community members. Your relationships are no longer about quantity but about quality and mutual support.

Contributing to others: Minimalism often leads people to give back to their communities—whether through volunteering, sharing resources or offering support. After 8 weeks of living with intention, you may feel more connected to your community and eager to contribute to the well-being of others, further reinforcing a sense of purpose and connectedness.

16. Increased Creativity and Innovation

Creative freedom: With a simpler life, you've created mental space for creativity. By removing distractions, you may notice that your creative pursuits have flourished. Whether it's writing, painting, designing or innovating in your career, minimalism can help clear the way for new ideas to flow freely.

Innovation at work: If you work in a field that requires problem-solving or innovation, the minimalist approach may help you approach challenges with fresh perspectives. Instead of focusing on complexity, you might begin to embrace simpler, more efficient solutions, boosting your productivity and innovation.

17. Enhanced Emotional Awareness

More self-reflection: With fewer distractions in your life, you may find yourself engaging in more self-reflection. You have time to understand your emotional responses, identify triggers and work on improving your emotional intelligence. This awareness can deepen your understanding of yourself and improve your relationships with others.

Letting go of emotional baggage: As you simplify your life, you might begin to let go of past emotional baggage, grudges or attachments that no longer serve you. This emotional clarity can lead to personal growth and an improved sense of well-being.

18. Spiritual Growth

Deeper connection with your beliefs: By creating a simpler, quieter life, you may find that you're able to connect more deeply with your spiritual or philosophical beliefs. Whether through meditation, prayer or other practices, minimalism can provide the space and time needed for spiritual growth and connection.

Living with purpose and intention: After 8 weeks of intentionally simplifying your life, you may have developed a greater understanding of your life's purpose. This can foster spiritual growth, providing you with a sense of inner peace and clarity about your journey.

19. Empathy and Compassion for Others

Increased compassion: By living simply and intentionally, you're likely to develop a greater sense of empathy and compassion for others. This may involve helping those in need, offering support to friends and family or simply becoming more patient and understanding in your day-to-day interactions.
Engaging in acts of kindness: You may feel more inclined to perform random acts of kindness, whether through small gestures like helping someone carry their groceries or offering emotional support to a friend. These actions create positive energy that is often reciprocated, creating a cycle of kindness in your life.

20. A Sustainable Lifestyle

Contributing to a sustainable future: By reducing your consumption and simplifying your life, you are likely reducing your environmental impact. Whether through mindful purchasing, reducing waste or embracing sustainable practices, you are contributing to a more sustainable world.
Living in harmony with nature: As you embrace minimalism, you might develop a deeper connection with nature and the environment. This connection can inspire more sustainable living choices and a sense of responsibility toward preserving the planet.

After 8 weeks of living a minimalist, intentional lifestyle, you may find that the benefits go far beyond just physical decluttering. You will have transformed not only your environment but your mindset and emotional state. The results will likely continue to unfold as you maintain these practices, leading to a more fulfilled, connected and purposeful life.

While minimalism may not be a one-size-fits-all solution, the shifts you've made toward a simpler and more intentional life can bring about lasting change that impacts every area of your life—your relationships, health, finances, creativity and emotional well-being. This journey of simplicity can be a continual process of growth, where you discover more about yourself and the world around you as you embrace the power of "less" in order to experience "more" of what truly matters.

Chapter 30: Story and Real-Life Examples of Minimalism

Aaron's Shift: A London Life, Finally Light

1) The Flat That Looked Full and a Life That Felt Even Fuller

On a rainy Tuesday evening in East London, Aaron returned to his one-bedroom flat near Stratford, shaking off the drizzle from his jacket. The elevator smelled faintly of takeaway and wet umbrellas — a scent he had quietly accepted as part of city living. His flat, however, had its own atmosphere: **full**. Not dirty, not messy - just full. The hallway had a shoe rack that groaned under seven pairs he rarely wore. The living room had shelves arranged with precision but packed with objects - travel souvenirs from trips taken years ago, multiple smart devices, candles he liked the *idea* of, not the use of.

The kitchen was the real confession. Three types of olive oil, two slow cookers, an air fryer he used once because "everyone in the office had one," and a drawer so packed with utensils that it needed a strategic hip-push to close. Everything had been bought for a version of himself he thought he needed to become.

And then there was the wardrobe. London seasons had justified purchases — jackets for drizzle, jackets for cold drizzle, jackets for pretending he might go hiking "sometime." But most days, he wore the same navy coat because it simply worked.

The place was aesthetically fine. But it quietly demanded tending — rearranging, maintaining, deciding. That was the part that wore him down.

The flat held everything he thought adulthood required. But walking into it each day, Aaron felt neither grown nor grounded — just crowded.

2) When London Began Feeling Smaller

The shift didn't start with stuff. It started with **time**.
London was a city he loved but increasingly felt like he was watching from the sidelines — too busy maintaining his life to actually live it. He declined weekend plans because laundry, reorganising, meal prepping and errands had become a full shift of their own.

He noticed the same fatigue which everyone recognise: Not from *big* work but from **micro-maintenance** of belongings.

The second sign was money. London rent was high, yes — but the silent drip of expenses felt higher: upgrades, duplicates, subscriptions for devices he barely used, impulse buys justified by convenience.

The third sign was noise. His flat felt visually loud — surfaces decorated, shelves loaded, every corner occupied. It reflected his inner clutter.

One night, while searching for a charger in a drawer that had everything except clarity, he found an old note he'd written when he first moved to London: **"Explore the city deeply. Live simply. Grow intentionally."**

He felt embarrassed by how far he had drifted.

3) The Tube Ride Realisation

A few days later, on the Central Line to Liverpool Street, Aaron noticed a man reading a paperback with a tiny backpack at his feet — no laptop bag, no accessories, no clutter. He looked… *unburdened.*

Aaron stared at his own seat: a large work bag, headphones case, glasses case, snack pouch, external battery, charger, umbrella, notebook and a gym outfit he carried daily but rarely used.

His life had become excess disguised as preparedness.

For the first time, the thought arose gently: **"Maybe I don't need this much."**

4) The Saturday Reset: His First Minimalist Action

Aaron blocked one Saturday — no brunch, no errands, no plans. Just an audit.
He took three large brown paper bags from the Tesco downstairs and labelled them:

- **Keep** – I use it weekly
- **Let Go** – I don't and someone else can
- **Maybe** – a 30-day quarantine

He began with kitchenware. Why did he own three chopping boards when he chopped 90% of things on one? Two slow cookers? Four travel mugs when he walked to Pret every morning anyway?

By noon, the kitchen felt lighter — like it could finally exhale.

In the wardrobe, he tried a new test: **"Would I pack this for a spontaneous weekend trip?"** Surprisingly, only a third of his clothes passed.

By evening, the flat didn't look empty. It looked honest. Not curated. Just functional.

5) The 30-Day Tube Rule

He gave himself one experiment: **If during the next 30 Tube rides, he wished he had something he decluttered, he would buy it again.**
Not once did that happen.

Instead, he enjoyed something unexpected:

- His commute bag was half the weight.
- His shoulders felt physically freer.
- He no longer rummaged through pockets and pouches.
- His mornings became smoother.

Minimalism was no longer an idea — it was a sensation.

6) The London Lifestyle Shift

Aaron reduced the friction around him:

- Kept one work bag that did everything
- Donated duplicates to a local charity shop in Hackney
- Sold old gadgets at a weekend market
- Cancelled three subscription services he barely touched
- Returned unused décor to let the flat breathe
- Replaced multiple hobby gear with one good quality version
- Made a weekly "reset hour" on Sunday evenings

The flat transformed. Not into a showroom — into a home.

And his savings quietly grew because for the first time in London… he wasn't bleeding money through tiny, needless purchases.

7) A New Rhythm in a Fast City

He began noticing changes:

- Coffee tasted better when drunk from the one mug he genuinely loved.
- His evenings opened up because tidying took minutes, not hours.
- He hosted friends more because he no longer feared clutter.
- He started exploring London properly — parks, rivers, bookshops, walking trails.
- He rediscovered the joy of doing nothing — a rare luxury in a loud city.

Minimalism didn't shrink his life. It expanded it.

8) The Identity Shift

Months in, Aaron wrote his new rule — a sentence he taped inside his hallway:
"I own what I use, choose what I value and live with what gives me peace."

This changed his behaviour naturally:

- No impulse purchases
- No buying for identity
- No filling space just because space existed
- No guilt over letting things go
- No hiding behind "just in case"

He wasn't performing minimalism. He was embodying it.

9) The Walk Home That Confirmed Everything

One evening, after a walk along the Thames near Tower Bridge, Aaron returned to his building. He unlocked his door and stood silently inside for a moment.

The flat was calm. Clean. Light.
Not perfect — but peaceful.

He noticed something deeply simple and profoundly rare: He *liked* being home because home no longer asked anything from him.

Minimalism, he realised, wasn't about decluttering. It was about creating **room** — in space, in time, in emotion, in self.

The After

Here is what Aaron's ordinary life looks like now:

- **Morning:** 20-minute routine, effortless dressing, quiet breakfast.
- **Workday:** Fewer tools, clearer focus, better outcomes.
- **Evenings:** Walks, reading, meeting a friend — without rushing.
- **Weekends:** Exploring London instead of organising his flat.
- **Finances:** Stronger savings through intentional living.
- **Mind:** Quieter. Steadier. Lighter.

Minimalism didn't make him extreme. It made him *present*.

He didn't end up living with nothing. He ended up living with **exactly what supported him**.

And that was enough. Enough to feel free — in a city that never stops moving.

Real-Life Examples of Minimalism

1. **Mission Statement** - A short mission statement gives clarity and direction. The fewer the words, the stronger the focus.
2. **People's Attention Time** - Human attention is limited. Short, meaningful messages are remembered far more than long explanations.
3. **Speech** - A concise speech creates impact. Listeners absorb more when you say less but say it well.
4. **Working Hours** - Working 12 hours doesn't make you 1.5 times more productive than 8 hours. Smart work beats long work; even major companies experiment with 4-day weeks.
5. **Friends** - A few genuine friends bring more joy than a large circle of shallow connections.
6. **Sleep** - Quality matters more than quantity. Deep, restful sleep for fewer hours can refresh you better than long, disturbed sleep.
7. **Tour – Items to Carry** - Travel light and you travel free. Fewer items mean less stress and more enjoyment.
8. **Picnic – Number of Friends** - Small groups create deeper conversations and stronger memories than large, chaotic gatherings.
9. **Big House** - A bigger house doesn't multiply happiness. The joy of space fades quickly; comfort and peace matter more.
10. **Spiritual Life – One God** - Focusing on one belief or practice brings clarity. Too many paths create confusion.
11. **Less Colour – More Beauty** - Minimal colours in art, design or fashion often create elegance. Simplicity highlights true beauty.
12. **Party – Food Variety** - A few high-quality dishes bring more satisfaction than a huge spread with average taste.
13. **Knowledge** - Depth beats width. Mastery in one or two subjects is more valuable than shallow awareness of many.
14. **Study Duration & Material** - Focused study with fewer books is more effective than drowning in endless material.

15. **One Good House** - Owning one comfortable home brings peace. Multiple properties bring maintenance, stress and responsibility.

16. **Speech Duration** - A powerful 5-minute talk can inspire more than a long, tiring 1-hour lecture.

17. **Helpers** - A few trusted professionals — doctor, teacher, barber, plumber — simplify life. Too many options create confusion.

18. **Less Words, More Impact** - Short, thoughtful communication carries more weight than long, unnecessary talk.

19. **Parties** - A simple roadside tea with 3–4 close friends often feel richer than a grand party with hundreds.

20. **Less Water, More for All** - Using less water ensures sustainability. Conservation creates abundance.

21. **Tea Sharing in Indian Shops** - Half-cup chai shared between two people shows how small portions can still create connection.

22. **Hi-Fi Gadget for an 80-Year-Old** - For elders, simple devices bring more comfort. Complexity adds stress, not value.

23. **Age & Experience** - With age, people naturally simplify life. Wisdom teaches that less complication means more peace.

24. **Speak Less, Be Heard More** - When you speak less, your words carry weight. People listen more carefully.

25. **Specialization** - One expert with deep knowledge is more valuable than someone with ten shallow skills.

26. **Start Action** - Waiting for perfect tools stops progress. Start with what you have; add only what's necessary.

27. **Less Paper, More Trees** - Using less paper protects nature. Small reductions create big environmental impact.

28. **Task Execution** - Whether given 10 days or 30, people often finish in the same time. Focus, not duration, drives results.

29. **Multitasking** - The brain performs best with one task at a time. Doing less improves quality.

30. **World Wants More in Less Time** - Efficiency is valued everywhere. Shorter processes with better results define modern success.

31. **National / Company Anthem** - Short anthems are easier to remember and unite people more effectively.

32. **Minimalism in Music** - Simple melodies often touch the heart more deeply than complex compositions.

33. **TED Talks** - TED Talks are powerful because they deliver big ideas in short, focused presentations.

34. **Poetry** - Great poets use few words to express deep emotions. Simplicity creates magic.

35. **Dashboard Monitoring** - ICU dashboards or scorecards show only essential data. Too much information creates confusion.

36. **Highly Paid People** - Top professionals focus on a few key skills. Their value comes from depth, not volume.

37. **Sports** - Fixed team sizes create structure and fairness. Too many players lead to chaos.

38. **Village Life** - Villages have fewer possessions but more peace. Simplicity brings contentment.

39. **Monk – Thailand** - Monks own very little yet live joyfully. Their happiness comes from simplicity, not possessions.

40. **Old Days** - Life without digital overload had fewer distractions. People lived slower, deeper and more connected lives.

Part XII: Conclusion: The Path to Lasting Change

Reflect on the journey from chaos to clarity and from excess to balance.

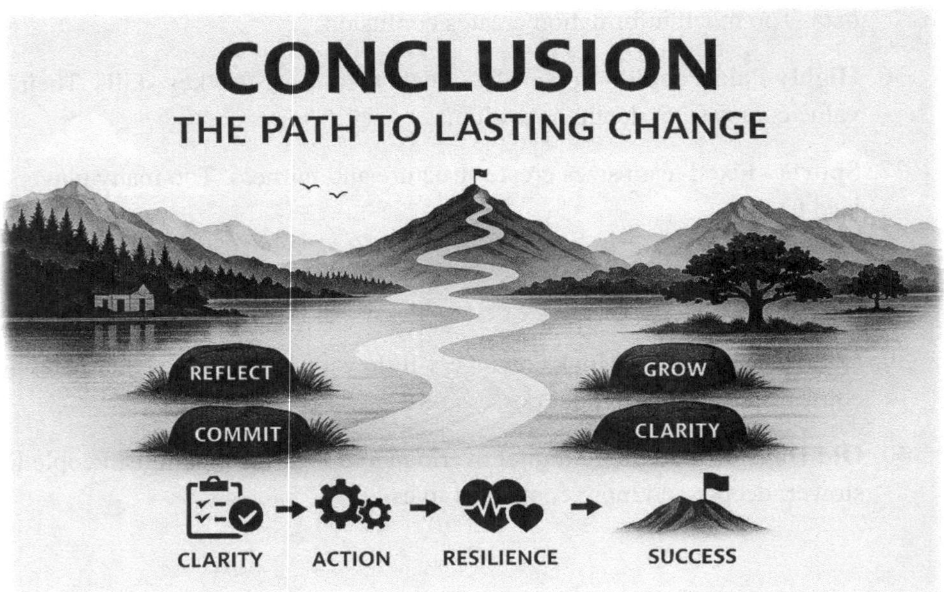

The Path to Lasting Change

"Small habits. Simple living. Lasting change."

The journey you've just completed

You began this book by holding up a mirror to modern life—its speed, choice overload, digital noise and the hidden costs of chasing "more." From there, you walked through practical simplicity, spiritual calm, health and well-being, relationships, everyday systems, happiness beyond possessions and finally the mindset and methods of minimalism applied to real life. Together, these chapters were designed to help you replace noise with **clarity**, clutter with **space** and pressure with **peace**—so you can start living by design, not by default.

Why a simple life works every single day

Simplicity isn't an aesthetic; it's a **system** for living. It frees your time, steadies your emotions and focuses your energy on what truly matters—your health, your people, your purpose. That's why this volume kept returning to a few core ideas: **intentional routines, mindful attention, honest reflection, fewer but better choices and consistent small steps**. You saw these rhythms repeated across chapters because the brain learns through repetition and practice—and because life actually changes **only** when the basics become daily habits.

This book is a life companion that walks with you quietly, guiding you toward a simpler way of living. Open it whenever a day feels heavy, a decision feels noisy or a moment calls for calm. It is written to be that pocket companion you can return to again and again.

From knowing to doing: choose one habit (and let it multiply)

Lasting change begins smaller than we think. **Take one good habit**—just one—and practice it daily. It could be the **One-Minute Pause** before you react, a **night-before plan** for tomorrow, ten minutes of **quiet breathing**, a **phone-free meal** or a **five-item declutter** every evening. Then trust this natural law of progress:

"Take one good habit—one good habit will invite others."

When a single habit becomes real in your life, it reduces friction for the next one. Focus deepens. Confidence grows. Energy returns. And progress stops feeling like a fight and starts feeling like flow. You've met this principle in many forms in the book—mini steps, gentle repetition, compounding effort and systems that make good choices automatic.

Why you noticed repetition (and why it matters)

If you felt certain themes echoing through these pages, that was deliberate. People don't change because they read something once. People change when ideas **sink in**, when language becomes **familiar**, when practices are **rehearsed** and when reminders arrive at the right time on an ordinary day. Repetition is not noise—it is a practical kindness that helps you **digest** the book and **implement** it in real life. This volume is meant to be **revisited**: open a chapter when you need it, underline a line that speaks to you and return to a practice until it becomes your new normal.

The arc of Volume I—and what it gives you to carry forward

- **A clearer map of modern pressures** so you can name them—and stop being shaped by them.
- **Simplicity as a practice**—less but better—so your days feel lighter and your mind feels free.
- **Inner steadiness** through presence, reflection and small rituals that guard peace in noisy times.
- **Body-first living**—sleep, nutrition, movement, nature—because health is the foundation of everything else.
- **Relationship sense**—rhythms, boundaries, kindness, community—because people are the point of life.
- **Everyday systems** that turn discipline into ease—so your life runs on rails, not reminders.
- **Money with meaning**—calm choices, purposeful spending, digital and financial minimalism—so freedom grows instead of pressure.
- **A minimalist lens** across home, work, design, communication and mental space—small shifts, big impact.

These are not boxes to tick; they're **anchors** to steady you while the world keeps moving.

Where the path continues—Volume II at a glance

When the **inside** grows calmer, you naturally want to strengthen the **outside**. That is why this series continues with ***Volume II: Mastering Success, Productivity & Personal Discipline*** —a direct extension of the same philosophy, applied to results. There, you'll translate inner clarity into **daily discipline**, **time mastery**, **deep work and focus**, **mindset and performance under pressure**, **decision-making** and **communication**. It's the same spirit of simplicity but aimed at productivity, capability and purposeful execution

How the two volumes fit together

- **Volume I:** Peace within. Simplicity in living. Foundations for health, relationships and clarity.
- **Volume II:** Progress outside. Simplicity in doing. Systems for focus, productivity and disciplined action.

Read them in a circle: whenever outer execution feels heavy, come home to inner simplicity; whenever inner life is steady, step forward into focused action.

A simple, human way to begin (and keep going)

- **Start tiny.** Choose one habit. Put it where it fits. Make it easier than you think.
- **Use cues.** Tie the habit to something you already do (after tea → 5-minute walk; before bed → 3 lines of gratitude).
- **Protect your mornings.** Even 15 calm minutes can steer the next 23 hours.
- **Make a system, not a promise.** Fix a time, a place and a method—then let the system carry the weight.
- **Expect the wobble.** Miss a day? It happens. **Never miss two.** Smile, restart, move.
- **Measure weekly.** Zoom out. Patterns matter more than perfect days.
- **Share it.** Tell one person what you're building; community makes discipline gentle.

Seven micro-shifts to try this week

1. **The One-Minute Pause** before you reply or decide. (Peace grows where reactivity ends.)
2. **Night-before planning**: Top-3 priorities on a sticky note. (Wake with clarity.)
3. **Phone-free meals**—single-task your food and your family. (Presence is happiness.)
4. **Five-item item release**: donate, discard or return five things daily. (Space invites calm.)
5. **Ten-minute walk in sunlight**—body first, mind follows. (Energy loves daylight.) [
6. **Gratitude in three lines** each night. (The mind becomes what it repeats.)
7. **Weekly mini-review**: What worked? What will I try next? (Progress is a pattern.)

When life gets noisy come back to this

You will have weeks when the world rushes again, when the calendar crowds and the mind feels full. On those days, **return to any page** that once made you breathe easier. Re-read the line you underlined. Re-start the one habit that steadies you. This is why the book repeats its truths from different angles: so that the right idea meets you at the right time and the practice becomes part of who you are.

Call to action

Choose **one** habit today—only one. Write it where you'll see it. Practice it for seven days. Tell someone you trust. Next week, let that one habit **invites another**.

Every day offers a small opportunity to choose better: to pause instead of rush to listen instead of argue to move instead of sit to speak gently to live consciously. These choices seem insignificant but they are seeds. One good choice today becomes the foundation for the next good one tomorrow.

A single good choice does more than change your day—it changes your state of mind. When you make one positive decision, your brain shifts into a mode of confidence and control. It reminds you that improvement is possible. It gives you momentum. Suddenly, the next good decision feels easier. Then the next. Slowly, almost invisibly, life begins to take a new shape.

Living Well: The Art of Simplicity and Success

Volume I: Foundations of a Simple, Happy and Healthy Life

Live lighter. Feel calmer. Grow stronger.

Today, life has become louder, faster and heavier than it should be.
We are surrounded by convenience, yet starved of calm. We achieve more, yet feel less fulfilled. We stay constantly connected yet rarely feel truly present. ***Living Well: The Art of Simplicity and Success* – *Volume I*** is a gentle but powerful invitation to slow down, clear the inner clutter and return to what truly matters.Written as a **life companion**, this book offers **simple, clear and actionable guidance** that can be applied immediately—at home, at work or in moments of selfreflection. Each chapter carries gentle insights and practical wisdom that help you move forward with **strength, focus and calm**, without overwhelm or pressure.

Rather than asking you to change everything, this book helps you remove what no longer serves you. Through **timeless principles, real life reflections and practical habits**, it addresses the inner foundations of a well lived life—mental clarity, emotional balance, health, relationships, mindfulness, spirituality and daily simplicity.

This is not a book to rush through. It is a book to keep close.
A book to open whenever life feels heavy, confusing or noisy.

Whether you are a **professional, student, leader, entrepreneur, homemaker or a seeker of growth**, this book is written for **every person who wishes to live a happy, healthy and peaceful life**.

A calm mind. A simpler life. A meaningful beginning. **A gift for your loved ones.**

Sandeep Shah is a seasoned professional and thought leader passionate about simplicity, personal growth and mindful living. He shares actionable insights to help readers thrive in today's fast-paced world. Blending decades of observation, learning and practical experience, he helps readers build lives filled with clarity, calm and meaningful success. ***Living Well: The Art of Simplicity and Success*** is his signature work — a guide for every stage of life.

Contact: sandeepsshah@icloud.com